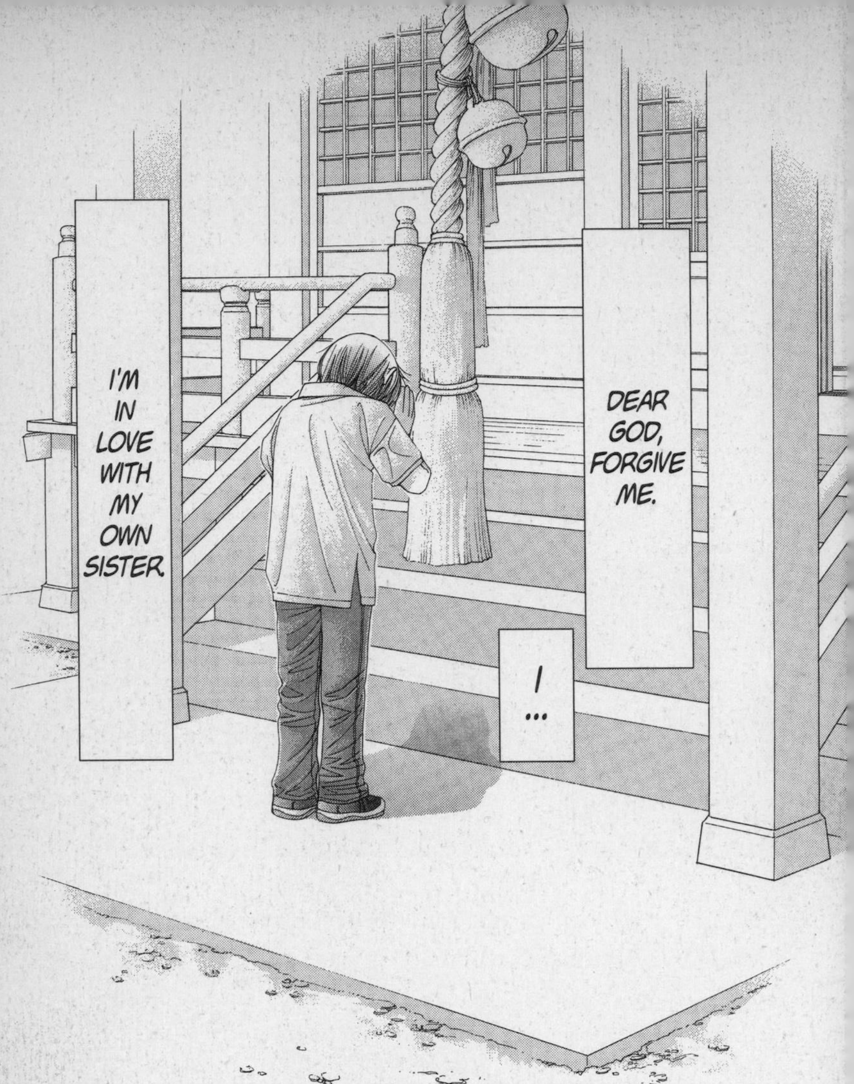
DEAR GOD, FORGIVE ME.
I ...
I'M IN LOVE WITH MY OWN SISTER.

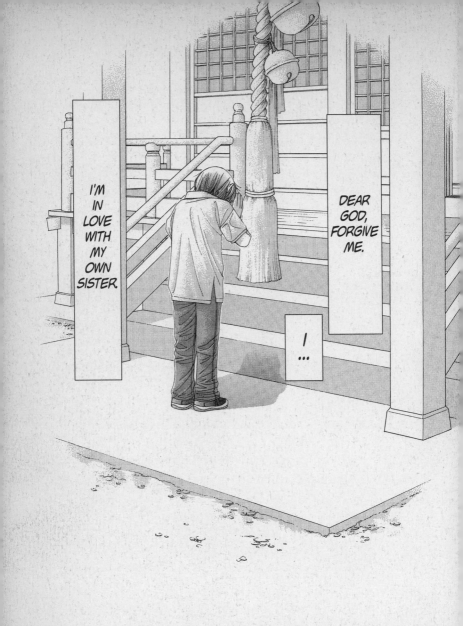

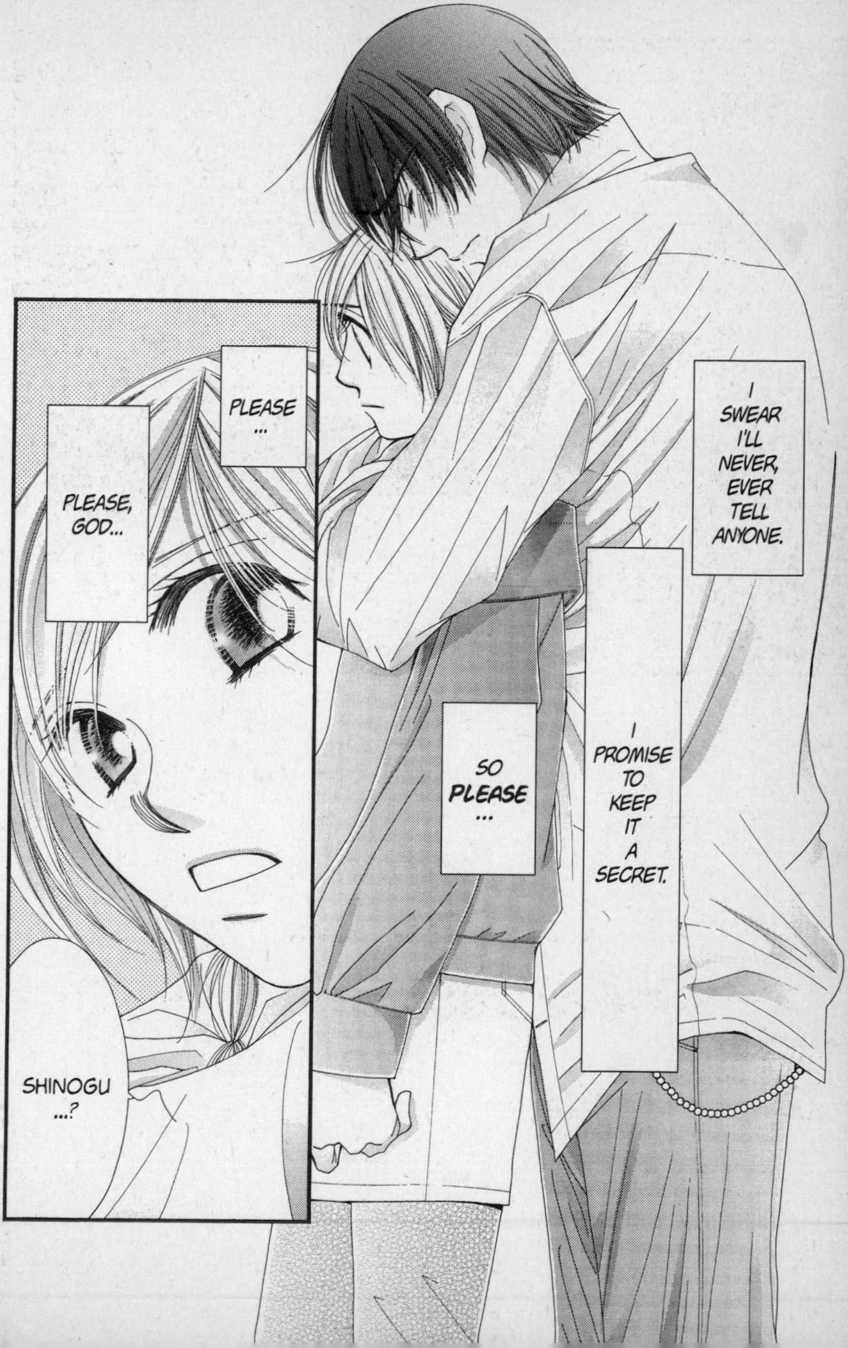
I SWEAR I'LL NEVER, EVER TELL ANYONE.
I PROMISE TO KEEP IT A SECRET.
SO PLEASE ...
PLEASE ...
PLEASE, GOD...
SHINOGU ...?

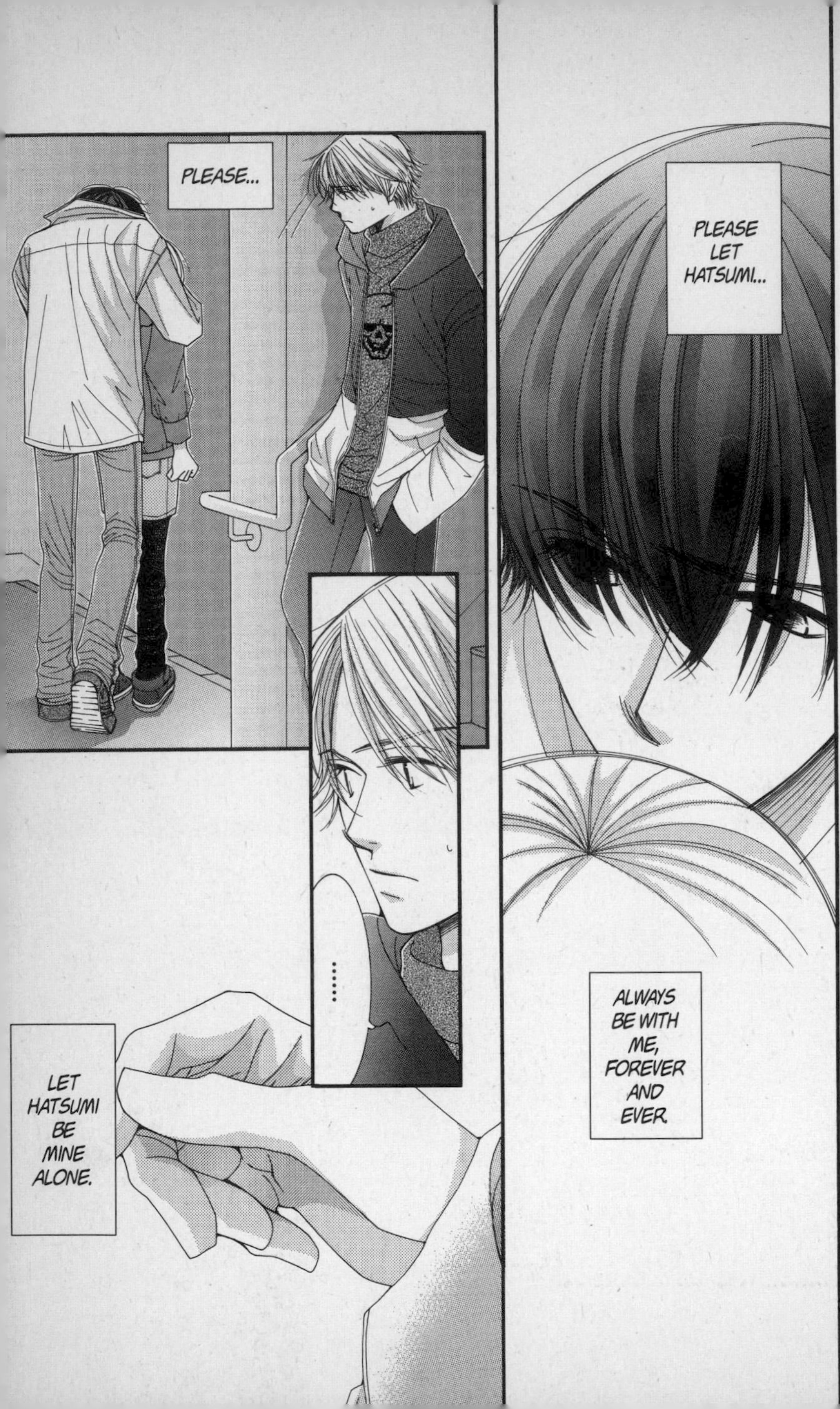
PLEASE LET HATSUMI...
ALWAYS BE WITH ME, FOREVER AND EVER.
PLEASE...
......
LET HATSUMI BE MINE ALONE.

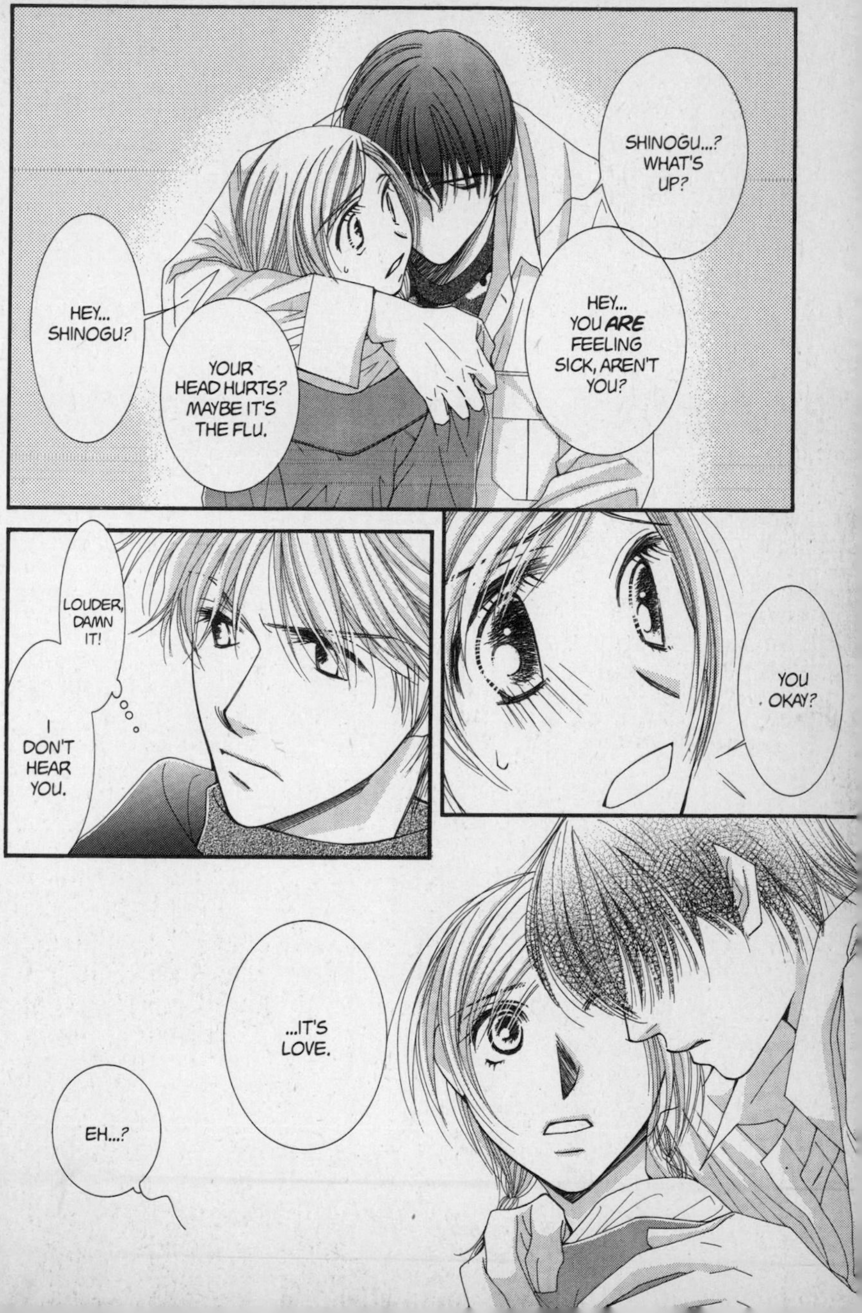
SHINOGU...? WHAT'S UP?
HEY... YOU **ARE** FEELING SICK, AREN'T YOU?
YOUR HEAD HURTS? MAYBE IT'S THE FLU.
HEY... SHINOGU?
YOU OKAY?
LOUDER, DAMN IT!
I DON'T HEAR YOU.
...IT'S LOVE.
EH...?

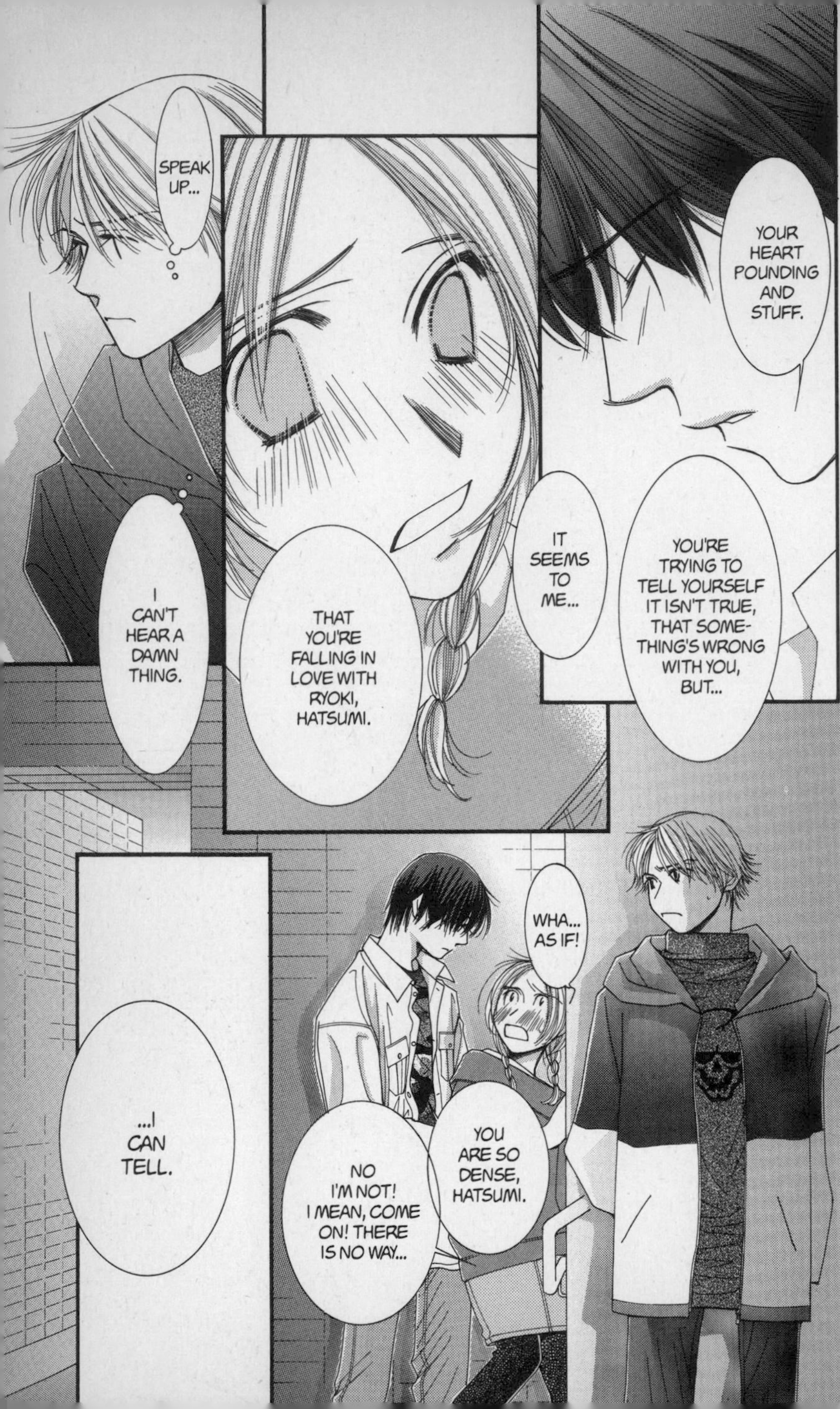
YOUR HEART POUNDING AND STUFF.
YOU'RE TRYING TO TELL YOURSELF IT ISN'T TRUE, THAT SOME-THING'S WRONG WITH YOU, BUT...
IT SEEMS TO ME...
THAT YOU'RE FALLING IN LOVE WITH RYOKI, HATSUMI.
SPEAK UP...
I CAN'T HEAR A DAMN THING.
WHA... AS IF!
YOU ARE SO DENSE, HATSUMI.
NO I'M NOT! I MEAN, COME ON! THERE IS NO WAY...
...I CAN TELL.

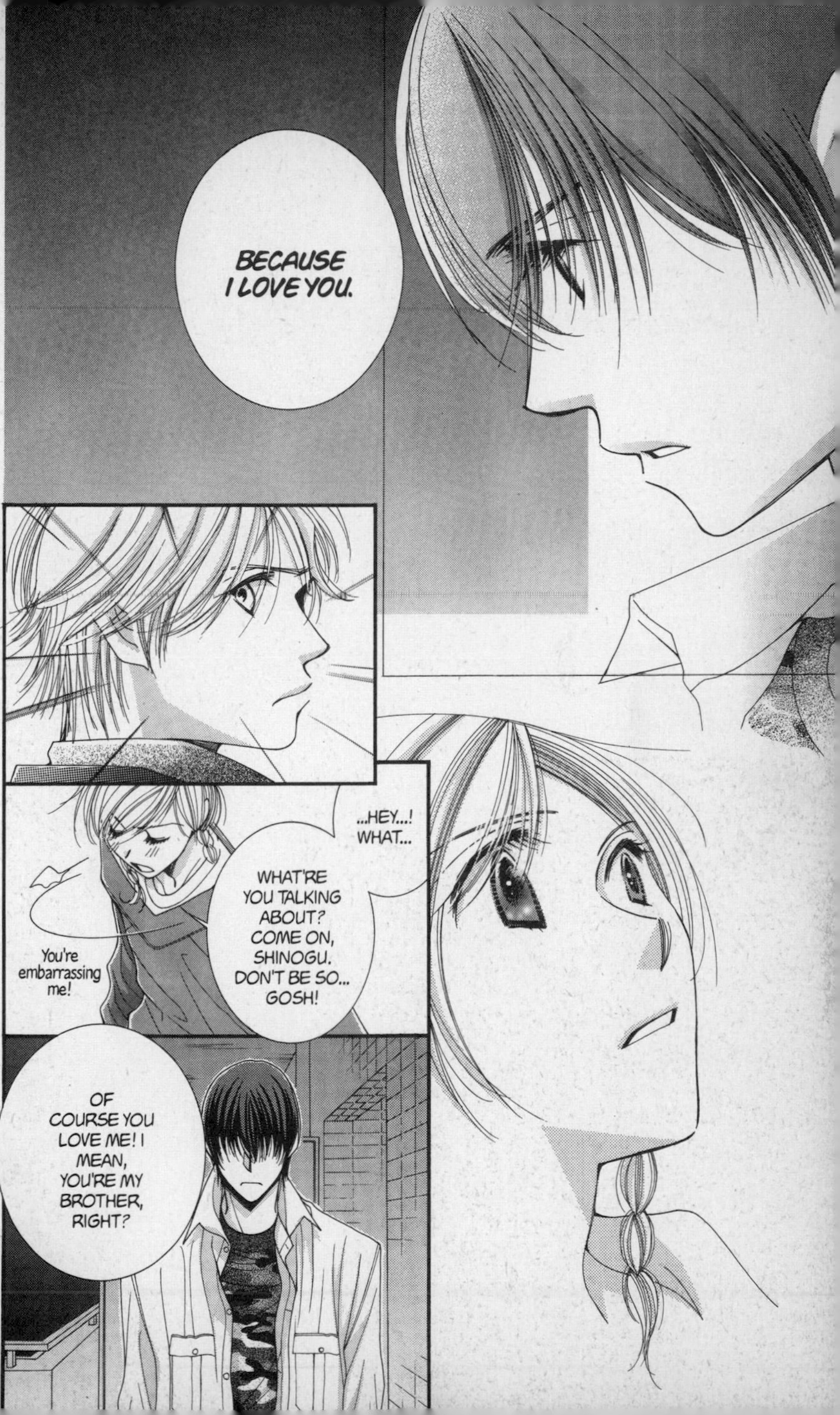
BECAUSE I LOVE YOU.
...HEY...! WHAT...
WHAT'RE YOU TALKING ABOUT? COME ON, SHINOGU. DON'T BE SO... GOSH!
You're embarrassing me!
OF COURSE YOU LOVE ME! I MEAN, YOU'RE MY BROTHER, RIGHT?

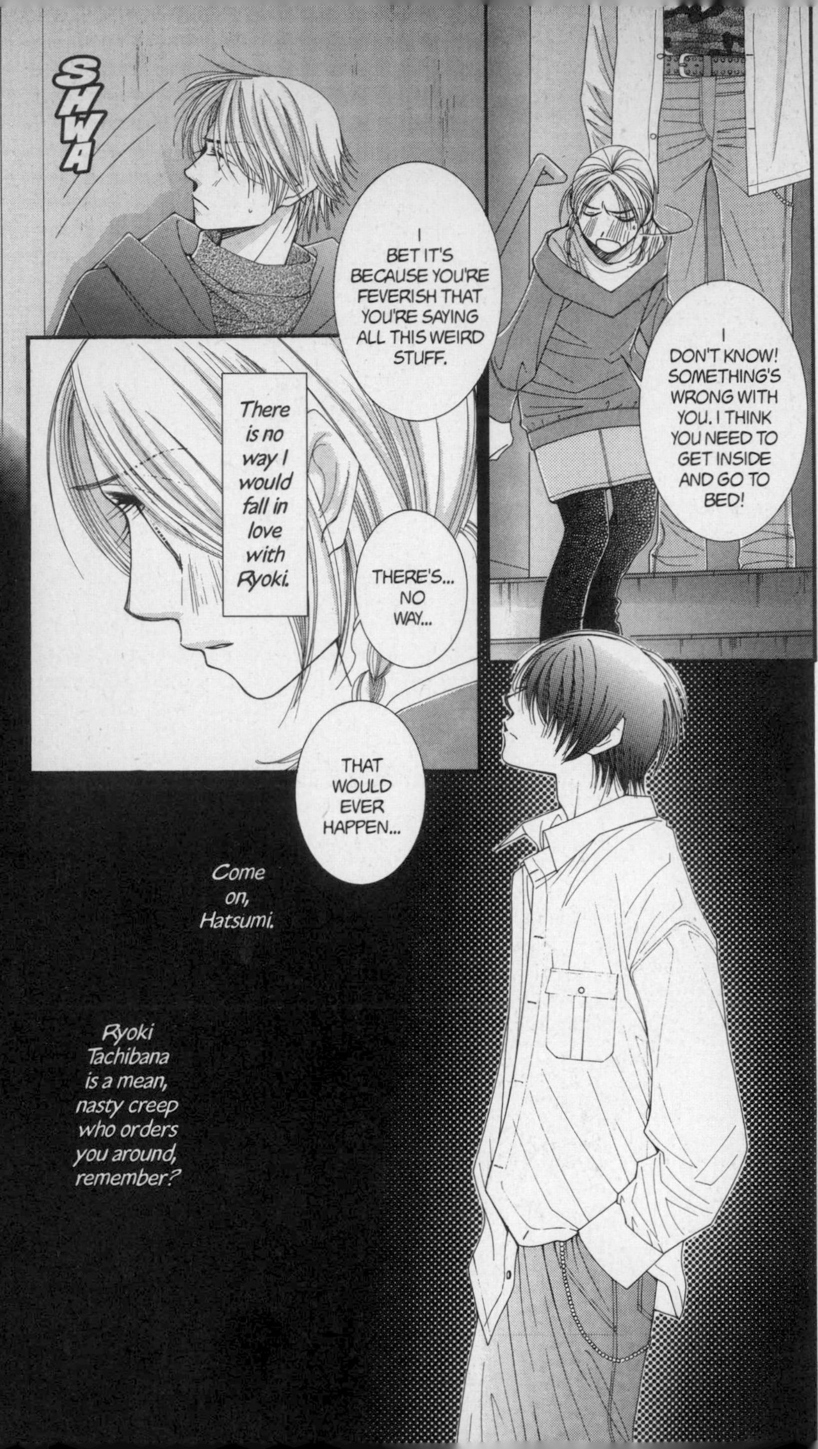
I BET IT'S BECAUSE YOU'RE FEVERISH THAT YOU'RE SAYING ALL THIS WEIRD STUFF.
I DON'T KNOW! SOMETHING'S WRONG WITH YOU. I THINK YOU NEED TO GET INSIDE AND GO TO BED!
SHWA
There is no way I would fall in love with Ryoki.
THERE'S... NO WAY...
THAT WOULD EVER HAPPEN...
Come on, Hatsumi.
Ryoki Tachibana is a mean, nasty creep who orders you around, remember?

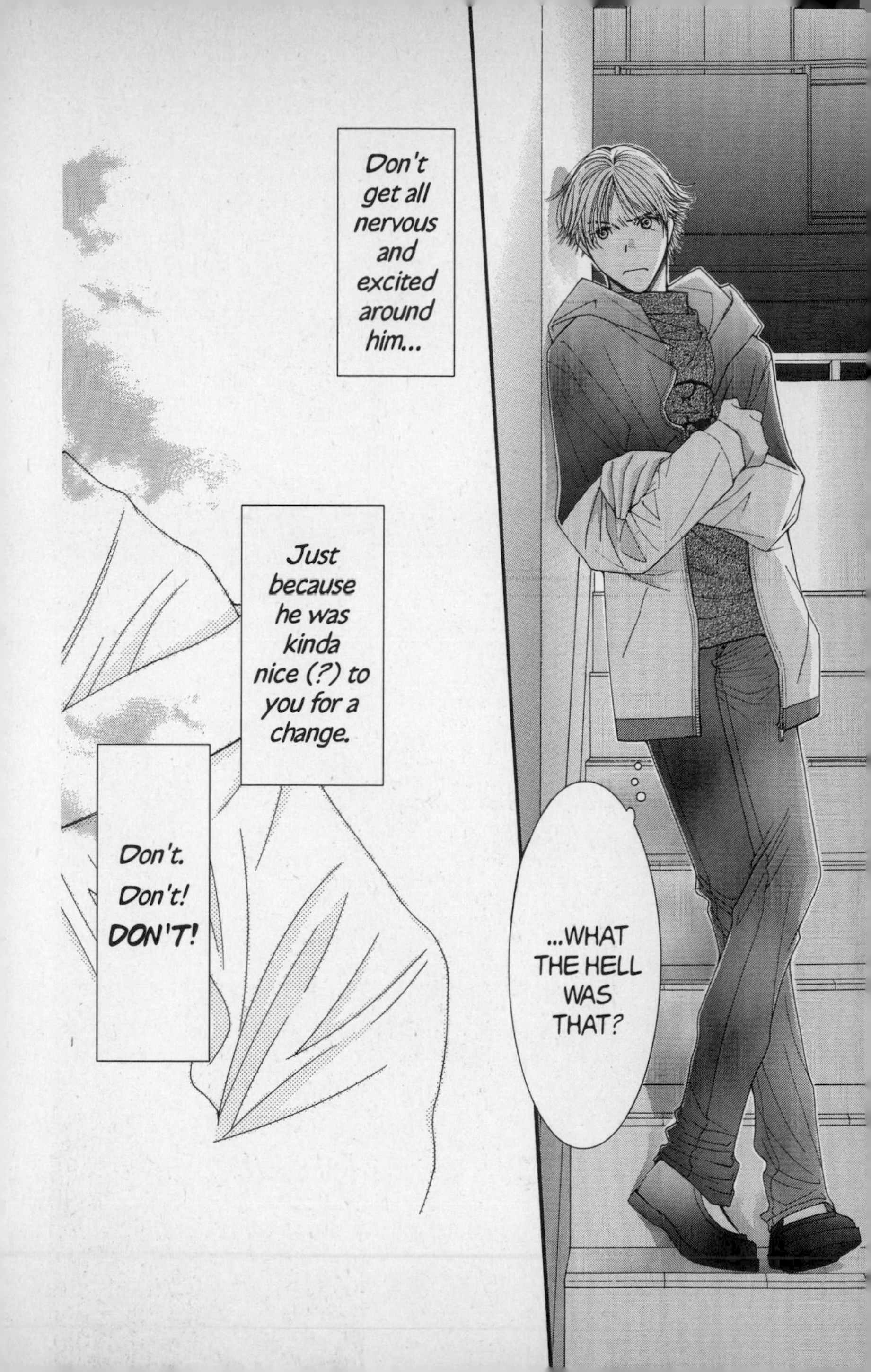

...WHAT THE HELL WAS THAT?
Don't get all nervous and excited around him...
Just because he was kinda nice (?) to you for a change.
Don't. Don't! DON'T!

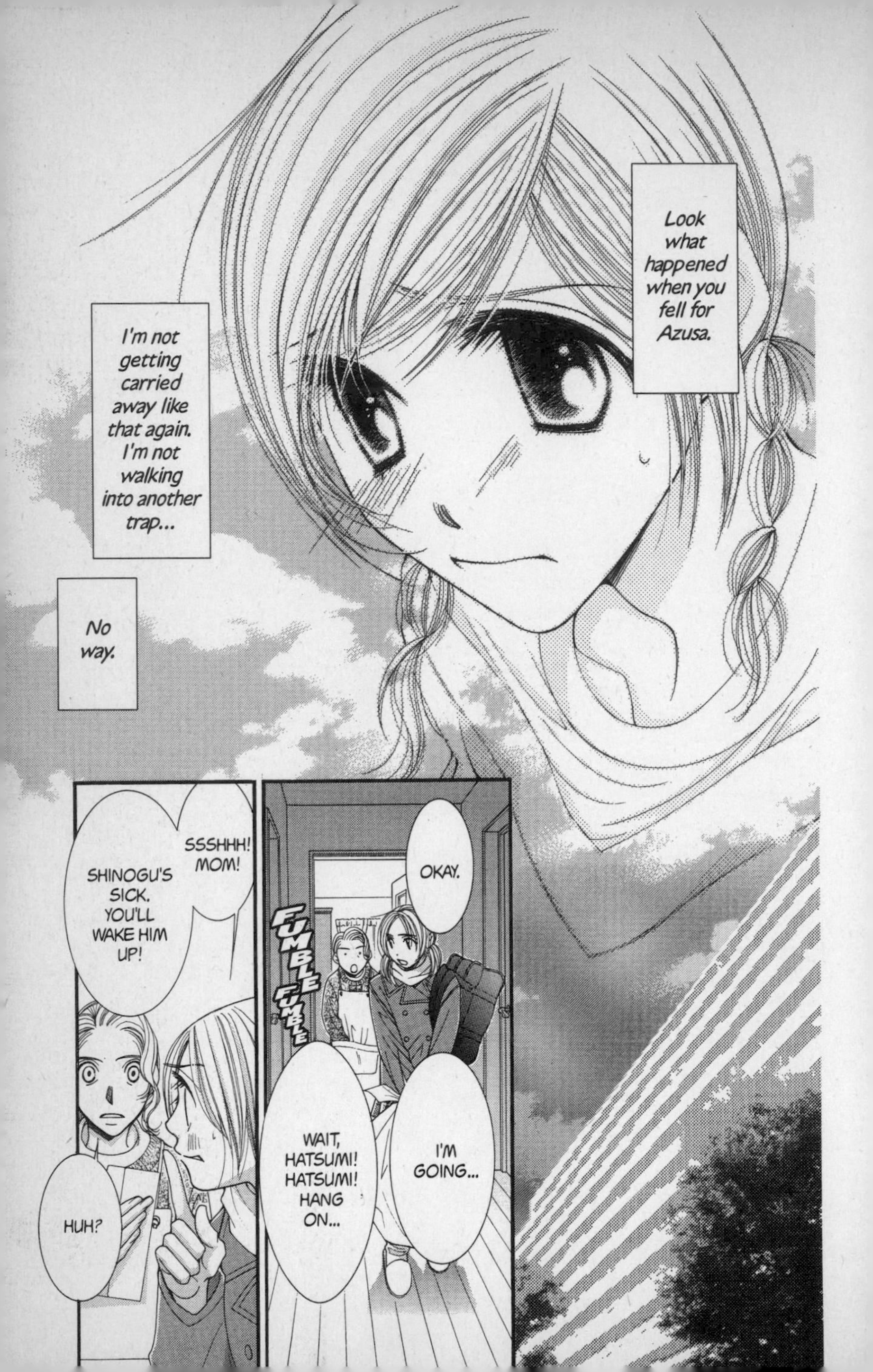

Look what happened when you fell for Azusa.
I'm not getting carried away like that again. I'm not walking into another trap...
No way.
OKAY.
FUMBLE FUMBLE
I'M GOING...
WAIT, HATSUMI! HATSUMI! HANG ON...
SSSHHH! MOM!
SHINOGU'S SICK. YOU'LL WAKE HIM UP!
HUH?

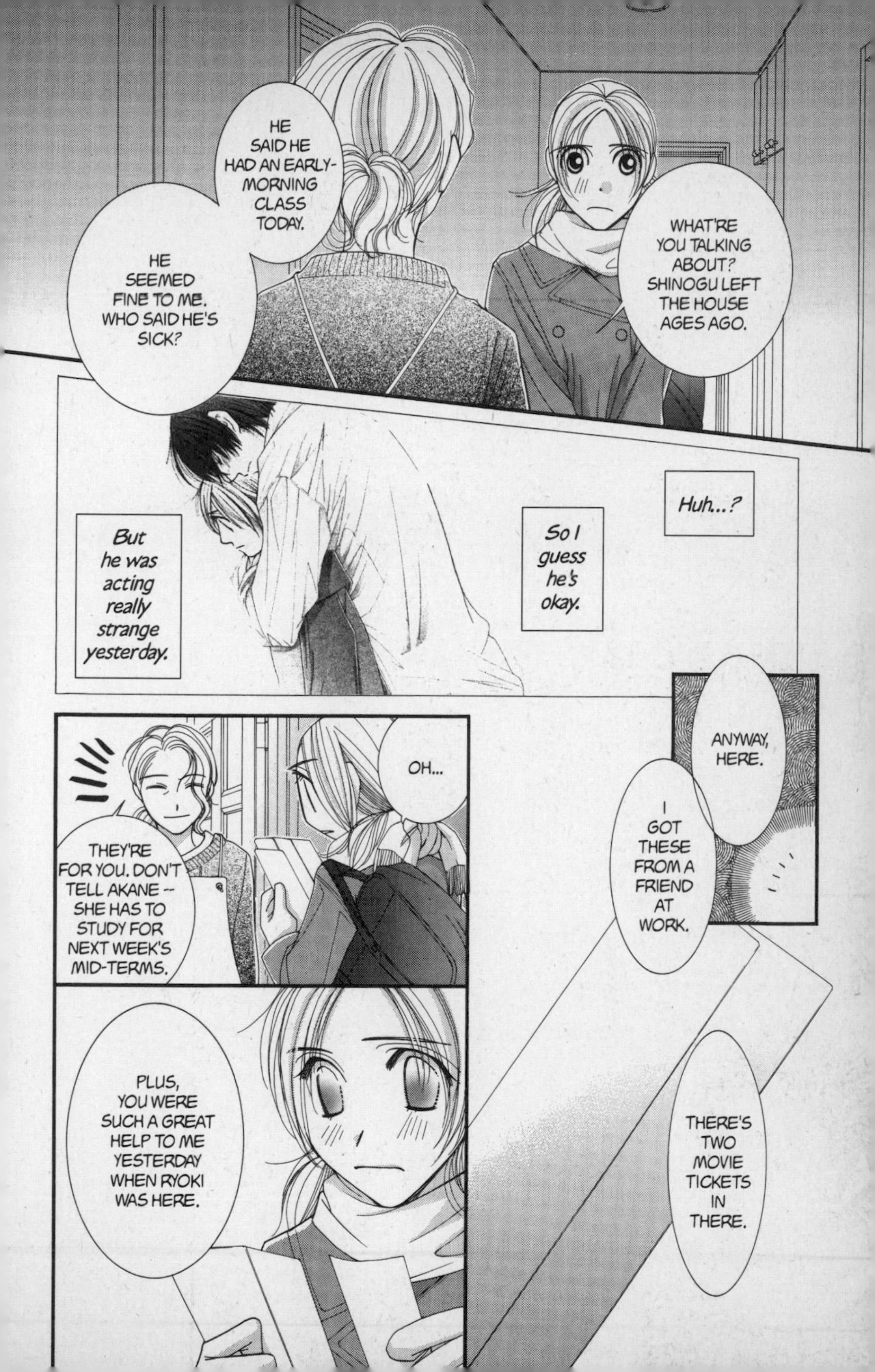
WHAT'RE YOU TALKING ABOUT? SHINOGU LEFT THE HOUSE AGES AGO.
HE SAID HE HAD AN EARLY-MORNING CLASS TODAY.
HE SEEMED FINE TO ME. WHO SAID HE'S SICK?
Huh...?
So I guess he's okay.
But he was acting really strange yesterday.
ANYWAY, HERE.
I GOT THESE FROM A FRIEND AT WORK.
THERE'S TWO MOVIE TICKETS IN THERE.
OH...
THEY'RE FOR YOU. DON'T TELL AKANE -- SHE HAS TO STUDY FOR NEXT WEEK'S MID-TERMS.
PLUS, YOU WERE SUCH A GREAT HELP TO ME YESTERDAY WHEN RYOKI WAS HERE.

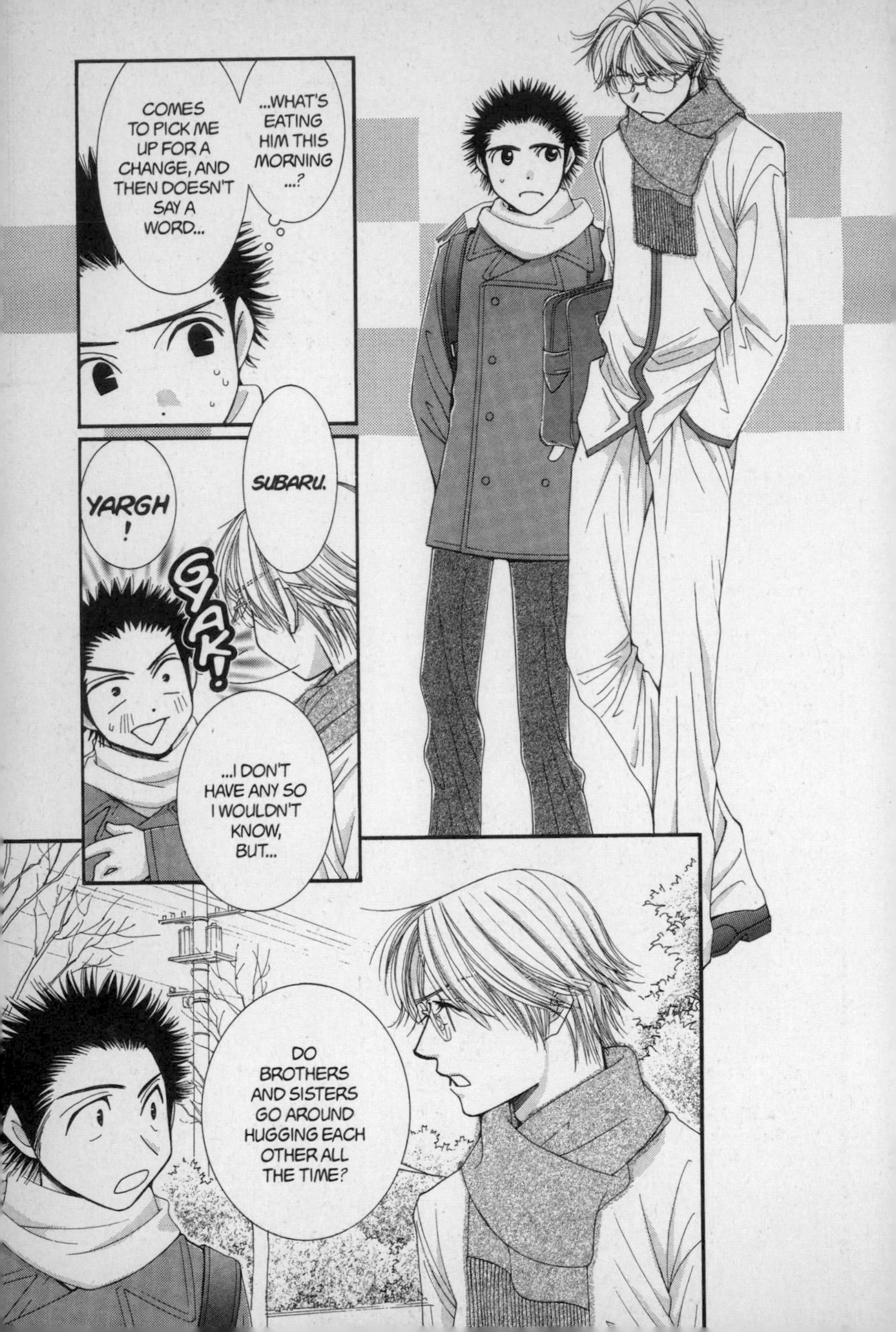
...WHAT'S EATING HIM THIS MORNING ...?
COMES TO PICK ME UP FOR A CHANGE, AND THEN DOESN'T SAY A WORD...
SUBARU.
YARGH!
GYAK!
...I DON'T HAVE ANY SO I WOULDN'T KNOW, BUT...
DO BROTHERS AND SISTERS GO AROUND HUGGING EACH OTHER ALL THE TIME?

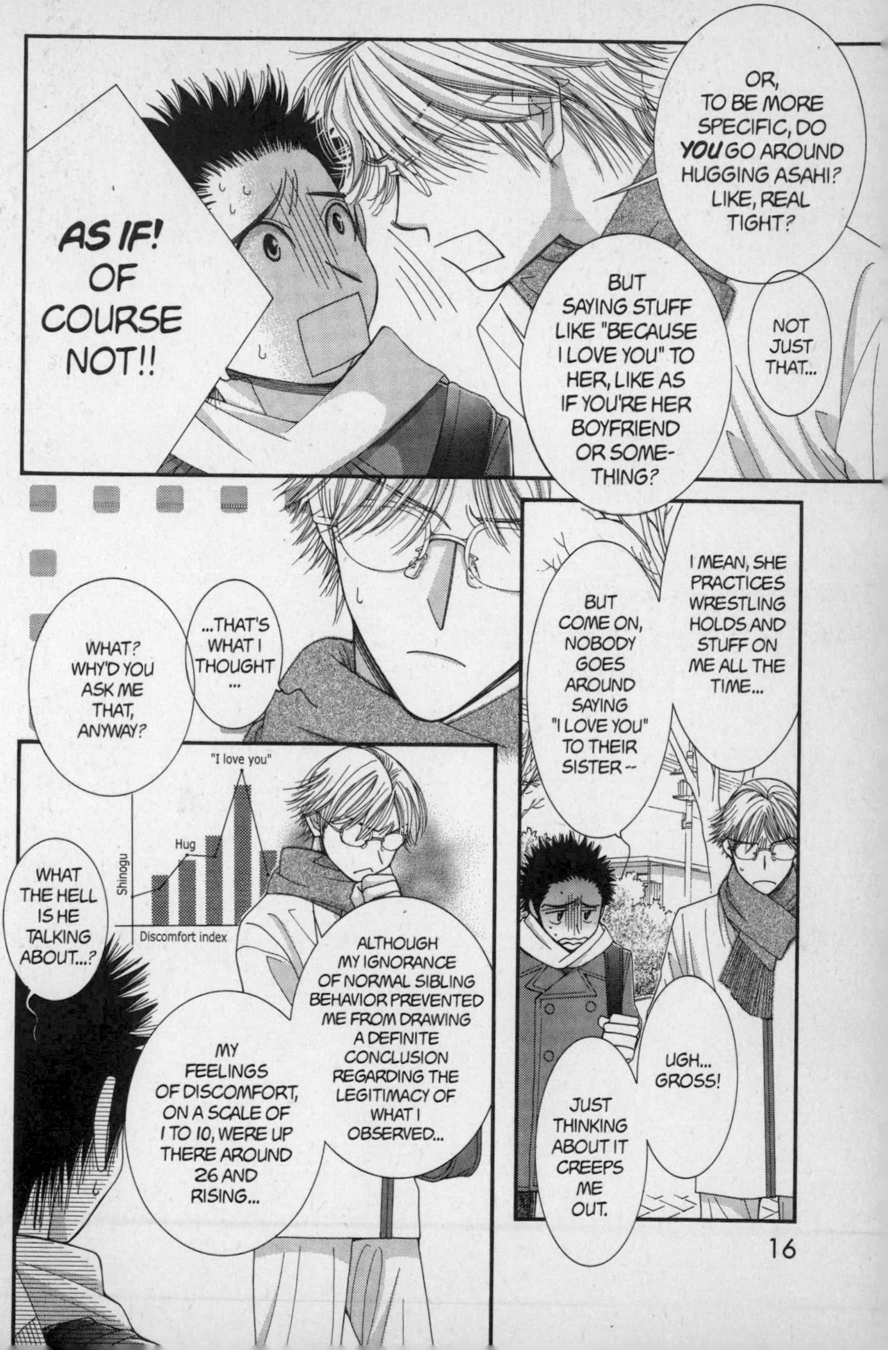
OR, TO BE MORE SPECIFIC, DO **YOU** GO AROUND HUGGING ASAHI? LIKE, REAL TIGHT?
NOT JUST THAT...
BUT SAYING STUFF LIKE "BECAUSE I LOVE YOU" TO HER, LIKE AS IF YOU'RE HER BOYFRIEND OR SOME-THING?
AS IF! OF COURSE NOT!!
I MEAN, SHE PRACTICES WRESTLING HOLDS AND STUFF ON ME ALL THE TIME...
BUT COME ON, NOBODY GOES AROUND SAYING "I LOVE YOU" TO THEIR SISTER --
UGH... GROSS!
JUST THINKING ABOUT IT CREEPS ME OUT.
...THAT'S WHAT I THOUGHT ...
WHAT? WHY'D YOU ASK ME THAT, ANYWAY?
"I love you"
Hug
Shinogu
Discomfort index
ALTHOUGH MY IGNORANCE OF NORMAL SIBLING BEHAVIOR PREVENTED ME FROM DRAWING A DEFINITE CONCLUSION REGARDING THE LEGITIMACY OF WHAT I OBSERVED...
MY FEELINGS OF DISCOMFORT, ON A SCALE OF 1 TO 10, WERE UP THERE AROUND 26 AND RISING...
WHAT THE HELL IS HE TALKING ABOUT...?

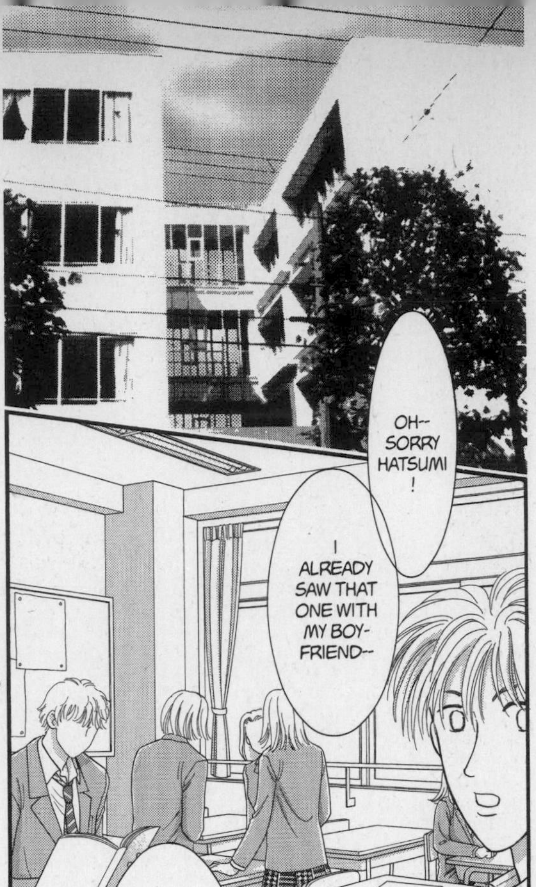
OH-- SORRY HATSUMI!
I ALREADY SAW THAT ONE WITH MY BOY-FRIEND--
IT WAS REALLY GOOD. YOU SHOULD TOTALLY GO--

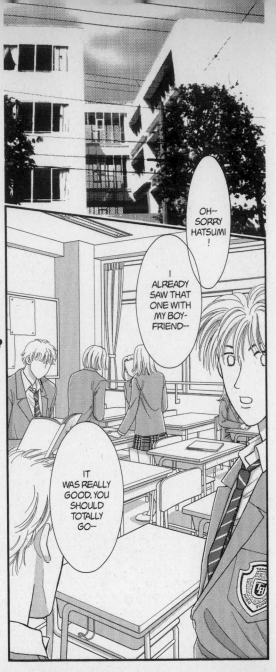

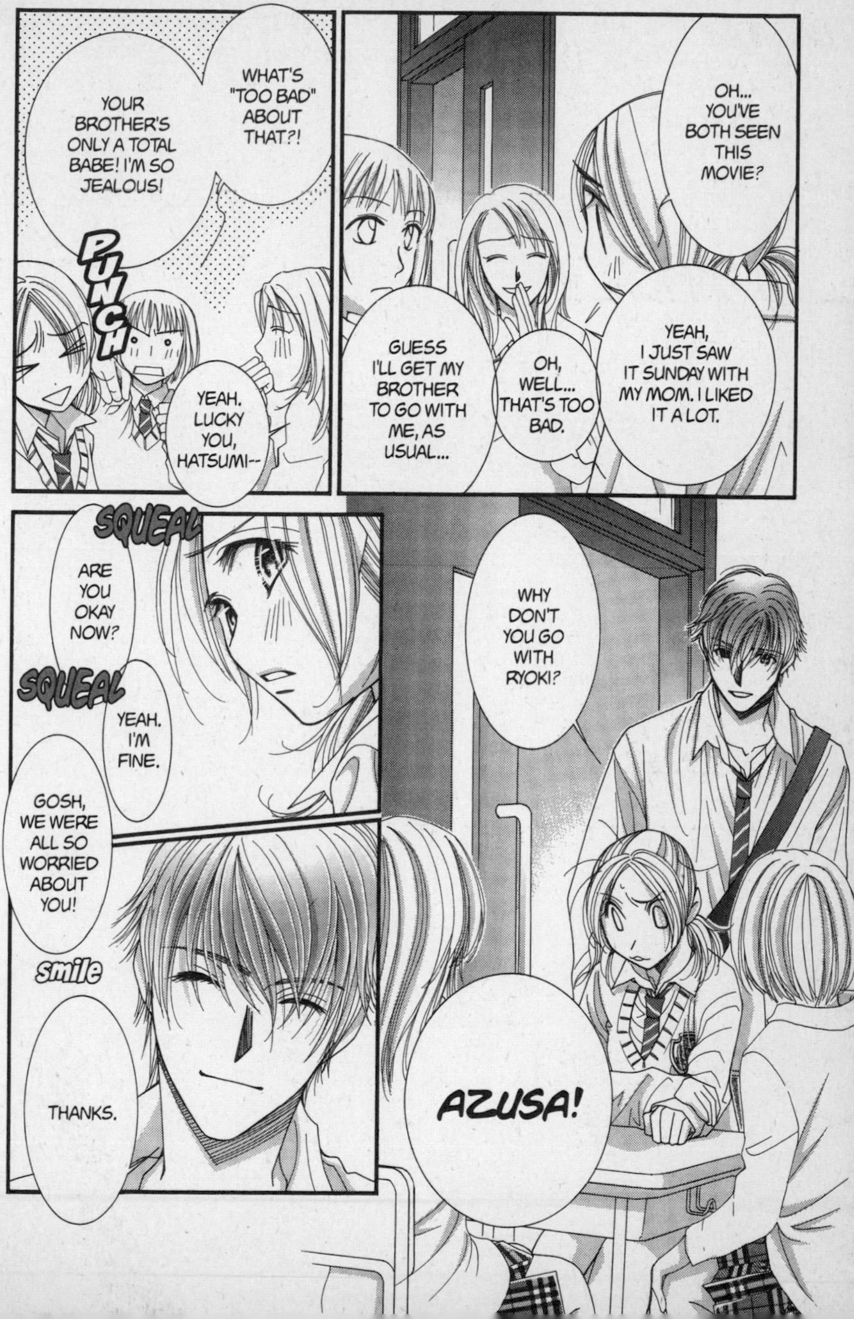
OH... YOU'VE BOTH SEEN THIS MOVIE?
YEAH, I JUST SAW IT SUNDAY WITH MY MOM. I LIKED IT A LOT.
OH, WELL... THAT'S TOO BAD.
GUESS I'LL GET MY BROTHER TO GO WITH ME, AS USUAL...
WHAT'S "TOO BAD" ABOUT THAT?!
YOUR BROTHER'S ONLY A TOTAL BABE! I'M SO JEALOUS!
PUNCH
YEAH. LUCKY YOU, HATSUMI--
WHY DON'T YOU GO WITH RYOKI?
AZUSA!
SQUEAL
ARE YOU OKAY NOW?
SQUEAL
YEAH. I'M FINE.
GOSH, WE WERE ALL SO WORRIED ABOUT YOU!
smile
THANKS.

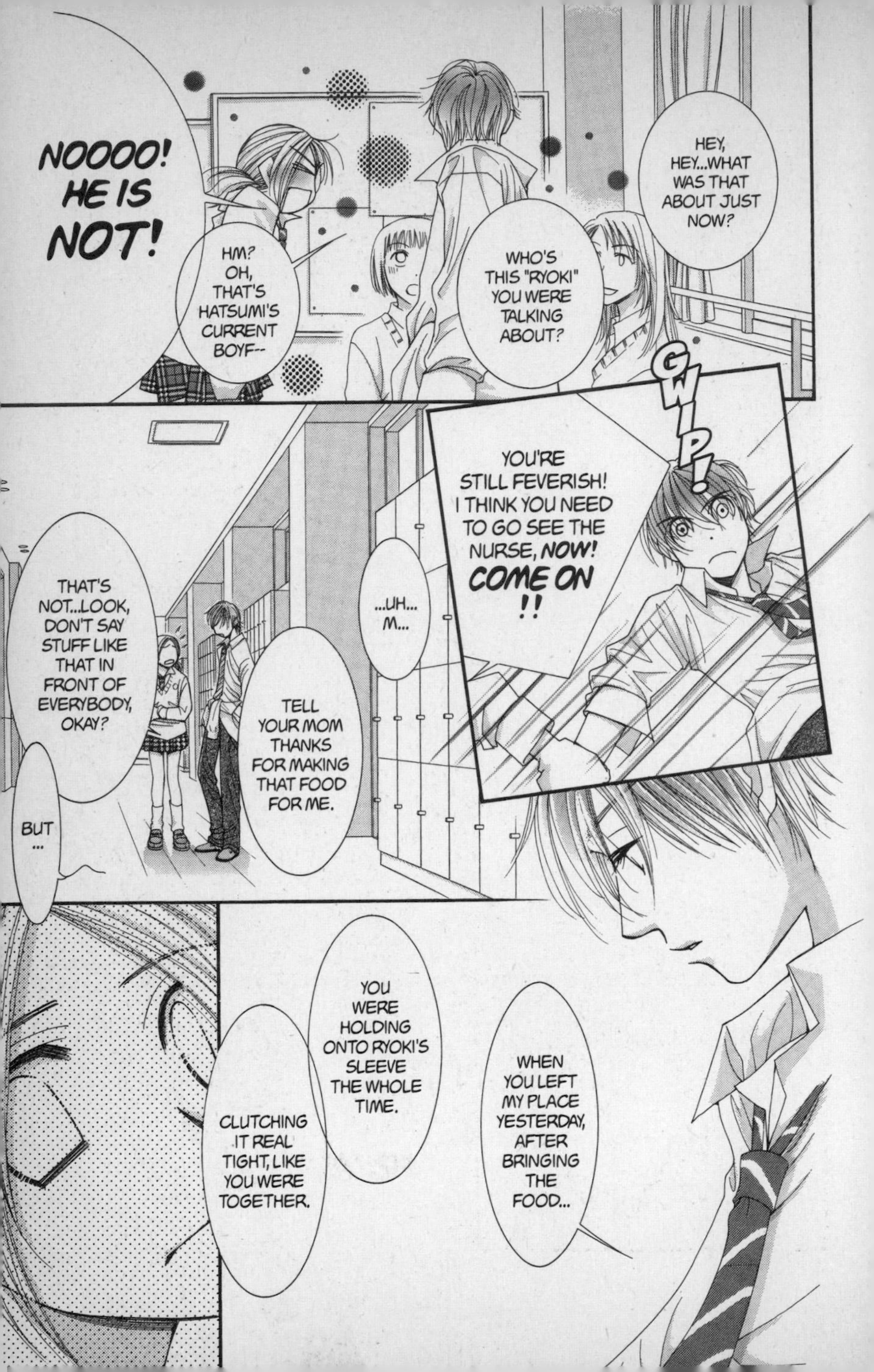
HEY, HEY...WHAT WAS THAT ABOUT JUST NOW?
WHO'S THIS "RYOKI" YOU WERE TALKING ABOUT?
HM? OH, THAT'S HATSUMI'S CURRENT BOYF--
NOOOO! HE IS NOT!
GWIP!
YOU'RE STILL FEVERISH! I THINK YOU NEED TO GO SEE THE NURSE, NOW! COME ON !!
...UH... M...
TELL YOUR MOM THANKS FOR MAKING THAT FOOD FOR ME.
THAT'S NOT...LOOK, DON'T SAY STUFF LIKE THAT IN FRONT OF EVERYBODY, OKAY?
BUT ...
WHEN YOU LEFT MY PLACE YESTERDAY, AFTER BRINGING THE FOOD...
YOU WERE HOLDING ONTO RYOKI'S SLEEVE THE WHOLE TIME.
CLUTCHING IT REAL TIGHT, LIKE YOU WERE TOGETHER.

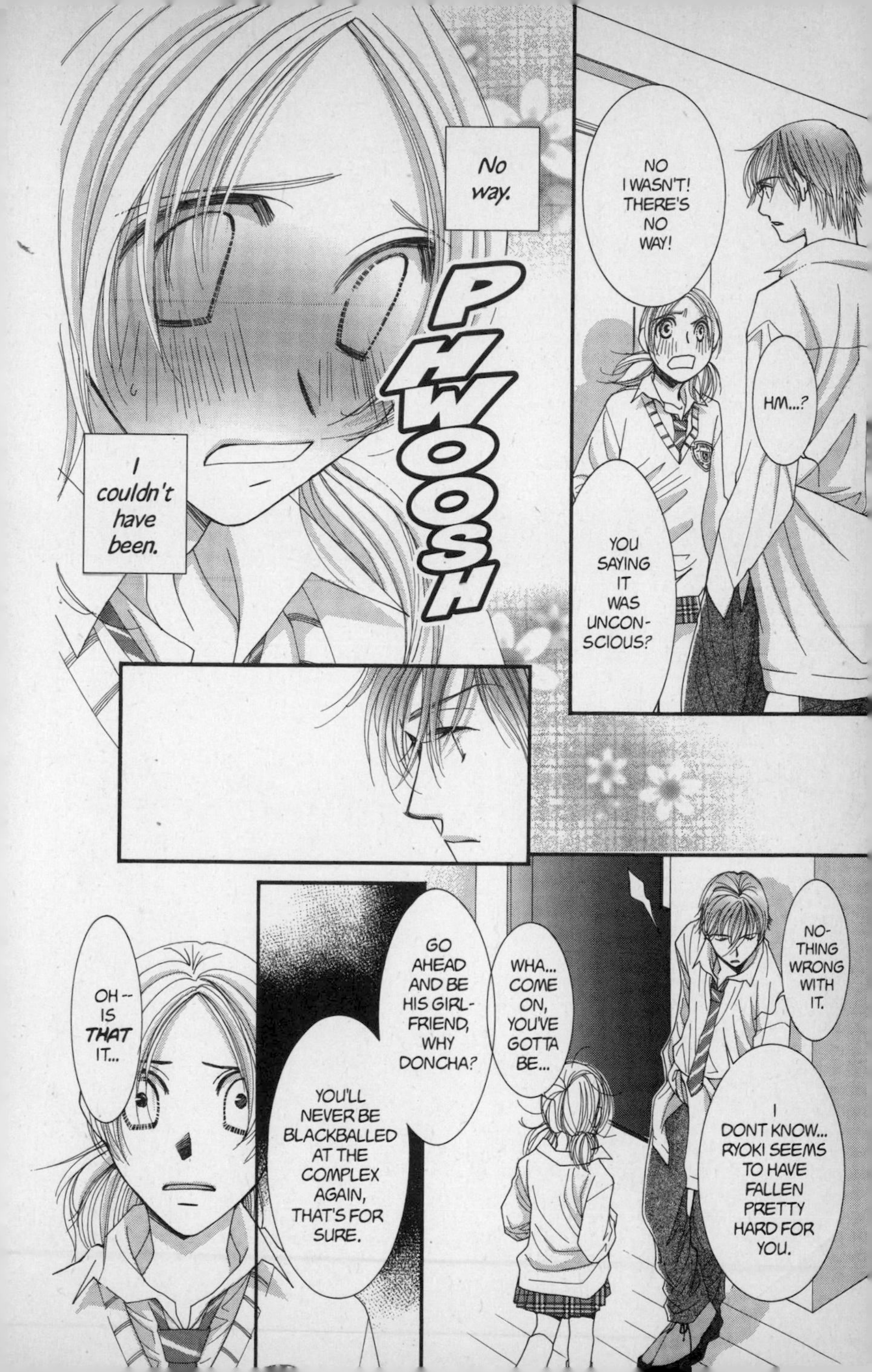
NO I WASN'T! THERE'S NO WAY!
HM...?
YOU SAYING IT WAS UNCONSCIOUS?
No way.
PHWOOSH
I couldn't have been.
NO-THING WRONG WITH IT.
I DONT KNOW... RYOKI SEEMS TO HAVE FALLEN PRETTY HARD FOR YOU.
WHA... COME ON, YOU'VE GOTTA BE...
GO AHEAD AND BE HIS GIRL-FRIEND, WHY DONCHA?
YOU'LL NEVER BE BLACKBALLED AT THE COMPLEX AGAIN, THAT'S FOR SURE.
OH -- IS THAT IT...

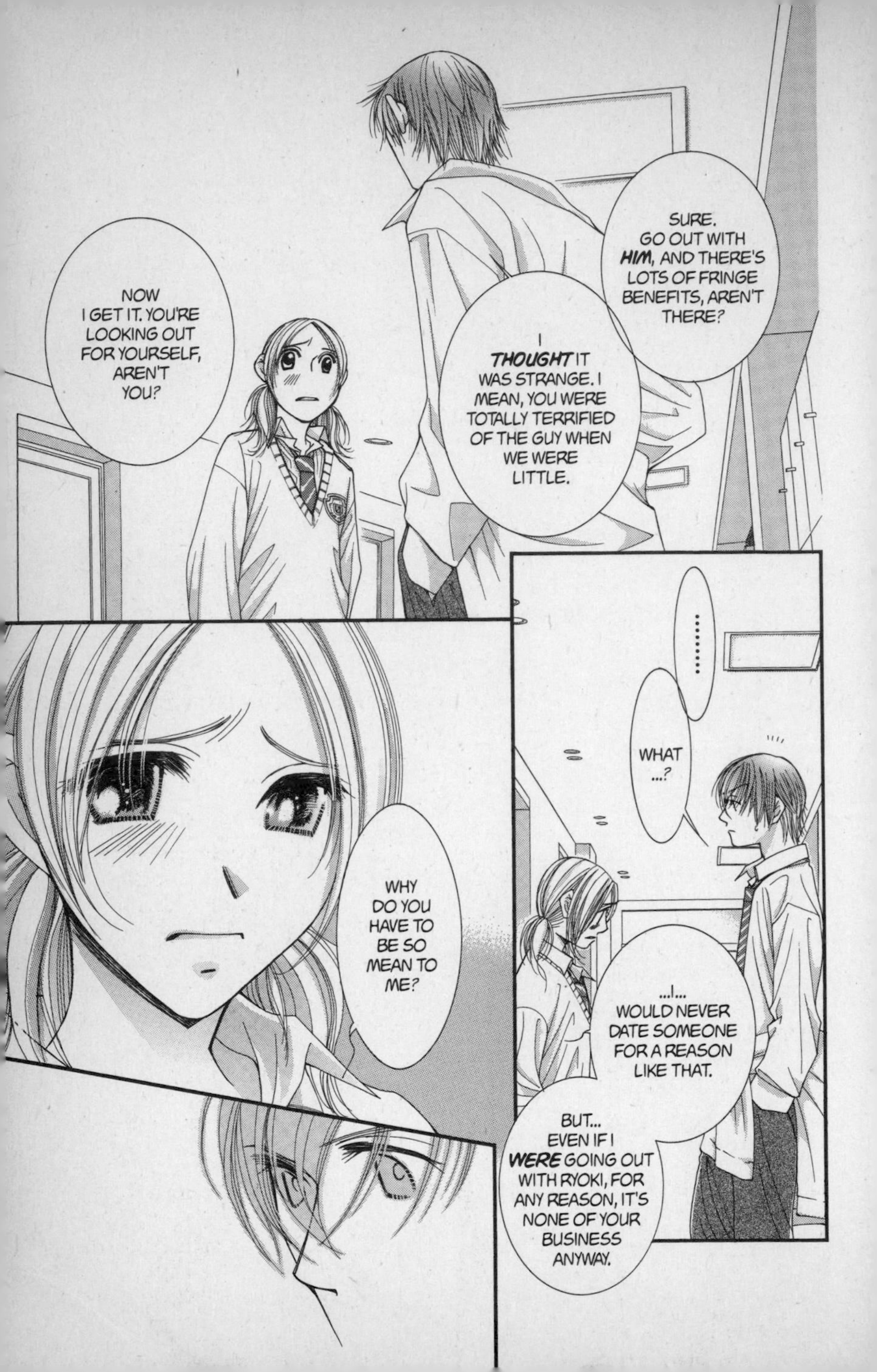

SURE. GO OUT WITH *HIM*, AND THERE'S LOTS OF FRINGE BENEFITS, AREN'T THERE?
I *THOUGHT* IT WAS STRANGE. I MEAN, YOU WERE TOTALLY TERRIFIED OF THE GUY WHEN WE WERE LITTLE.
NOW I GET IT. YOU'RE LOOKING OUT FOR YOURSELF, AREN'T YOU?
......
WHAT ...?
WHY DO YOU HAVE TO BE SO MEAN TO ME?
...I... WOULD NEVER DATE SOMEONE FOR A REASON LIKE THAT.
BUT... EVEN IF I *WERE* GOING OUT WITH RYOKI, FOR ANY REASON, IT'S NONE OF YOUR BUSINESS ANYWAY.

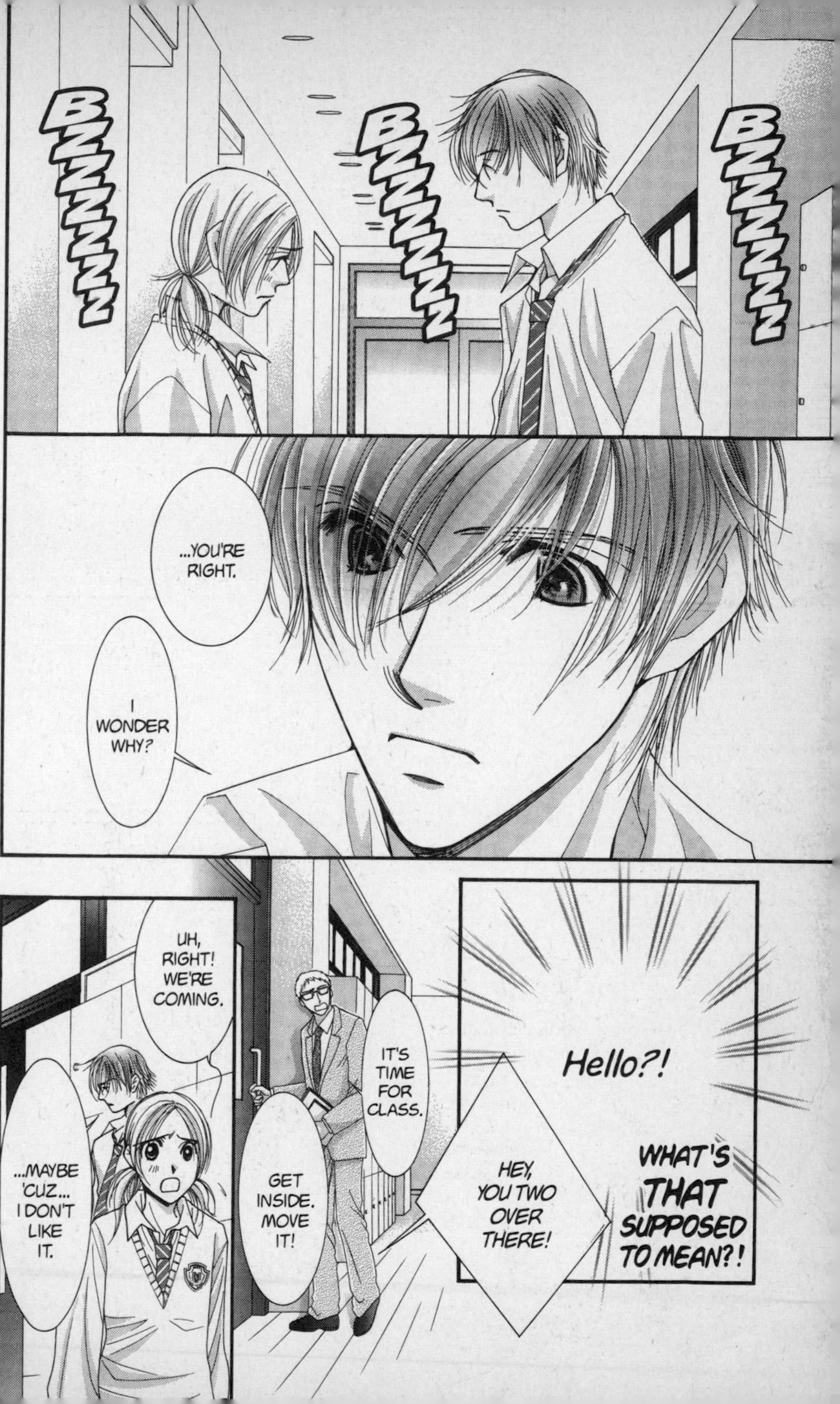
BZZZZZZ
BZZZZZZ
BZZZZZZ
...YOU'RE RIGHT.
I WONDER WHY?
Hello?!
WHAT'S THAT SUPPOSED TO MEAN?!
HEY, YOU TWO OVER THERE!
IT'S TIME FOR CLASS.
GET INSIDE. MOVE IT!
UH, RIGHT! WE'RE COMING.
...MAYBE 'CUZ... I DON'T LIKE IT.

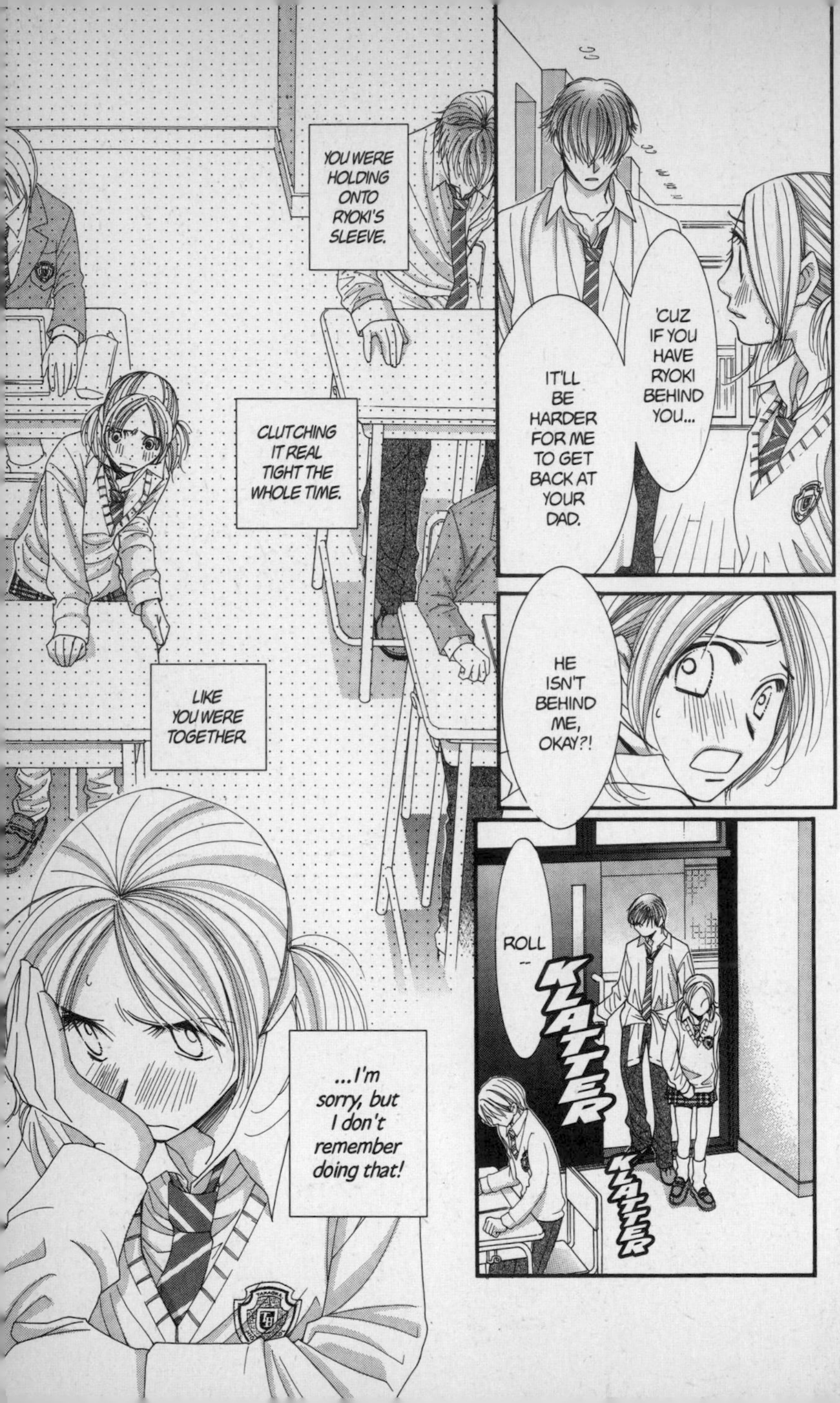
'CUZ IF YOU HAVE RYOKI BEHIND YOU...
IT'LL BE HARDER FOR ME TO GET BACK AT YOUR DAD.
HE ISN'T BEHIND ME, OKAY?!
ROLL --
KLATTER
KLATTER
YOU WERE HOLDING ONTO RYOKI'S SLEEVE.
CLUTCHING IT REAL TIGHT THE WHOLE TIME.
LIKE YOU WERE TOGETHER.
...I'm sorry, but I don't remember doing that!

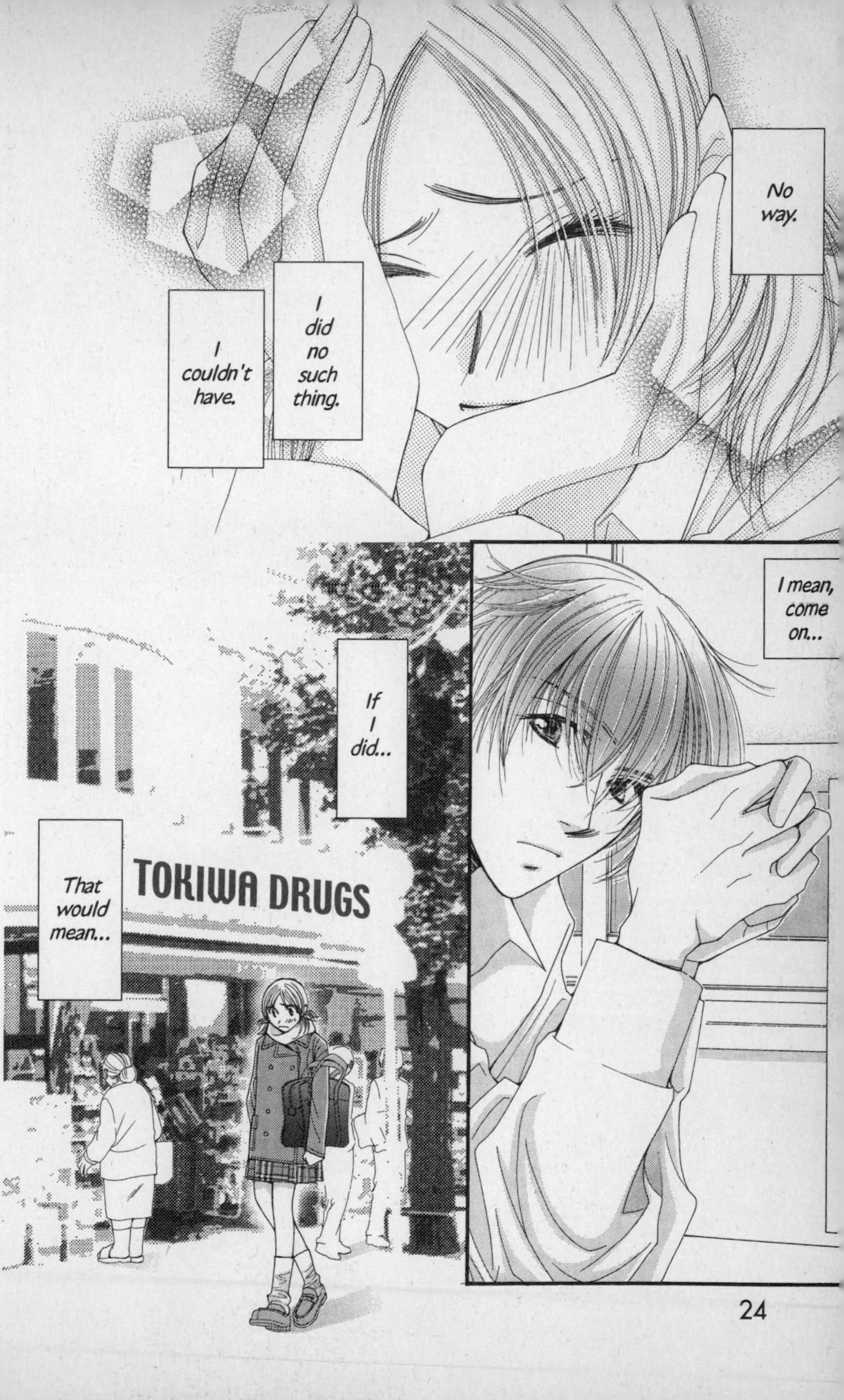
No way.
I did no such thing.
I couldn't have.
I mean, come on...
If I did...
That would mean...
TOKIWA DRUGS

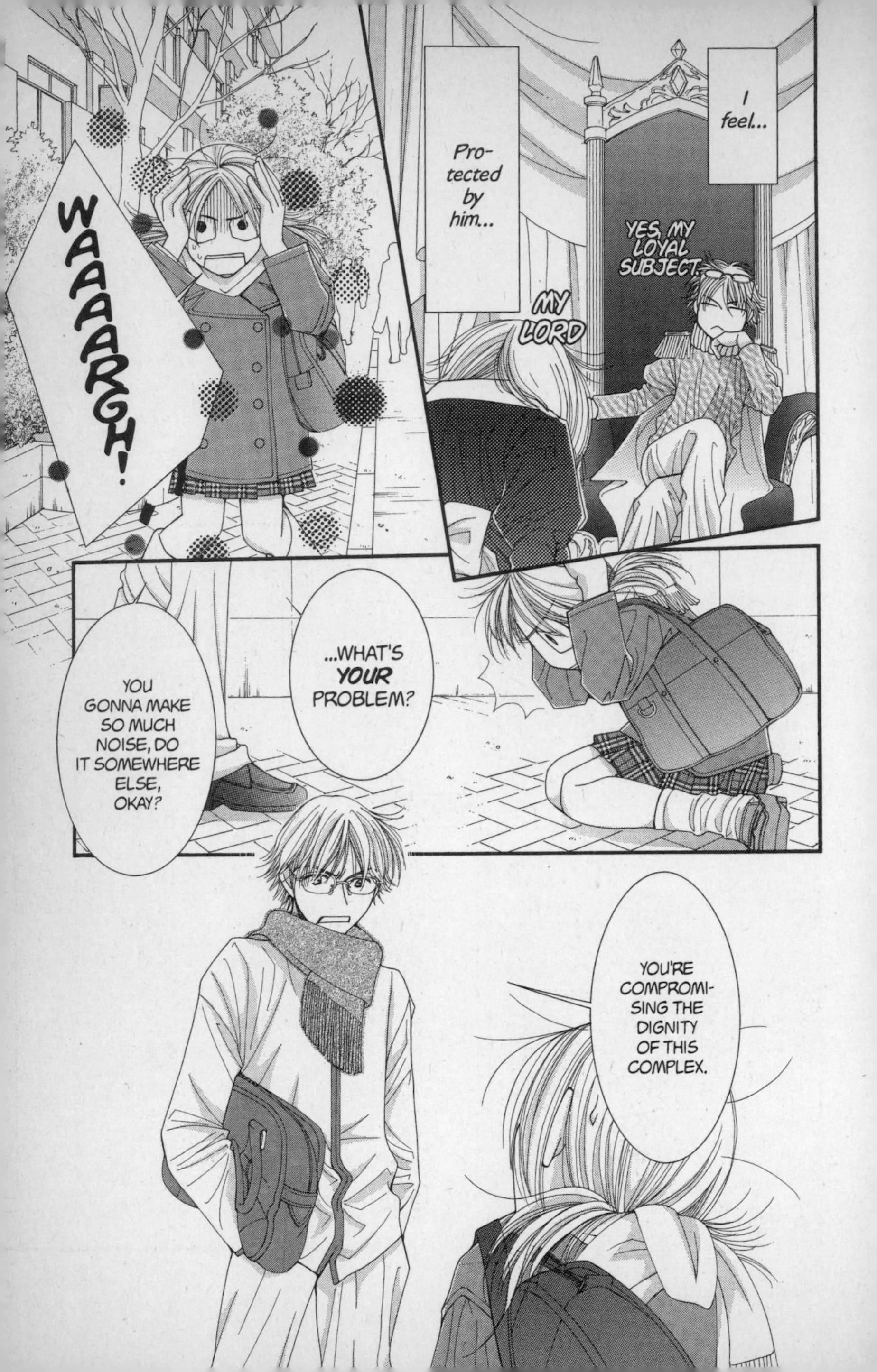
I feel...
Pro-tected by him...
YES, MY LOYAL SUBJECT.
MY LORD
WAAAARGH!
...WHAT'S YOUR PROBLEM?
YOU GONNA MAKE SO MUCH NOISE, DO IT SOMEWHERE ELSE, OKAY?
YOU'RE COMPROMI-SING THE DIGNITY OF THIS COMPLEX.

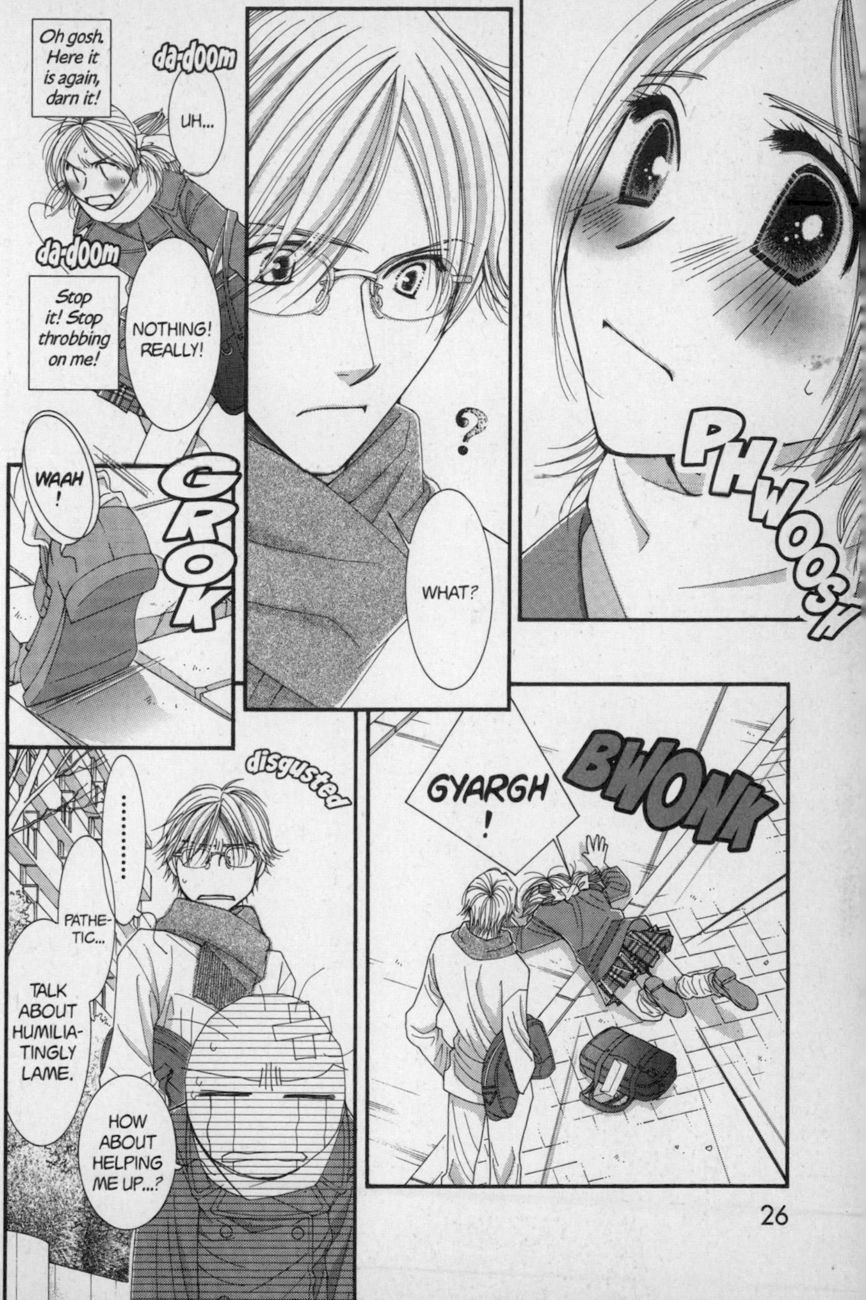
PHWOOSH
?
WHAT?
Oh gosh. Here it is again, darn it!
da-doom
UH...
da-doom
Stop it! Stop throbbing on me!
NOTHING! REALLY!
WAAH!
GROK
BWONK
GYARGH!
disgusted
......
PATHETIC...
TALK ABOUT HUMILIATINGLY LAME.
HOW ABOUT HELPING ME UP...?

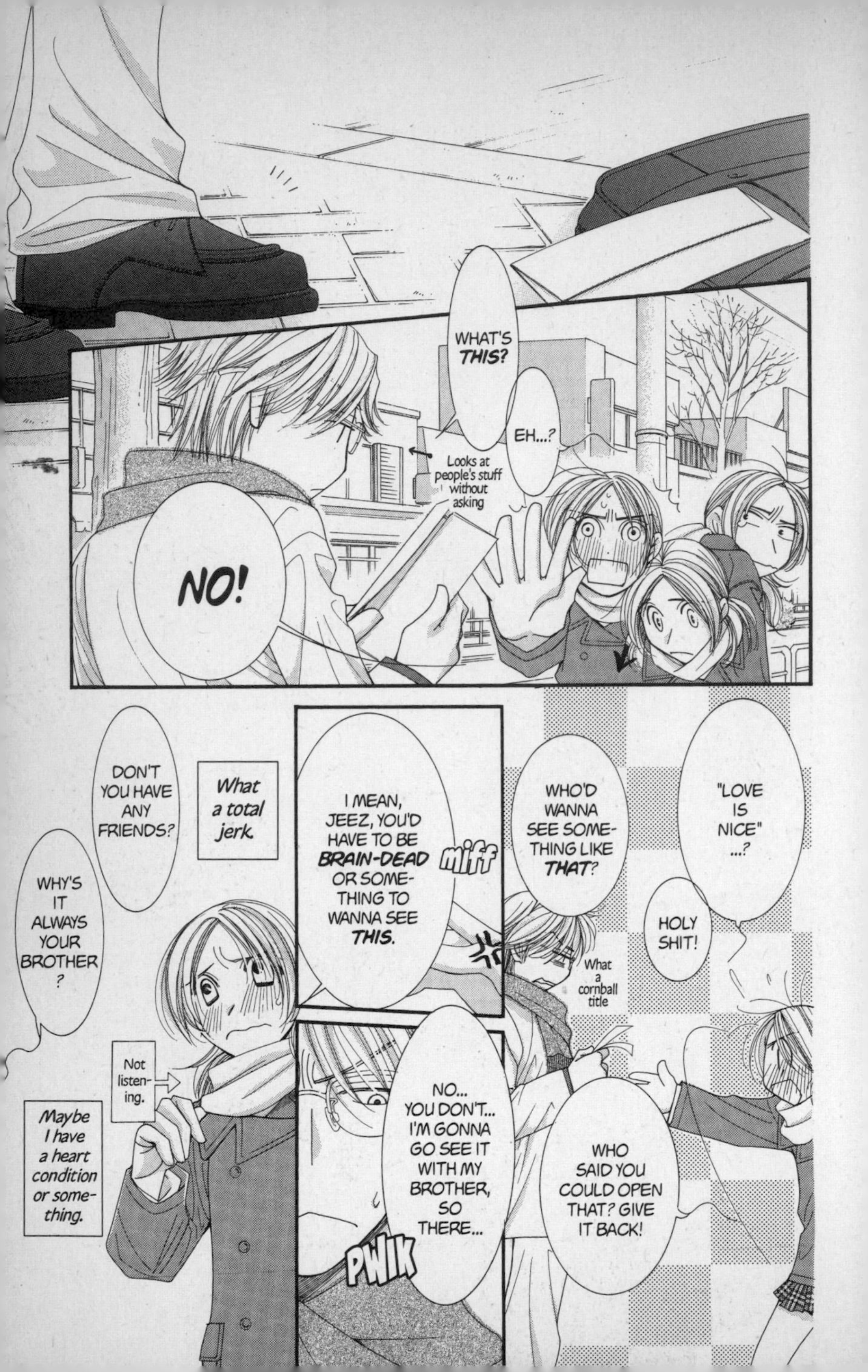
WHAT'S THIS?
EH...?
Looks at people's stuff without asking
NO!
"LOVE IS NICE" ...?
HOLY SHIT!
WHO'D WANNA SEE SOMETHING LIKE THAT?
What a cornball title
WHO SAID YOU COULD OPEN THAT? GIVE IT BACK!
I MEAN, JEEZ, YOU'D HAVE TO BE BRAIN-DEAD OR SOMETHING TO WANNA SEE THIS.
miff
NO... YOU DON'T... I'M GONNA GO SEE IT WITH MY BROTHER, SO THERE...
PWIK
What a total jerk.
DON'T YOU HAVE ANY FRIENDS?
WHY'S IT ALWAYS YOUR BROTHER?
Not listening.
Maybe I have a heart condition or something.

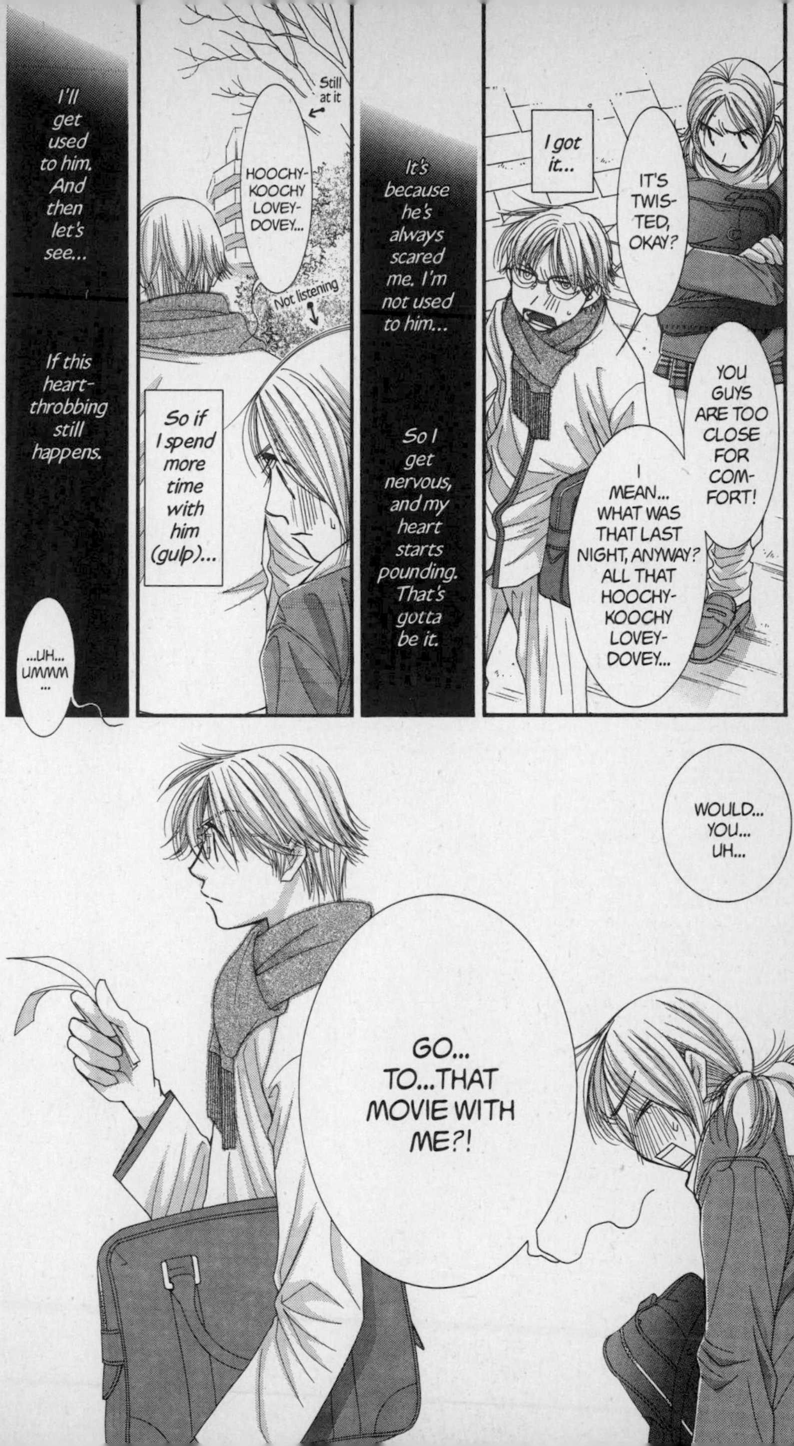
IT'S TWISTED, OKAY?
I got it...
YOU GUYS ARE TOO CLOSE FOR COMFORT!
I MEAN... WHAT WAS THAT LAST NIGHT, ANYWAY? ALL THAT HOOCHY-KOOCHY LOVEY-DOVEY...
It's because he's always scared me. I'm not used to him...
So I get nervous, and my heart starts pounding. That's gotta be it.
Still at it
HOOCHY-KOOCHY LOVEY-DOVEY...
Not listening
So if I spend more time with him (gulp)...
I'll get used to him. And then let's see...
If this heart-throbbing still happens.
...UH... UMMM...
WOULD... YOU... UH...
GO... TO...THAT MOVIE WITH ME?!

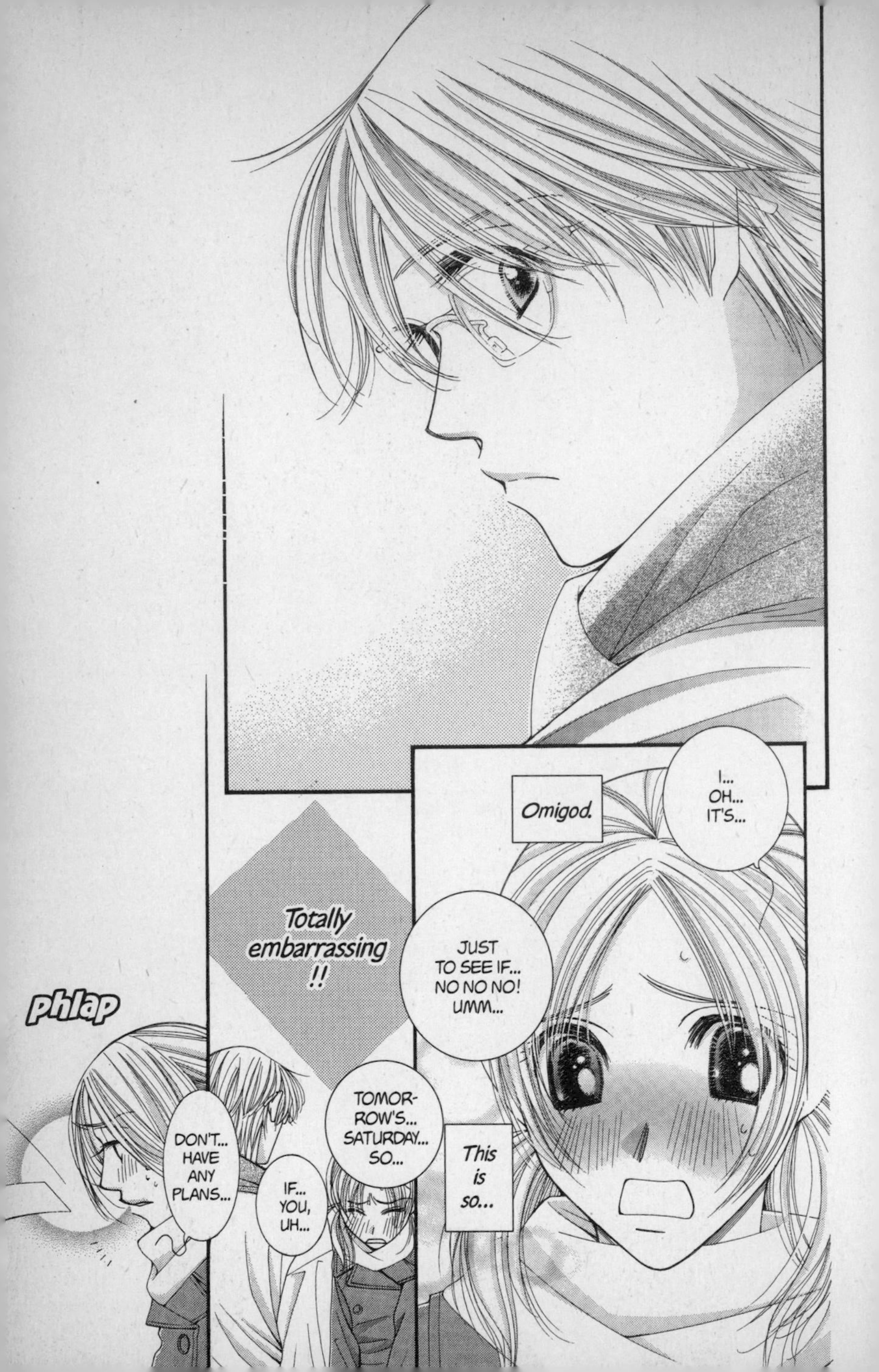
I... OH... IT'S...
Omigod.
JUST TO SEE IF... NO NO NO! UMM...
This is so...
Totally embarrassing !!
TOMOR-ROW'S... SATURDAY... SO...
IF... YOU, UH...
DON'T... HAVE ANY PLANS...
phlap

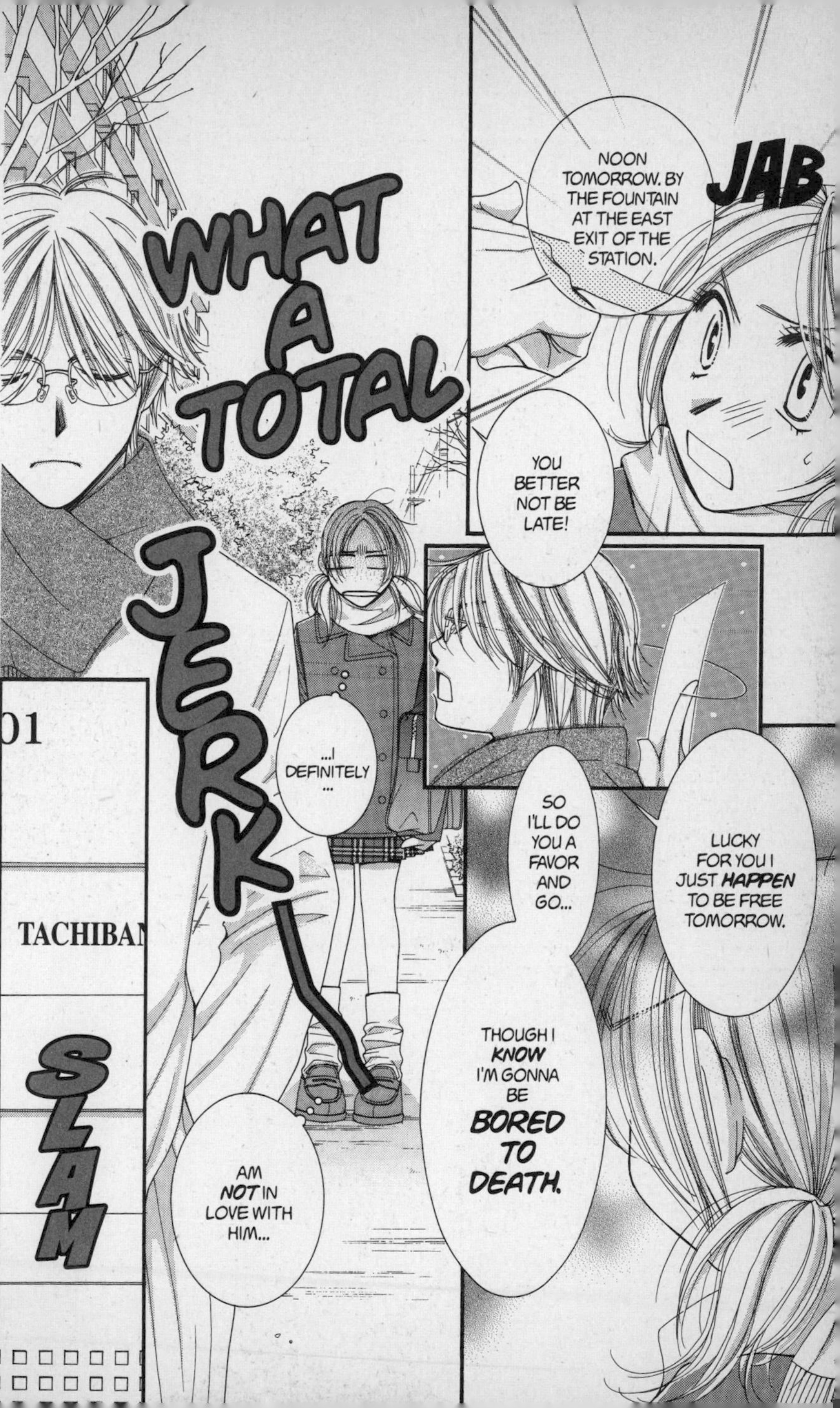
JAB
NOON TOMORROW. BY THE FOUNTAIN AT THE EAST EXIT OF THE STATION.
YOU BETTER NOT BE LATE!
LUCKY FOR YOU I JUST HAPPEN TO BE FREE TOMORROW.
SO I'LL DO YOU A FAVOR AND GO...
THOUGH I KNOW I'M GONNA BE BORED TO DEATH.
WHAT A TOTAL JERK
...I DEFINITELY ...
AM NOT IN LOVE WITH HIM...
01
TACHIBAN
SLAM

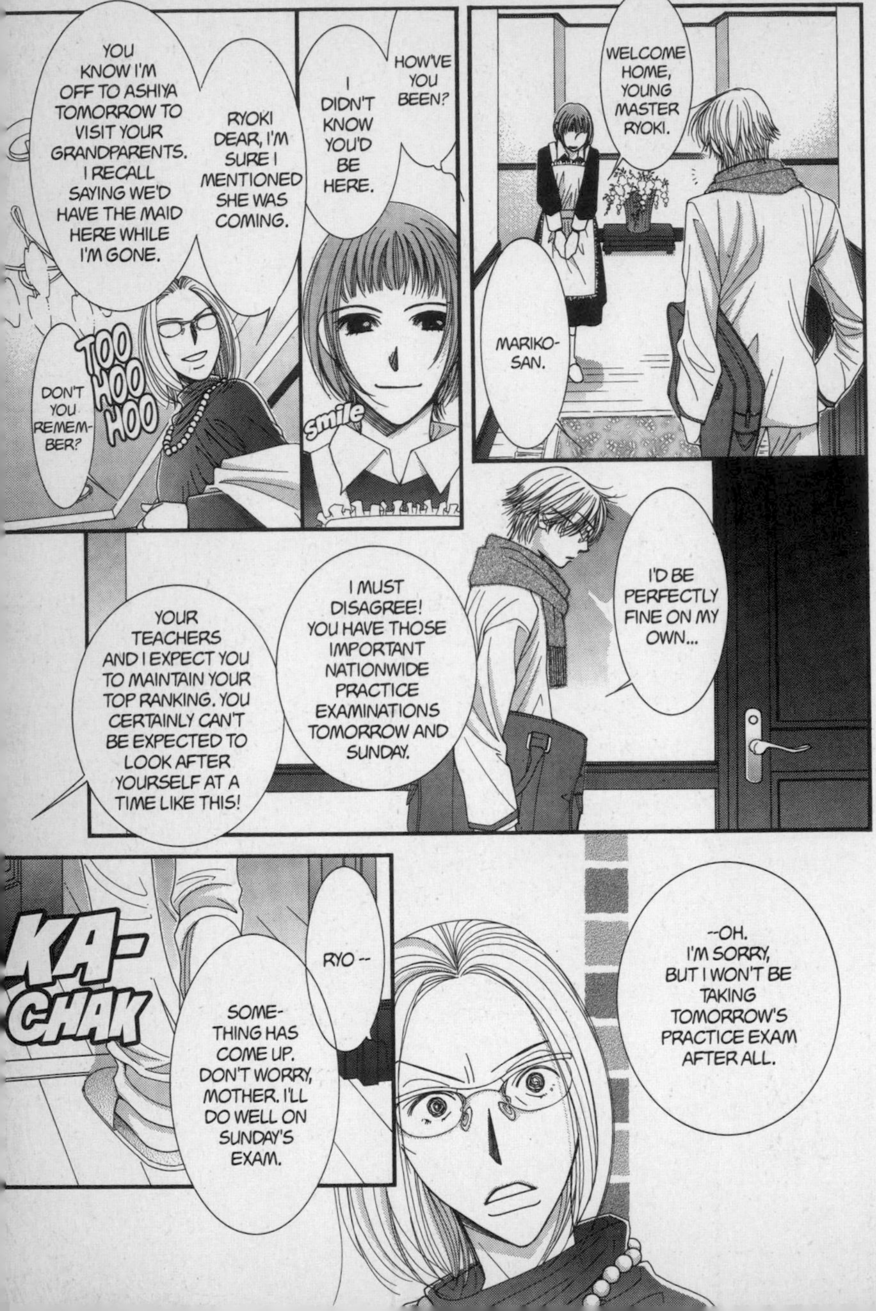
WELCOME HOME, YOUNG MASTER RYOKI.
MARIKO-SAN.
HOW'VE YOU BEEN?
I DIDN'T KNOW YOU'D BE HERE.
Smile
RYOKI DEAR, I'M SURE I MENTIONED SHE WAS COMING.
YOU KNOW I'M OFF TO ASHIYA TOMORROW TO VISIT YOUR GRANDPARENTS. I RECALL SAYING WE'D HAVE THE MAID HERE WHILE I'M GONE.
TOO HOO HOO
DON'T YOU REMEM-BER?
I'D BE PERFECTLY FINE ON MY OWN...
I MUST DISAGREE! YOU HAVE THOSE IMPORTANT NATIONWIDE PRACTICE EXAMINATIONS TOMORROW AND SUNDAY.
YOUR TEACHERS AND I EXPECT YOU TO MAINTAIN YOUR TOP RANKING. YOU CERTAINLY CAN'T BE EXPECTED TO LOOK AFTER YOURSELF AT A TIME LIKE THIS!
--OH. I'M SORRY, BUT I WON'T BE TAKING TOMORROW'S PRACTICE EXAM AFTER ALL.
RYO --
SOME-THING HAS COME UP. DON'T WORRY, MOTHER. I'LL DO WELL ON SUNDAY'S EXAM.
KA-CHAK

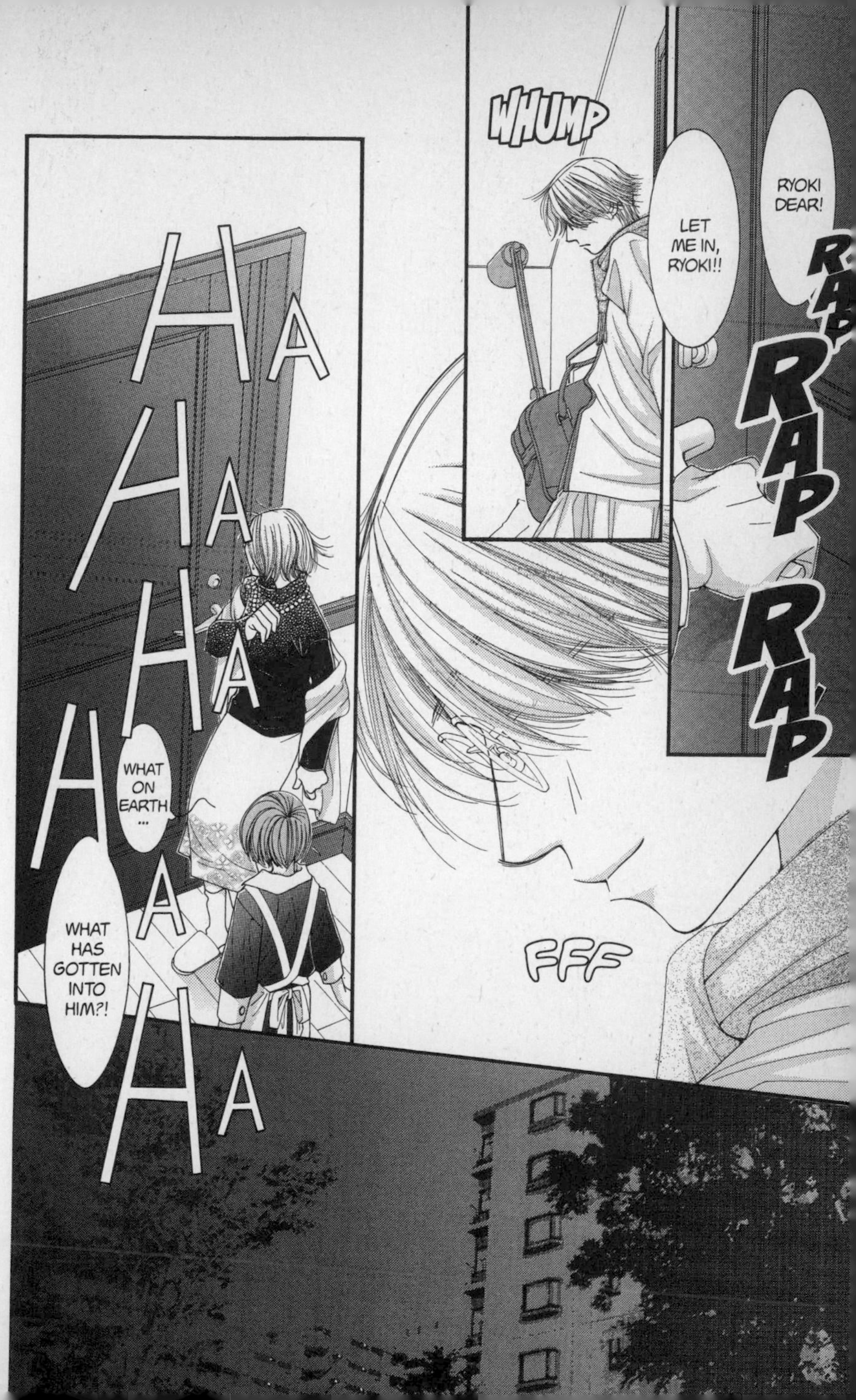
RYOKI DEAR!
LET ME IN, RYOKI!!
RAP RAP RAP RAP
WHUMP
FFF
HAAAHAHAHAHAHA
WHAT ON EARTH ...
WHAT HAS GOTTEN INTO HIM?!

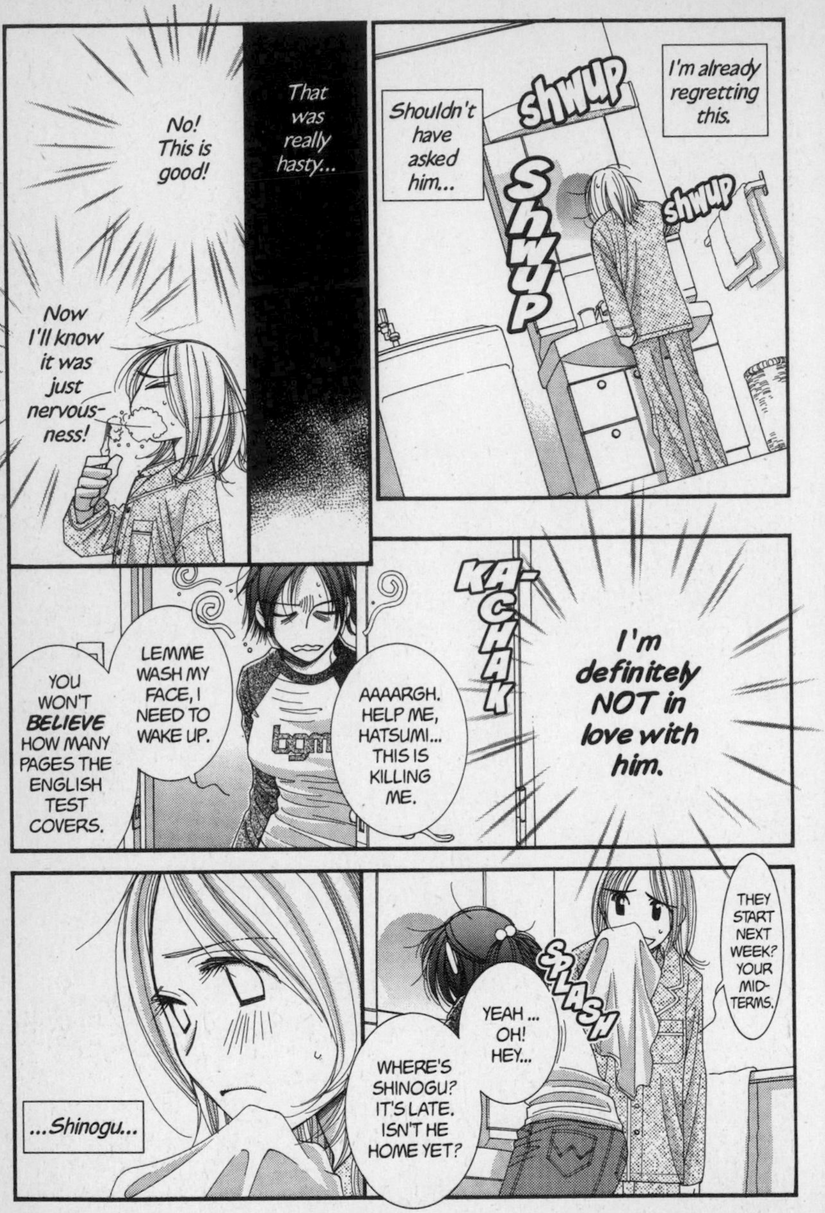
I'm already regretting this.
shwup
Shouldn't have asked him...
SHWUP
shwup
That was really hasty...
No! This is good!
Now I'll know it was just nervous-ness!
KA-CHAK
I'm definitely NOT in love with him.
AAAARGH. HELP ME, HATSUMI... THIS IS KILLING ME.
LEMME WASH MY FACE, I NEED TO WAKE UP.
YOU WON'T BELIEVE HOW MANY PAGES THE ENGLISH TEST COVERS.
THEY START NEXT WEEK? YOUR MID-TERMS.
SPLASH
YEAH ... OH! HEY...
WHERE'S SHINOGU? IT'S LATE. ISN'T HE HOME YET?
...Shinogu...

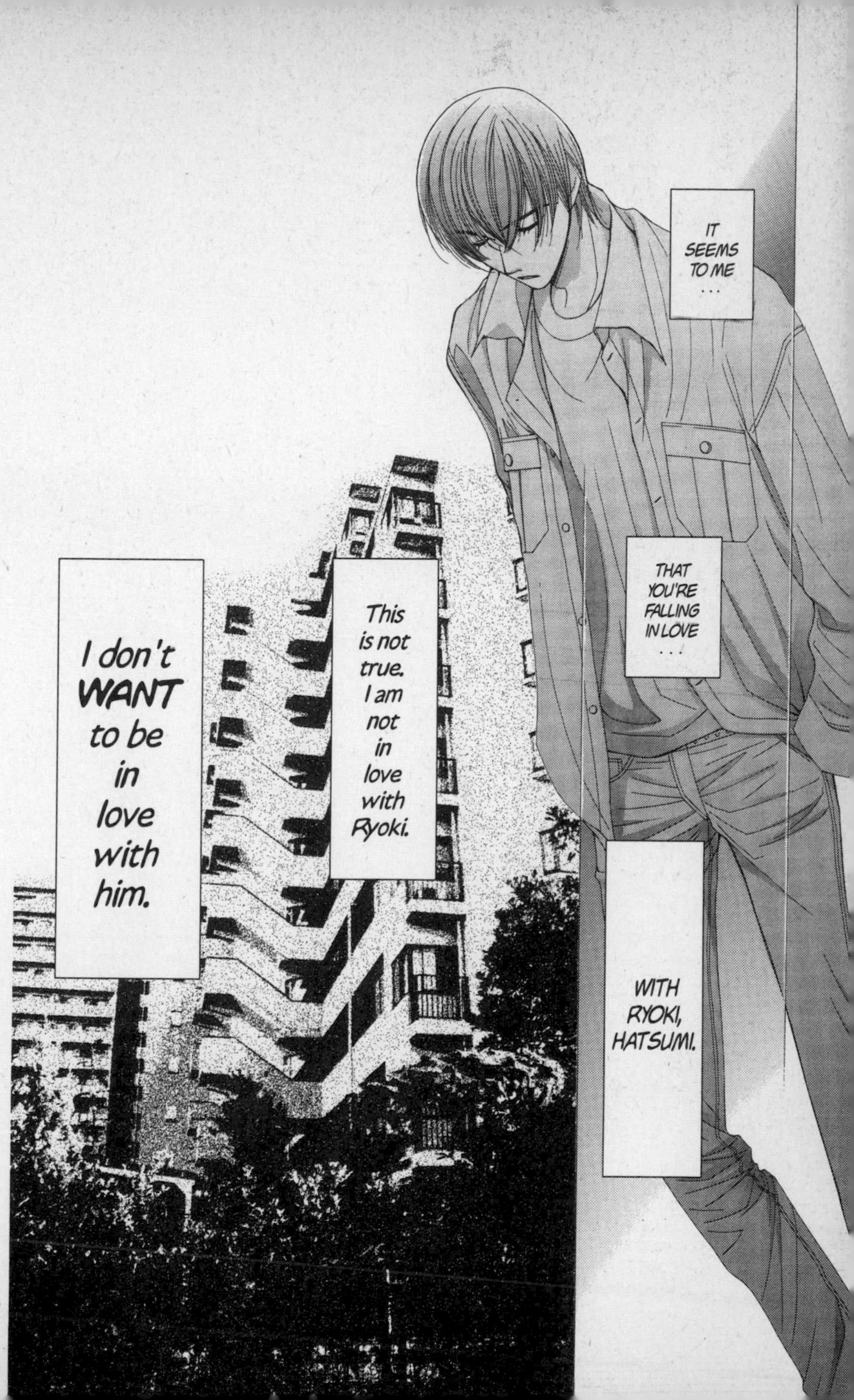
IT SEEMS TO ME . . .
THAT YOU'RE FALLING IN LOVE . . .
WITH RYOKI, HATSUMI.
This is not true. I am not in love with Ryoki.
I don't WANT to be in love with him.

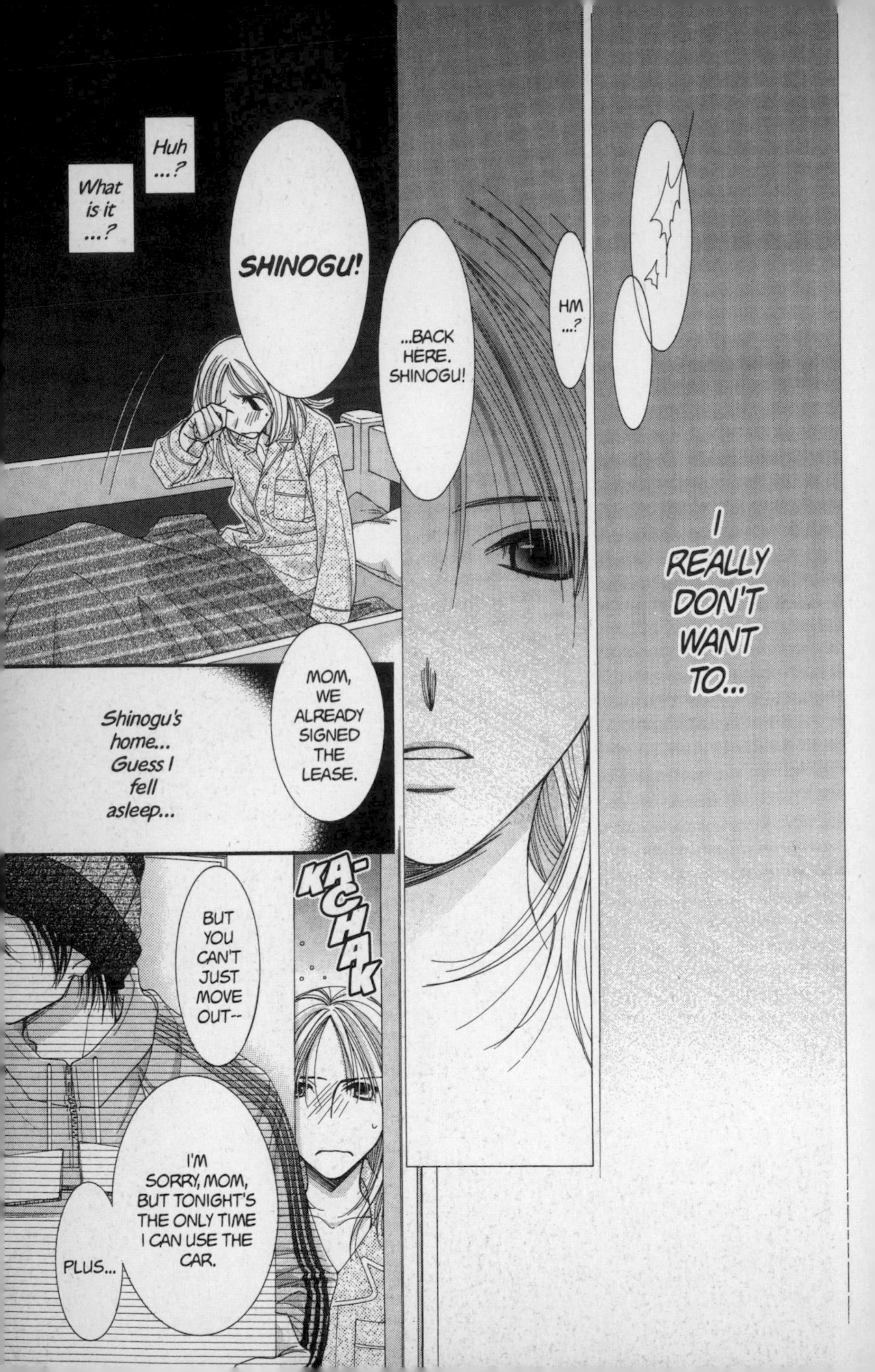
I REALLY DON'T WANT TO...
HM ...?
...BACK HERE. SHINOGU!
SHINOGU!
Huh ...?
What is it ...?
MOM, WE ALREADY SIGNED THE LEASE.
Shinogu's home... Guess I fell asleep...
KA-CHAK
BUT YOU CAN'T JUST MOVE OUT--
I'M SORRY, MOM, BUT TONIGHT'S THE ONLY TIME I CAN USE THE CAR.
PLUS...

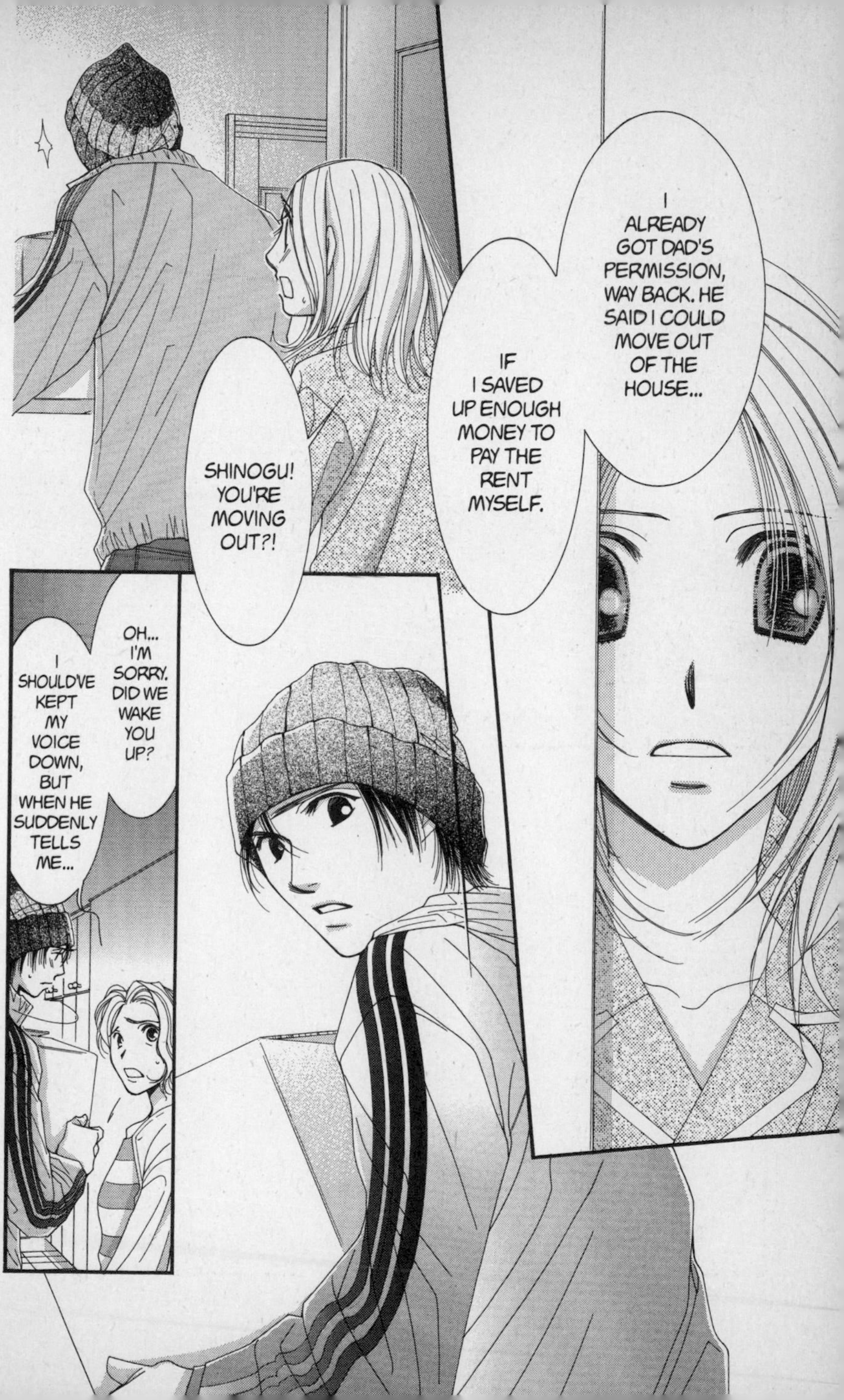
SHINOGU! YOU'RE MOVING OUT?!
I ALREADY GOT DAD'S PERMISSION, WAY BACK. HE SAID I COULD MOVE OUT OF THE HOUSE...
IF I SAVED UP ENOUGH MONEY TO PAY THE RENT MYSELF.
OH... I'M SORRY. DID WE WAKE YOU UP?
I SHOULD'VE KEPT MY VOICE DOWN, BUT WHEN HE SUDDENLY TELLS ME...

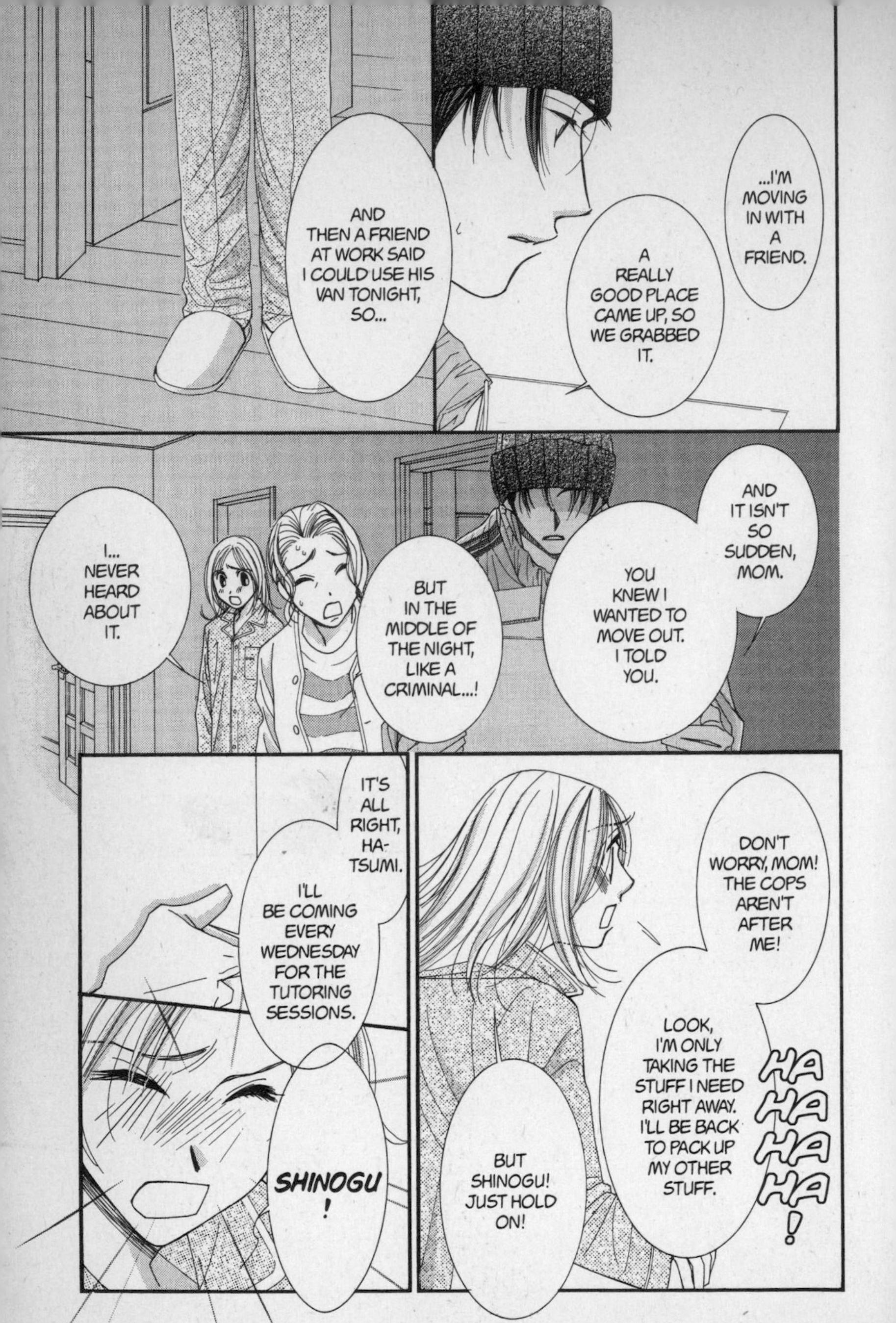
...I'M MOVING IN WITH A FRIEND.
A REALLY GOOD PLACE CAME UP, SO WE GRABBED IT.
AND THEN A FRIEND AT WORK SAID I COULD USE HIS VAN TONIGHT, SO...
AND IT ISN'T SO SUDDEN, MOM.
YOU KNEW I WANTED TO MOVE OUT. I TOLD YOU.
BUT IN THE MIDDLE OF THE NIGHT, LIKE A CRIMINAL...!
I... NEVER HEARD ABOUT IT.
DON'T WORRY, MOM! THE COPS AREN'T AFTER ME!
LOOK, I'M ONLY TAKING THE STUFF I NEED RIGHT AWAY. I'LL BE BACK TO PACK UP MY OTHER STUFF.
HA HA HA HA!
BUT SHINOGU! JUST HOLD ON!
IT'S ALL RIGHT, HA-TSUMI.
I'LL BE COMING EVERY WEDNESDAY FOR THE TUTORING SESSIONS.
SHINOGU!

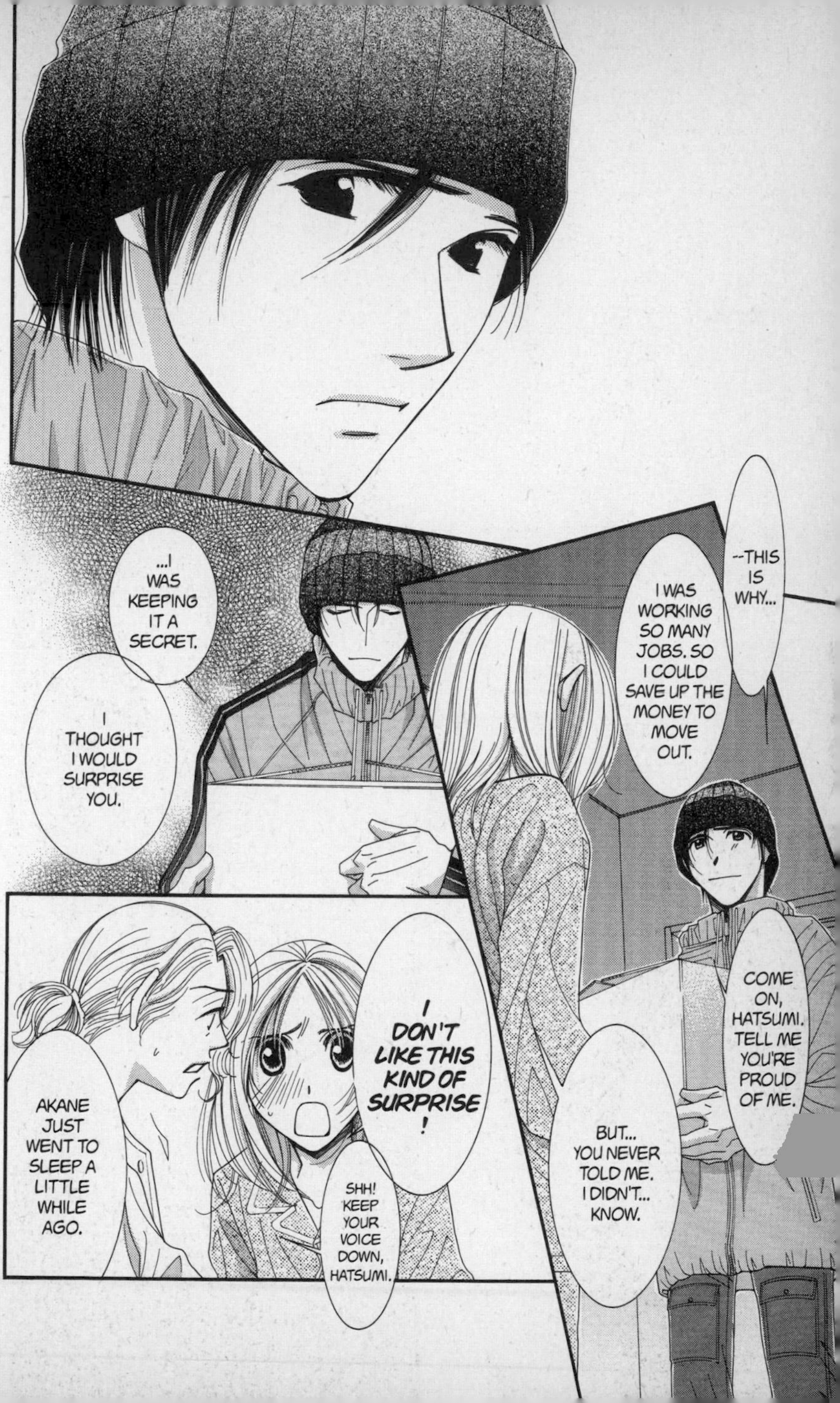
--THIS IS WHY...
I WAS WORKING SO MANY JOBS. SO I COULD SAVE UP THE MONEY TO MOVE OUT.
COME ON, HATSUMI. TELL ME YOU'RE PROUD OF ME.
BUT... YOU NEVER TOLD ME. I DIDN'T... KNOW.
...I WAS KEEPING IT A SECRET.
I THOUGHT I WOULD SURPRISE YOU.
I DON'T LIKE THIS KIND OF SURPRISE!
SHH! KEEP YOUR VOICE DOWN, HATSUMI.
AKANE JUST WENT TO SLEEP A LITTLE WHILE AGO.

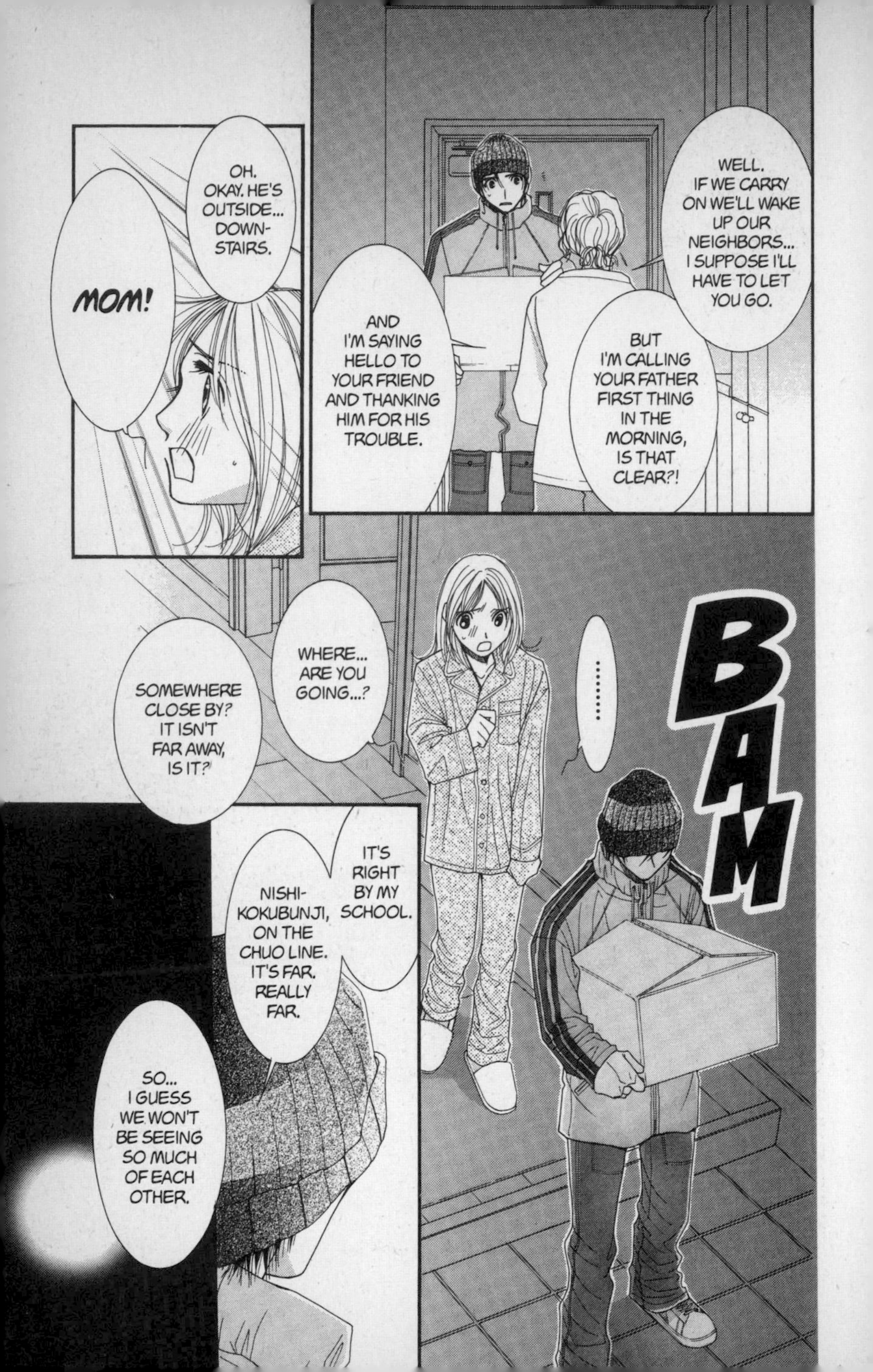
WELL. IF WE CARRY ON WE'LL WAKE UP OUR NEIGHBORS... I SUPPOSE I'LL HAVE TO LET YOU GO.
BUT I'M CALLING YOUR FATHER FIRST THING IN THE MORNING, IS THAT CLEAR?!
AND I'M SAYING HELLO TO YOUR FRIEND AND THANKING HIM FOR HIS TROUBLE.
OH. OKAY. HE'S OUTSIDE... DOWN-STAIRS.
MOM!
BAM
....
WHERE... ARE YOU GOING...?
SOMEWHERE CLOSE BY? IT ISN'T FAR AWAY, IS IT?
IT'S RIGHT BY MY SCHOOL.
NISHI-KOKUBUNJI, ON THE CHUO LINE. IT'S FAR. REALLY FAR.
SO... I GUESS WE WON'T BE SEEING SO MUCH OF EACH OTHER.

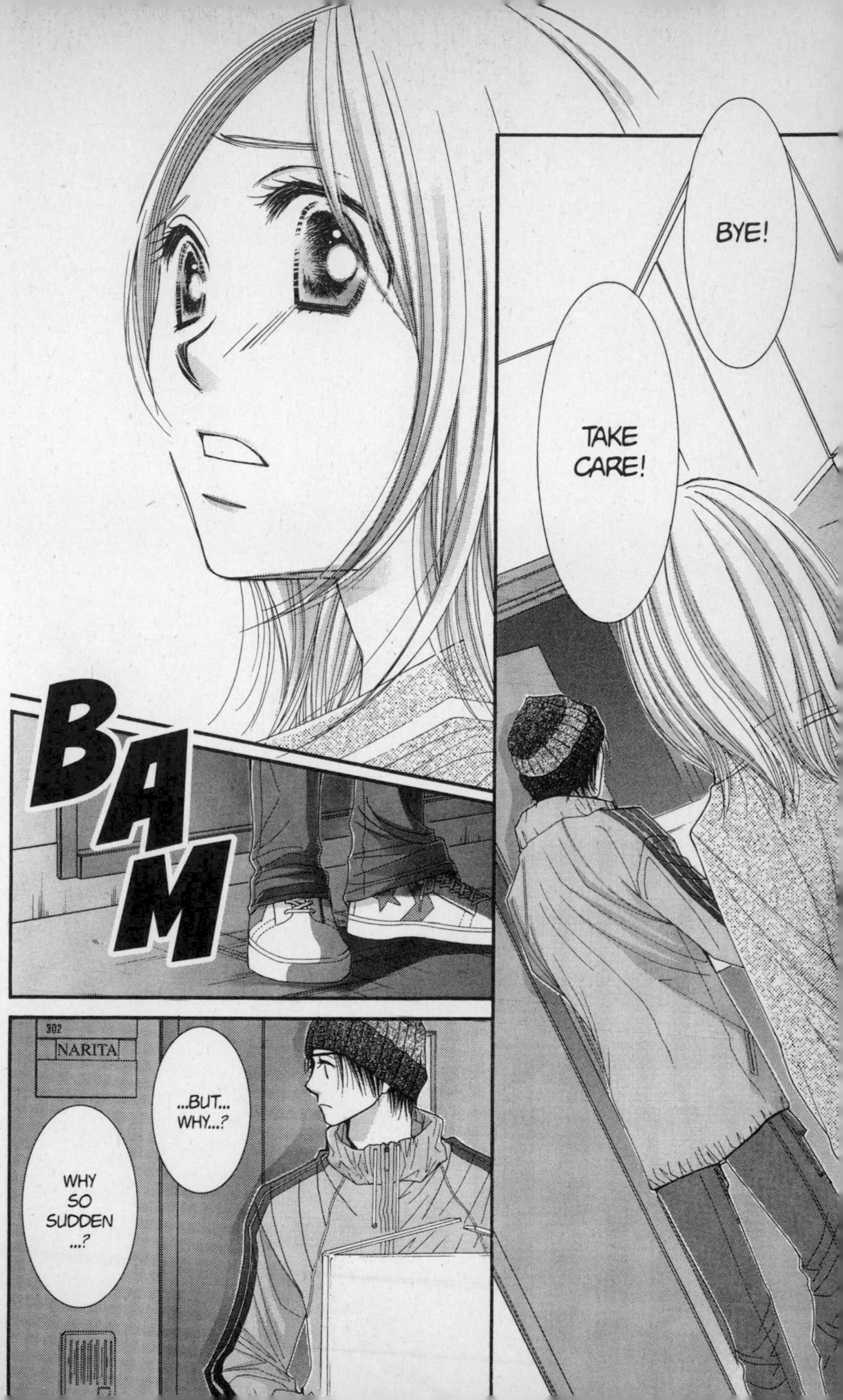
BYE!
TAKE CARE!
BAM
NARITA
...BUT... WHY...?
WHY SO SUDDEN ...?

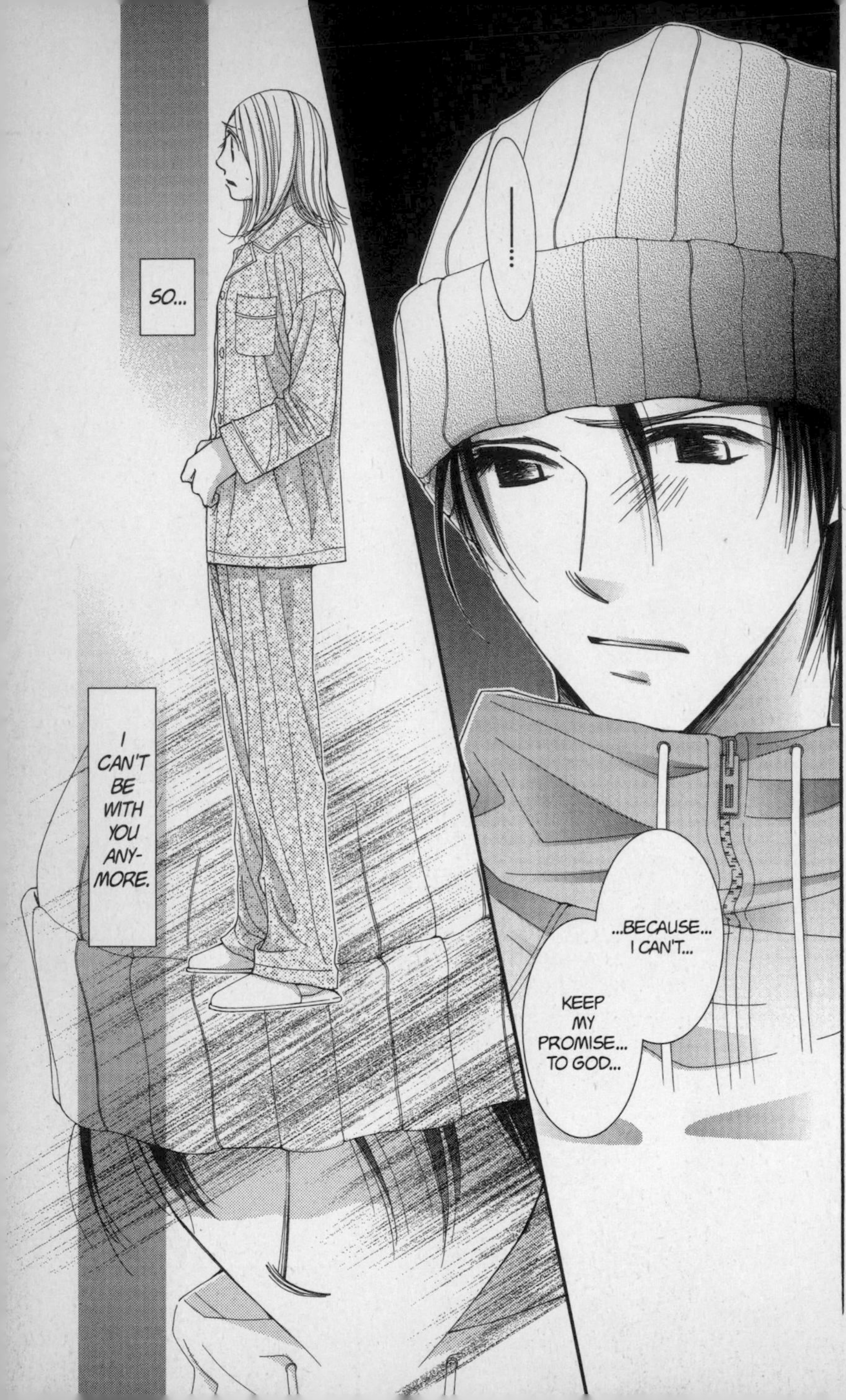
—……
...BECAUSE... I CAN'T...
KEEP MY PROMISE... TO GOD...
SO...
I CAN'T BE WITH YOU ANYMORE.

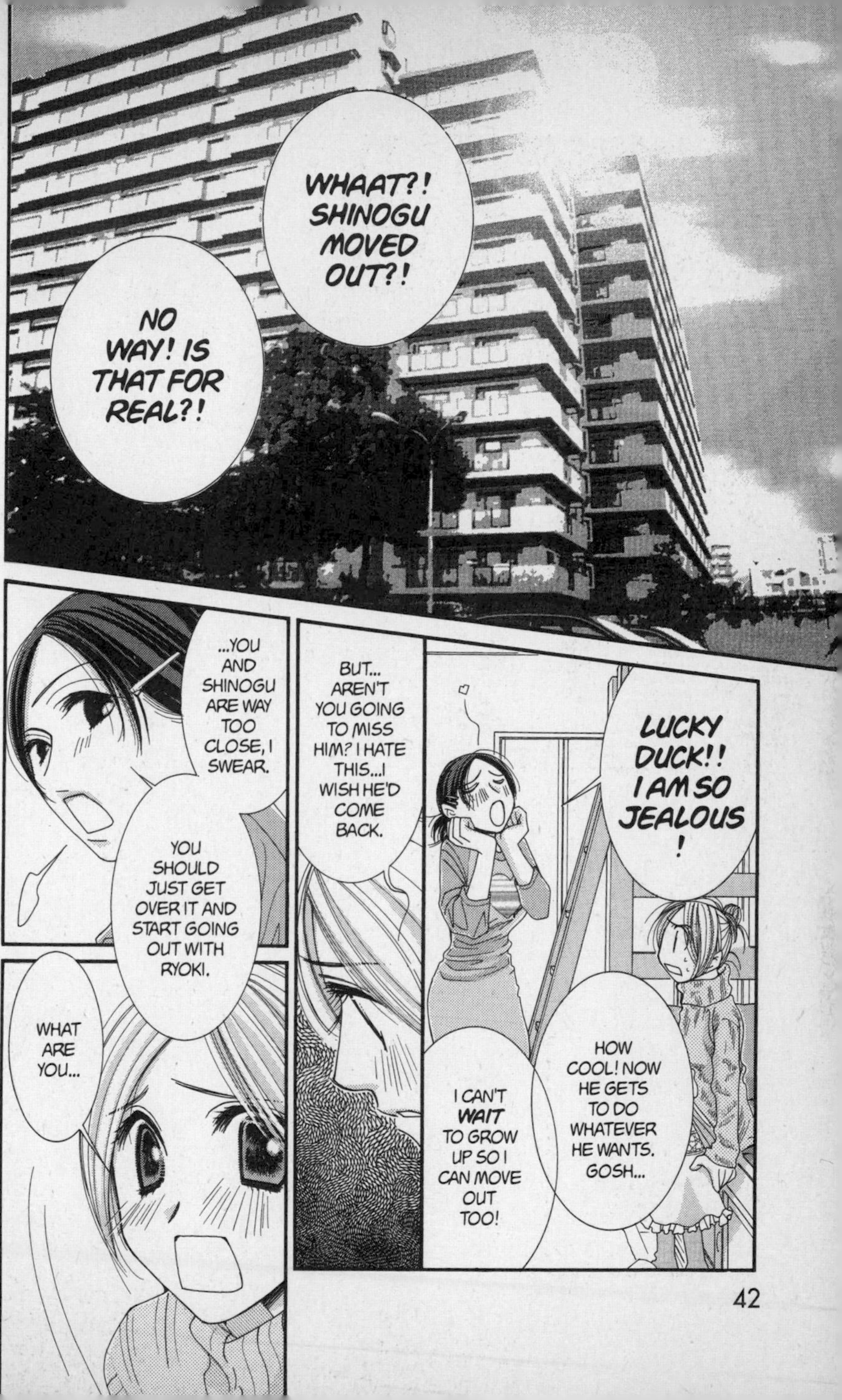
WHAAT?! SHINOGU MOVED OUT?!
NO WAY! IS THAT FOR REAL?!
LUCKY DUCK!! I AM SO JEALOUS!
HOW COOL! NOW HE GETS TO DO WHATEVER HE WANTS. GOSH...
I CAN'T WAIT TO GROW UP SO I CAN MOVE OUT TOO!
BUT... AREN'T YOU GOING TO MISS HIM? I HATE THIS...I WISH HE'D COME BACK.
...YOU AND SHINOGU ARE WAY TOO CLOSE, I SWEAR.
YOU SHOULD JUST GET OVER IT AND START GOING OUT WITH RYOKI.
WHAT ARE YOU...

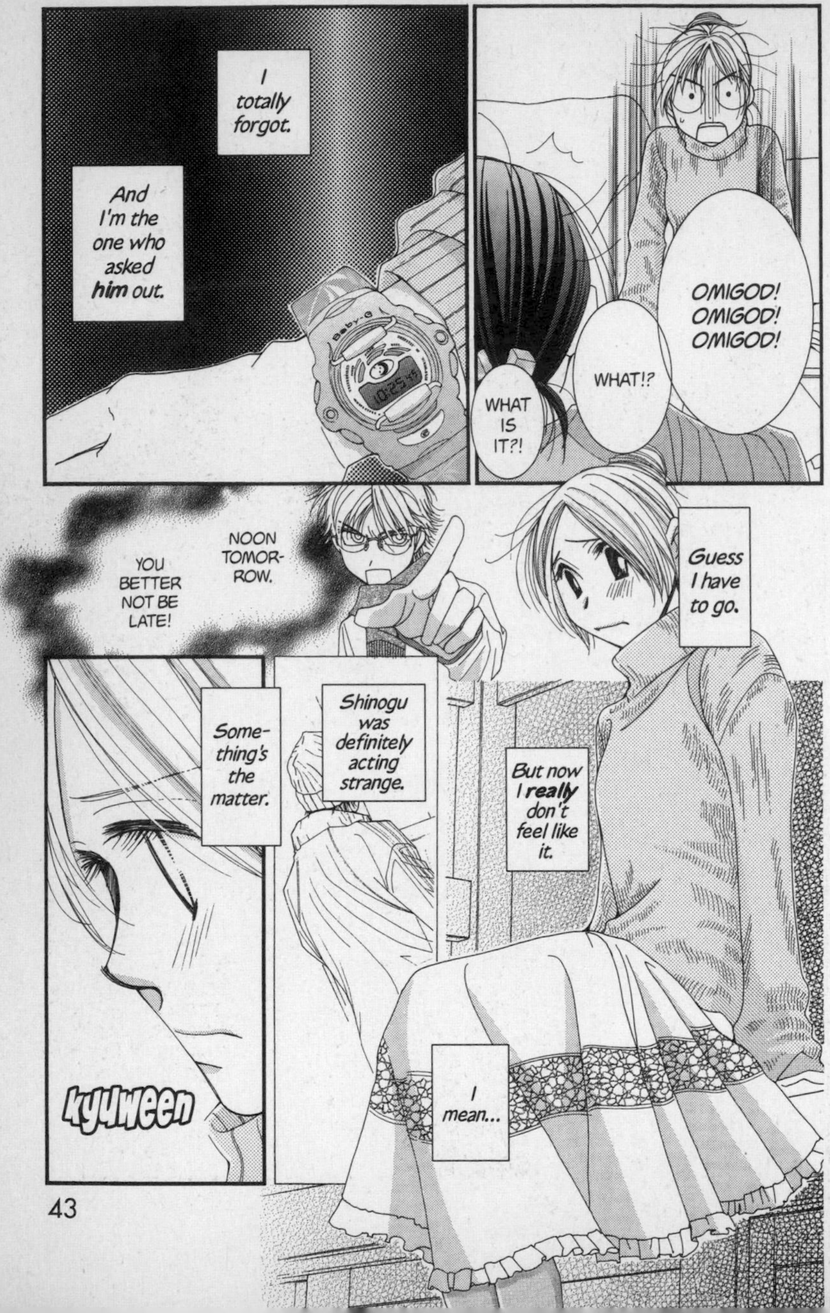
OMIGOD! OMIGOD! OMIGOD!
WHAT!?
WHAT IS IT?!
I totally forgot.
And I'm the one who asked **him** out.
Guess I have to go.
NOON TOMORROW.
YOU BETTER NOT BE LATE!
But now I **really** don't feel like it.
I mean...
Shinogu was definitely acting strange.
Something's the matter.
kyuween

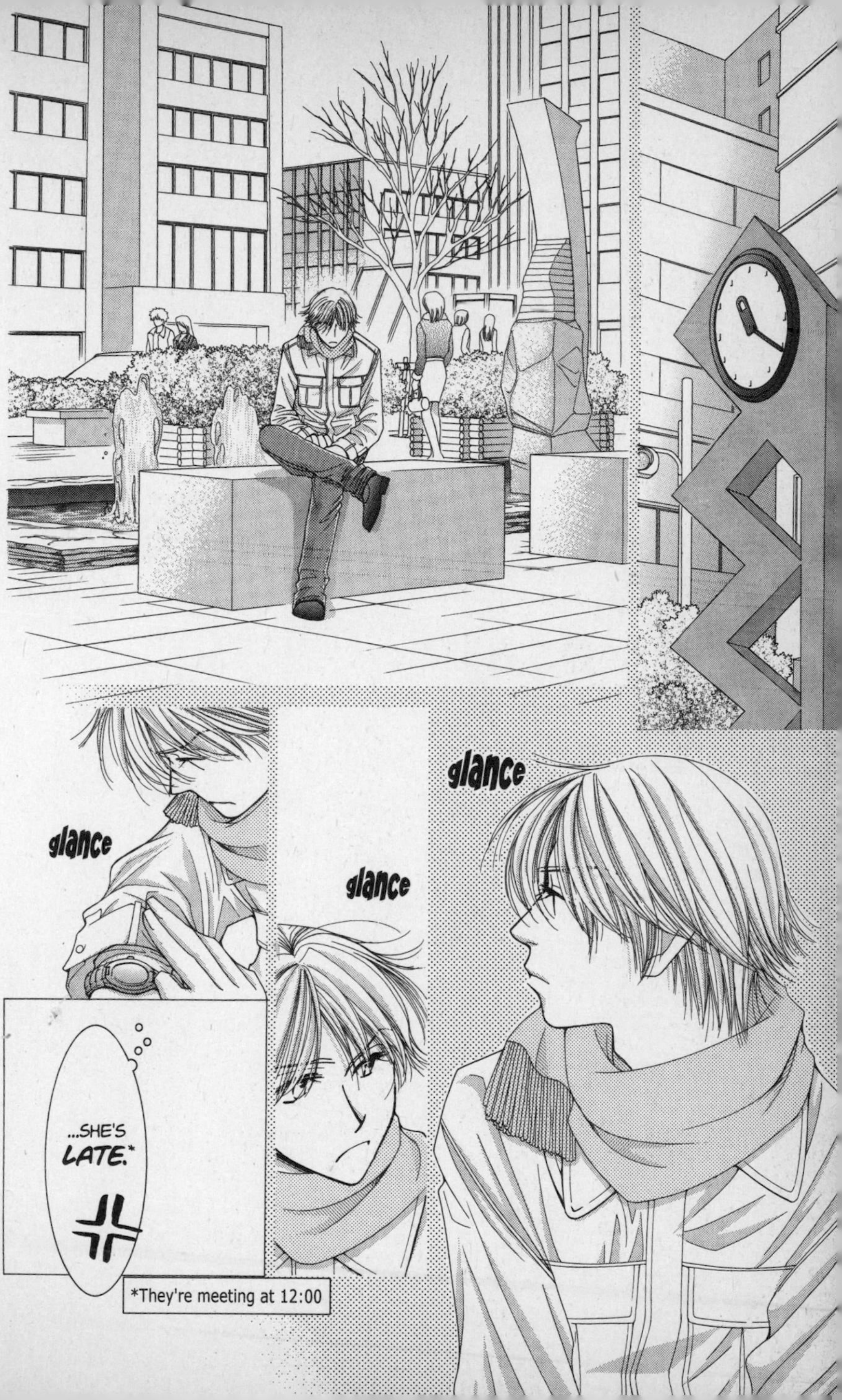
glance
glance
glance
...SHE'S LATE.*
*They're meeting at 12:00

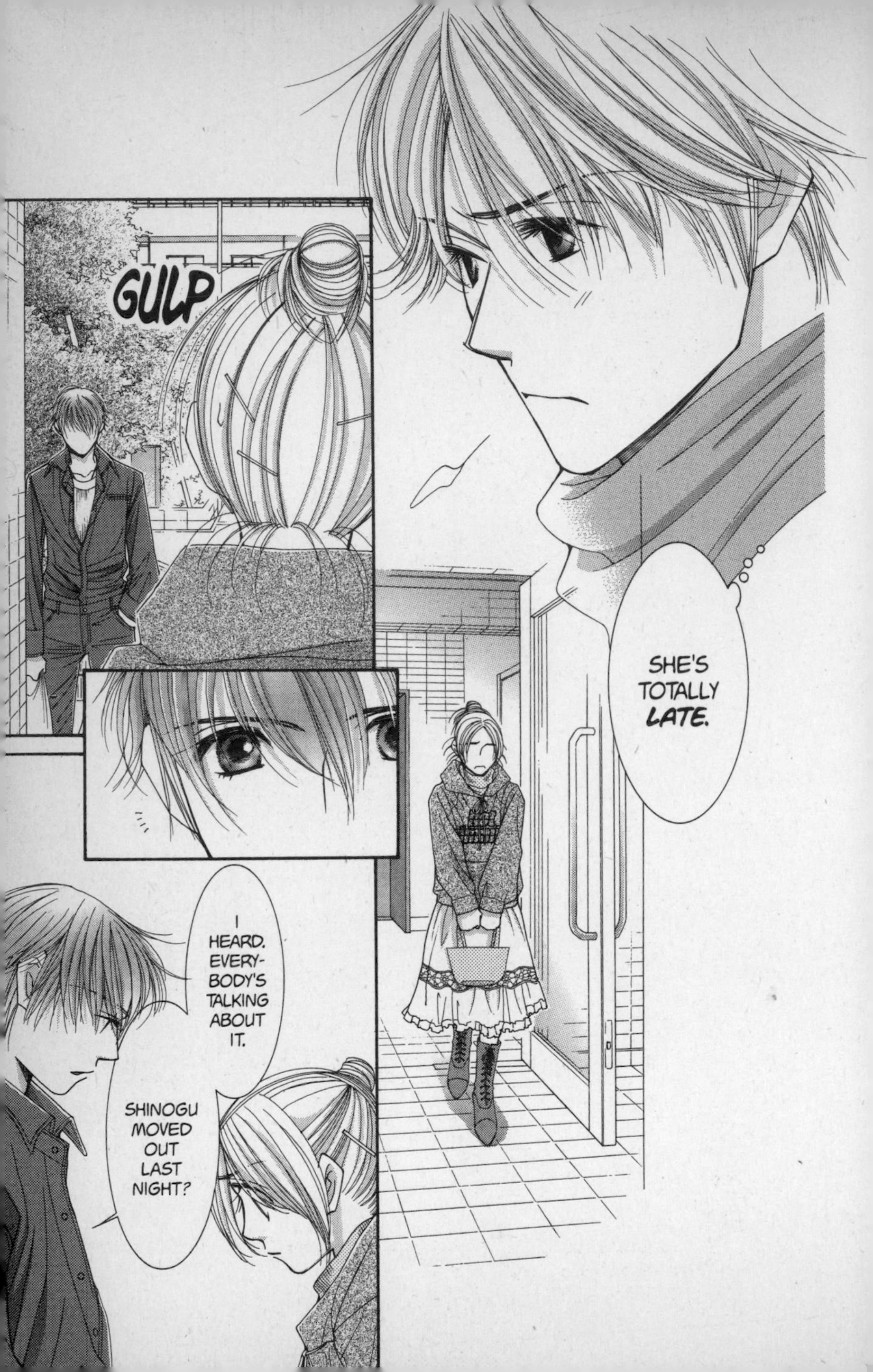
SHE'S TOTALLY LATE.
GULP
I HEARD. EVERY-BODY'S TALKING ABOUT IT.
SHINOGU MOVED OUT LAST NIGHT?

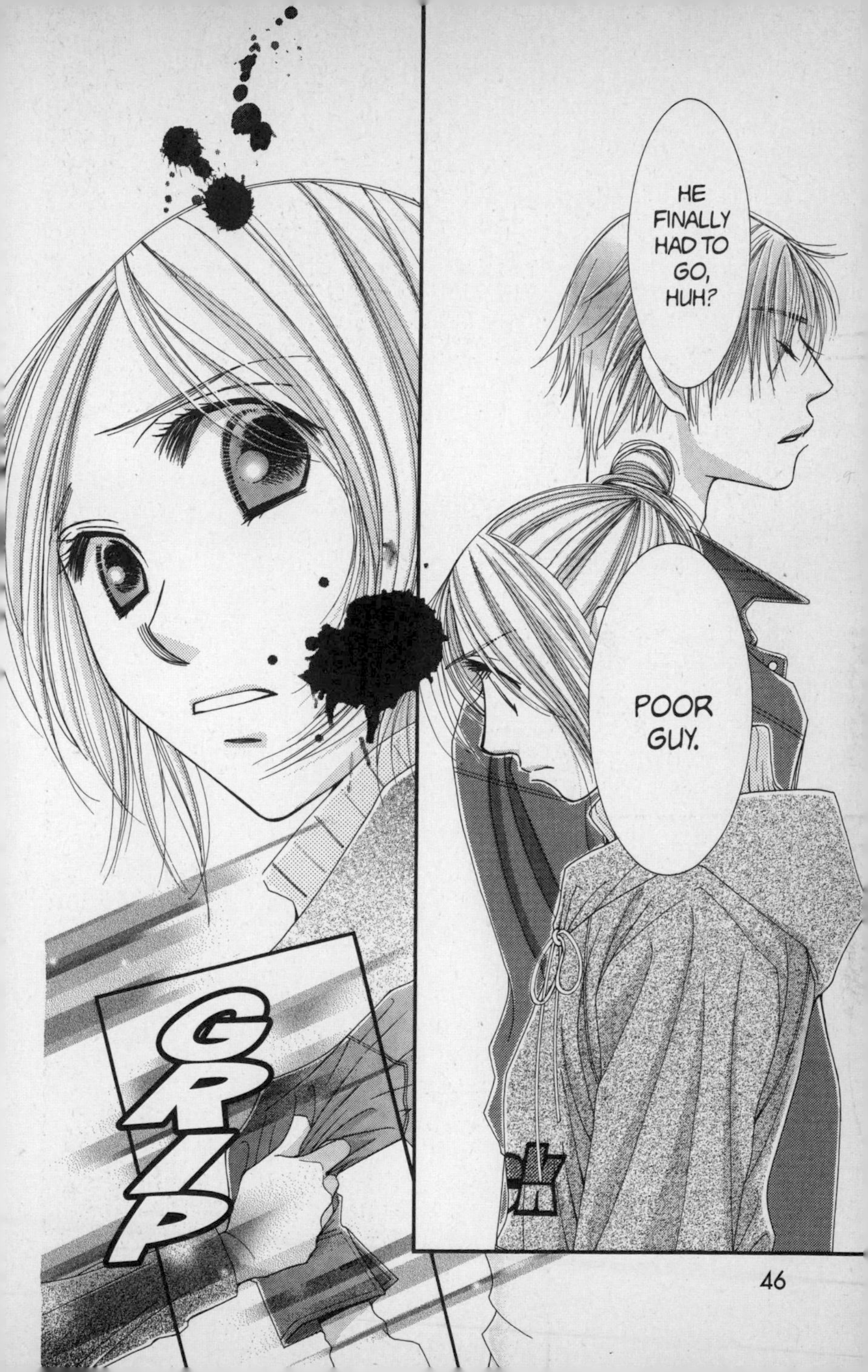
HE FINALLY HAD TO GO, HUH?
POOR GUY.
GRIP

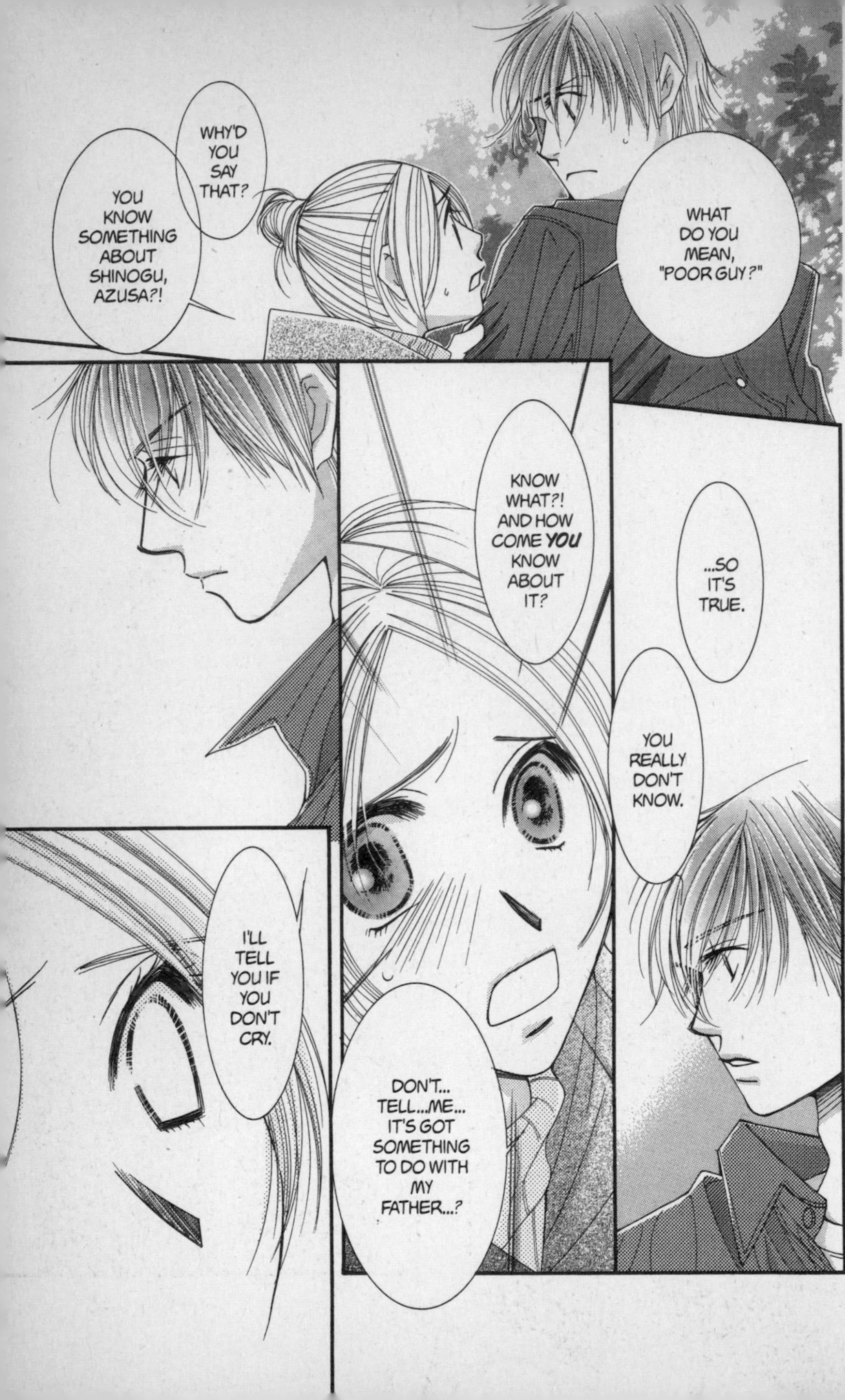
WHAT DO YOU MEAN, "POOR GUY?"
WHY'D YOU SAY THAT?
YOU KNOW SOMETHING ABOUT SHINOGU, AZUSA?!
...SO IT'S TRUE.
YOU REALLY DON'T KNOW.
KNOW WHAT?! AND HOW COME *YOU* KNOW ABOUT IT?
DON'T... TELL...ME... IT'S GOT SOMETHING TO DO WITH MY FATHER...?
I'LL TELL YOU IF YOU DON'T CRY.

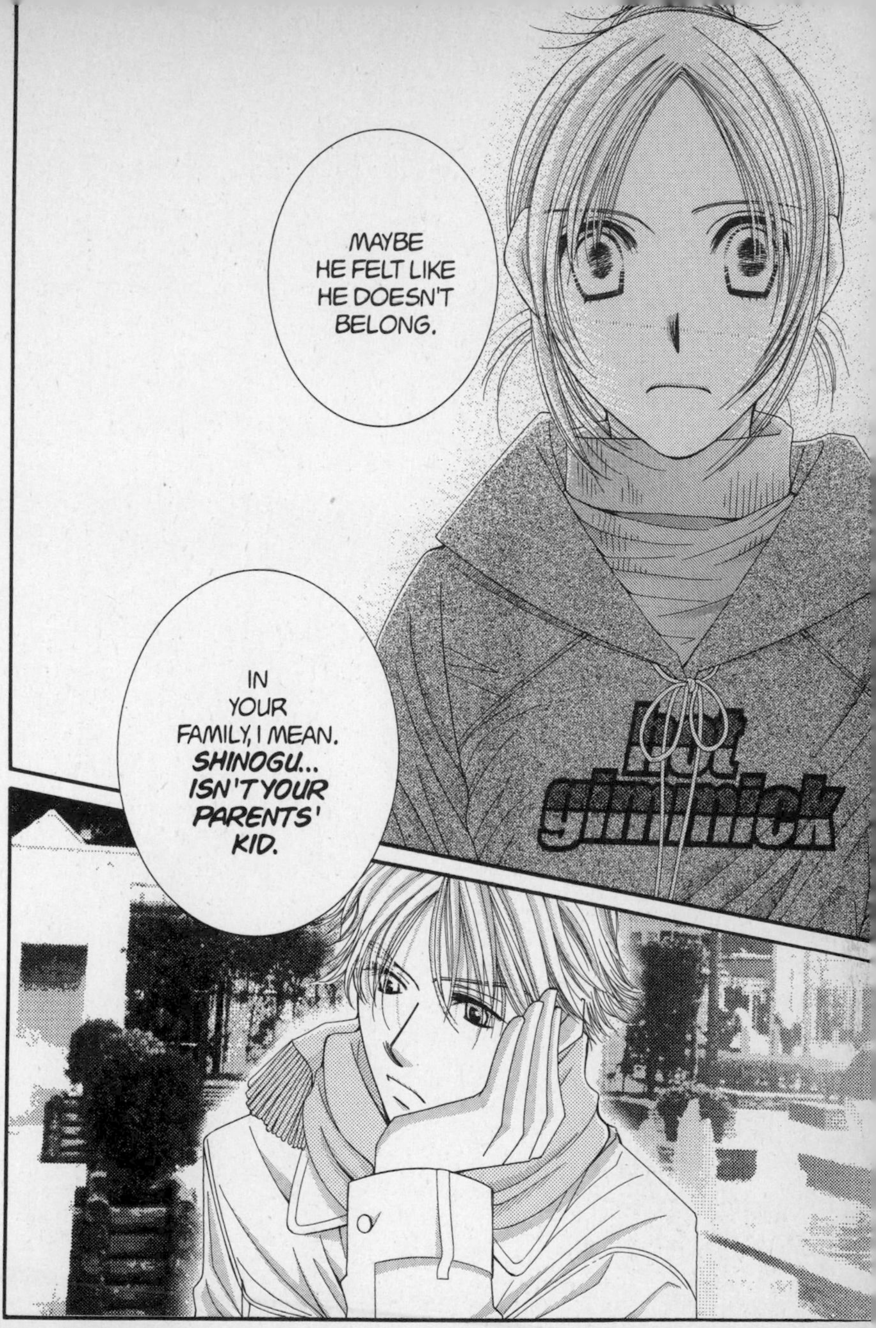
MAYBE HE FELT LIKE HE DOESN'T BELONG.
IN YOUR FAMILY, I MEAN. SHINOGU... ISN'T YOUR PARENTS' KID.
gimmick

Chapter 21

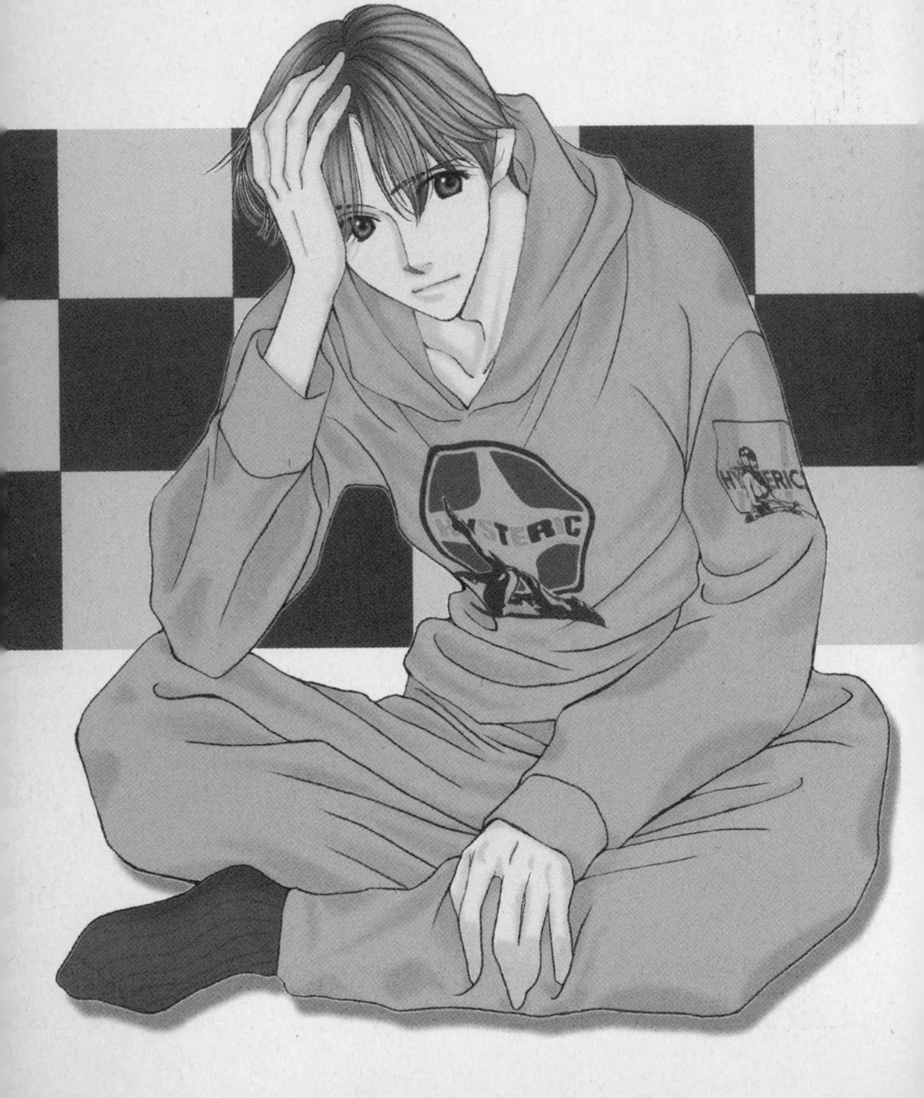

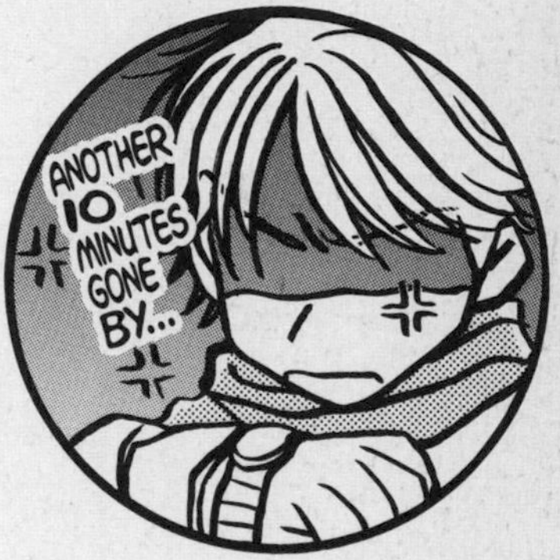
ANOTHER 10 MINUTES GONE BY...

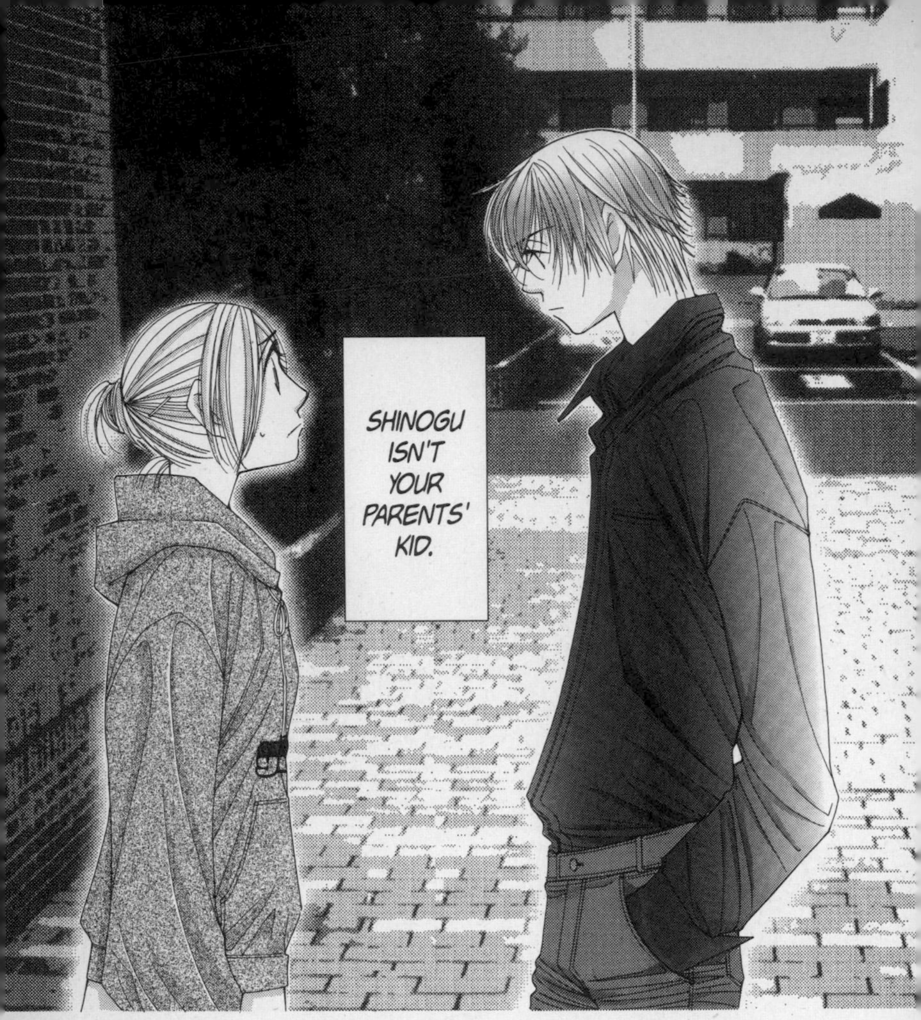
SHINOGU ISN'T YOUR PARENTS' KID.

hot gimmick

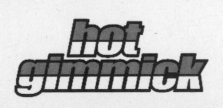

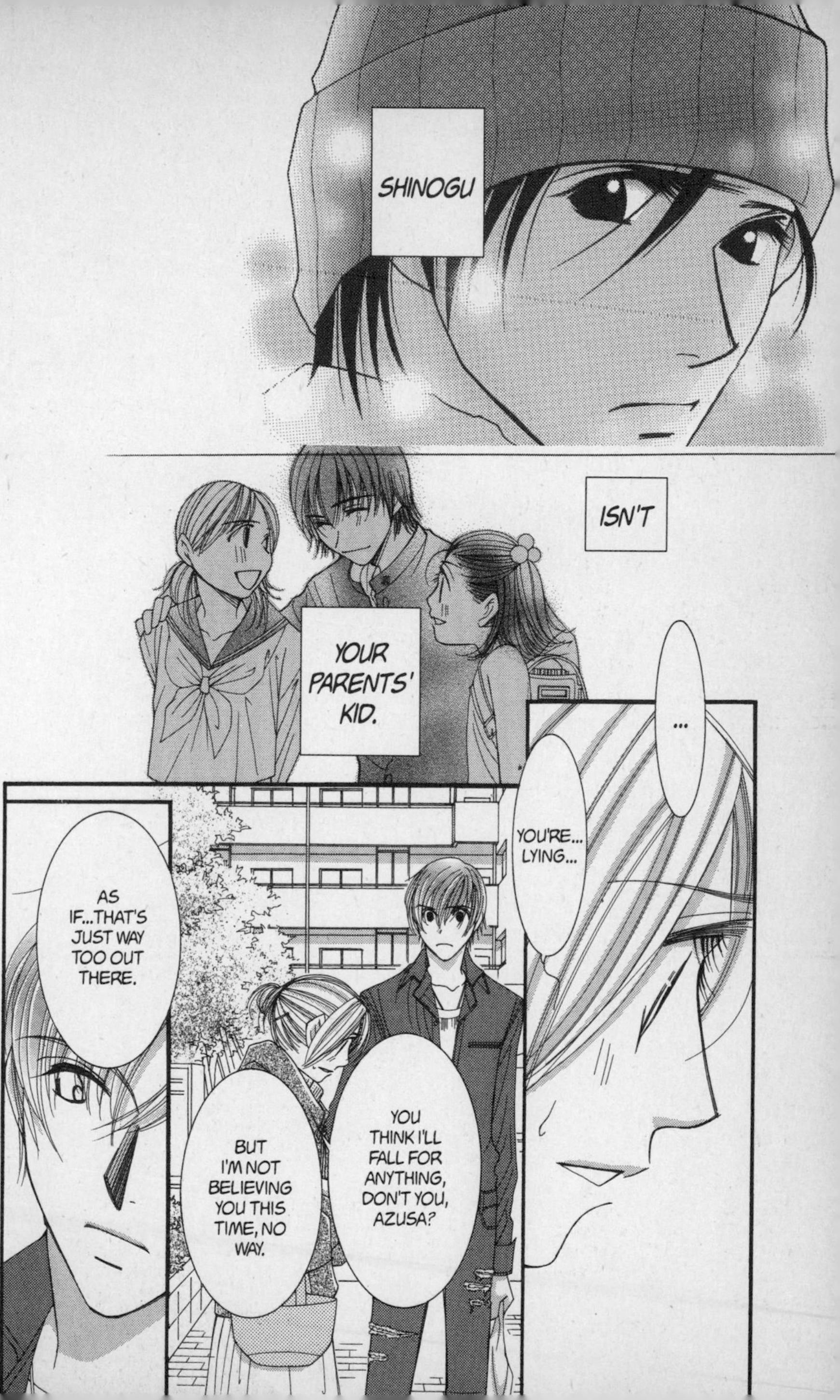
SHINOGU
ISN'T
YOUR PARENTS' KID.
...
YOU'RE... LYING...
YOU THINK I'LL FALL FOR ANYTHING, DON'T YOU, AZUSA?
BUT I'M NOT BELIEVING YOU THIS TIME, NO WAY.
AS IF...THAT'S JUST WAY TOO OUT THERE.

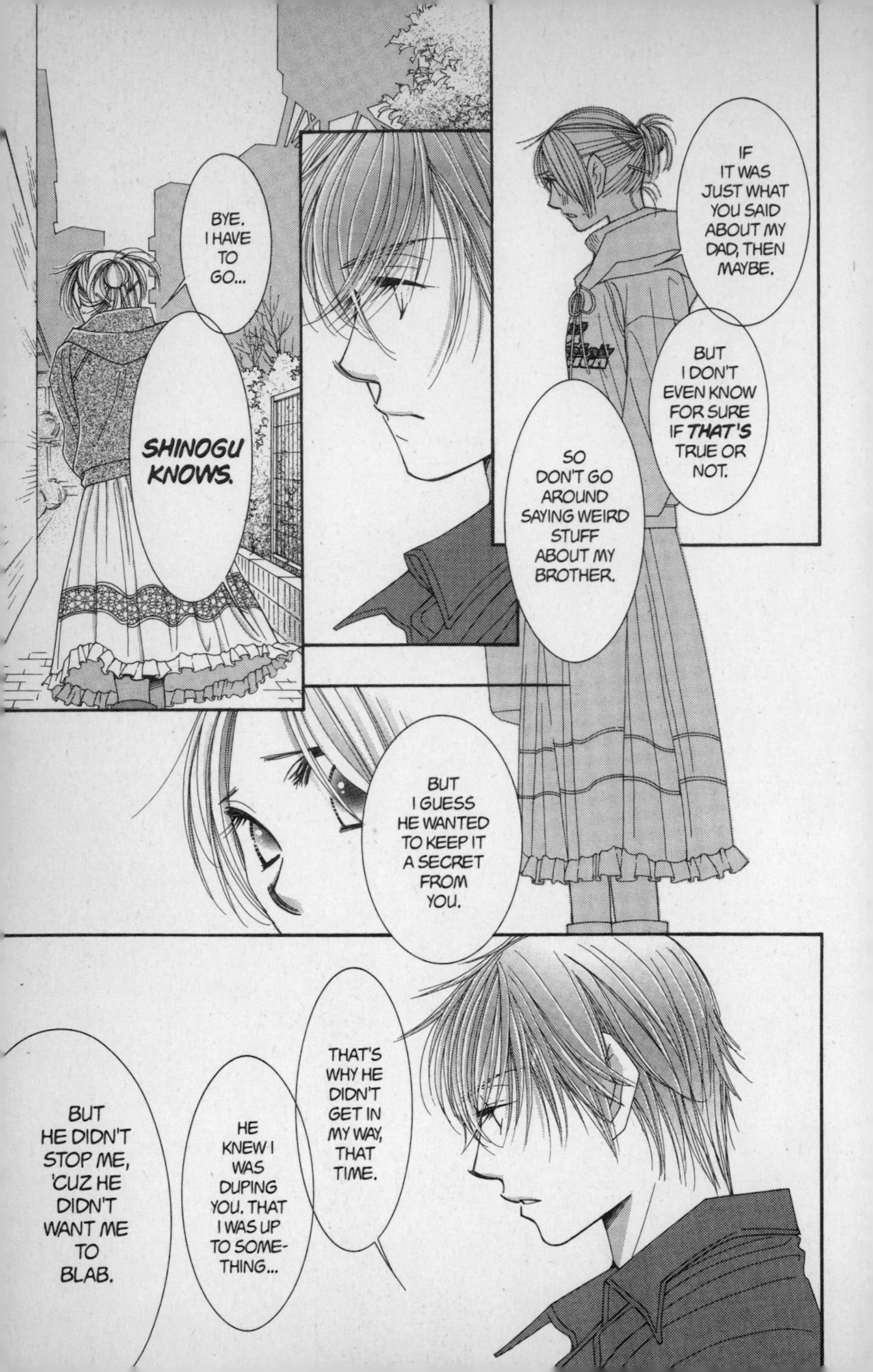
IF IT WAS JUST WHAT YOU SAID ABOUT MY DAD, THEN MAYBE.
BUT I DON'T EVEN KNOW FOR SURE IF *THAT'S* TRUE OR NOT.
SO DON'T GO AROUND SAYING WEIRD STUFF ABOUT MY BROTHER.
BYE. I HAVE TO GO...
SHINOGU KNOWS.
BUT I GUESS HE WANTED TO KEEP IT A SECRET FROM YOU.
THAT'S WHY HE DIDN'T GET IN MY WAY, THAT TIME.
HE KNEW I WAS DUPING YOU. THAT I WAS UP TO SOME-THING...
BUT HE DIDN'T STOP ME, 'CUZ HE DIDN'T WANT ME TO BLAB.

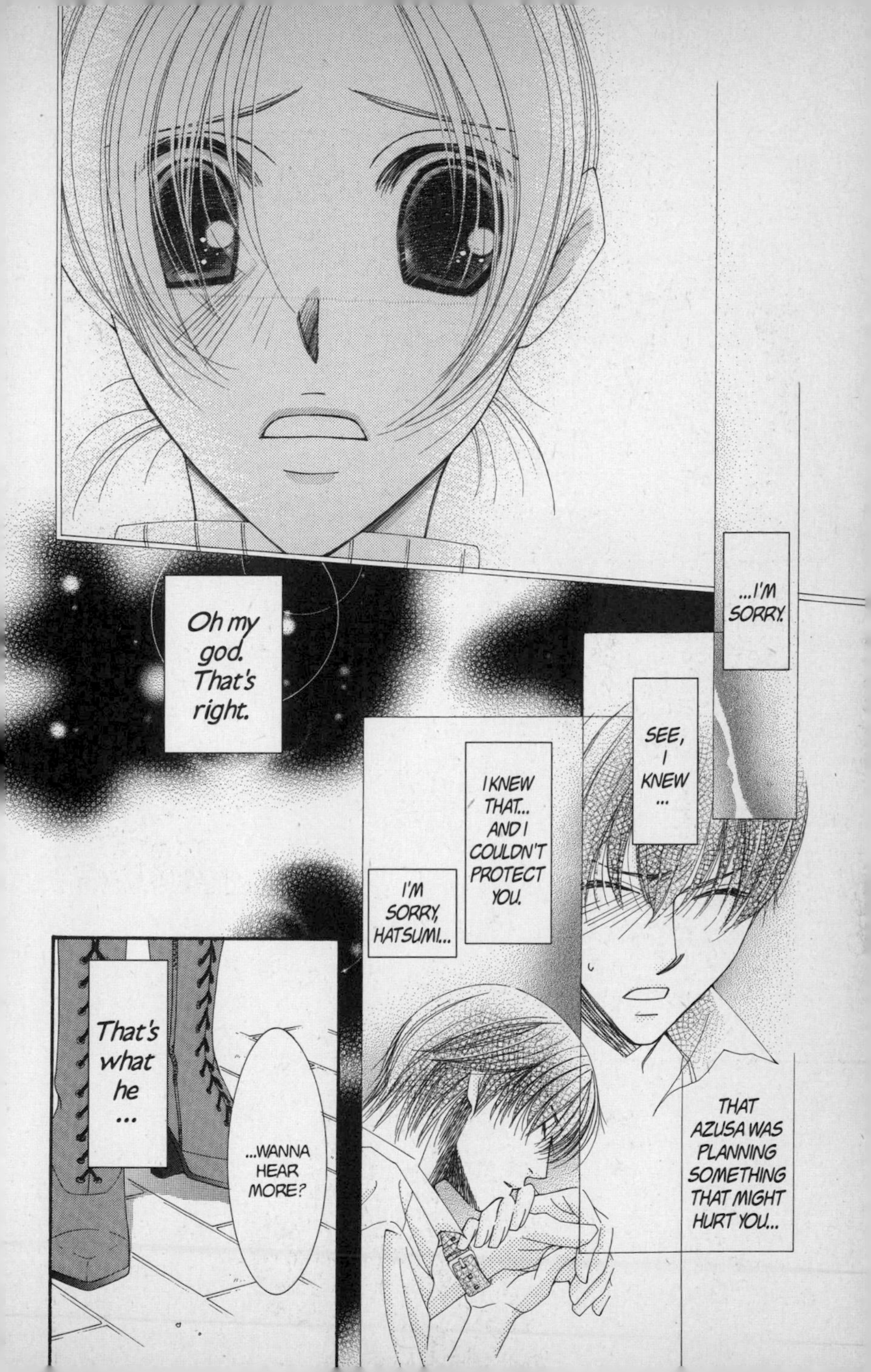
...I'M SORRY.
SEE, I KNEW ...
THAT AZUSA WAS PLANNING SOMETHING THAT MIGHT HURT YOU...
I KNEW THAT... AND I COULDN'T PROTECT YOU.
I'M SORRY, HATSUMI...
Oh my god. That's right.
That's what he ...
...WANNA HEAR MORE?

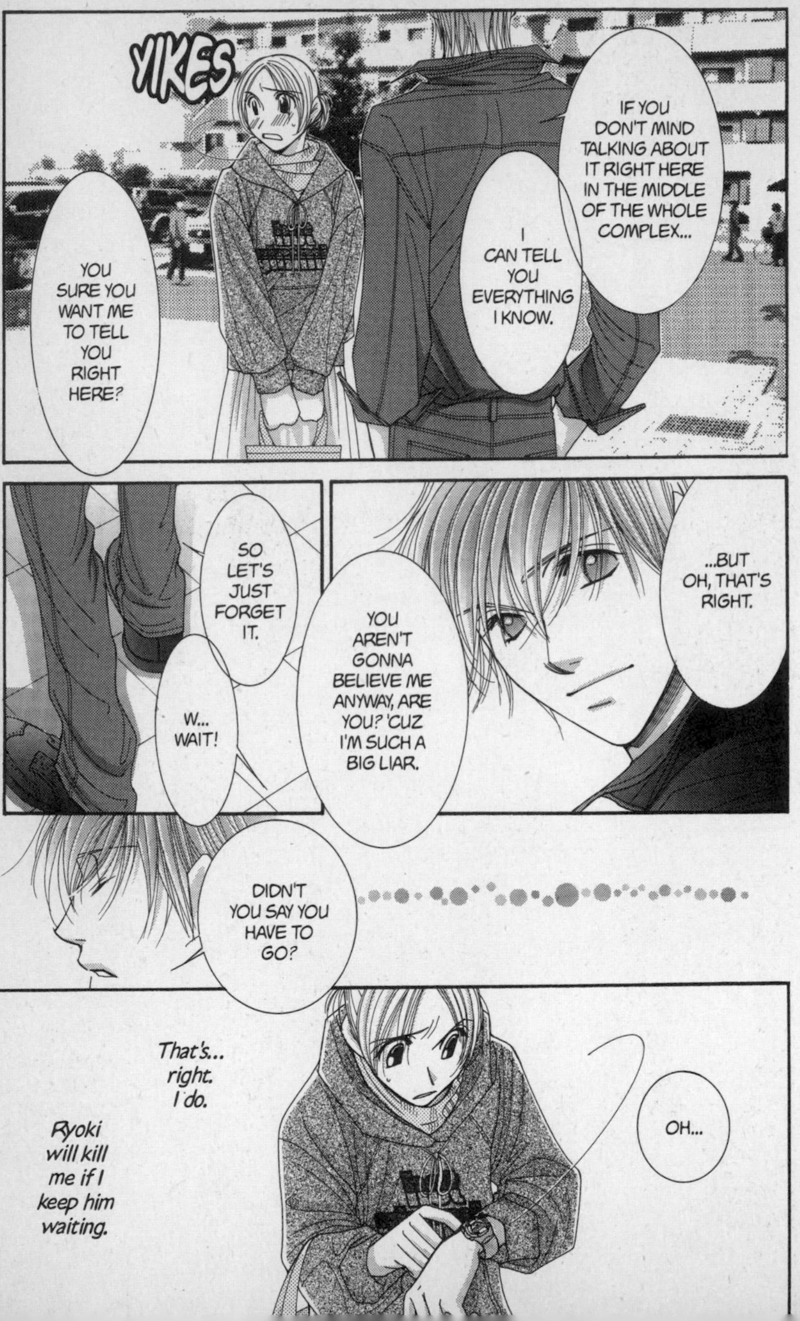
IF YOU DON'T MIND TALKING ABOUT IT RIGHT HERE IN THE MIDDLE OF THE WHOLE COMPLEX...
I CAN TELL YOU EVERYTHING I KNOW.
YIKES
YOU SURE YOU WANT ME TO TELL YOU RIGHT HERE?
...BUT OH, THAT'S RIGHT.
YOU AREN'T GONNA BELIEVE ME ANYWAY, ARE YOU? 'CUZ I'M SUCH A BIG LIAR.
SO LET'S JUST FORGET IT.
W... WAIT!
DIDN'T YOU SAY YOU HAVE TO GO?
OH...
That's... right. I do.
Ryoki will kill me if I keep him waiting.

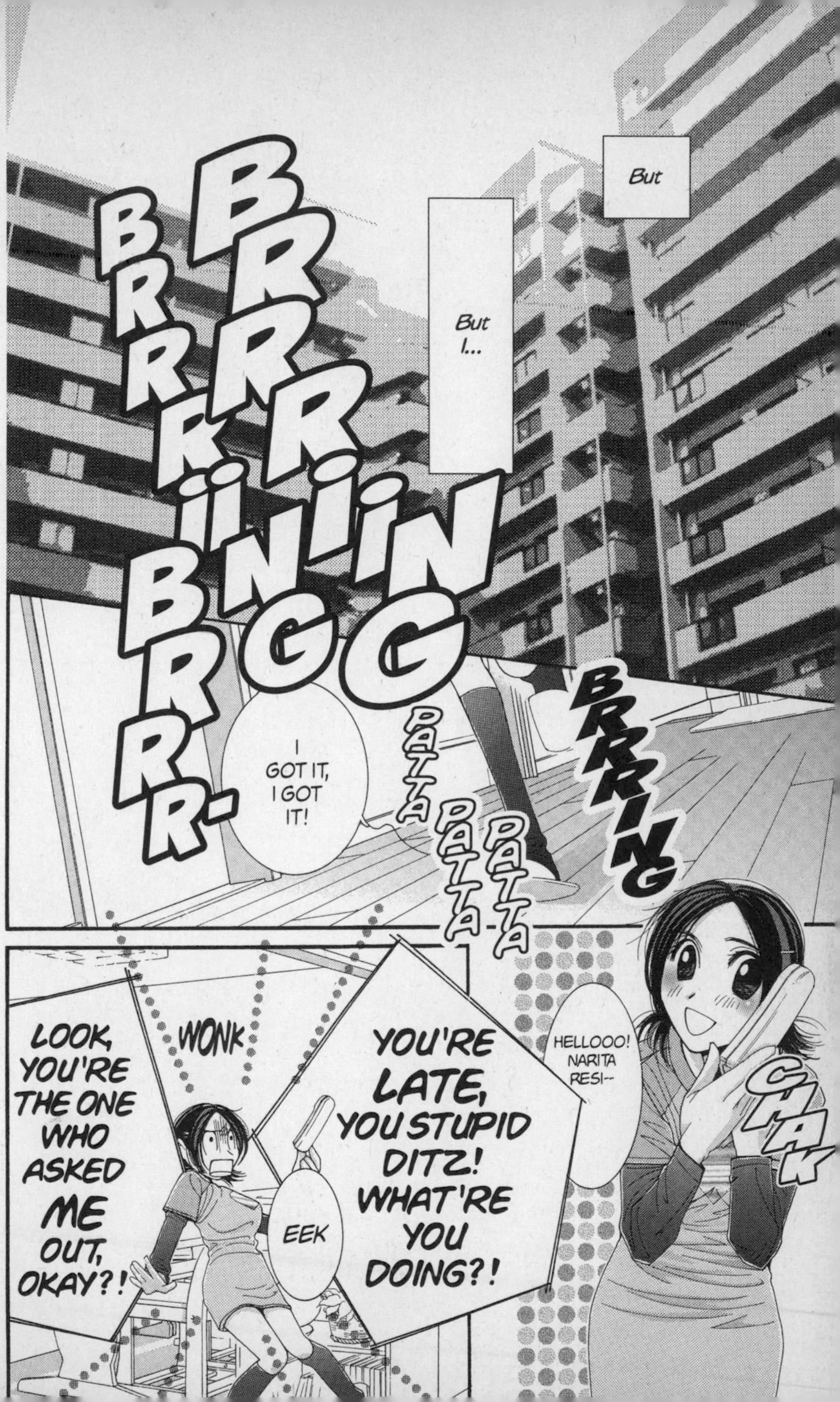
But
But I...
BRRRIIING
BRRRRIIING
BRRR-
PATTA
I GOT IT, I GOT IT!
PATTA
PATTA
BRRRING
CHAK
HELLOOO! NARITA RESI--
YOU'RE LATE, YOU STUPID DITZ! WHAT'RE YOU DOING?!
WONK
EEK
LOOK, YOU'RE THE ONE WHO ASKED ME OUT, OKAY?!

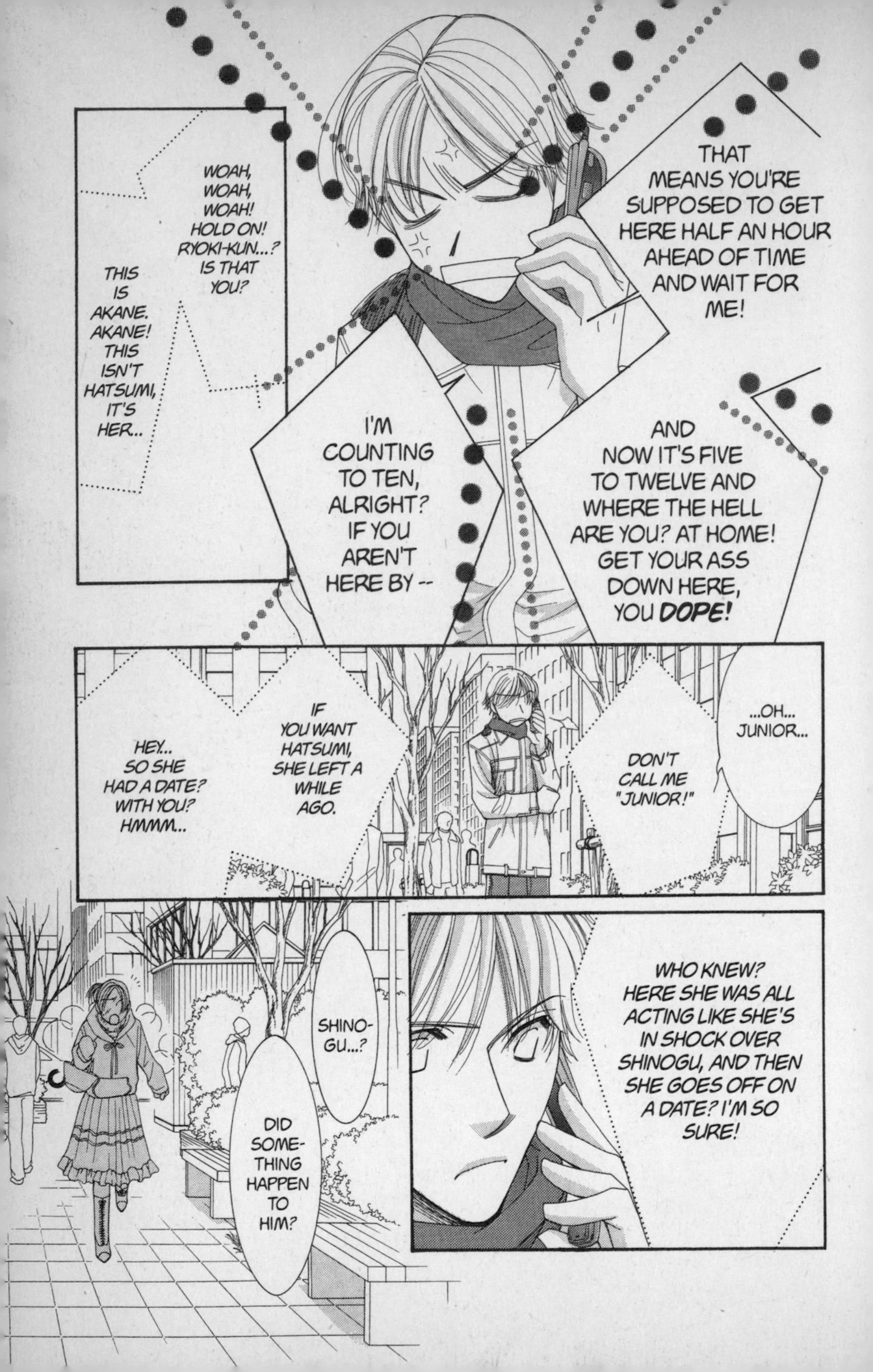
THAT MEANS YOU'RE SUPPOSED TO GET HERE HALF AN HOUR AHEAD OF TIME AND WAIT FOR ME!
AND NOW IT'S FIVE TO TWELVE AND WHERE THE HELL ARE YOU? AT HOME! GET YOUR ASS DOWN HERE, YOU **DOPE!**
I'M COUNTING TO TEN, ALRIGHT? IF YOU AREN'T HERE BY --
WOAH, WOAH, WOAH! HOLD ON! RYOKI-KUN...? IS THAT YOU?
THIS IS AKANE. AKANE! THIS ISN'T HATSUMI, IT'S HER...
...OH... JUNIOR...
DON'T CALL ME "JUNIOR!"
IF YOU WANT HATSUMI, SHE LEFT A WHILE AGO.
HEY... SO SHE HAD A DATE? WITH YOU? HMMM...
WHO KNEW? HERE SHE WAS ALL ACTING LIKE SHE'S IN SHOCK OVER SHINOGU, AND THEN SHE GOES OFF ON A DATE? I'M SO SURE!
SHINO-GU...?
DID SOME-THING HAPPEN TO HIM?

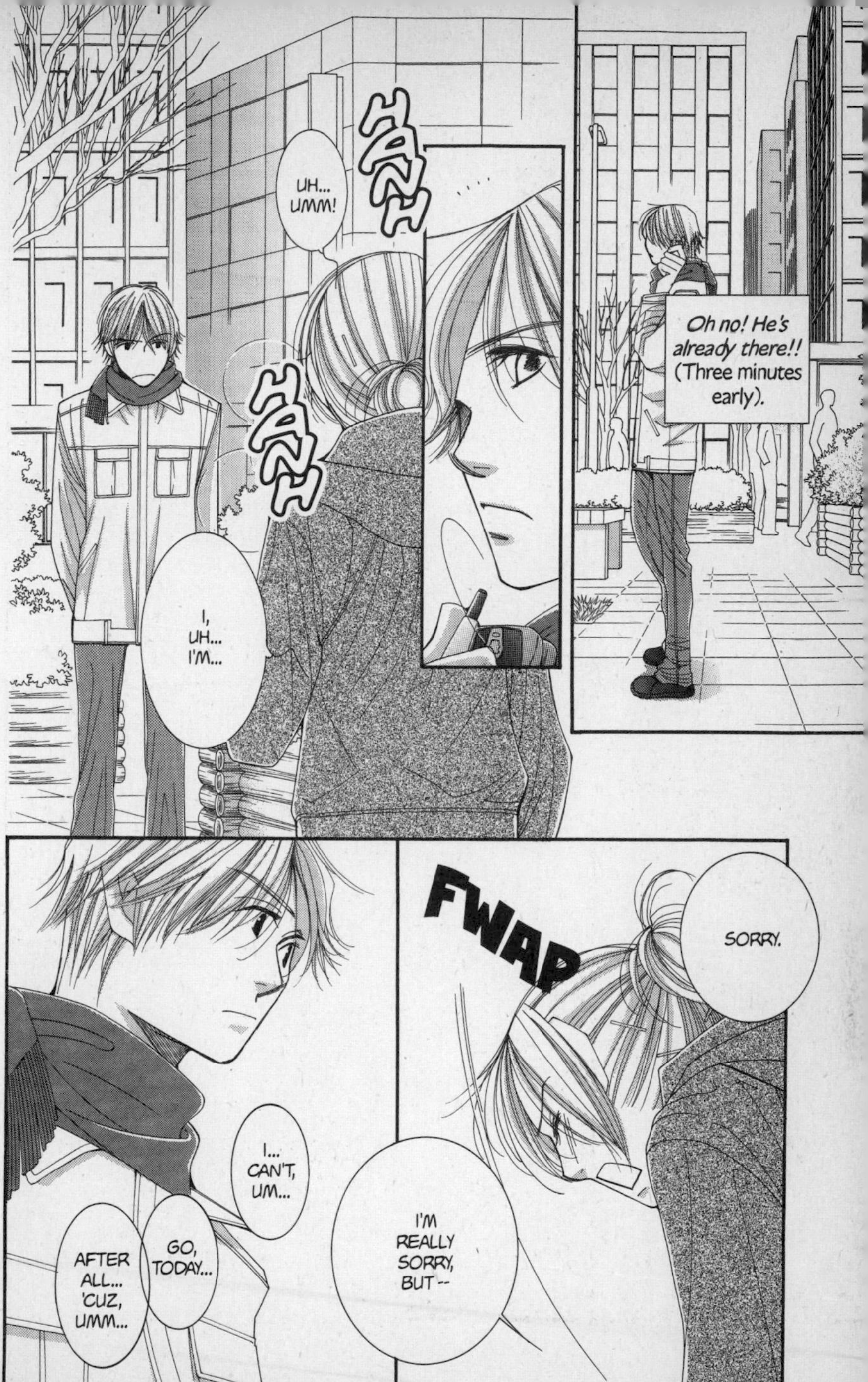
Oh no! He's already there!! (Three minutes early).
HAH
HAH
UH... UMM!
I, UH... I'M...
FWAP
SORRY.
I'M REALLY SORRY, BUT --
I... CAN'T, UM...
GO, TODAY...
AFTER ALL... 'CUZ, UMM...

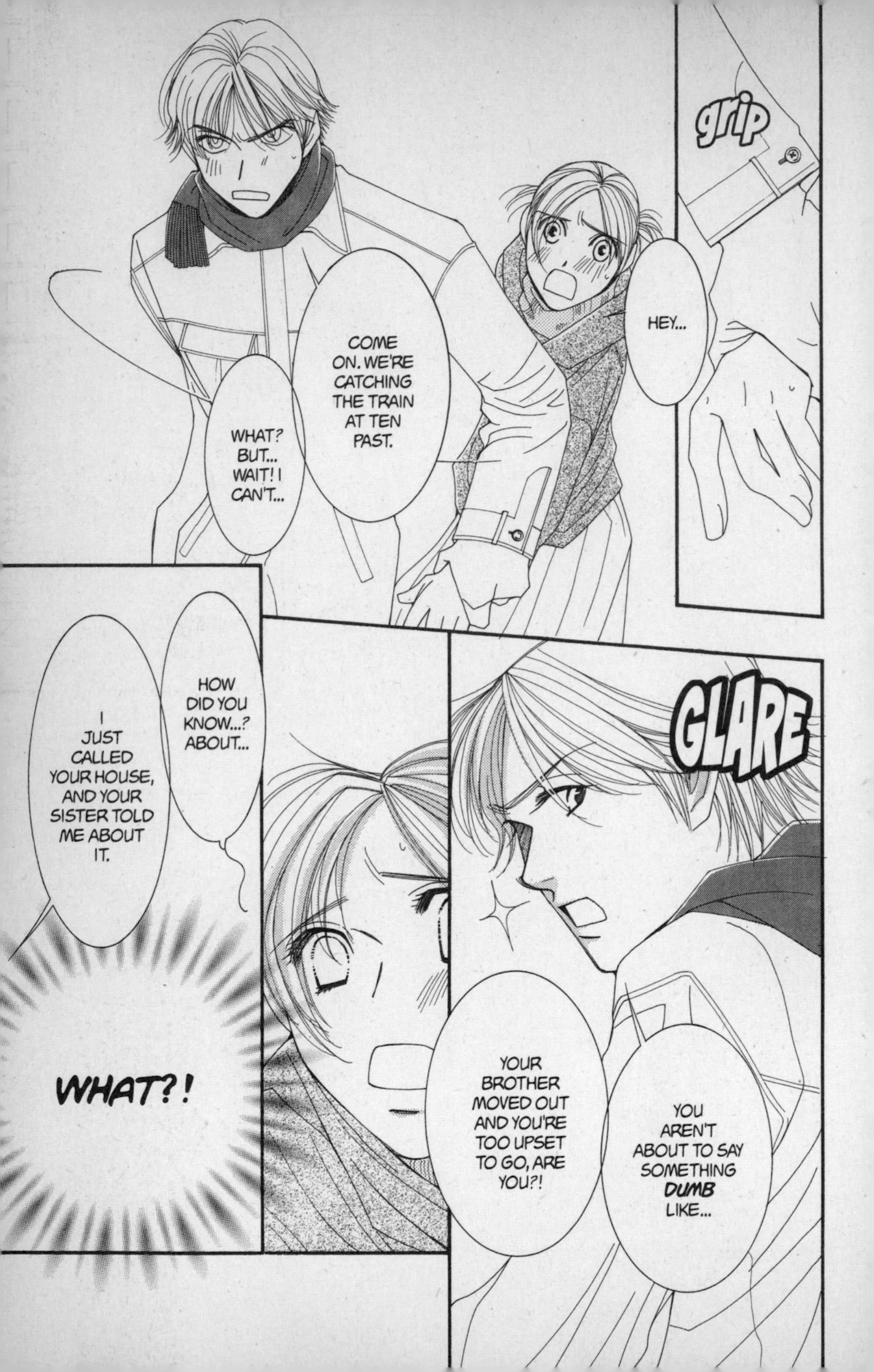
grip
HEY...
COME ON. WE'RE CATCHING THE TRAIN AT TEN PAST.
WHAT? BUT... WAIT! I CAN'T...
GLARE
YOU AREN'T ABOUT TO SAY SOMETHING **DUMB** LIKE...
YOUR BROTHER MOVED OUT AND YOU'RE TOO UPSET TO GO, ARE YOU?!
HOW DID YOU KNOW...? ABOUT...
I JUST CALLED YOUR HOUSE, AND YOUR SISTER TOLD ME ABOUT IT.
WHAT?!

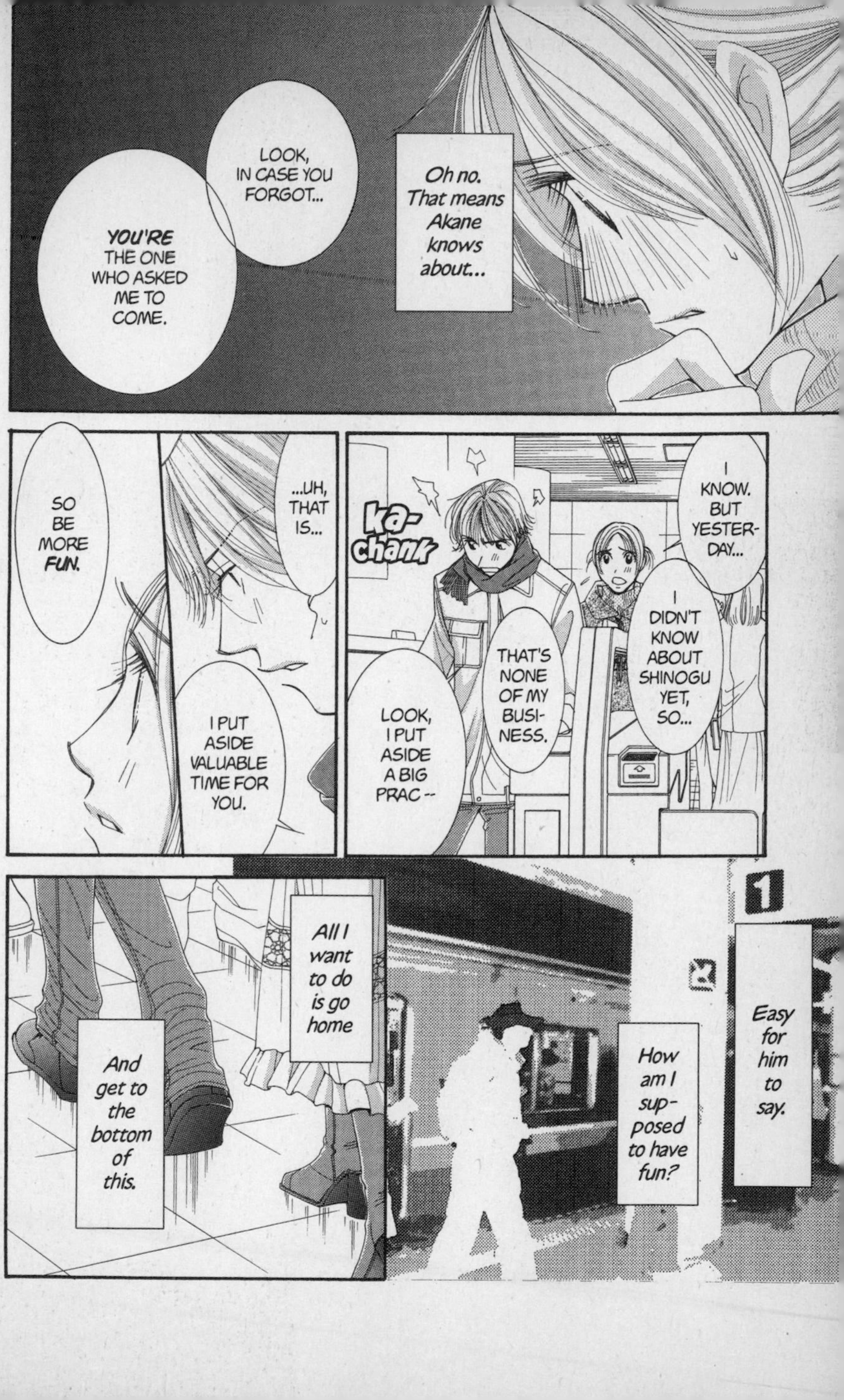
Oh no. That means Akane knows about...
LOOK, IN CASE YOU FORGOT...
YOU'RE THE ONE WHO ASKED ME TO COME.
I KNOW. BUT YESTER-DAY...
I DIDN'T KNOW ABOUT SHINOGU YET, SO...
THAT'S NONE OF MY BUSI-NESS.
ka-chank
LOOK, I PUT ASIDE A BIG PRAC --
...UH, THAT IS...
I PUT ASIDE VALUABLE TIME FOR YOU.
SO BE MORE FUN.
1
Easy for him to say.
How am I sup-posed to have fun?
All I want to do is go home
And get to the bottom of this.

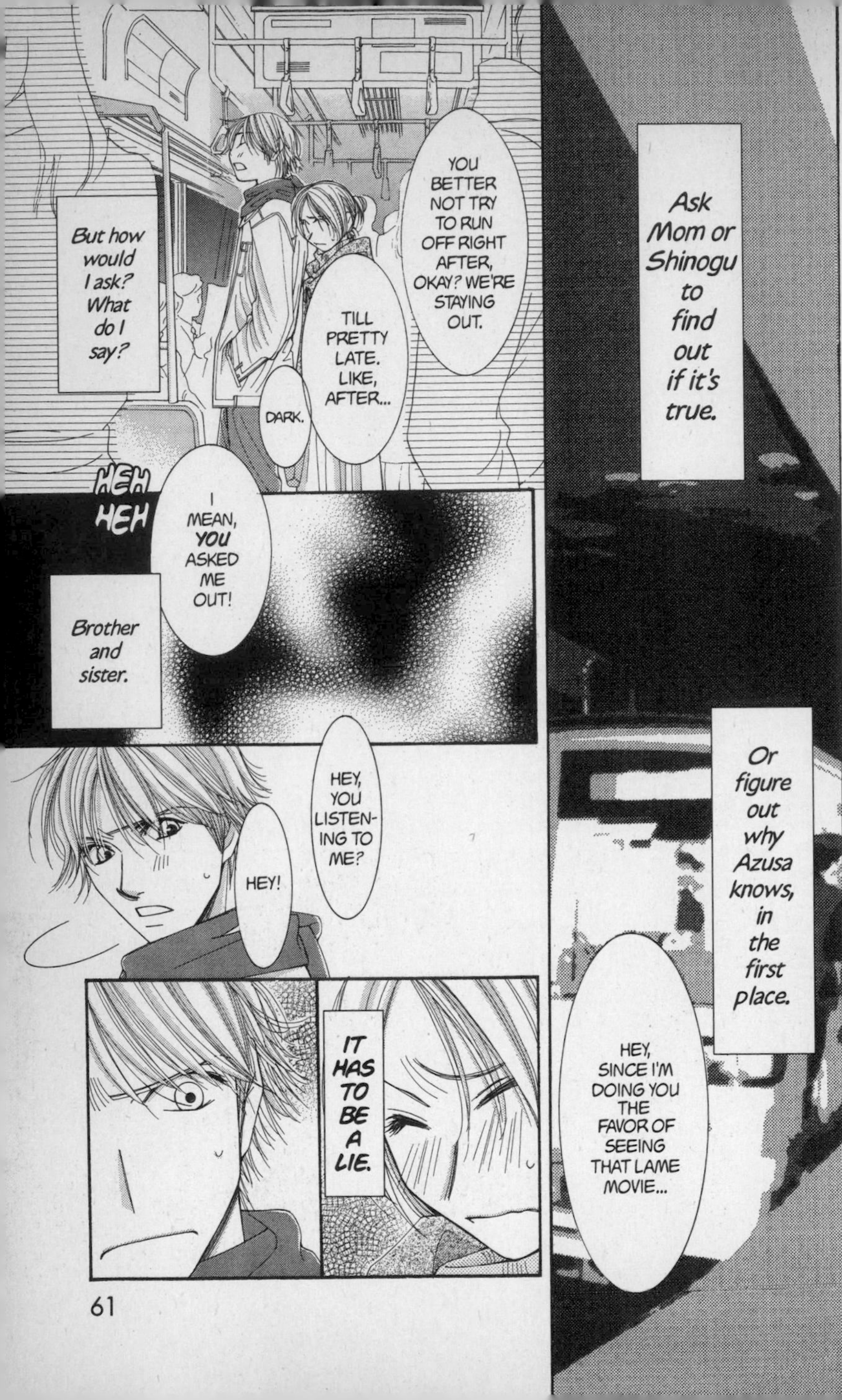
Ask Mom or Shinogu to find out if it's true.
Or figure out why Azusa knows, in the first place.
HEY, SINCE I'M DOING YOU THE FAVOR OF SEEING THAT LAME MOVIE...
YOU BETTER NOT TRY TO RUN OFF RIGHT AFTER, OKAY? WE'RE STAYING OUT.
TILL PRETTY LATE. LIKE, AFTER...
DARK.
But how would I ask? What do I say?
HEH HEH
I MEAN, YOU ASKED ME OUT!
Brother and sister.
HEY, YOU LISTENING TO ME?
HEY!
IT HAS TO BE A LIE.

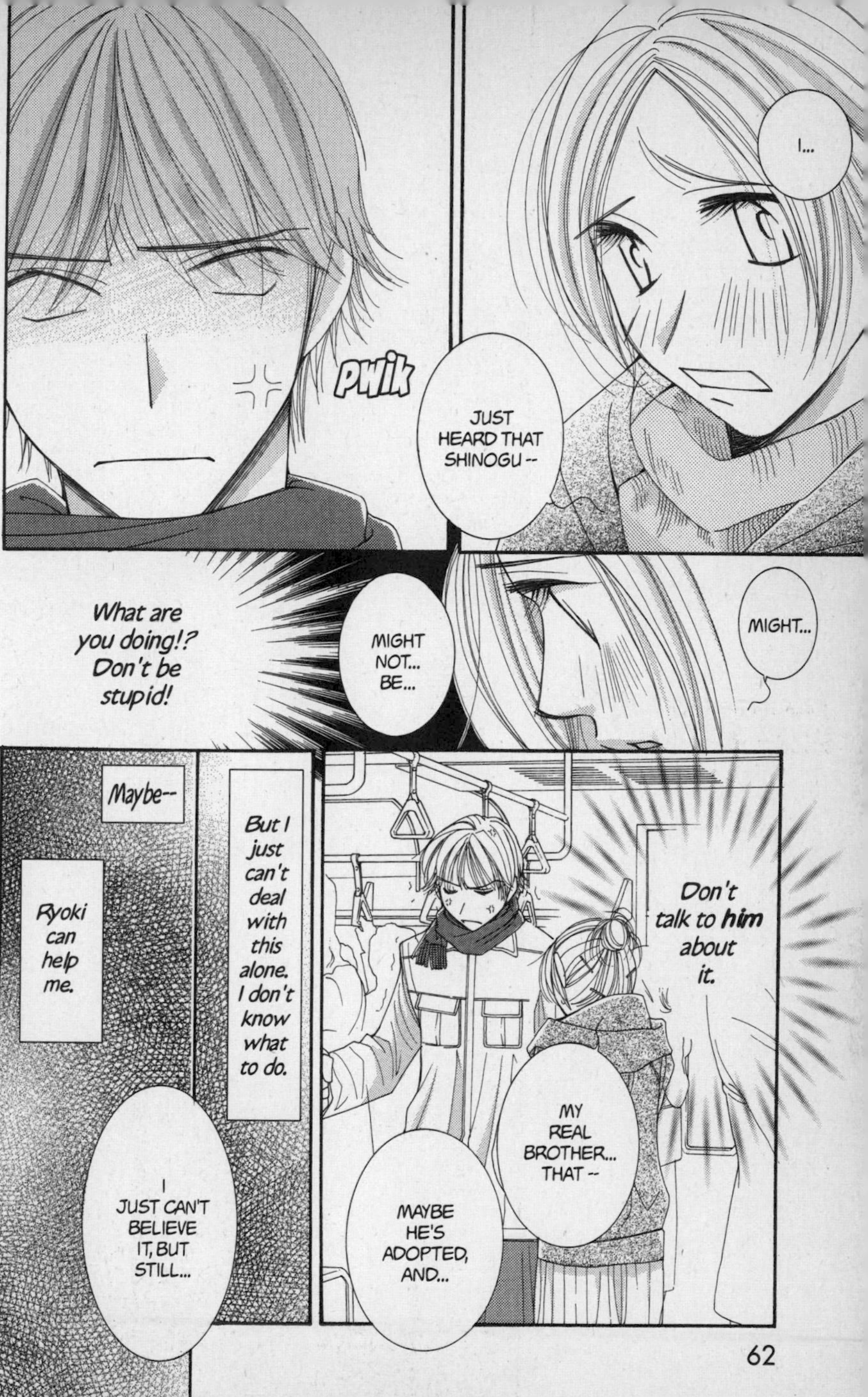
I...
JUST HEARD THAT SHINOGU --
PWIK
MIGHT...
MIGHT NOT... BE...
What are you doing!? Don't be stupid!
Don't talk to **him** about it.
MY REAL BROTHER... THAT --
MAYBE HE'S ADOPTED, AND...
But I just can't deal with this alone. I don't know what to do.
Maybe--
Ryoki can help me.
I JUST CAN'T BELIEVE IT, BUT STILL...

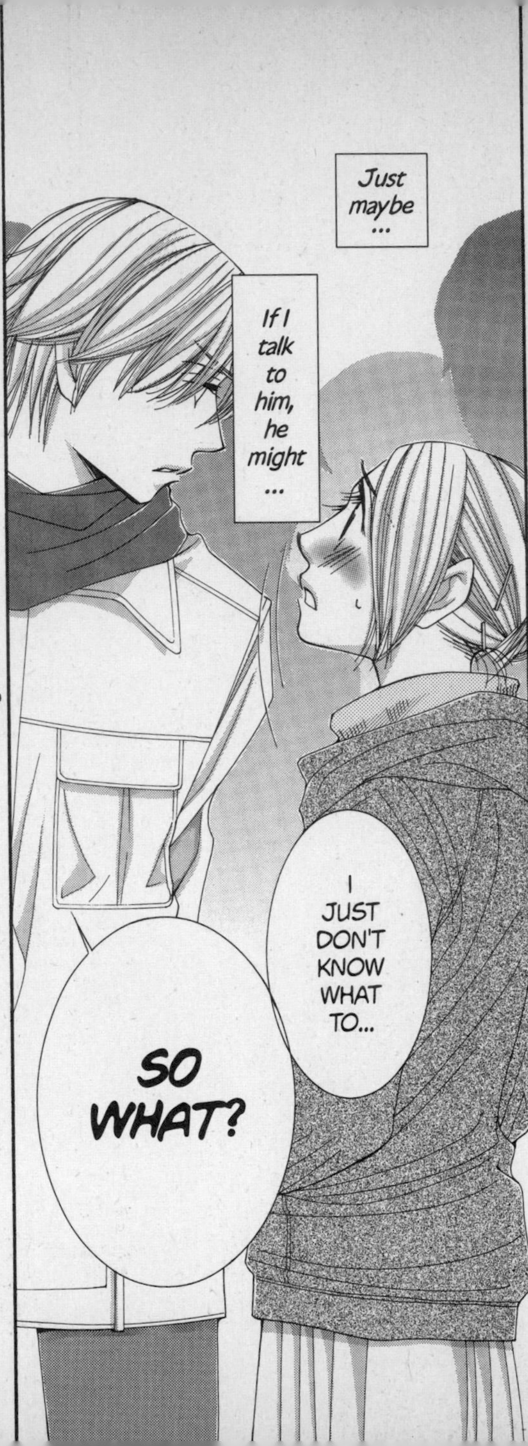
Just maybe ...
If I talk to him, he might ...
I JUST DON'T KNOW WHAT TO...
SO WHAT?

hotgimmick

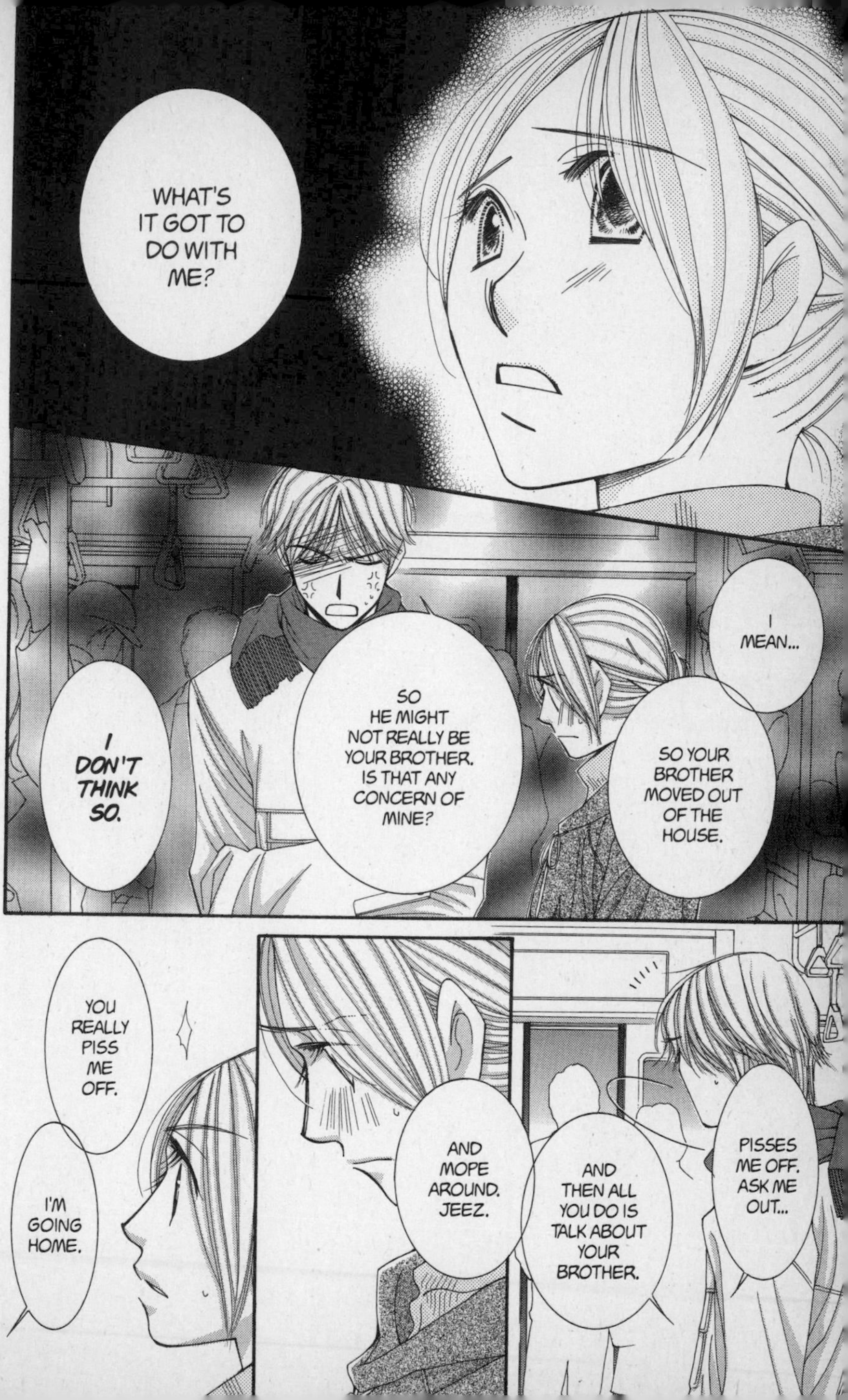
WHAT'S IT GOT TO DO WITH ME?
I MEAN...
SO YOUR BROTHER MOVED OUT OF THE HOUSE.
SO HE MIGHT NOT REALLY BE YOUR BROTHER. IS THAT ANY CONCERN OF MINE?
I DON'T THINK SO.
PISSES ME OFF. ASK ME OUT...
AND THEN ALL YOU DO IS TALK ABOUT YOUR BROTHER.
AND MOPE AROUND. JEEZ.
YOU REALLY PISS ME OFF.
I'M GOING HOME.

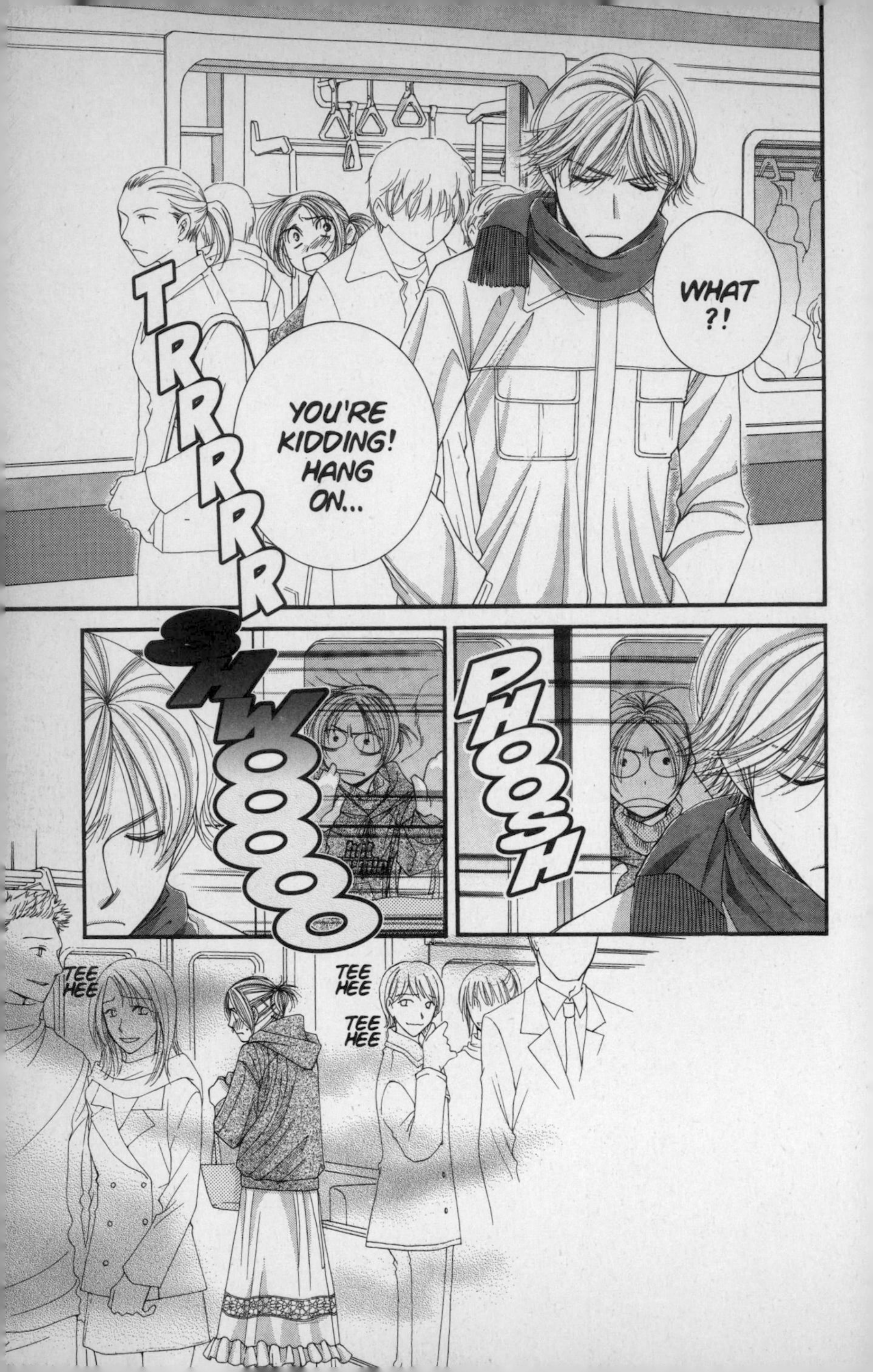
WHAT?!
YOU'RE KIDDING! HANG ON...
TRRRRR
PHOOSH
SHWOOOOO
TEE HEE
TEE HEE
TEE HEE

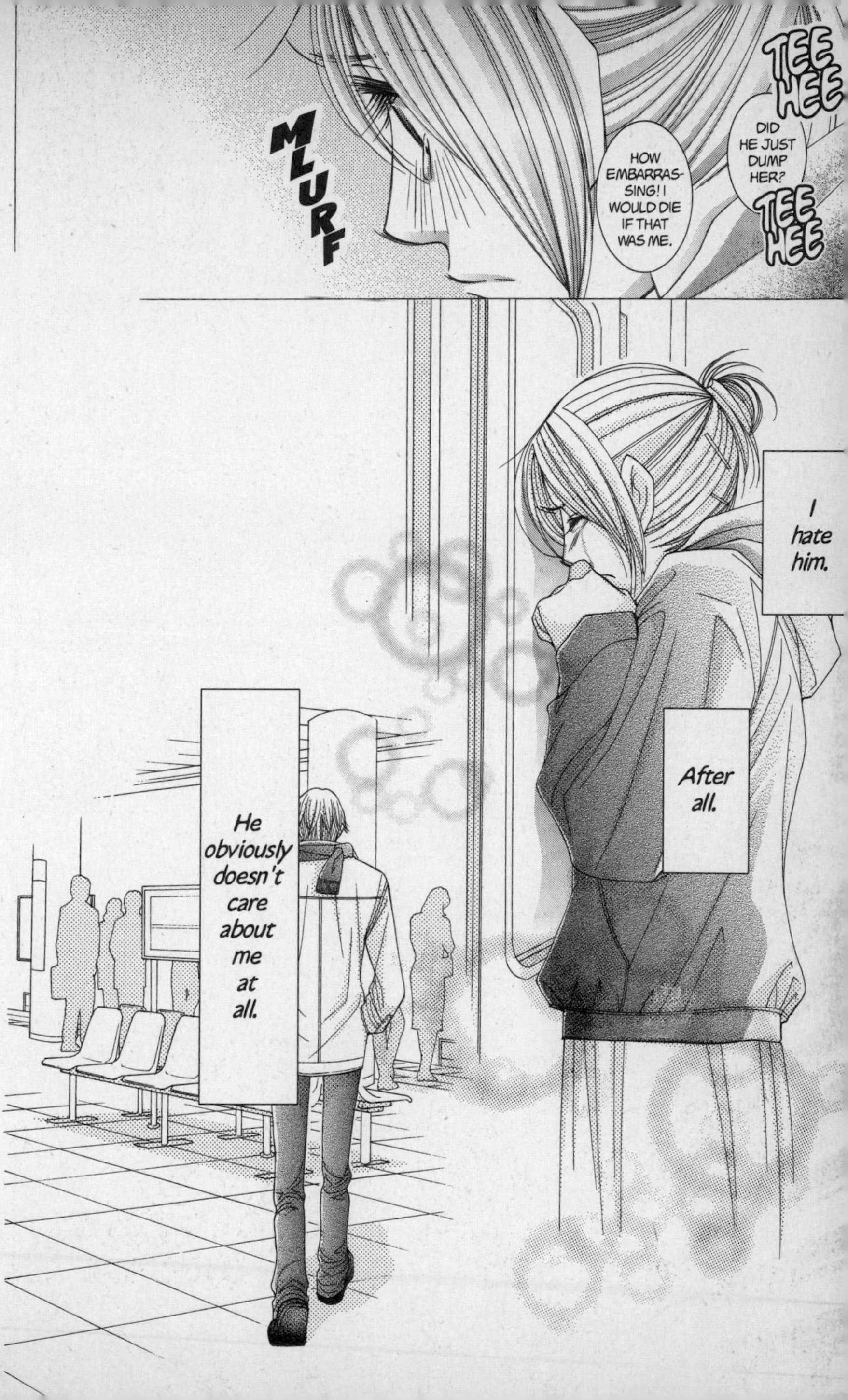
TEE HEE
DID HE JUST DUMP HER?
TEE HEE
HOW EMBARRASSING! I WOULD DIE IF THAT WAS ME.
MLURF
I hate him.
After all.
He obviously doesn't care about me at all.

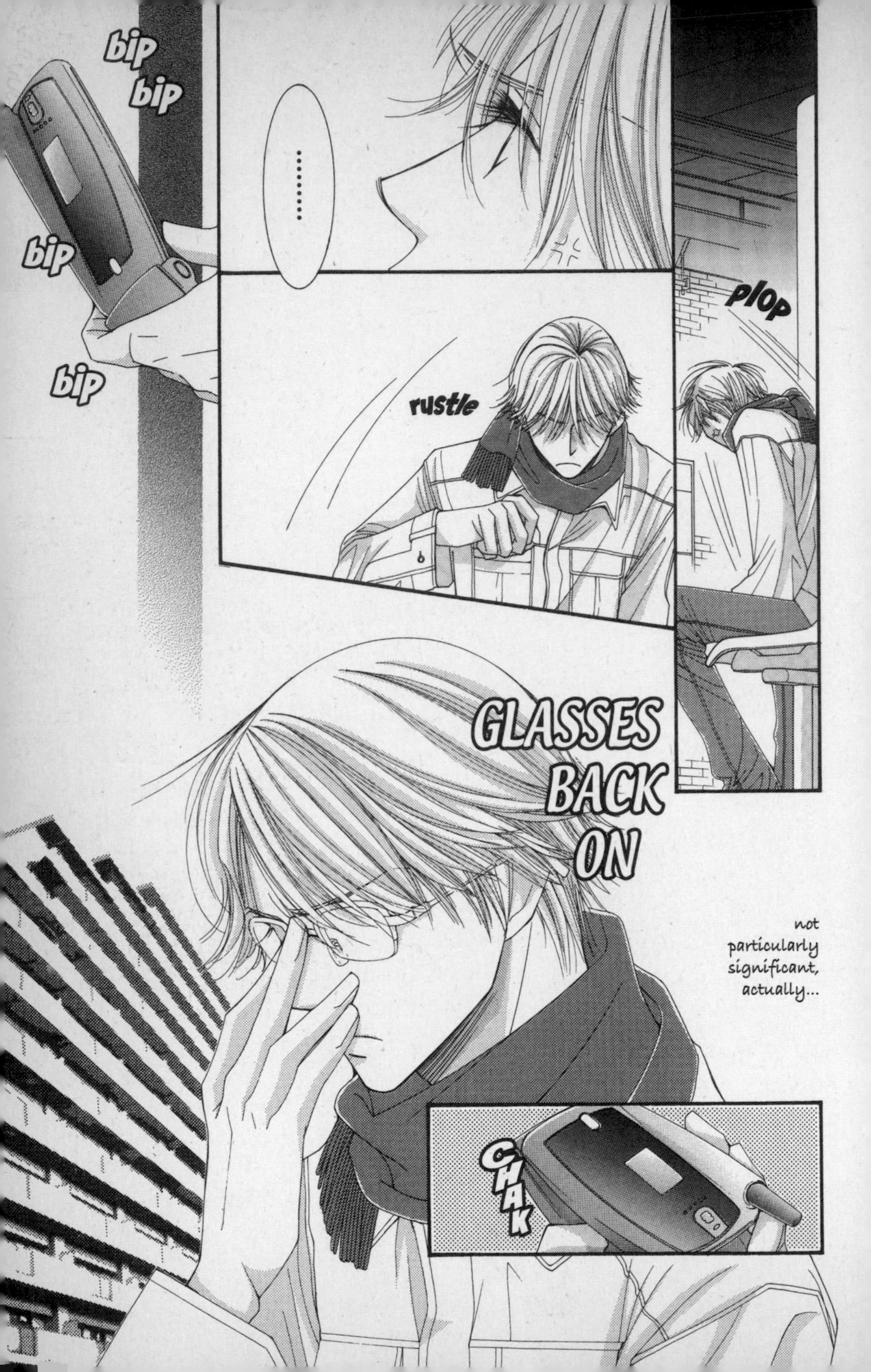

PLOP
......
rustle
bip
bip
bip
bip
GLASSES BACK ON
not particularly significant, actually...
CHAK

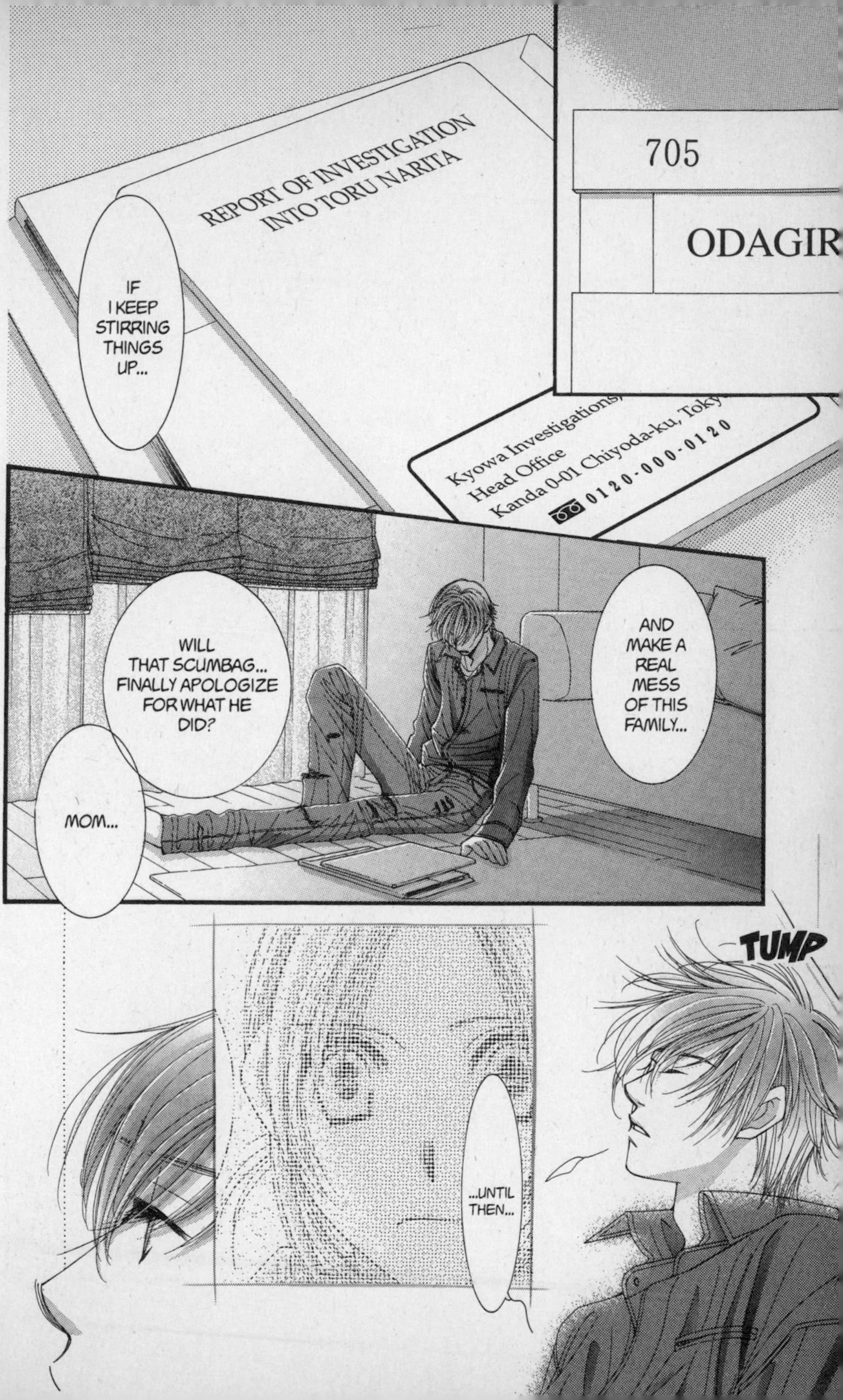
705
ODAGIR
Kyowa Investigations,
Head Office
Kanda 0-01 Chiyoda-ku, Toky
0120-000-0120
REPORT OF INVESTIGATION INTO TORU NARITA
IF I KEEP STIRRING THINGS UP...
AND MAKE A REAL MESS OF THIS FAMILY...
WILL THAT SCUMBAG... FINALLY APOLOGIZE FOR WHAT HE DID?
MOM...
TUMP
...UNTIL THEN...

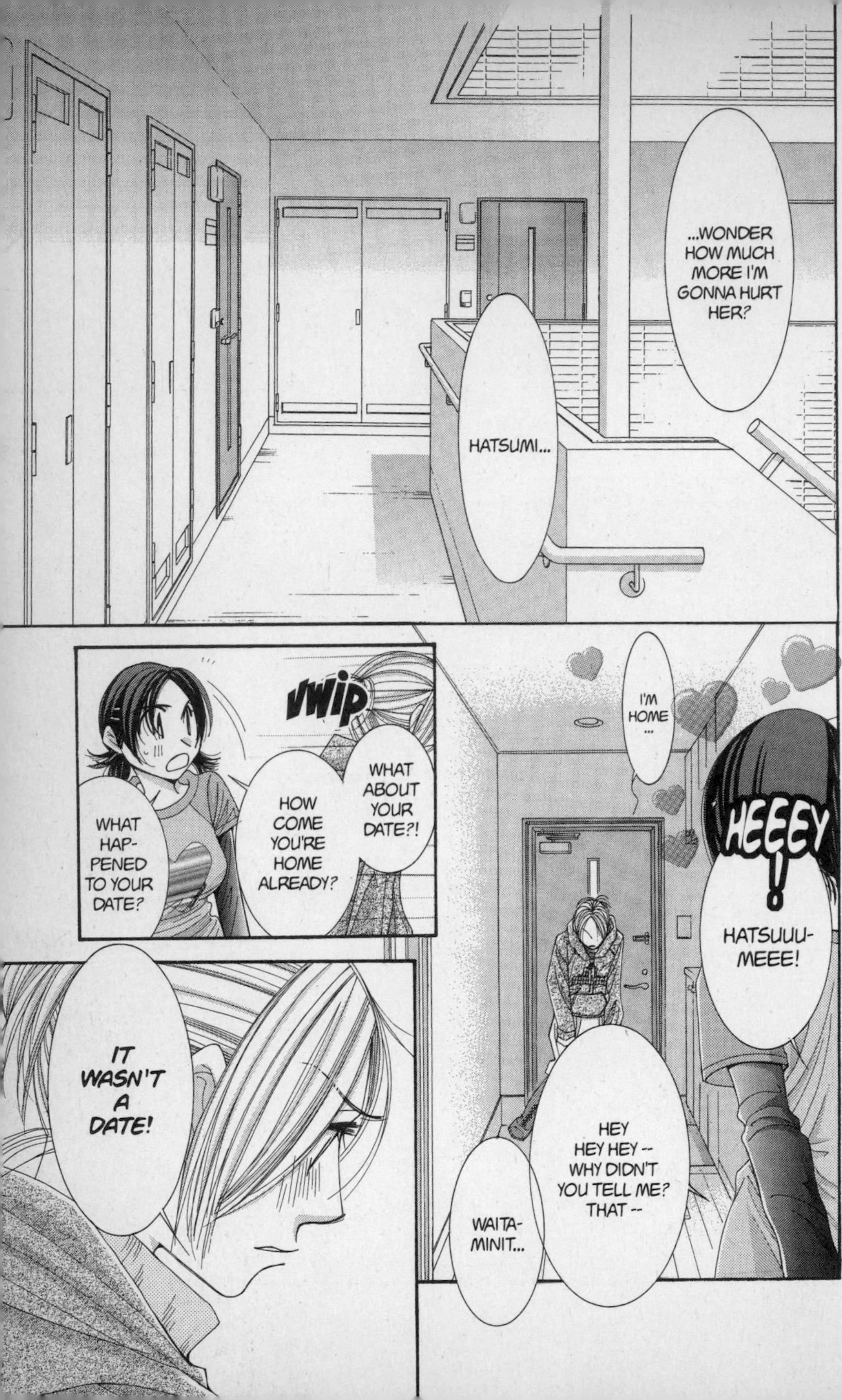
...WONDER HOW MUCH MORE I'M GONNA HURT HER?
HATSUMI...
I'M HOME ...
HEEEY!
HATSUUU-MEEE!
HEY HEY HEY -- WHY DIDN'T YOU TELL ME? THAT --
WAITA-MINIT...
WHAT ABOUT YOUR DATE?!
HOW COME YOU'RE HOME ALREADY?
VWIP
WHAT HAP-PENED TO YOUR DATE?
IT WASN'T A DATE!

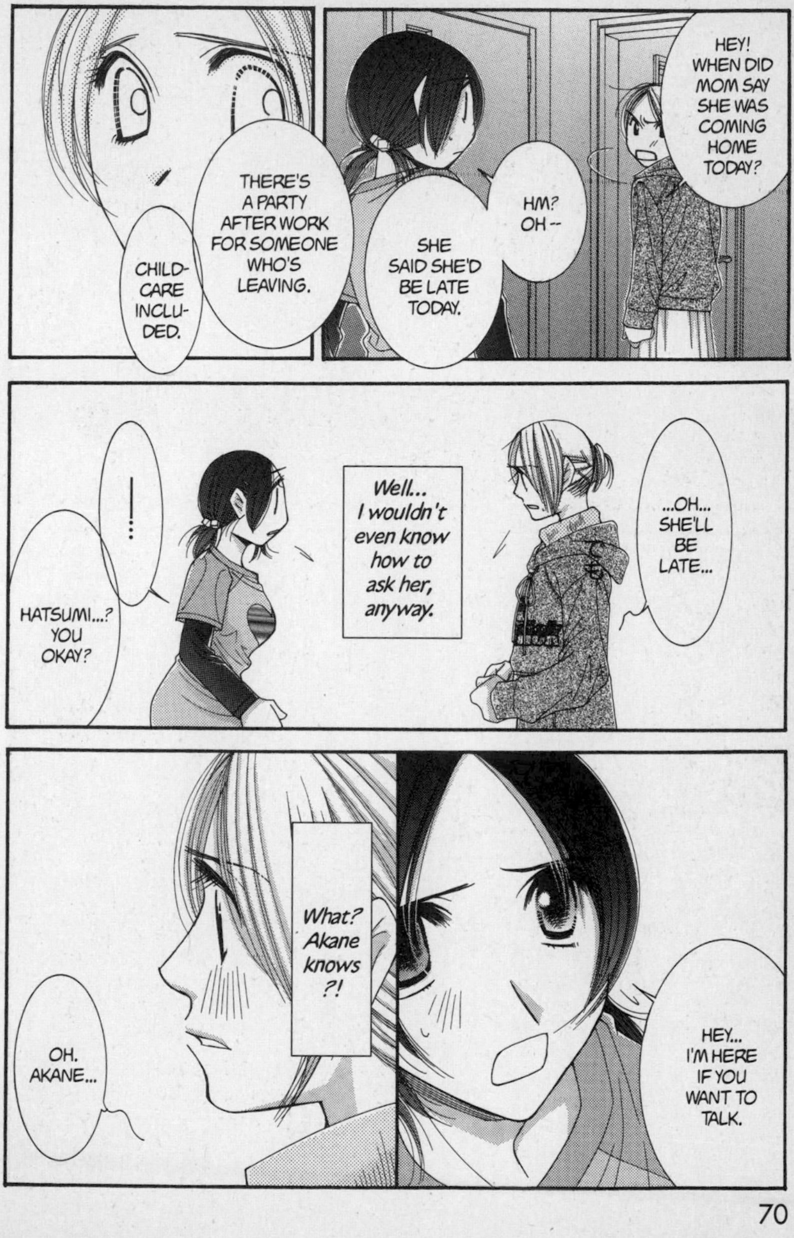
HEY! WHEN DID MOM SAY SHE WAS COMING HOME TODAY?
HM? OH --
SHE SAID SHE'D BE LATE TODAY.
THERE'S A PARTY AFTER WORK FOR SOMEONE WHO'S LEAVING.
CHILD-CARE INCLUDED.
...OH... SHE'LL BE LATE...
Well... I wouldn't even know how to ask her, anyway.
...!
HATSUMI...? YOU OKAY?
HEY... I'M HERE IF YOU WANT TO TALK.
What? Akane knows?!
OH. AKANE...

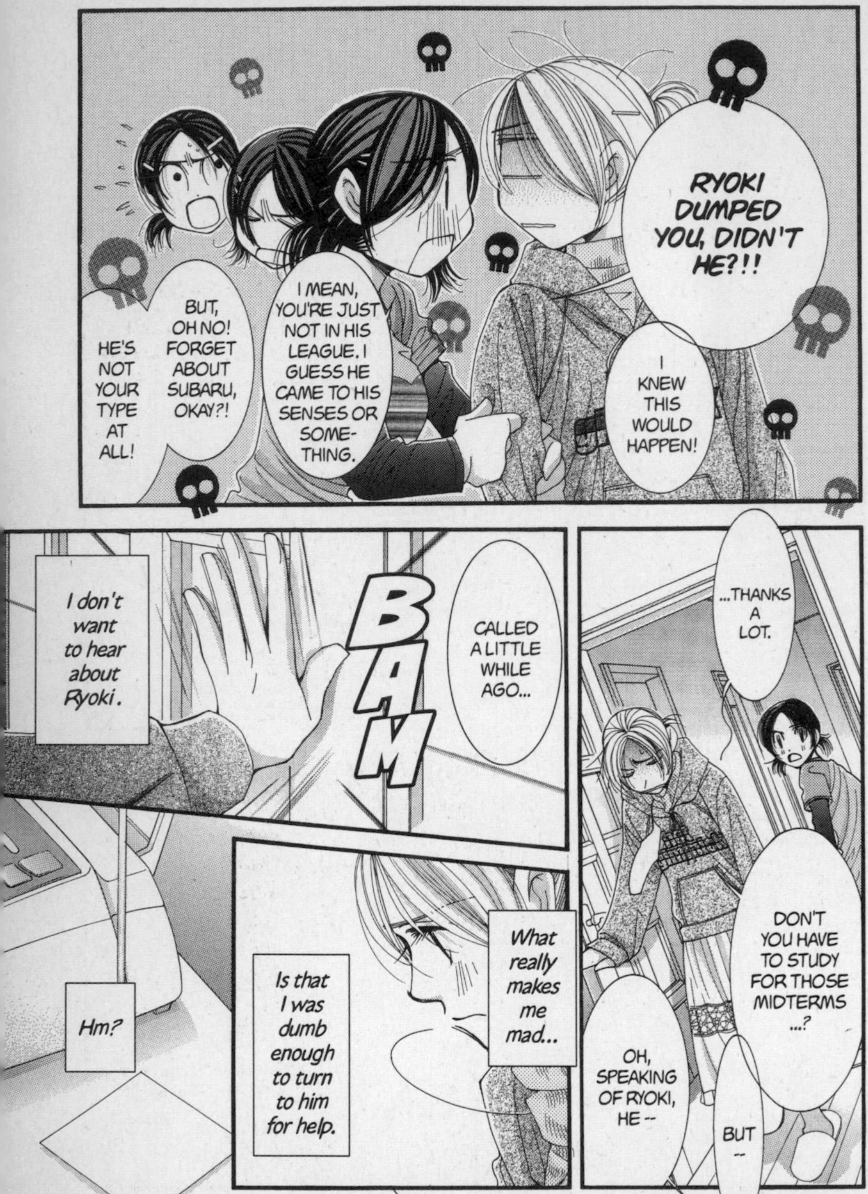
RYOKI DUMPED YOU, DIDN'T HE?!!
I KNEW THIS WOULD HAPPEN!
I MEAN, YOU'RE JUST NOT IN HIS LEAGUE. I GUESS HE CAME TO HIS SENSES OR SOME-THING.
BUT, OH NO! FORGET ABOUT SUBARU, OKAY?!
HE'S NOT YOUR TYPE AT ALL!
...THANKS A LOT.
DON'T YOU HAVE TO STUDY FOR THOSE MIDTERMS ...?
BUT --
OH, SPEAKING OF RYOKI, HE --
CALLED A LITTLE WHILE AGO...
BAM
I don't want to hear about Ryoki.
What really makes me mad...
Is that I was dumb enough to turn to him for help.
Hm?

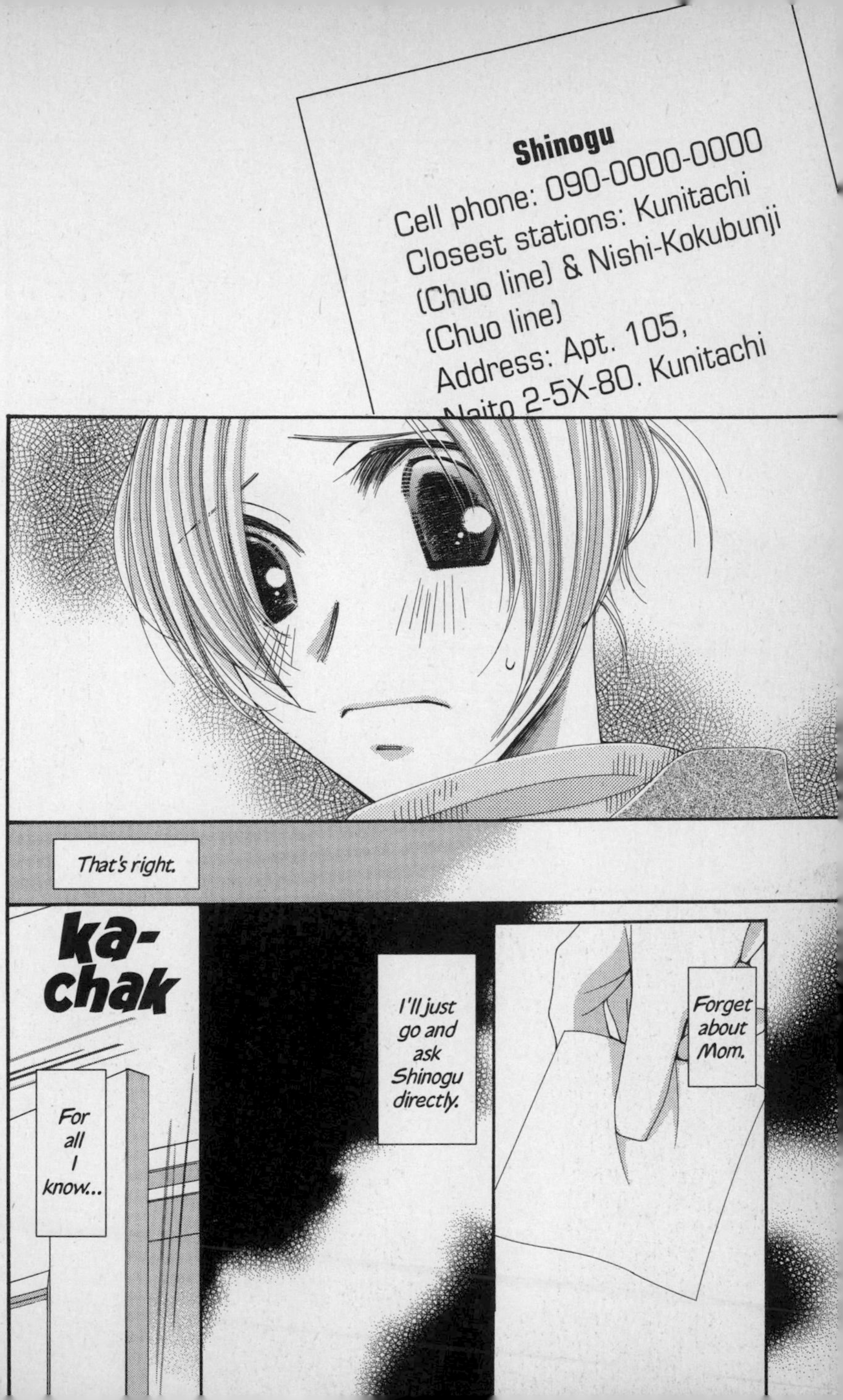
Shinogu
Cell phone: 090-0000-0000
Closest stations: Kunitachi
(Chuo line) & Nishi-Kokubunji
(Chuo line)
Address: Apt. 105,
Naito 2-5X-80. Kunitachi
That's right.
Forget about Mom.
I'll just go and ask Shinogu directly.
ka-chak
For all I know...

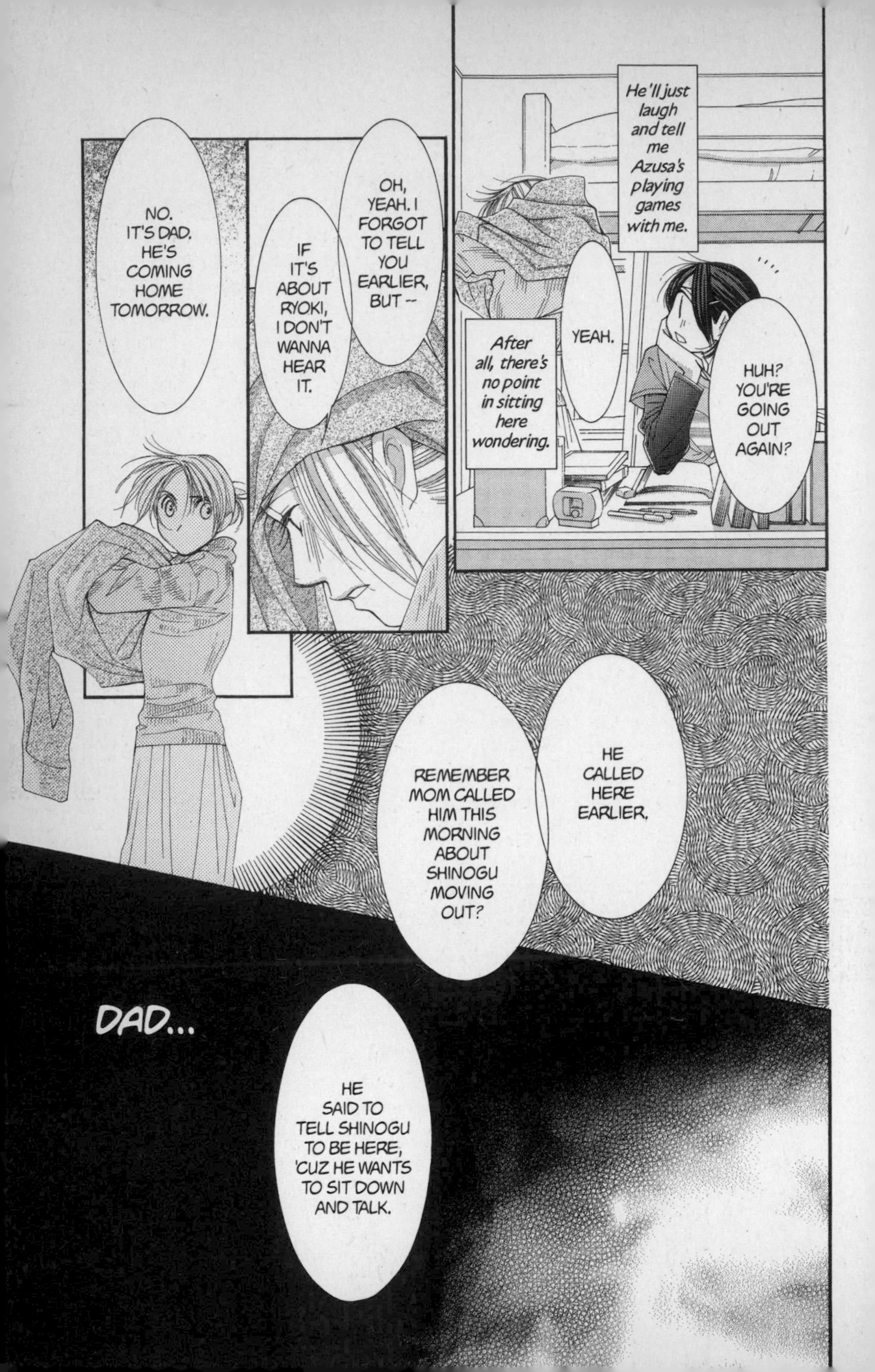
He'll just laugh and tell me Azusa's playing games with me.
HUH? YOU'RE GOING OUT AGAIN?
YEAH.
After all, there's no point in sitting here wondering.
OH, YEAH. I FORGOT TO TELL YOU EARLIER, BUT --
IF IT'S ABOUT RYOKI, I DON'T WANNA HEAR IT.
NO. IT'S DAD. HE'S COMING HOME TOMORROW.
HE CALLED HERE EARLIER.
REMEMBER MOM CALLED HIM THIS MORNING ABOUT SHINOGU MOVING OUT?
HE SAID TO TELL SHINOGU TO BE HERE, 'CUZ HE WANTS TO SIT DOWN AND TALK.
DAD...

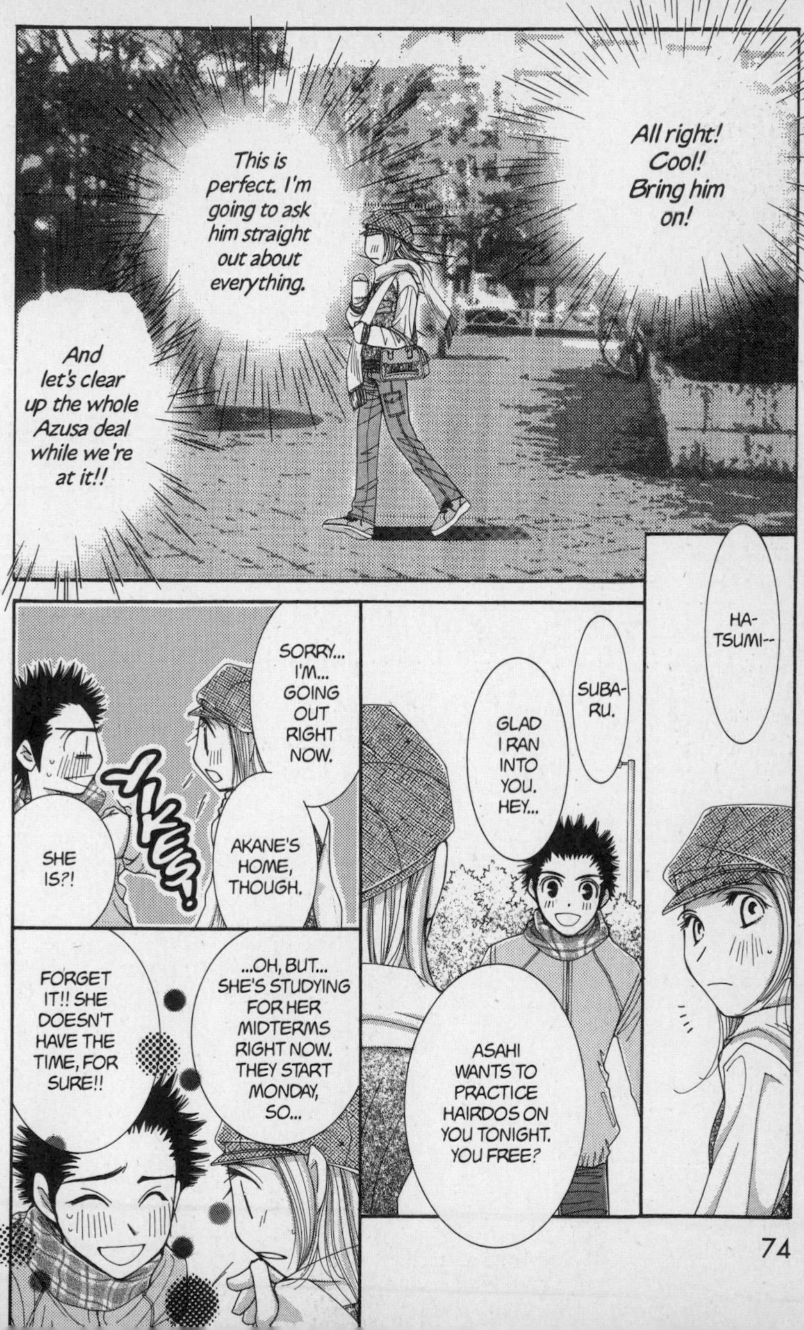
All right! Cool! Bring him on!
This is perfect. I'm going to ask him straight out about everything.
And let's clear up the whole Azusa deal while we're at it!!
HA-TSUMI--
SUBA-RU.
GLAD I RAN INTO YOU. HEY...
ASAHI WANTS TO PRACTICE HAIRDOS ON YOU TONIGHT. YOU FREE?
SORRY... I'M... GOING OUT RIGHT NOW.
AKANE'S HOME, THOUGH.
YIKES!
SHE IS?!
...OH, BUT... SHE'S STUDYING FOR HER MIDTERMS RIGHT NOW. THEY START MONDAY, SO...
FORGET IT!! SHE DOESN'T HAVE THE TIME, FOR SURE!!

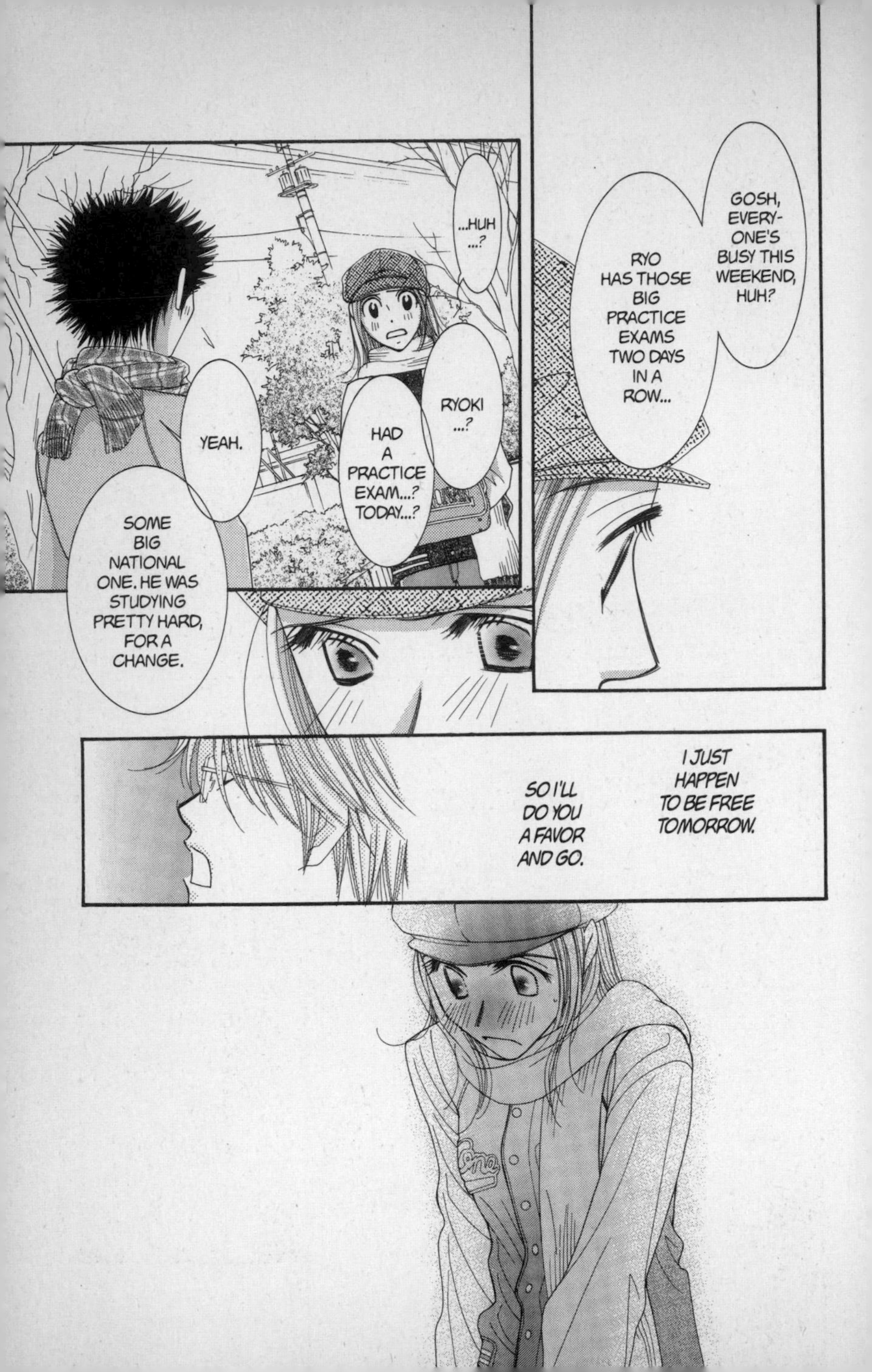
GOSH, EVERY-ONE'S BUSY THIS WEEKEND, HUH?
RYO HAS THOSE BIG PRACTICE EXAMS TWO DAYS IN A ROW...
...HUH ...?
RYOKI ...?
HAD A PRACTICE EXAM...? TODAY...?
YEAH.
SOME BIG NATIONAL ONE. HE WAS STUDYING PRETTY HARD, FOR A CHANGE.
I JUST HAPPEN TO BE FREE TOMORROW.
SO I'LL DO YOU A FAVOR AND GO.

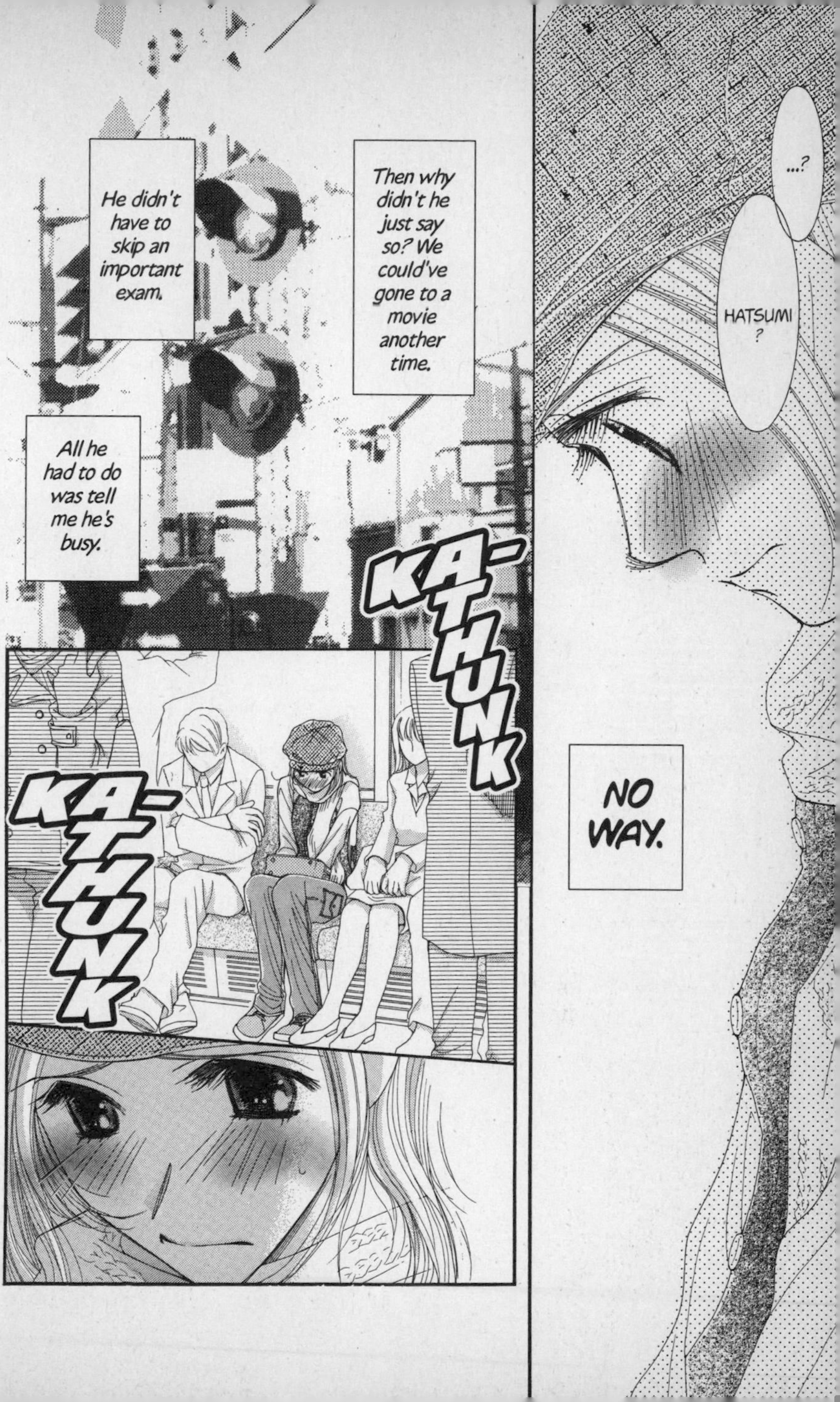
...?
HATSUMI?
NO WAY.
Then why didn't he just say so? We could've gone to a movie another time.
He didn't have to skip an important exam.
All he had to do was tell me he's busy.
KA-THUNK
KA-THUNK

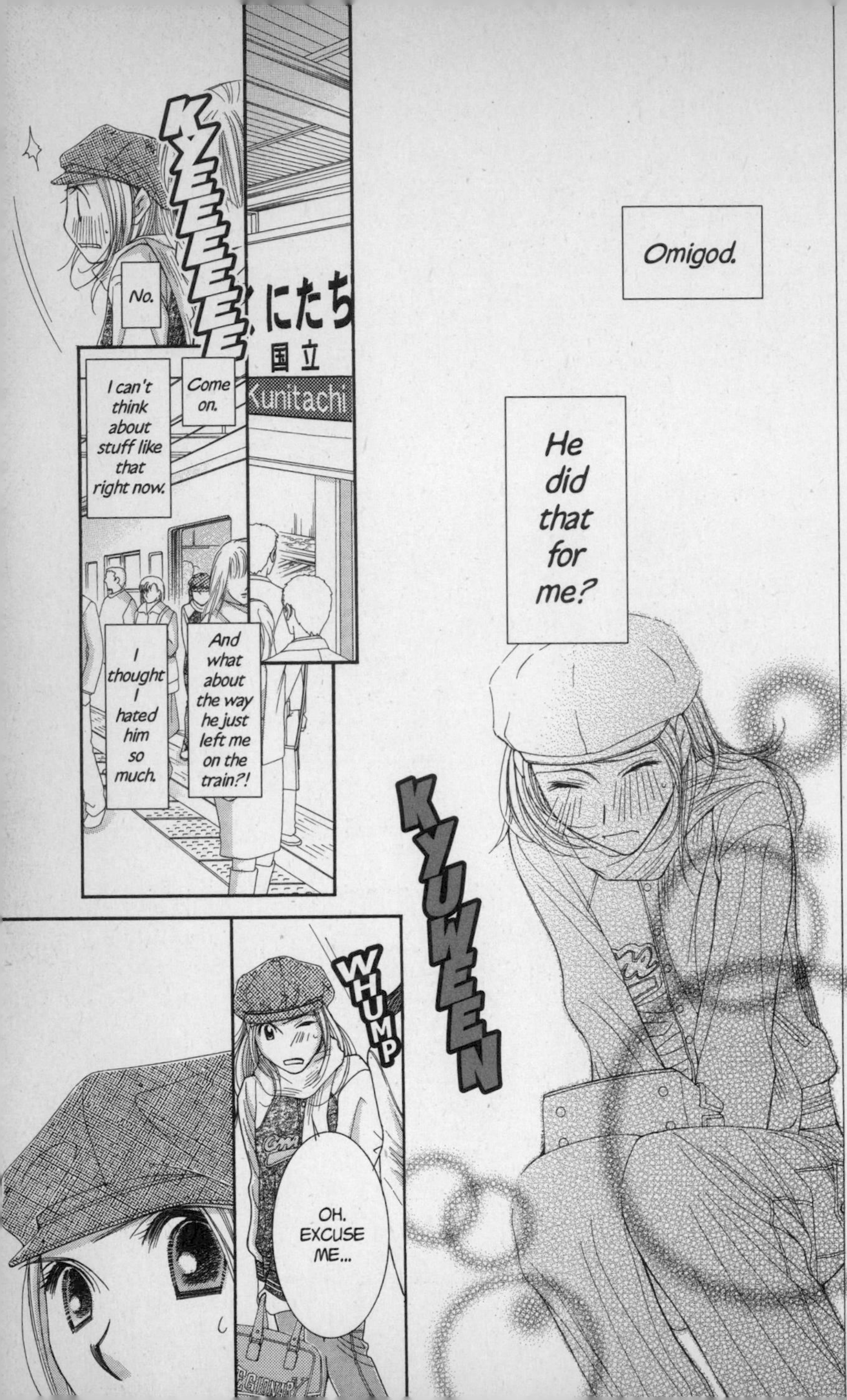
Omigod.
He did that for me?
KYUWEEN
KYEEEEE
にたち
国立
Kunitachi
No.
Come on.
I can't think about stuff like that right now.
And what about the way he just left me on the train?!
I thought I hated him so much.
WHUMP
OH. EXCUSE ME...

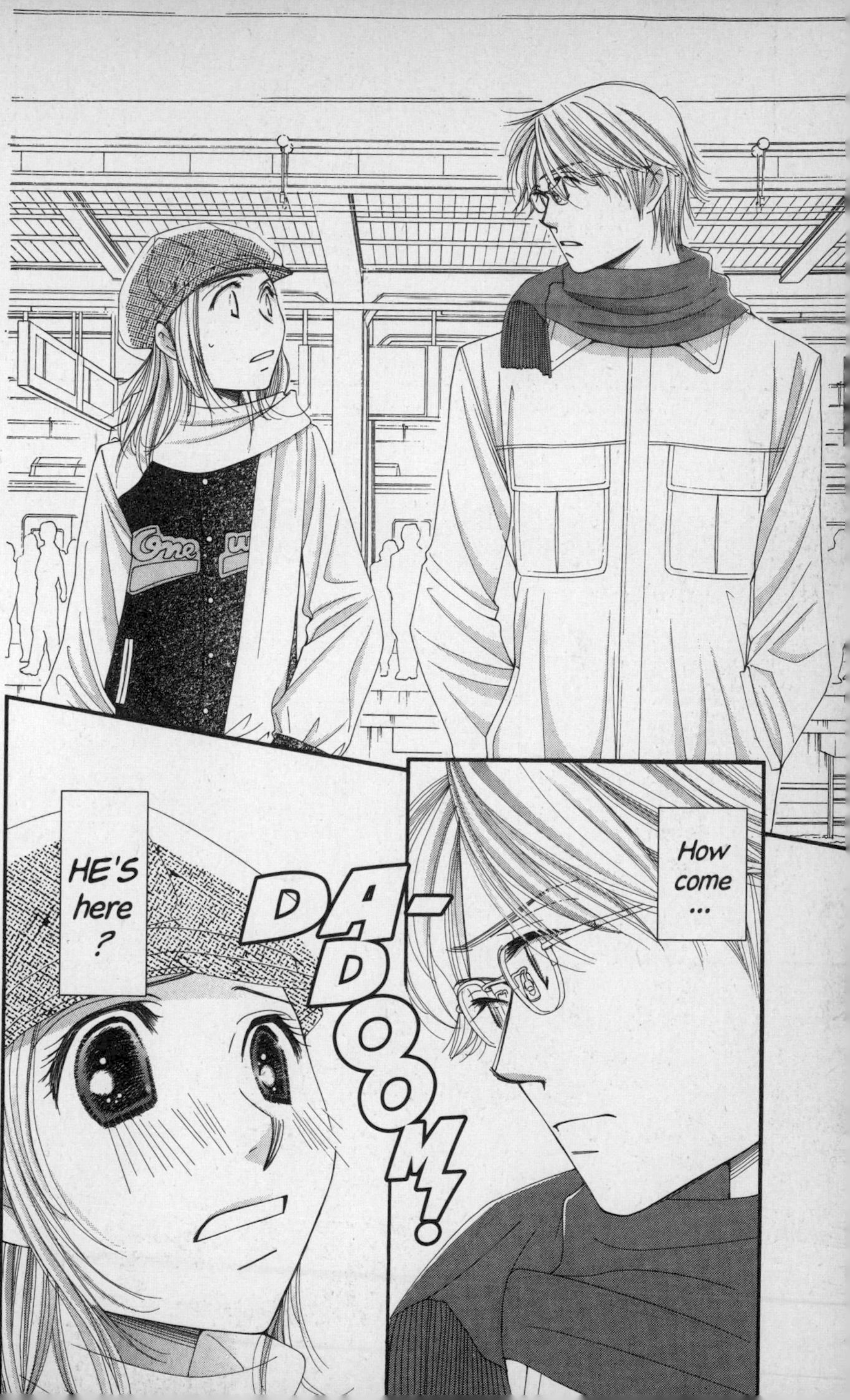
How come ...
DA-DOOM!
HE'S here ?

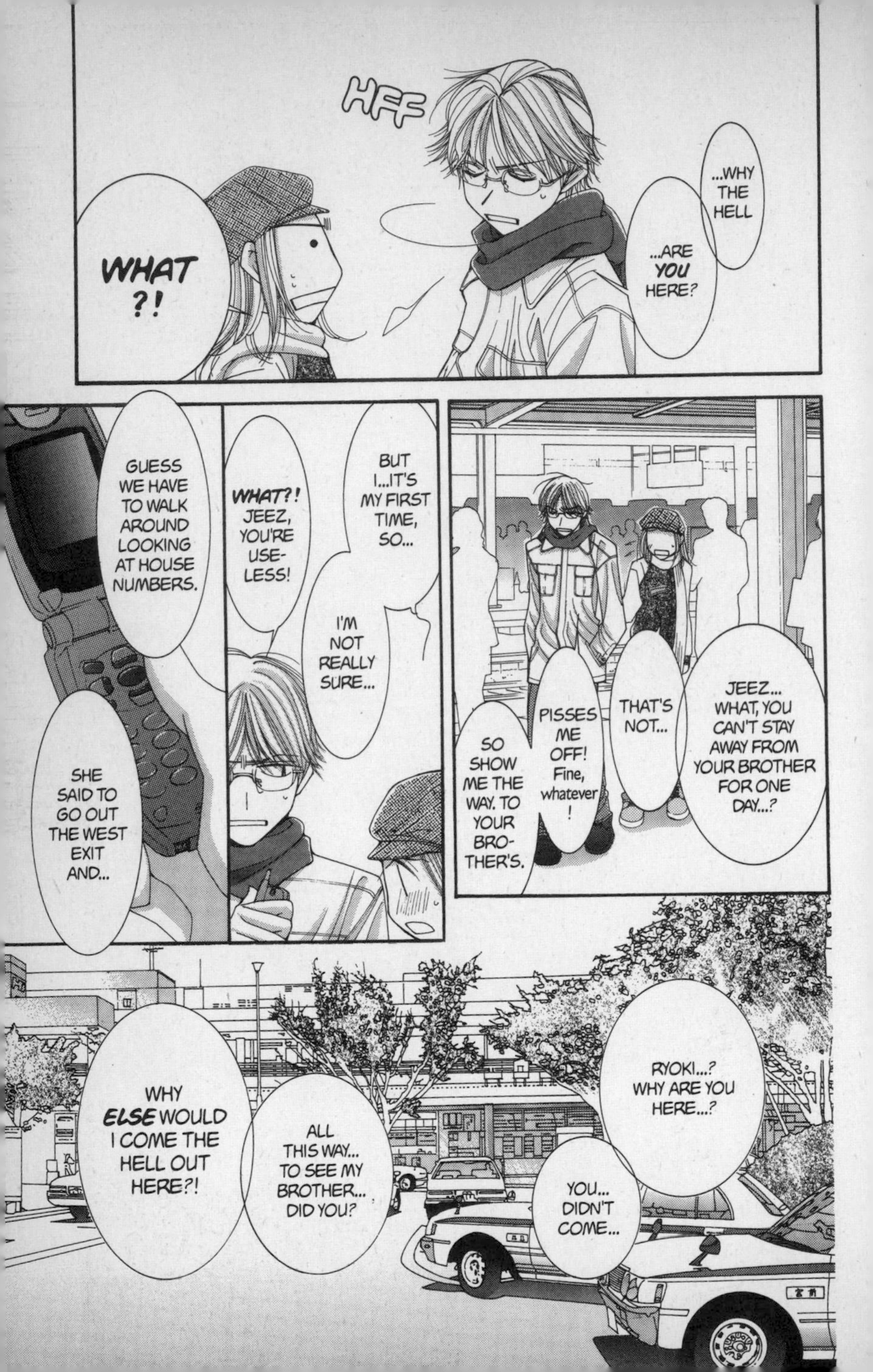
HFF
...WHY THE HELL
...ARE YOU HERE?
WHAT?!
JEEZ... WHAT, YOU CAN'T STAY AWAY FROM YOUR BROTHER FOR ONE DAY...?
THAT'S NOT...
PISSES ME OFF! Fine, whatever!
SO SHOW ME THE WAY. TO YOUR BROTHER'S.
BUT I...IT'S MY FIRST TIME, SO...
I'M NOT REALLY SURE...
WHAT?! JEEZ, YOU'RE USELESS!
GUESS WE HAVE TO WALK AROUND LOOKING AT HOUSE NUMBERS.
SHE SAID TO GO OUT THE WEST EXIT AND...
RYOKI...? WHY ARE YOU HERE...?
YOU... DIDN'T COME...
ALL THIS WAY... TO SEE MY BROTHER... DID YOU?
WHY ELSE WOULD I COME THE HELL OUT HERE?!

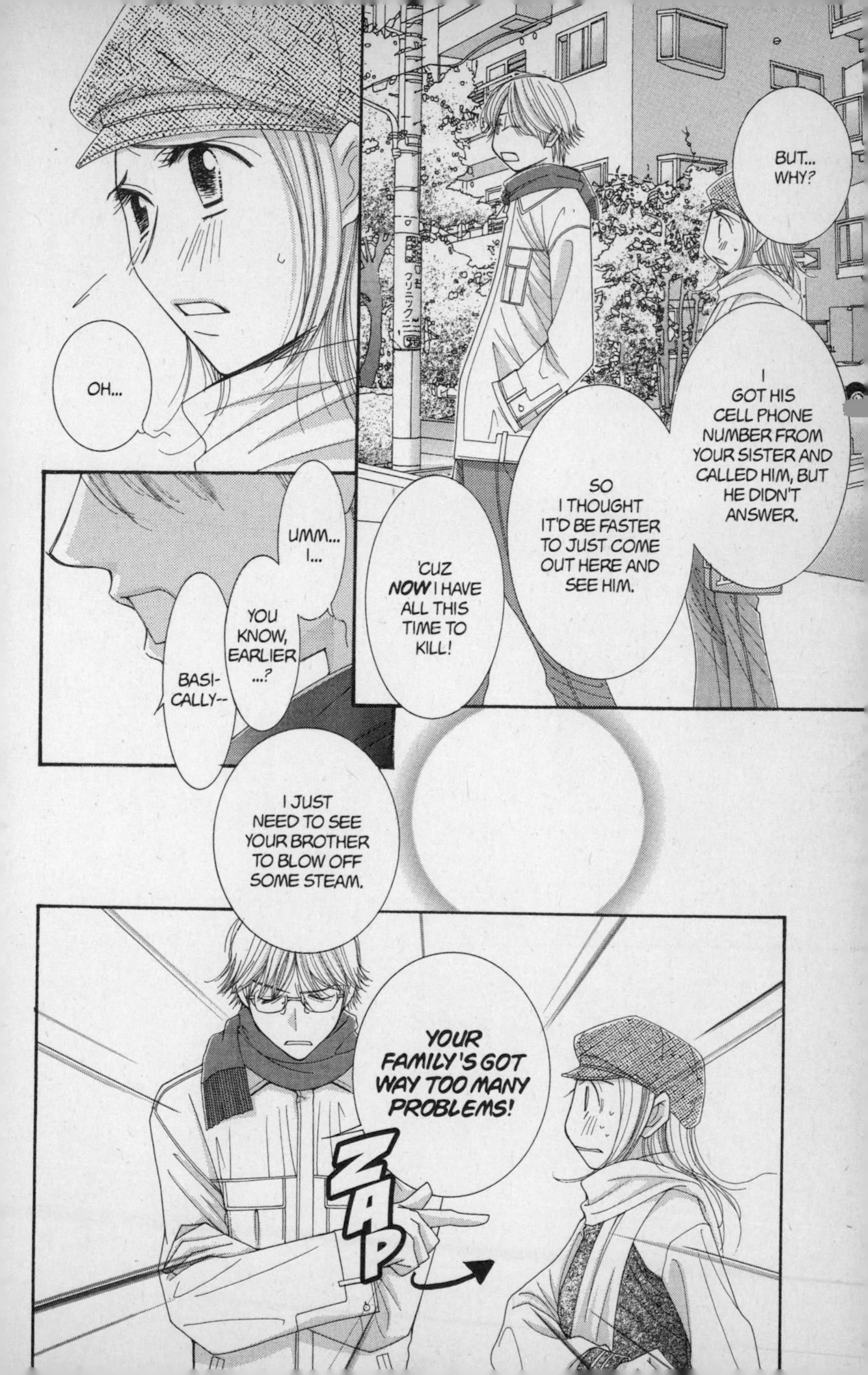
BUT... WHY?
I GOT HIS CELL PHONE NUMBER FROM YOUR SISTER AND CALLED HIM, BUT HE DIDN'T ANSWER.
SO I THOUGHT IT'D BE FASTER TO JUST COME OUT HERE AND SEE HIM.
'CUZ NOW I HAVE ALL THIS TIME TO KILL!
OH...
UMM... I...
YOU KNOW, EARLIER...?
BASI-CALLY--
I JUST NEED TO SEE YOUR BROTHER TO BLOW OFF SOME STEAM.
YOUR FAMILY'S GOT WAY TOO MANY PROBLEMS!
ZAP

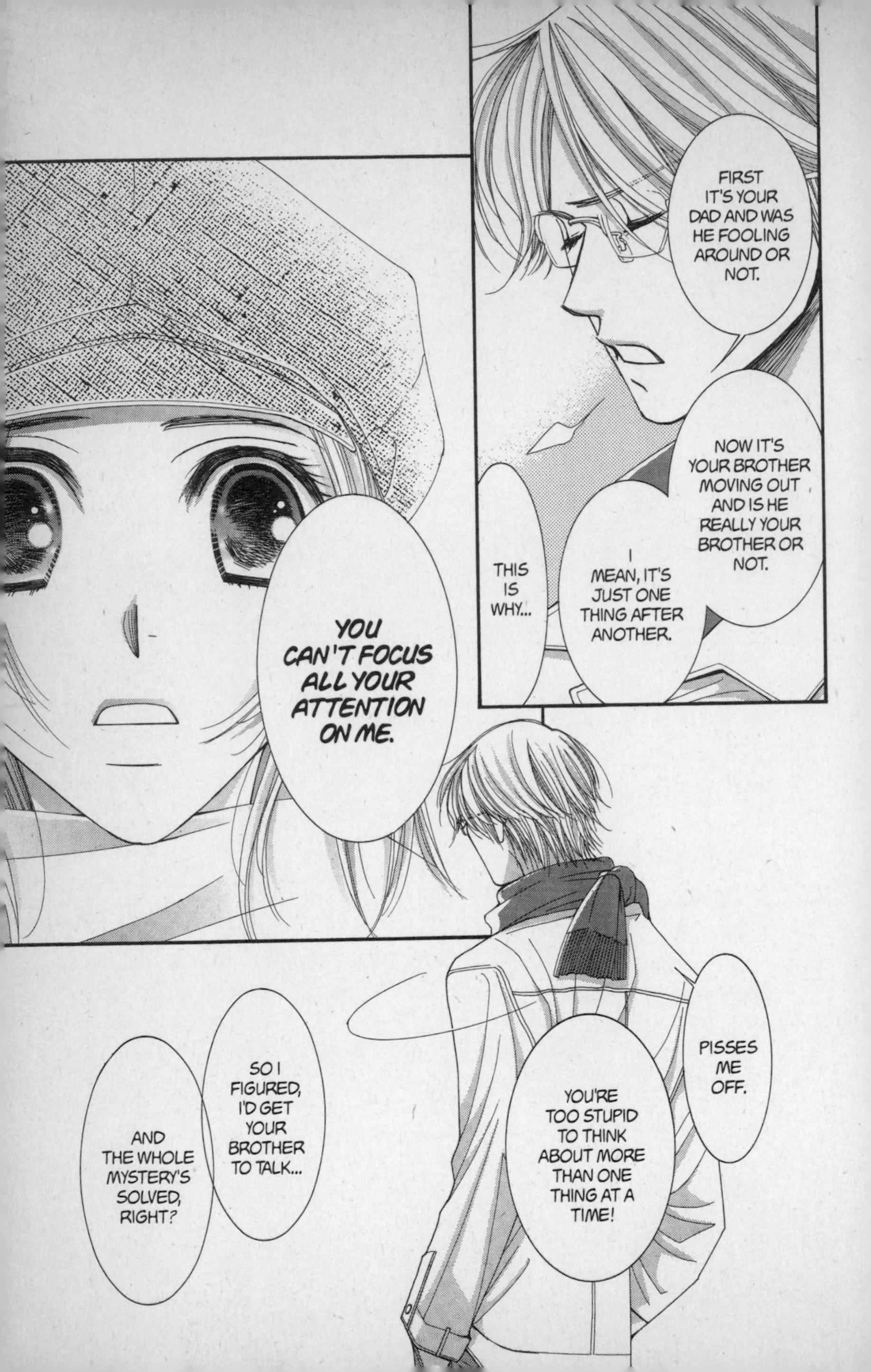
FIRST IT'S YOUR DAD AND WAS HE FOOLING AROUND OR NOT.
NOW IT'S YOUR BROTHER MOVING OUT AND IS HE REALLY YOUR BROTHER OR NOT.
I MEAN, IT'S JUST ONE THING AFTER ANOTHER.
THIS IS WHY...
YOU CAN'T FOCUS ALL YOUR ATTENTION ON ME.
PISSES ME OFF.
YOU'RE TOO STUPID TO THINK ABOUT MORE THAN ONE THING AT A TIME!
SO I FIGURED, I'D GET YOUR BROTHER TO TALK...
AND THE WHOLE MYSTERY'S SOLVED, RIGHT?

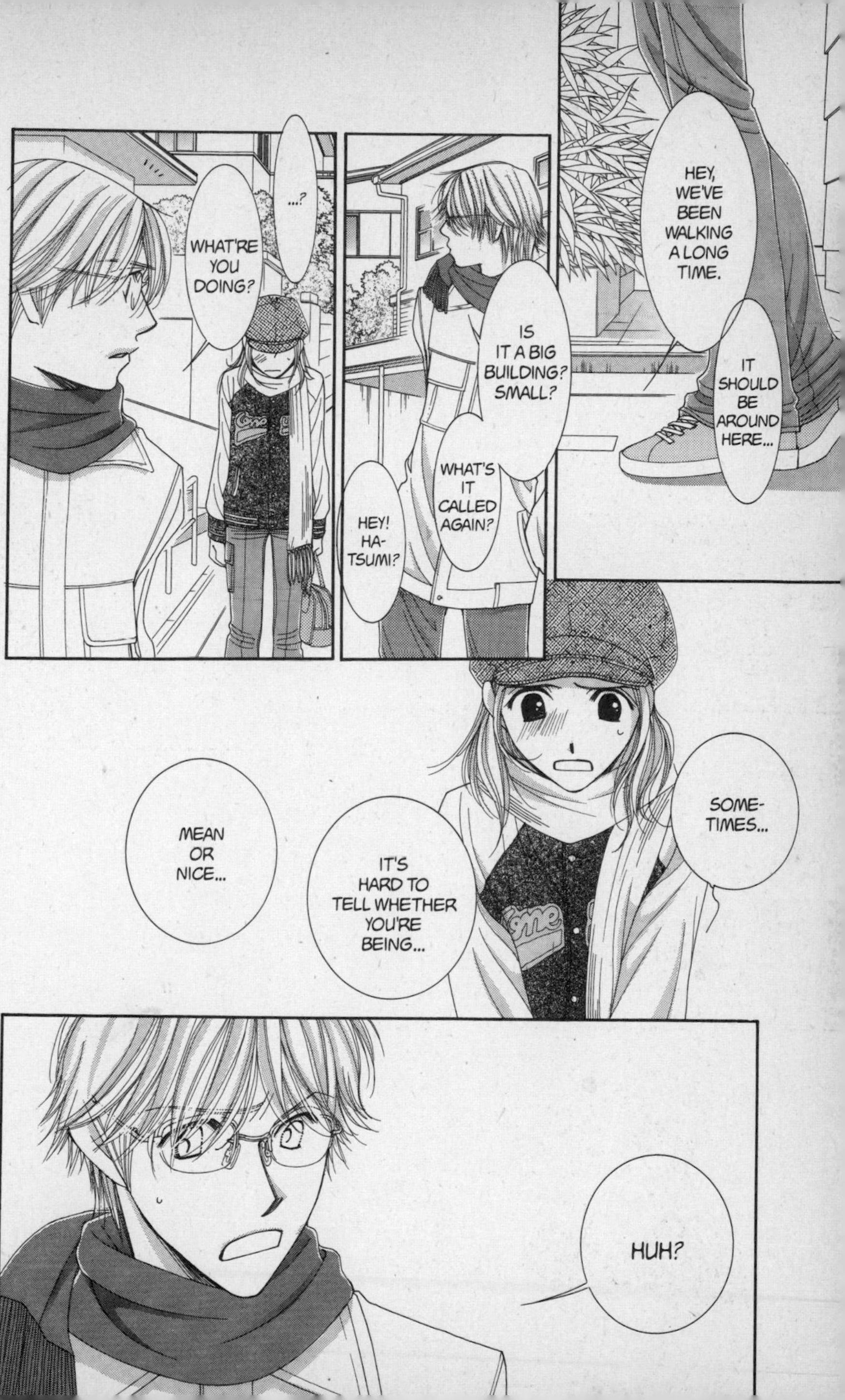
HEY, WE'VE BEEN WALKING A LONG TIME.
IT SHOULD BE AROUND HERE...
IS IT A BIG BUILDING? SMALL?
WHAT'S IT CALLED AGAIN?
HEY! HA-TSUMI?
...?
WHAT'RE YOU DOING?
SOME-TIMES...
IT'S HARD TO TELL WHETHER YOU'RE BEING...
MEAN OR NICE...
HUH?

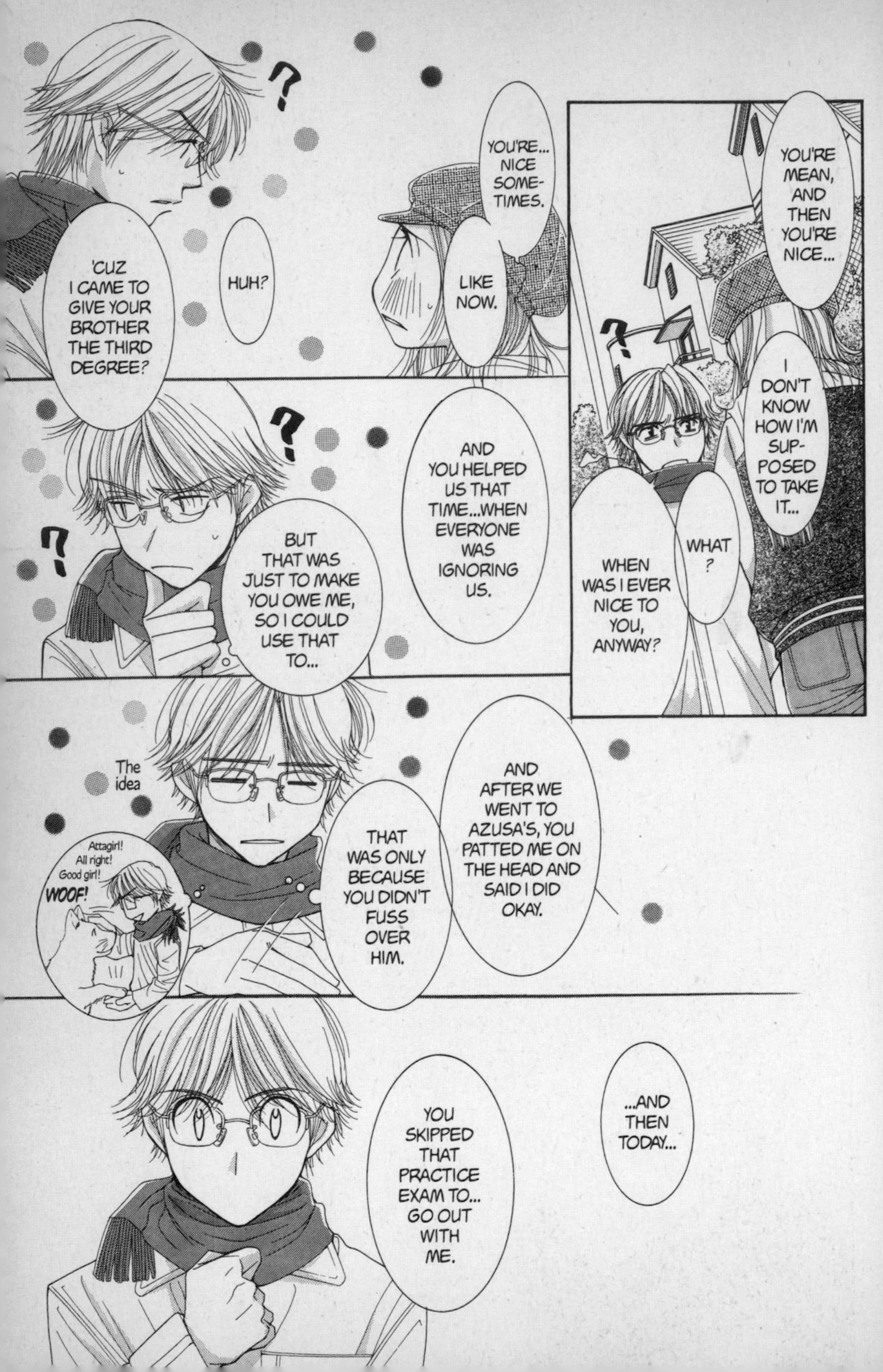
YOU'RE MEAN, AND THEN YOU'RE NICE...
I DON'T KNOW HOW I'M SUPPOSED TO TAKE IT...
WHAT?
WHEN WAS I EVER NICE TO YOU, ANYWAY?
YOU'RE... NICE SOMETIMES.
LIKE NOW.
HUH?
'CUZ I CAME TO GIVE YOUR BROTHER THE THIRD DEGREE?
AND YOU HELPED US THAT TIME...WHEN EVERYONE WAS IGNORING US.
BUT THAT WAS JUST TO MAKE YOU OWE ME, SO I COULD USE THAT TO...
AND AFTER WE WENT TO AZUSA'S, YOU PATTED ME ON THE HEAD AND SAID I DID OKAY.
THAT WAS ONLY BECAUSE YOU DIDN'T FUSS OVER HIM.
The idea
Attagirl! All right! Good girl!
WOOF!
...AND THEN TODAY...
YOU SKIPPED THAT PRACTICE EXAM TO... GO OUT WITH ME.

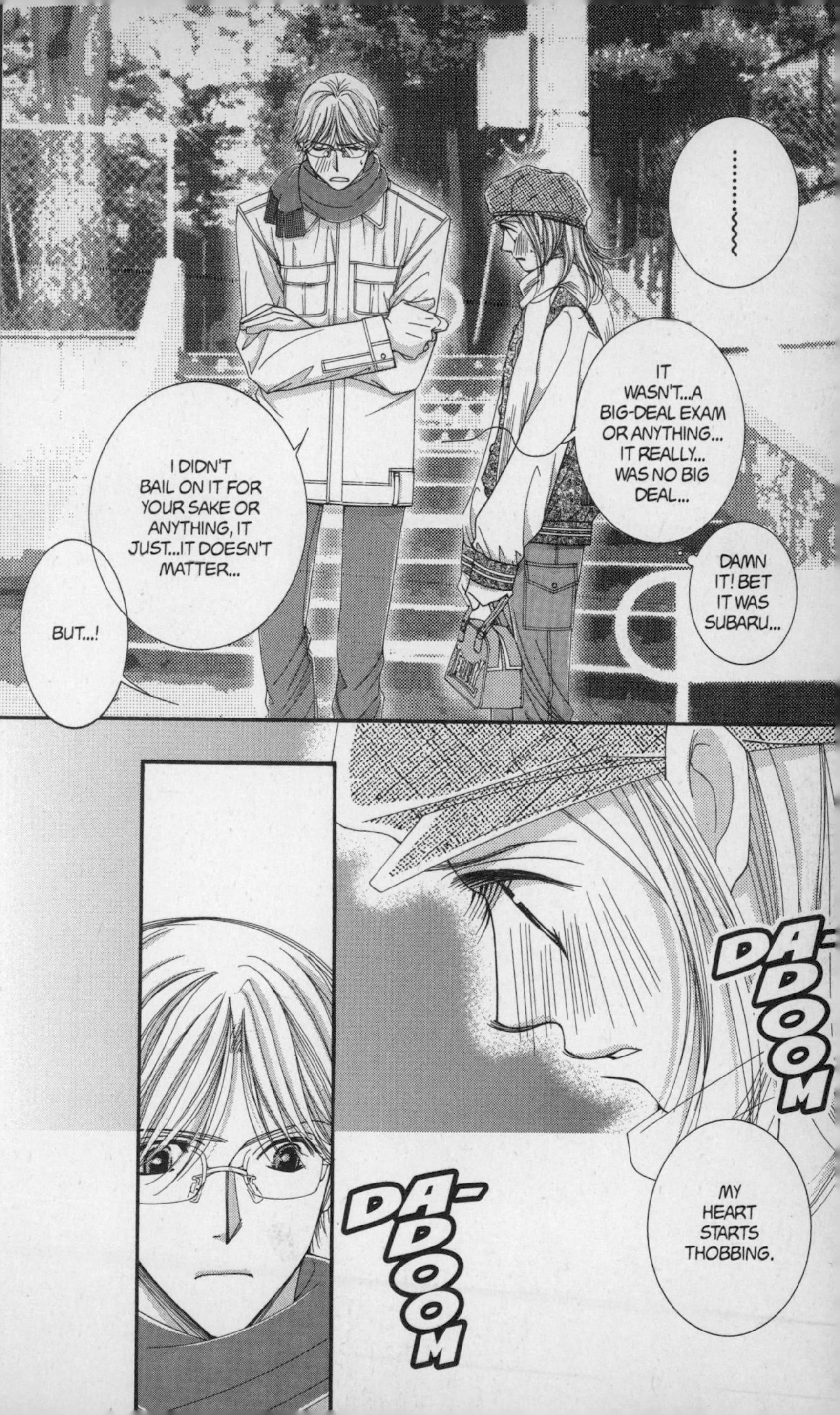
......
IT WASN'T...A BIG-DEAL EXAM OR ANYTHING... IT REALLY... WAS NO BIG DEAL...
DAMN IT! BET IT WAS SUBARU...
I DIDN'T BAIL ON IT FOR YOUR SAKE OR ANYTHING, IT JUST...IT DOESN'T MATTER...
BUT...!
DA-DOOM
MY HEART STARTS THOBBING.
DA-DOOM

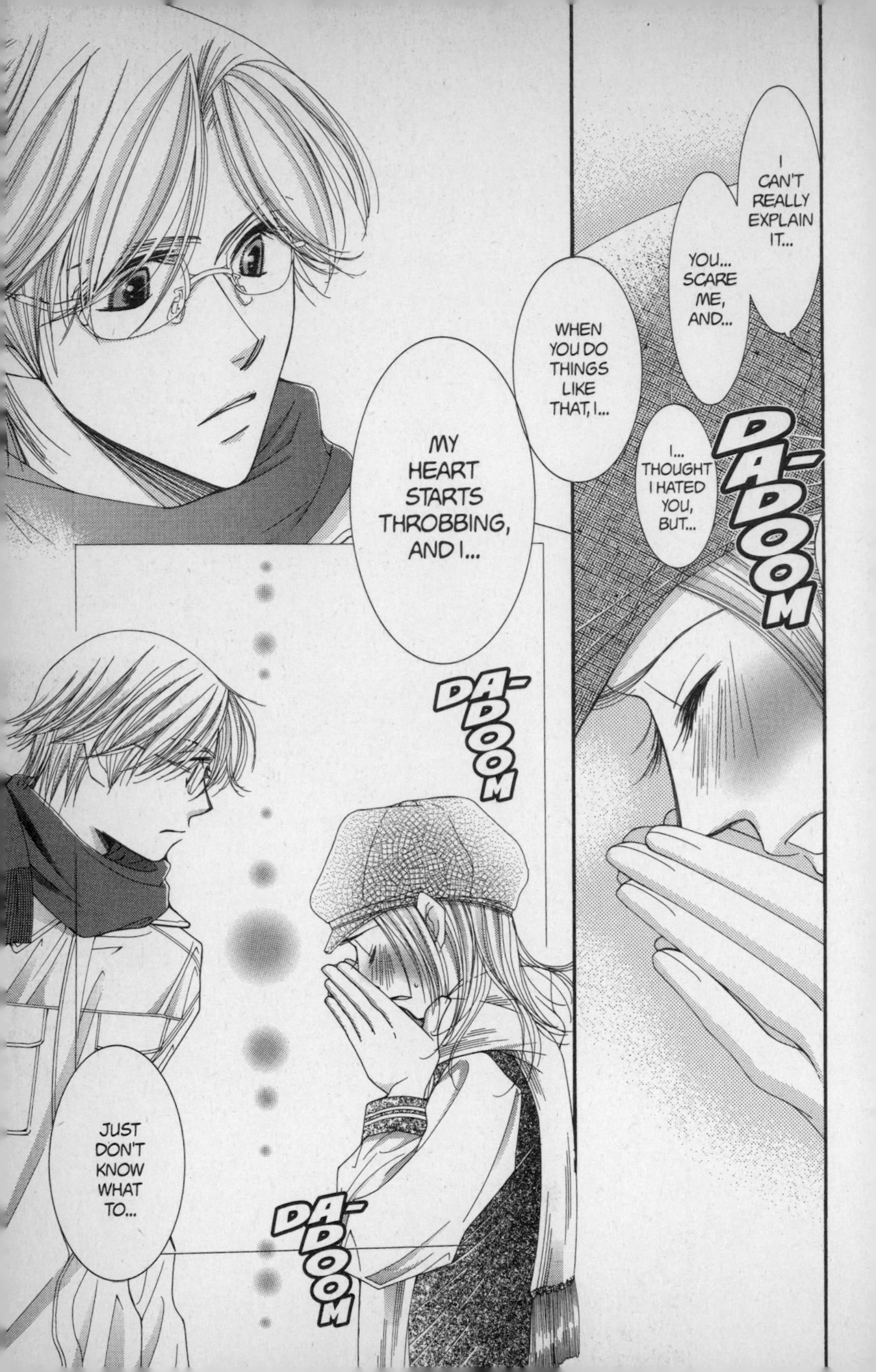
I CAN'T REALLY EXPLAIN IT...
YOU... SCARE ME, AND...
I... THOUGHT I HATED YOU, BUT...
DA-DOOM
WHEN YOU DO THINGS LIKE THAT, I...
MY HEART STARTS THROBBING, AND I...
DA-DOOM
DA-DOOM
JUST DON'T KNOW WHAT TO...

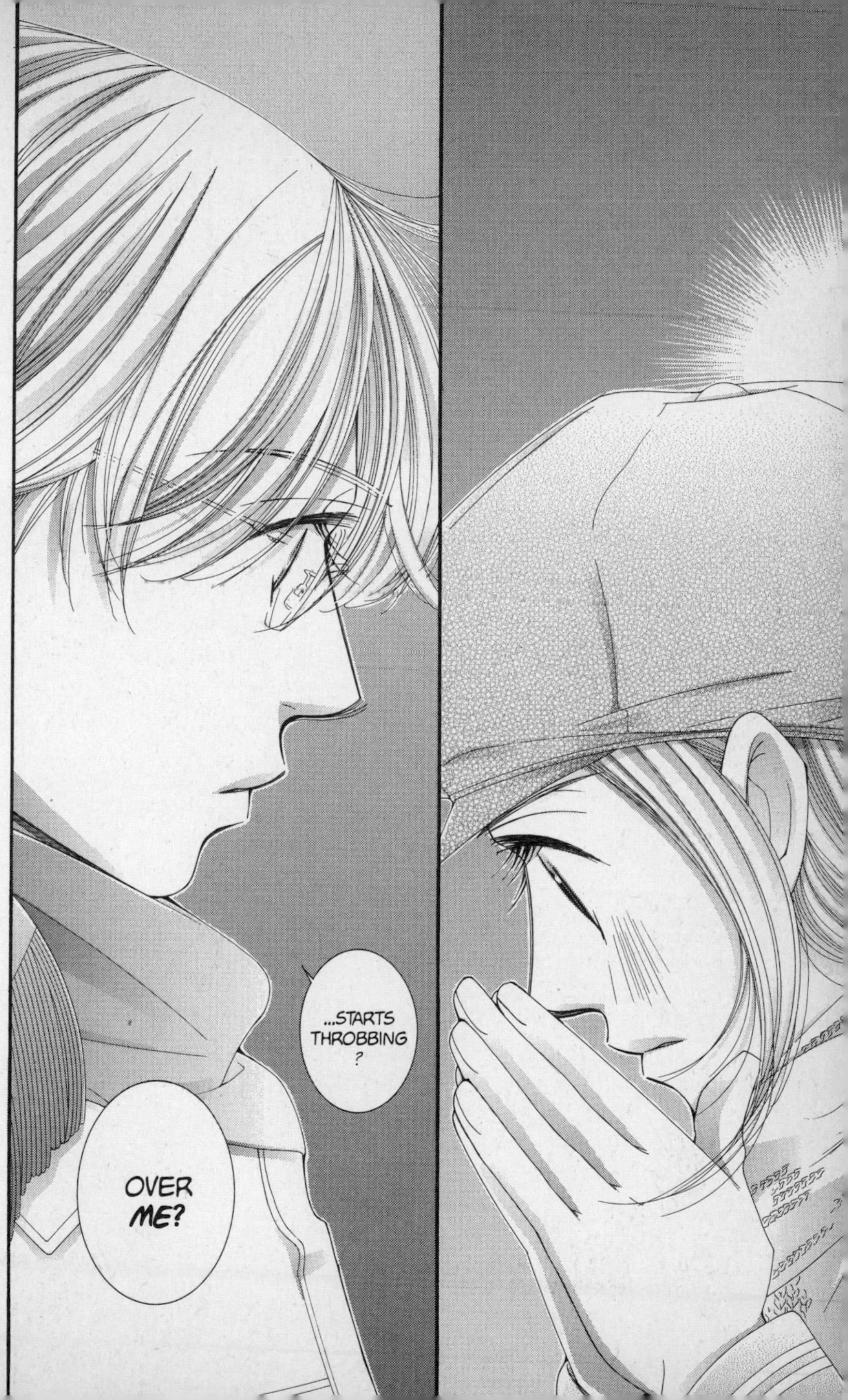
...STARTS THROBBING ?
OVER ME?

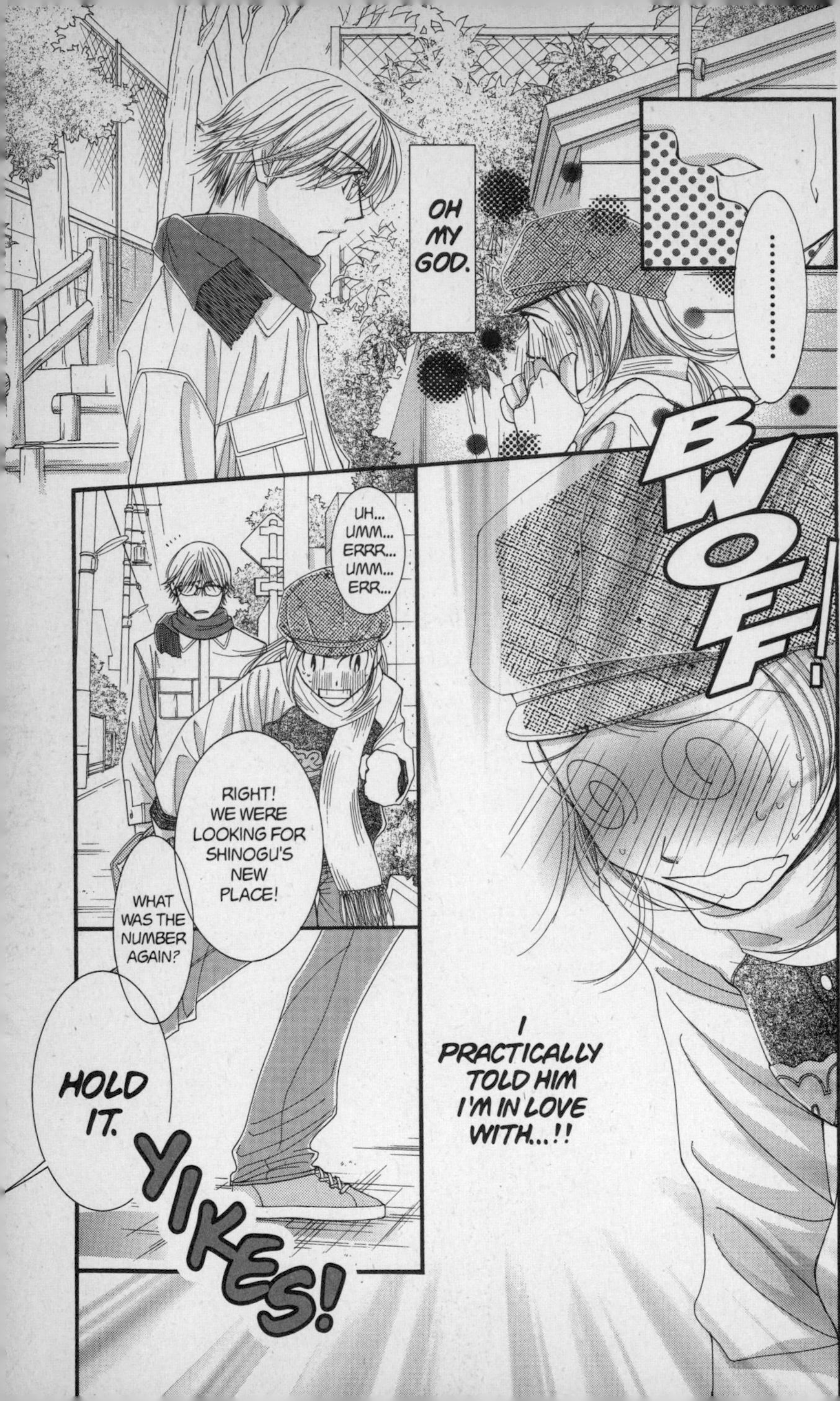
......
OH MY GOD.
BWOFF!
I PRACTICALLY TOLD HIM I'M IN LOVE WITH...!!
UH... UMM... ERRR... UMM... ERR...
RIGHT! WE WERE LOOKING FOR SHINOGU'S NEW PLACE!
WHAT WAS THE NUMBER AGAIN?
HOLD IT.
YIKES!

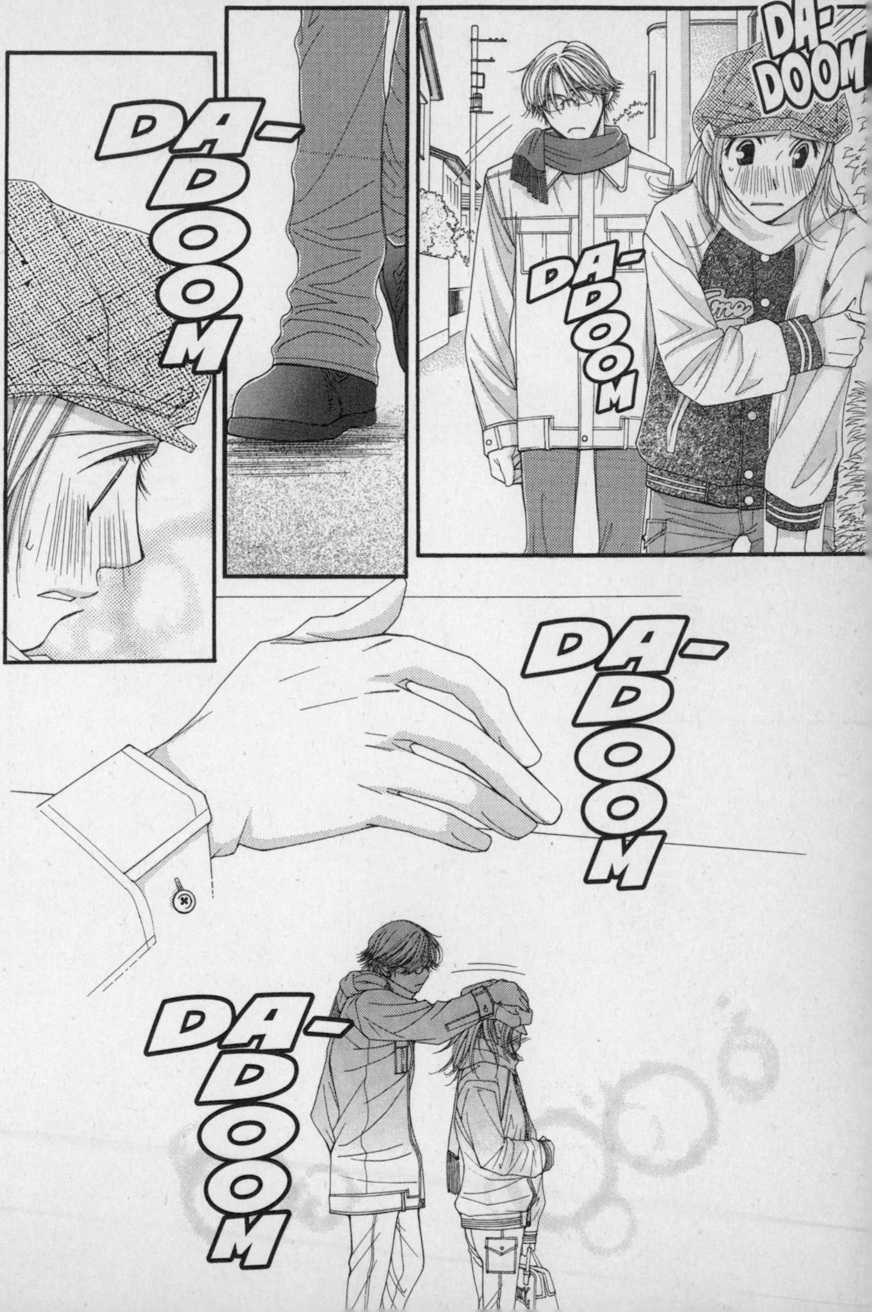
DA-DOOM
DA-DOOM
DA-DOOM
DA-DOOM
DA-DOOM

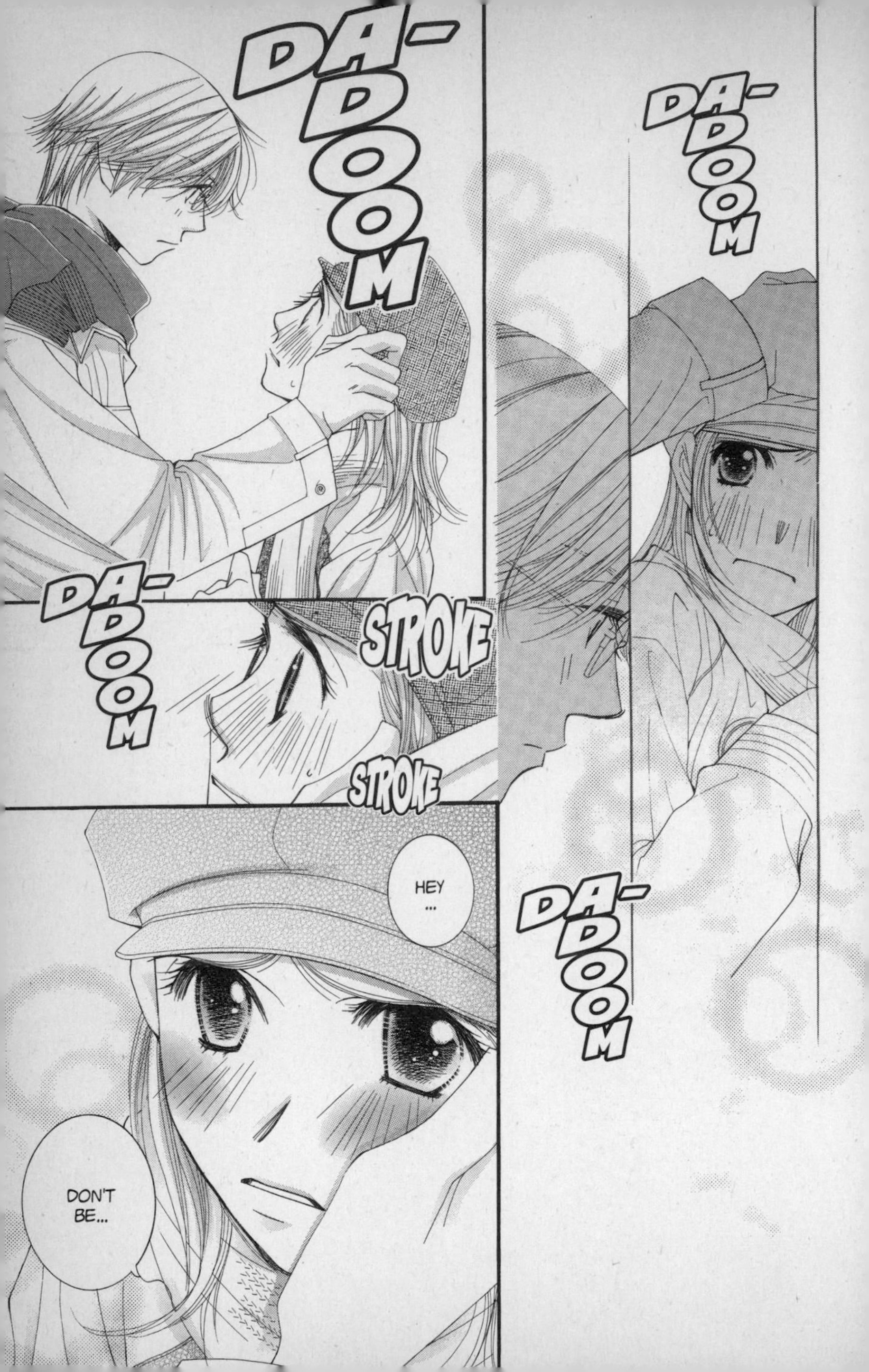
DA-DOOM
DA-DOOM
DA-DOOM
STROKE
DA-DOOM
STROKE
HEY ...
DON'T BE...

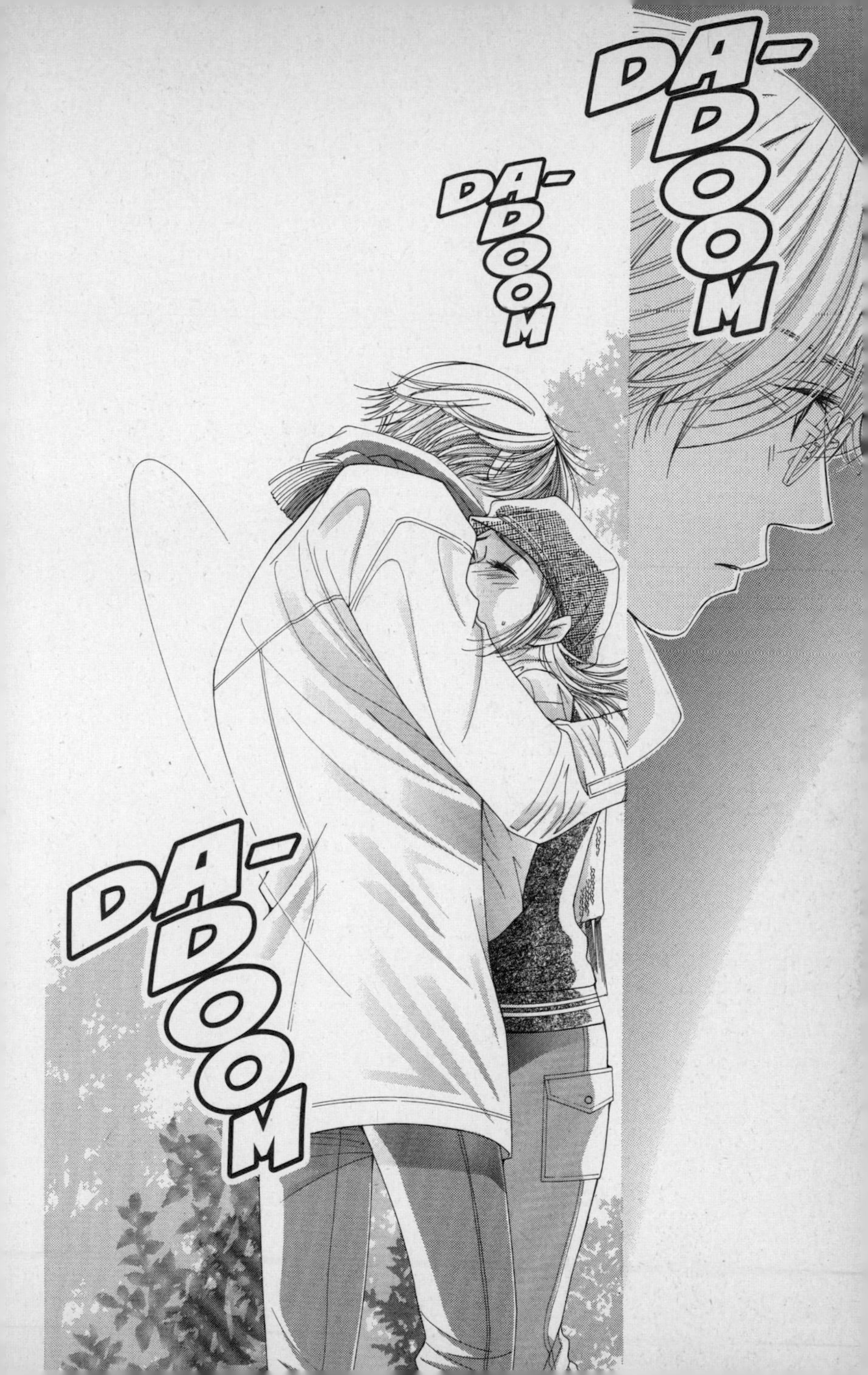
DA-DOOM
DA-DOOM
DA-DOOM

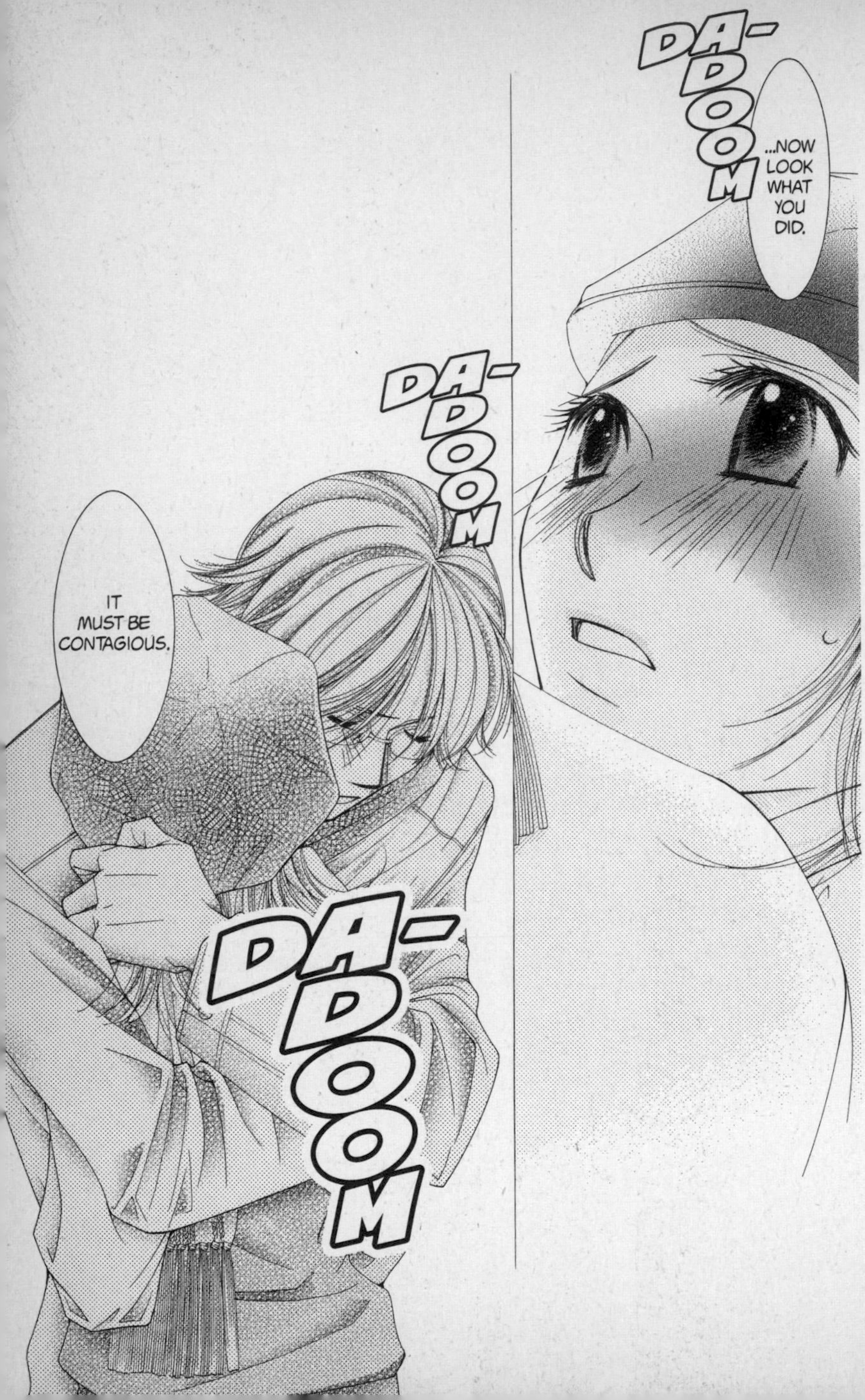

DA-DOOM
...NOW LOOK WHAT YOU DID.
DA-DOOM
IT MUST BE CONTAGIOUS.
DA-DOOM

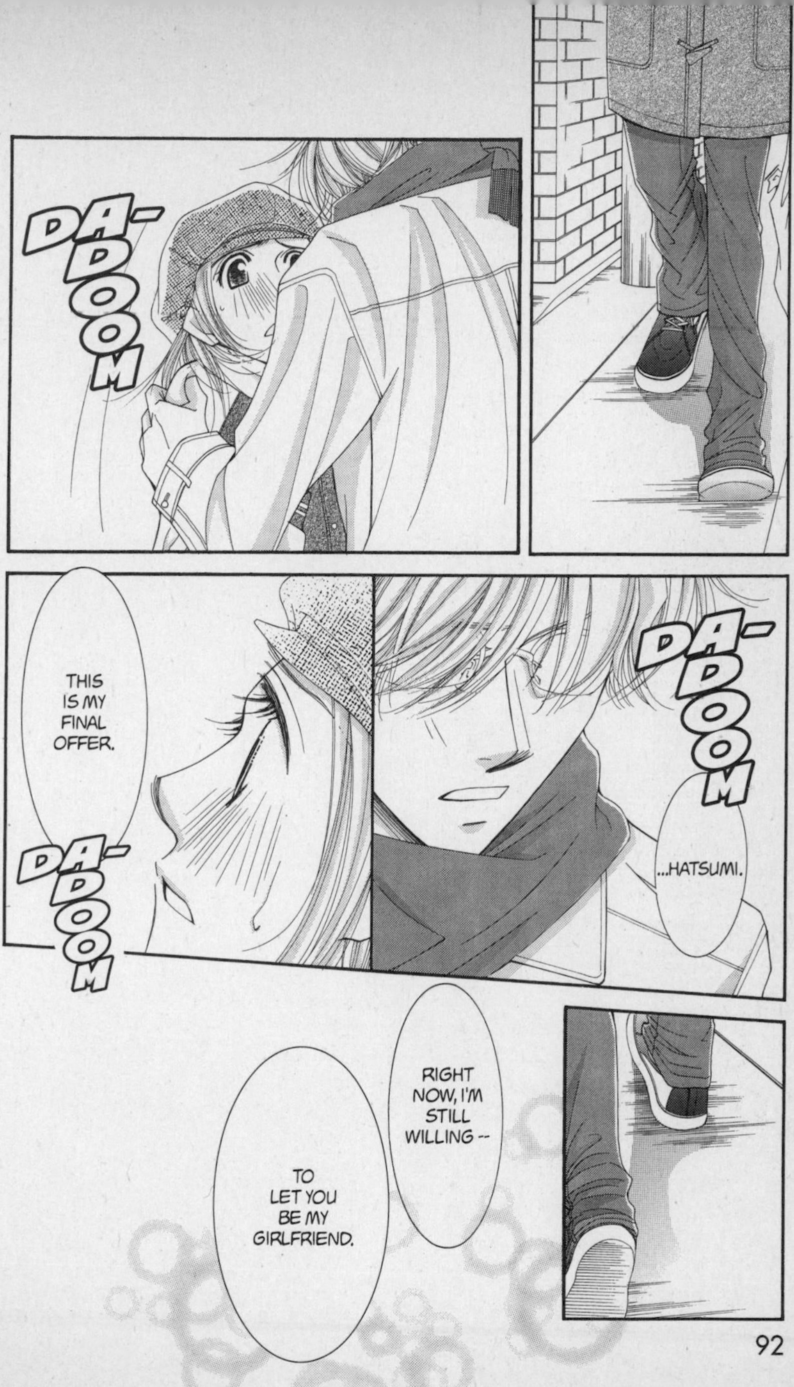
DA-DOOM
DA-DOOM
...HATSUMI.
THIS IS MY FINAL OFFER.
DA-DOOM
RIGHT NOW, I'M STILL WILLING --
TO LET YOU BE MY GIRLFRIEND.

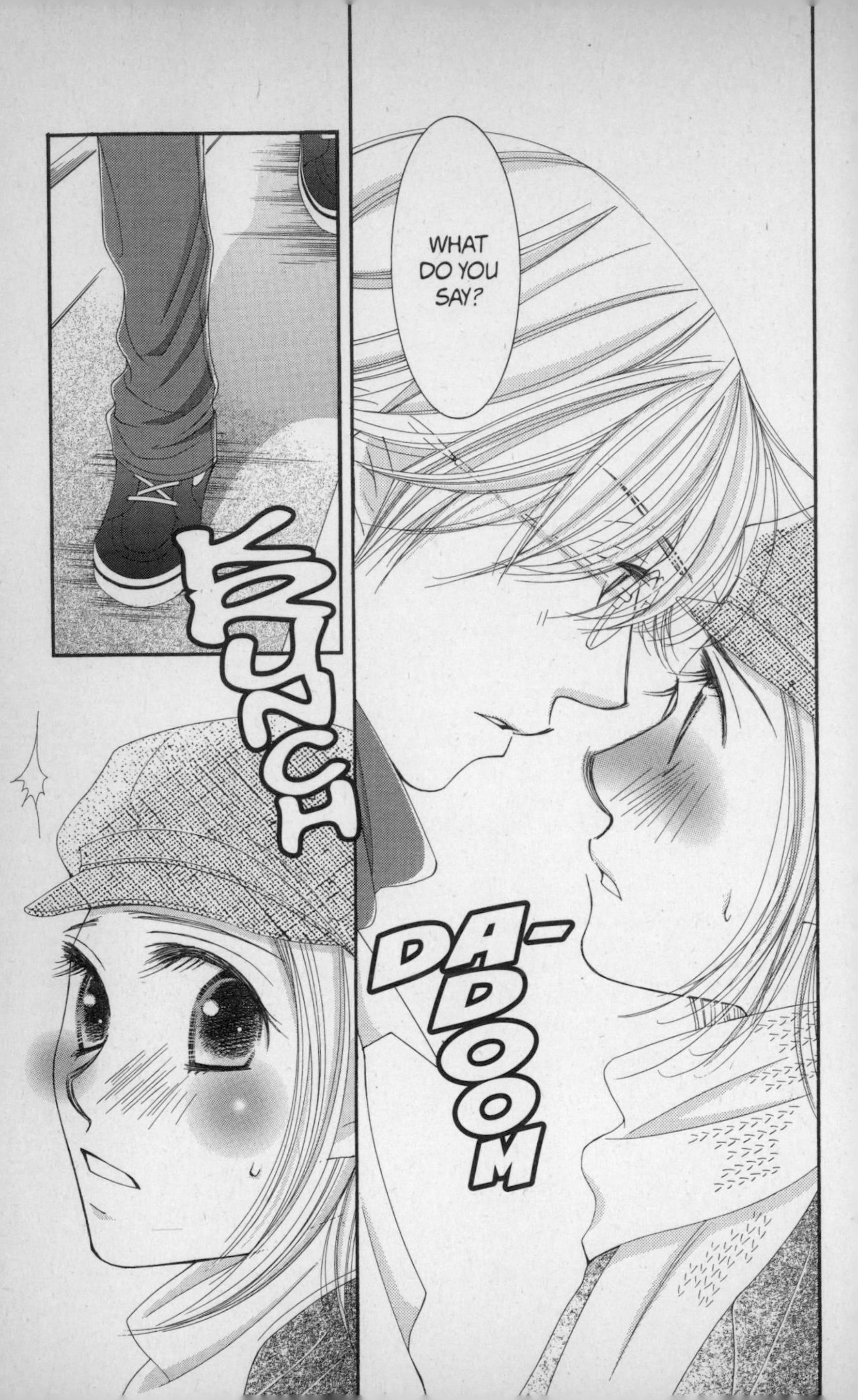
WHAT DO YOU SAY?
DA-DOOM

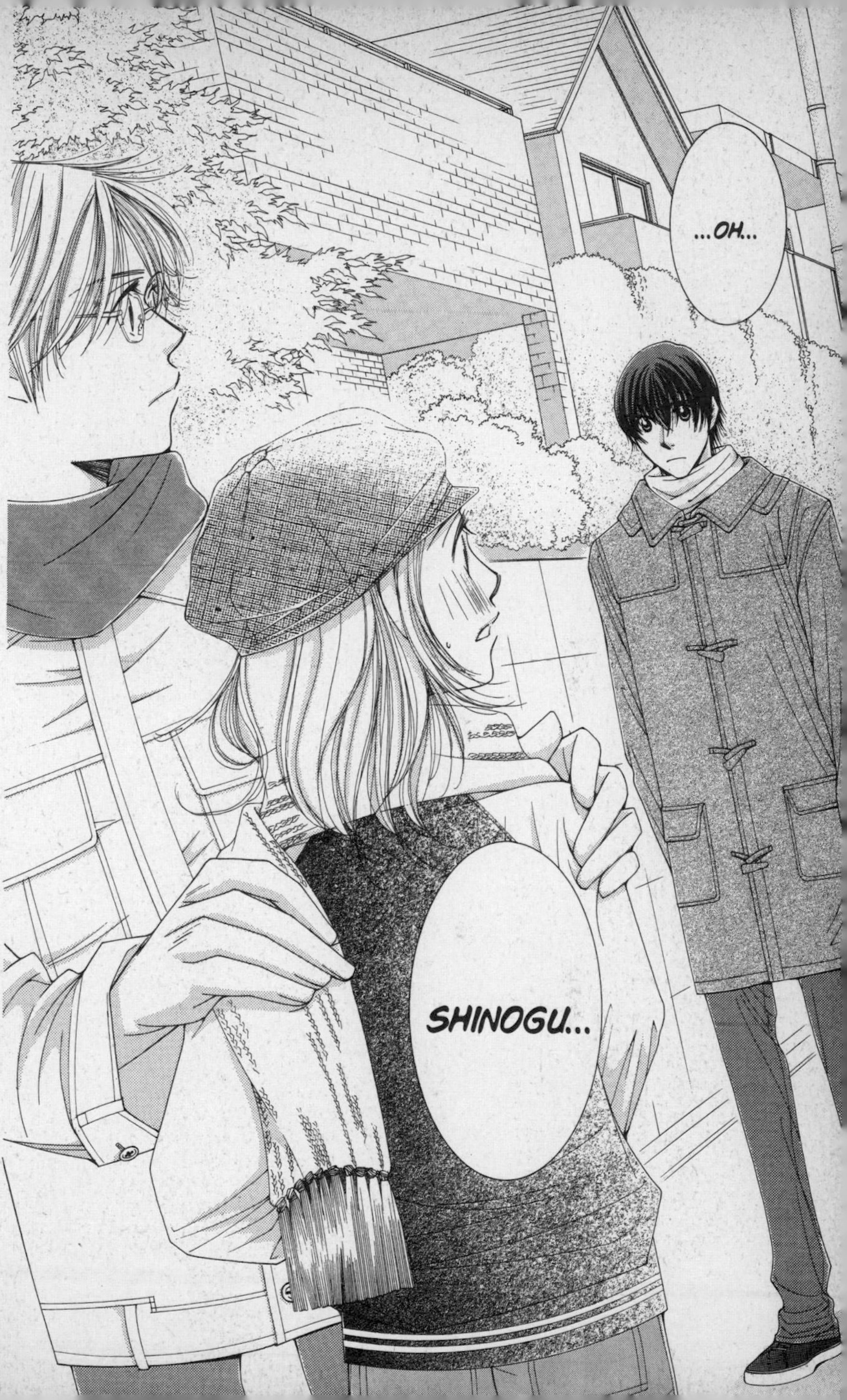
...OH...
SHINOGU...

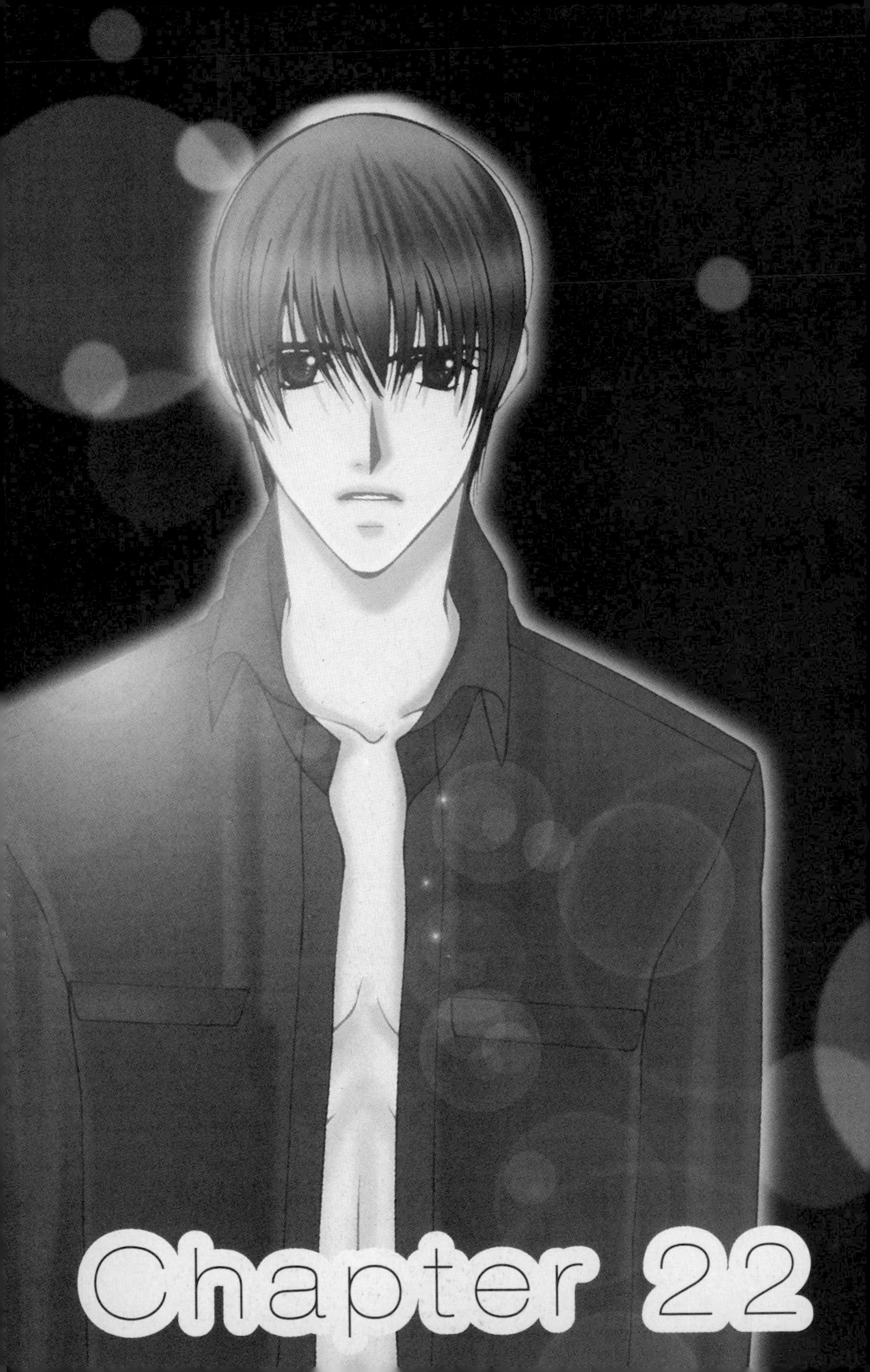
Chapter 22

Shinogu
vision
Ryoki's
hand
Locked on
Hatsumi!

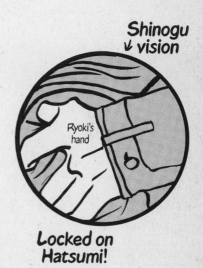

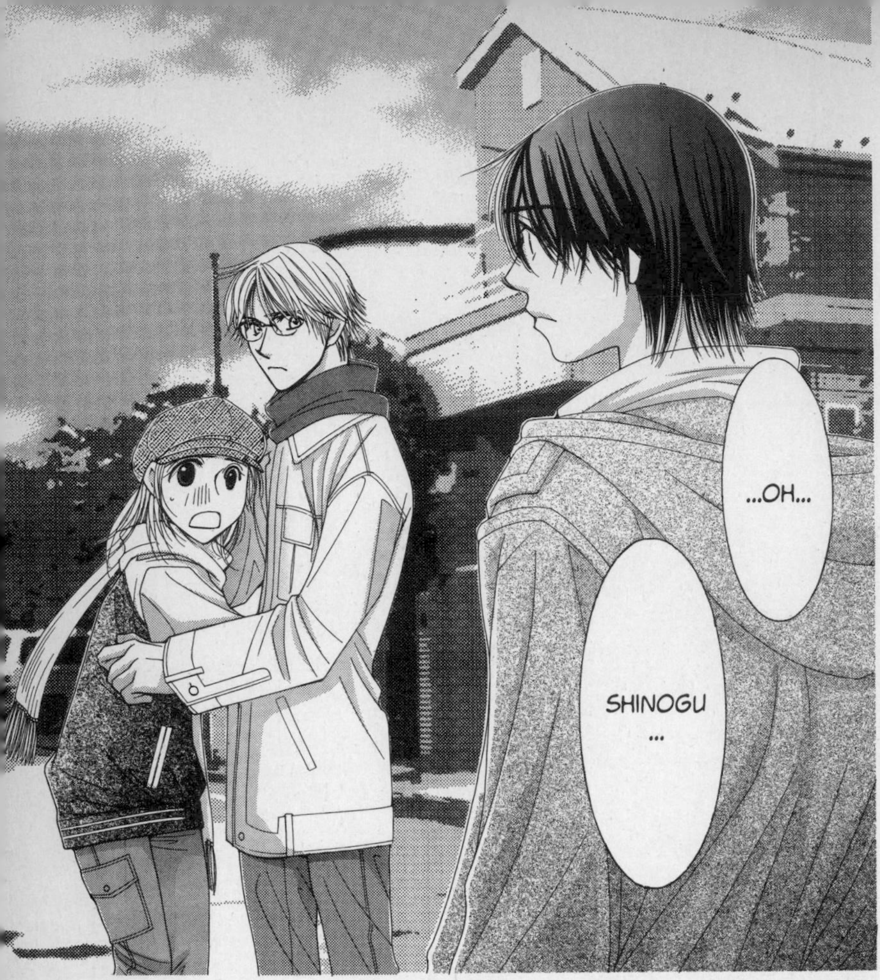
...OH...
SHINOGU ...

hot gimmick

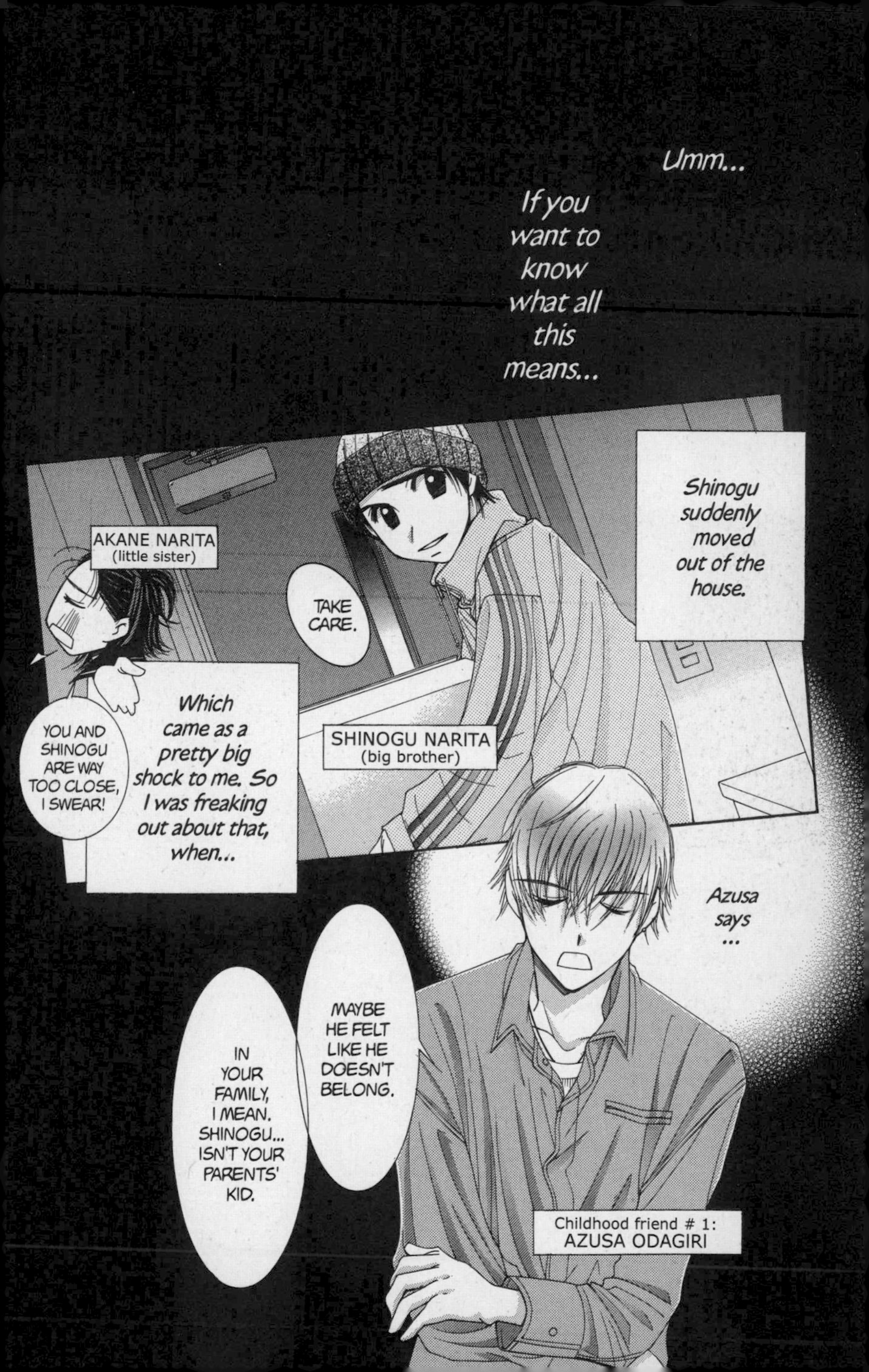
Umm...
If you want to know what all this means...
Shinogu suddenly moved out of the house.
SHINOGU NARITA (big brother)
TAKE CARE.
AKANE NARITA (little sister)
Which came as a pretty big shock to me. So I was freaking out about that, when...
YOU AND SHINOGU ARE WAY TOO CLOSE, I SWEAR!
Azusa says ...
Childhood friend # 1: AZUSA ODAGIRI
MAYBE HE FELT LIKE HE DOESN'T BELONG.
IN YOUR FAMILY, I MEAN. SHINOGU... ISN'T YOUR PARENTS' KID.

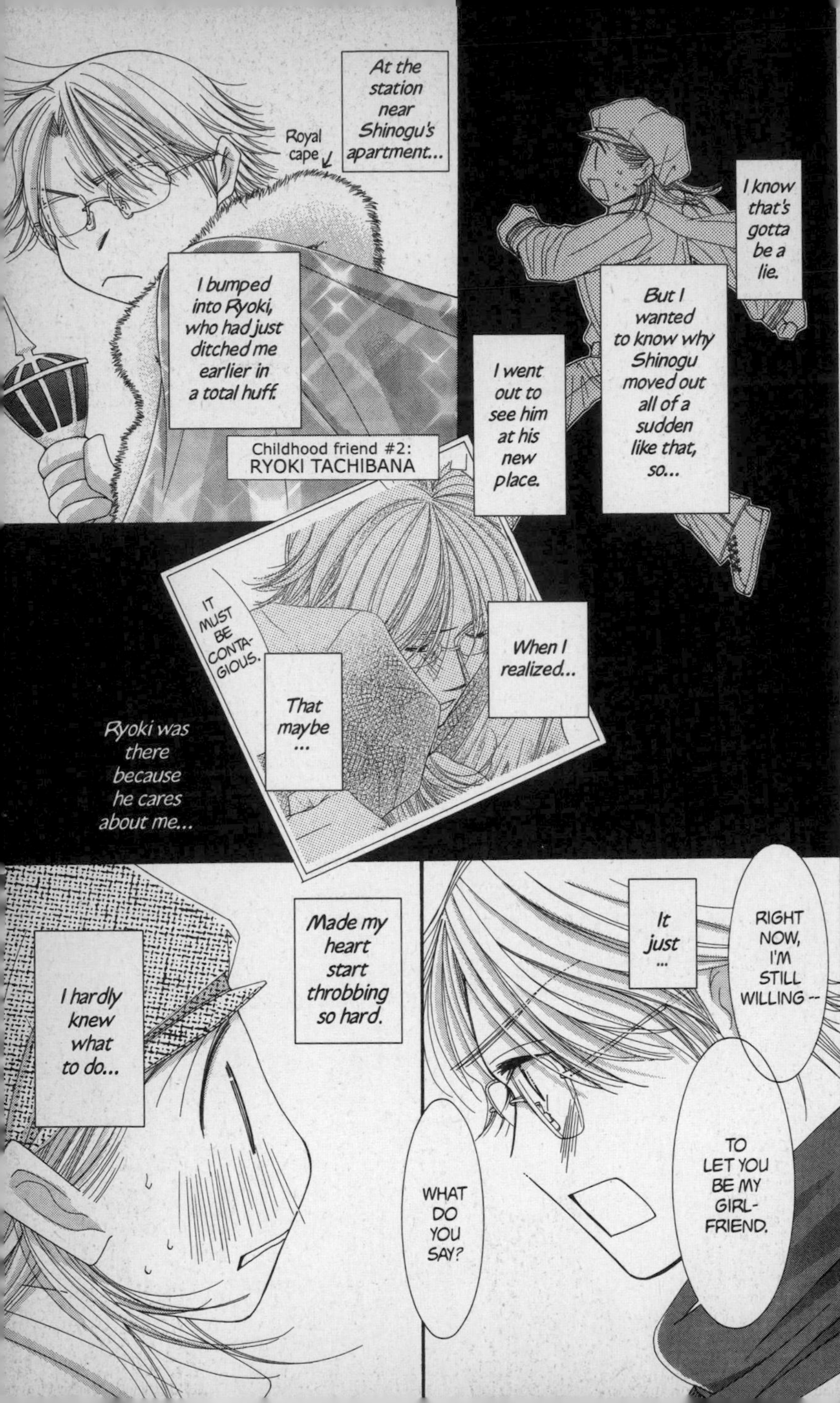
I know that's gotta be a lie.
But I wanted to know why Shinogu moved out all of a sudden like that, so...
I went out to see him at his new place.
At the station near Shinogu's apartment...
Royal cape
I bumped into Ryoki, who had just ditched me earlier in a total huff.
Childhood friend #2: RYOKI TACHIBANA
When I realized...
IT MUST BE CONTAGIOUS.
That maybe ...
Ryoki was there because he cares about me...
RIGHT NOW, I'M STILL WILLING --
It just ...
TO LET YOU BE MY GIRLFRIEND.
WHAT DO YOU SAY?
Made my heart start throbbing so hard.
I hardly knew what to do...

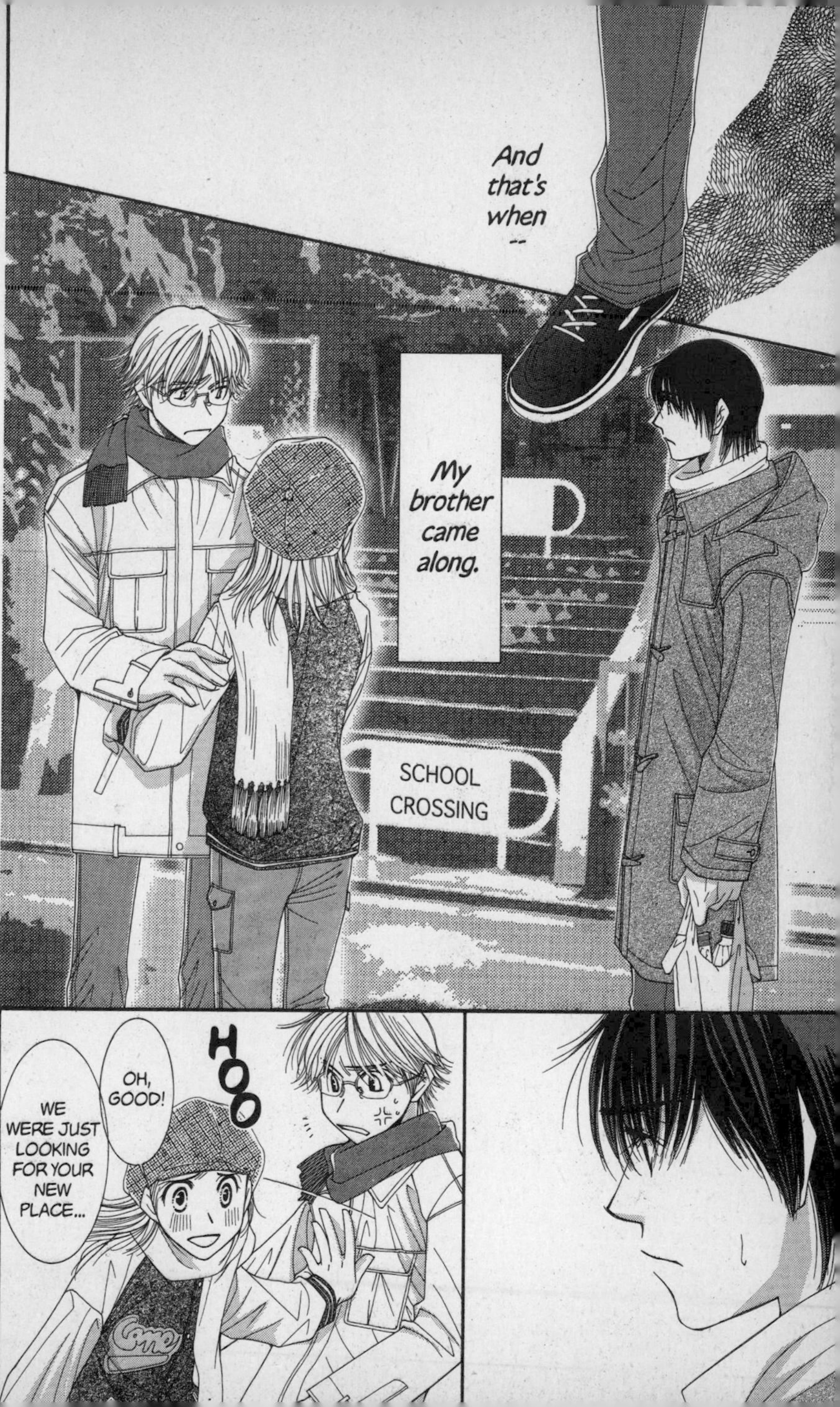
And that's when --
My brother came along.
SCHOOL CROSSING
HOO
OH, GOOD!
WE WERE JUST LOOKING FOR YOUR NEW PLACE...

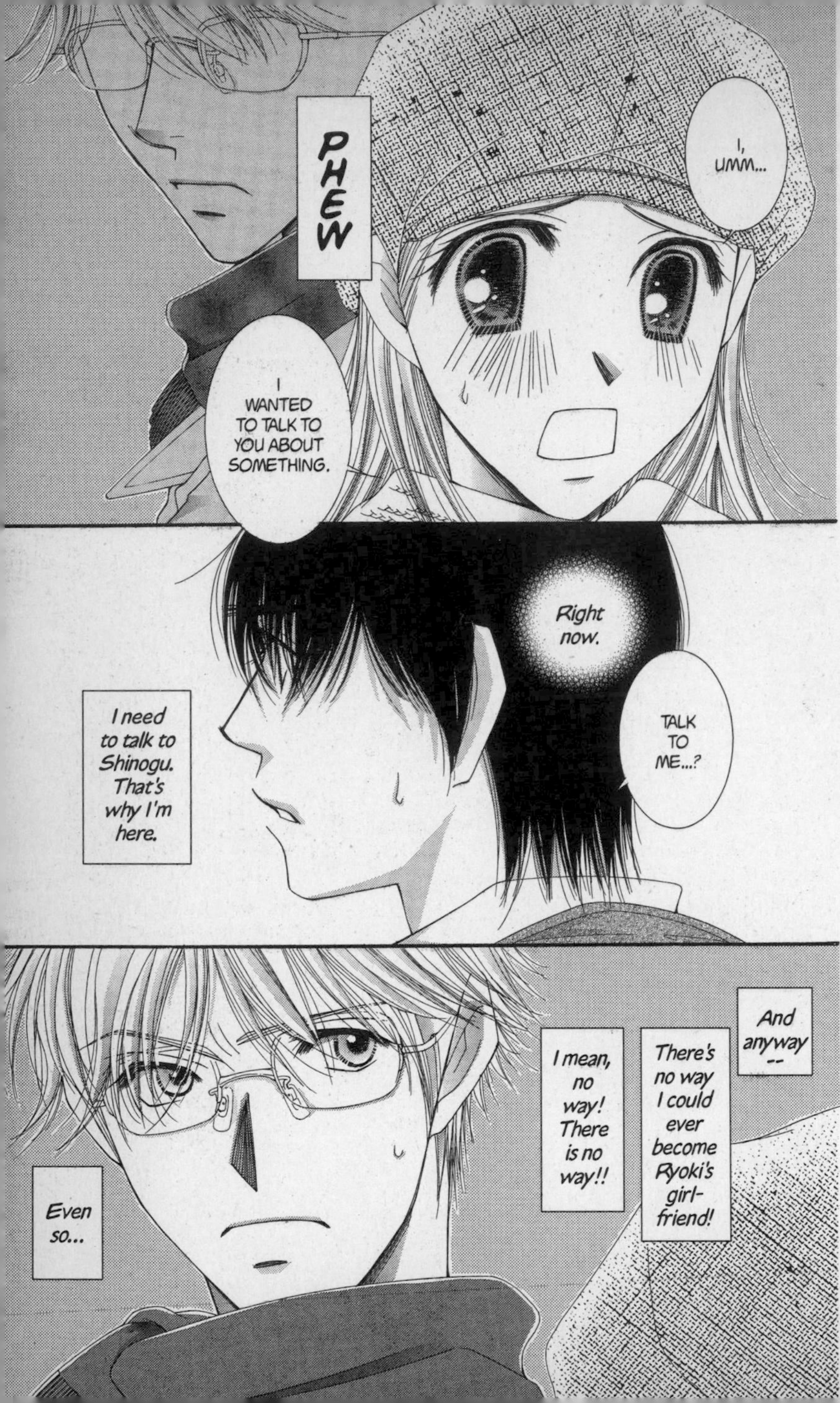
I, UMM...
PHEW
I WANTED TO TALK TO YOU ABOUT SOMETHING.
TALK TO ME...?
Right now.
I need to talk to Shinogu. That's why I'm here.
And anyway --
There's no way I could ever become Ryoki's girl-friend!
I mean, no way! There is no way!!
Even so...

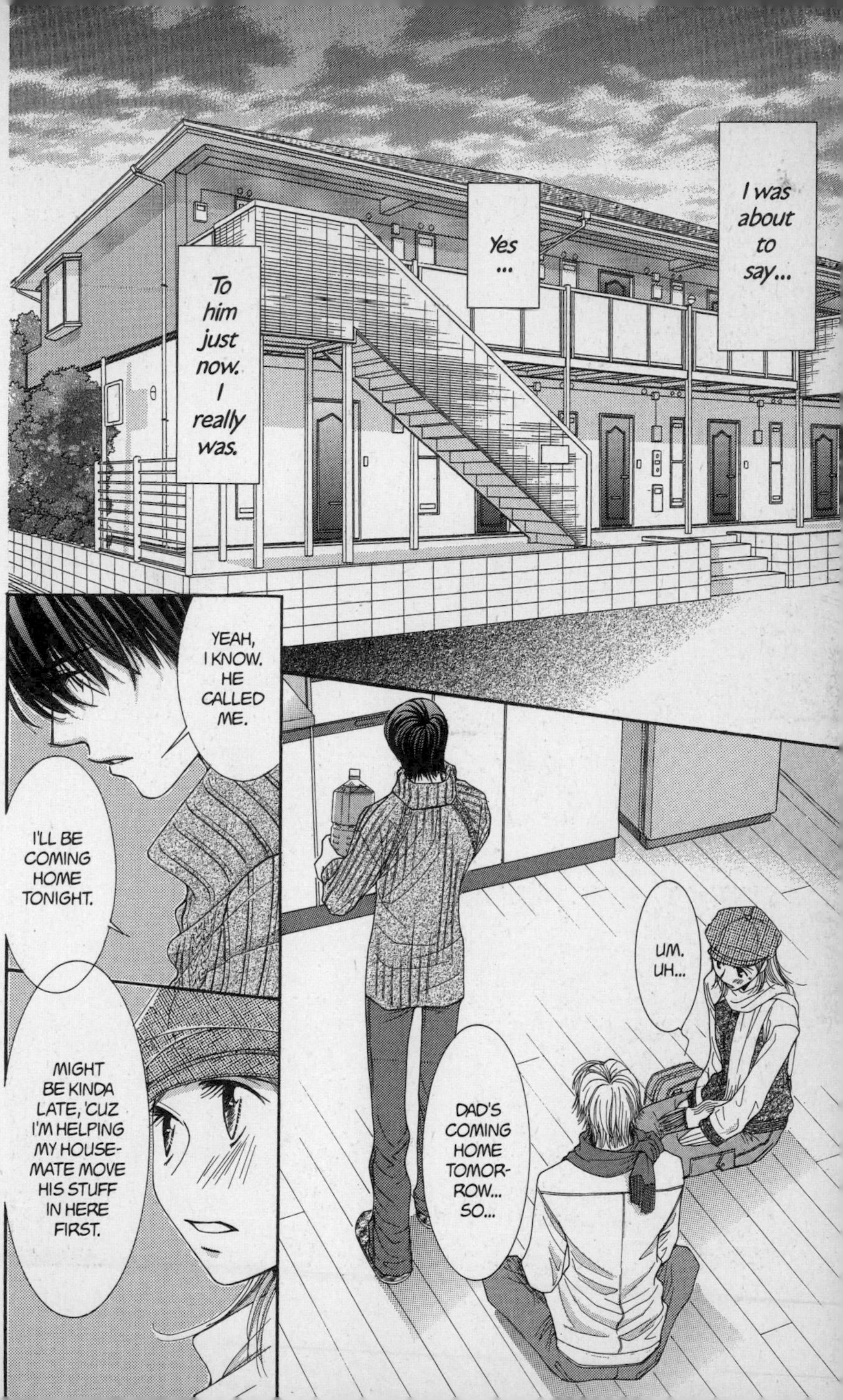
I was about to say...
Yes ...
To him just now. I really was.
UM. UH...
DAD'S COMING HOME TOMORROW... SO...
YEAH, I KNOW. HE CALLED ME.
I'LL BE COMING HOME TONIGHT.
MIGHT BE KINDA LATE, 'CUZ I'M HELPING MY HOUSE-MATE MOVE HIS STUFF IN HERE FIRST.

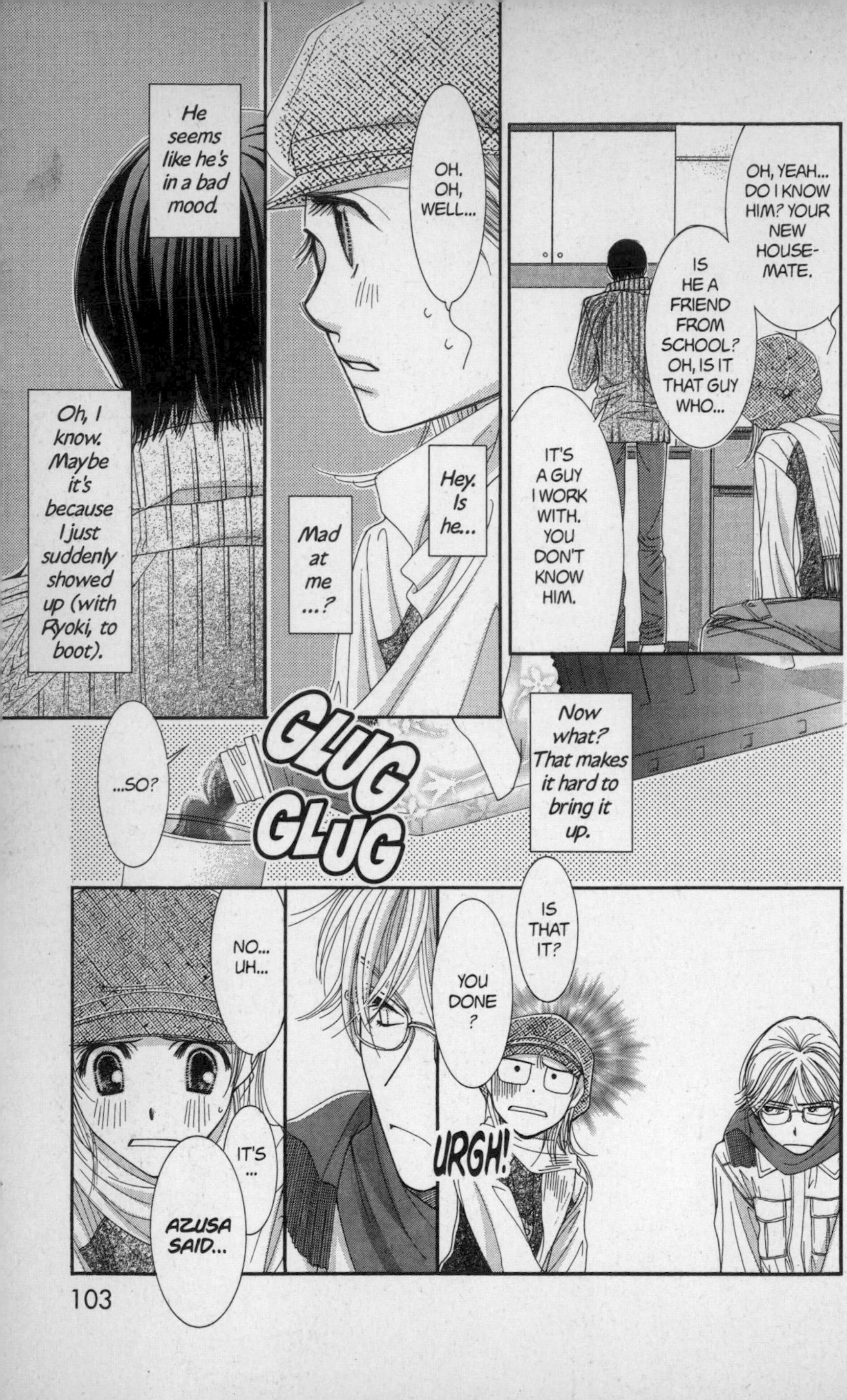

OH, YEAH... DO I KNOW HIM? YOUR NEW HOUSE-MATE.
IS HE A FRIEND FROM SCHOOL? OH, IS IT THAT GUY WHO...
IT'S A GUY I WORK WITH. YOU DON'T KNOW HIM.
OH. OH, WELL...
Hey. Is he...
Mad at me ...?
He seems like he's in a bad mood.
Oh, I know. Maybe it's because I just suddenly showed up (with Ryoki, to boot).
Now what? That makes it hard to bring it up.
GLUG GLUG
...SO?
IS THAT IT?
YOU DONE?
URGH!
NO... UH...
IT'S ...
AZUSA SAID...

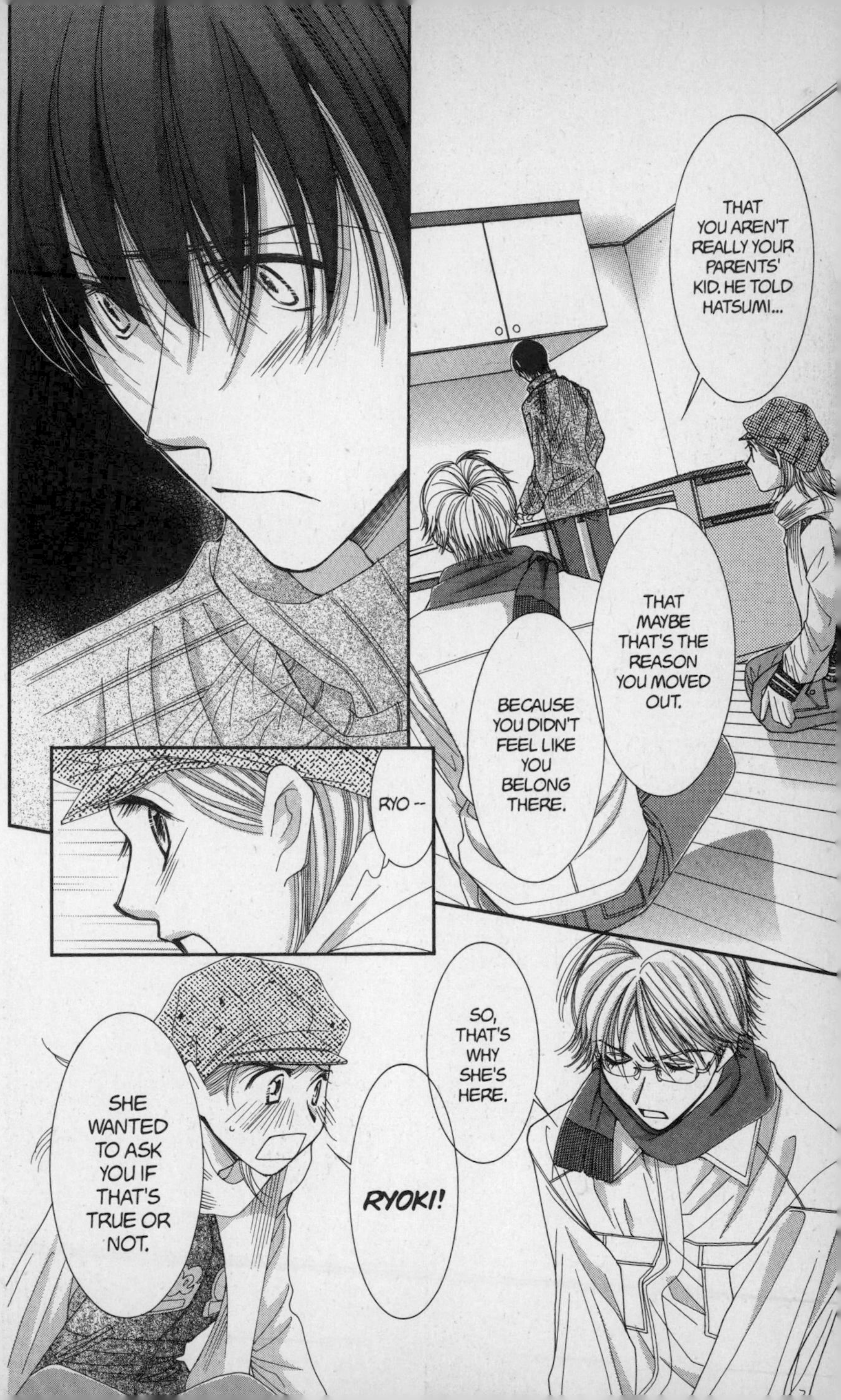
THAT YOU AREN'T REALLY YOUR PARENTS' KID. HE TOLD HATSUMI...
THAT MAYBE THAT'S THE REASON YOU MOVED OUT.
BECAUSE YOU DIDN'T FEEL LIKE YOU BELONG THERE.
RYO --
SO, THAT'S WHY SHE'S HERE.
RYOKI!
SHE WANTED TO ASK YOU IF THAT'S TRUE OR NOT.

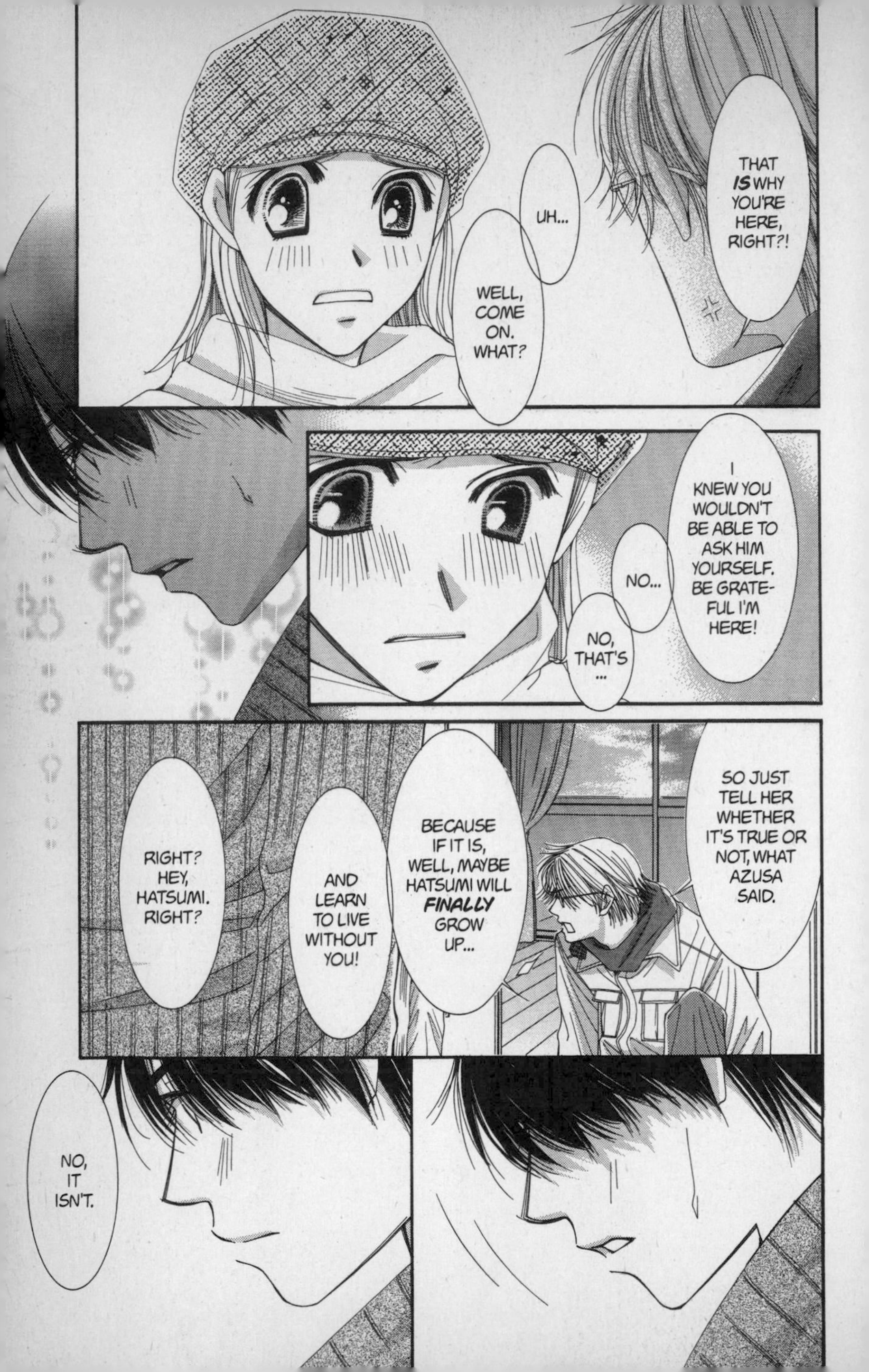
THAT **IS** WHY YOU'RE HERE, RIGHT?!
UH...
WELL, COME ON. WHAT?
I KNEW YOU WOULDN'T BE ABLE TO ASK HIM YOURSELF. BE GRATEFUL I'M HERE!
NO...
NO, THAT'S ...
SO JUST TELL HER WHETHER IT'S TRUE OR NOT, WHAT AZUSA SAID.
BECAUSE IF IT IS, WELL, MAYBE HATSUMI WILL **FINALLY** GROW UP...
AND LEARN TO LIVE WITHOUT YOU!
RIGHT? HEY, HATSUMI. RIGHT?
NO, IT ISN'T.

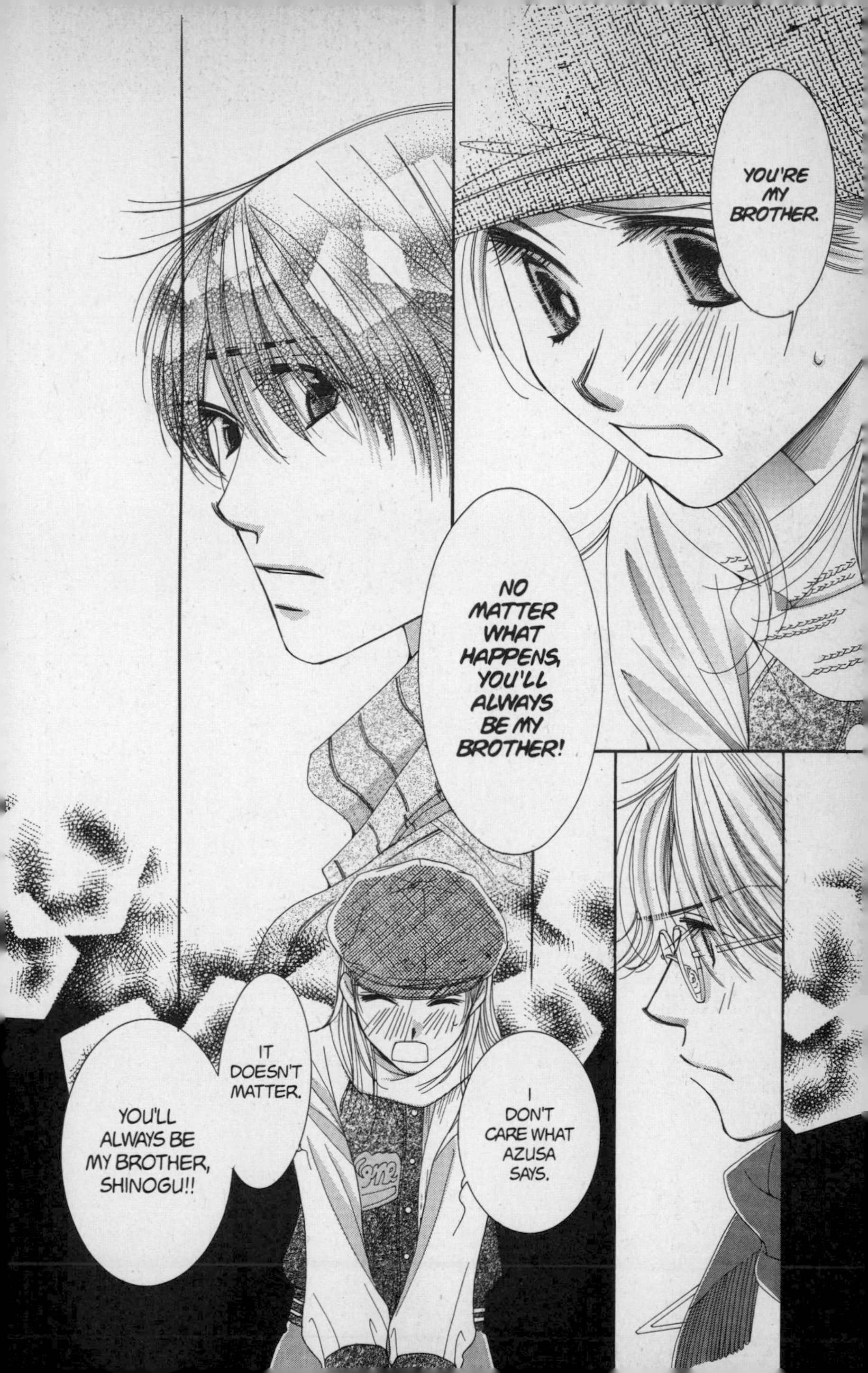
YOU'RE MY BROTHER.
NO MATTER WHAT HAPPENS, YOU'LL ALWAYS BE MY BROTHER!
I DON'T CARE WHAT AZUSA SAYS.
IT DOESN'T MATTER.
YOU'LL ALWAYS BE MY BROTHER, SHINOGU!!

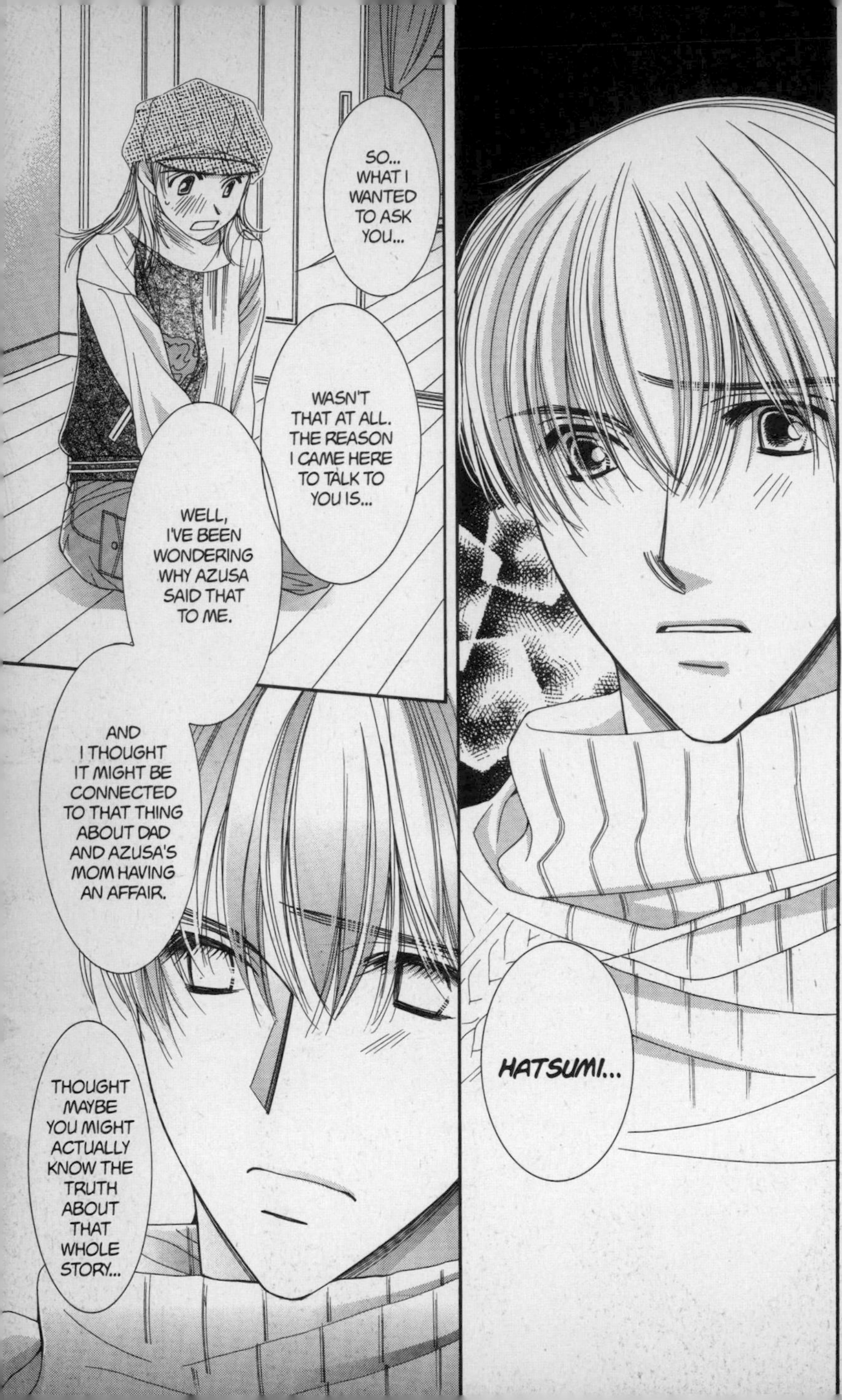
HATSUMI...
SO... WHAT I WANTED TO ASK YOU...
WASN'T THAT AT ALL. THE REASON I CAME HERE TO TALK TO YOU IS...
WELL, I'VE BEEN WONDERING WHY AZUSA SAID THAT TO ME.
AND I THOUGHT IT MIGHT BE CONNECTED TO THAT THING ABOUT DAD AND AZUSA'S MOM HAVING AN AFFAIR.
THOUGHT MAYBE YOU MIGHT ACTUALLY KNOW THE TRUTH ABOUT THAT WHOLE STORY...

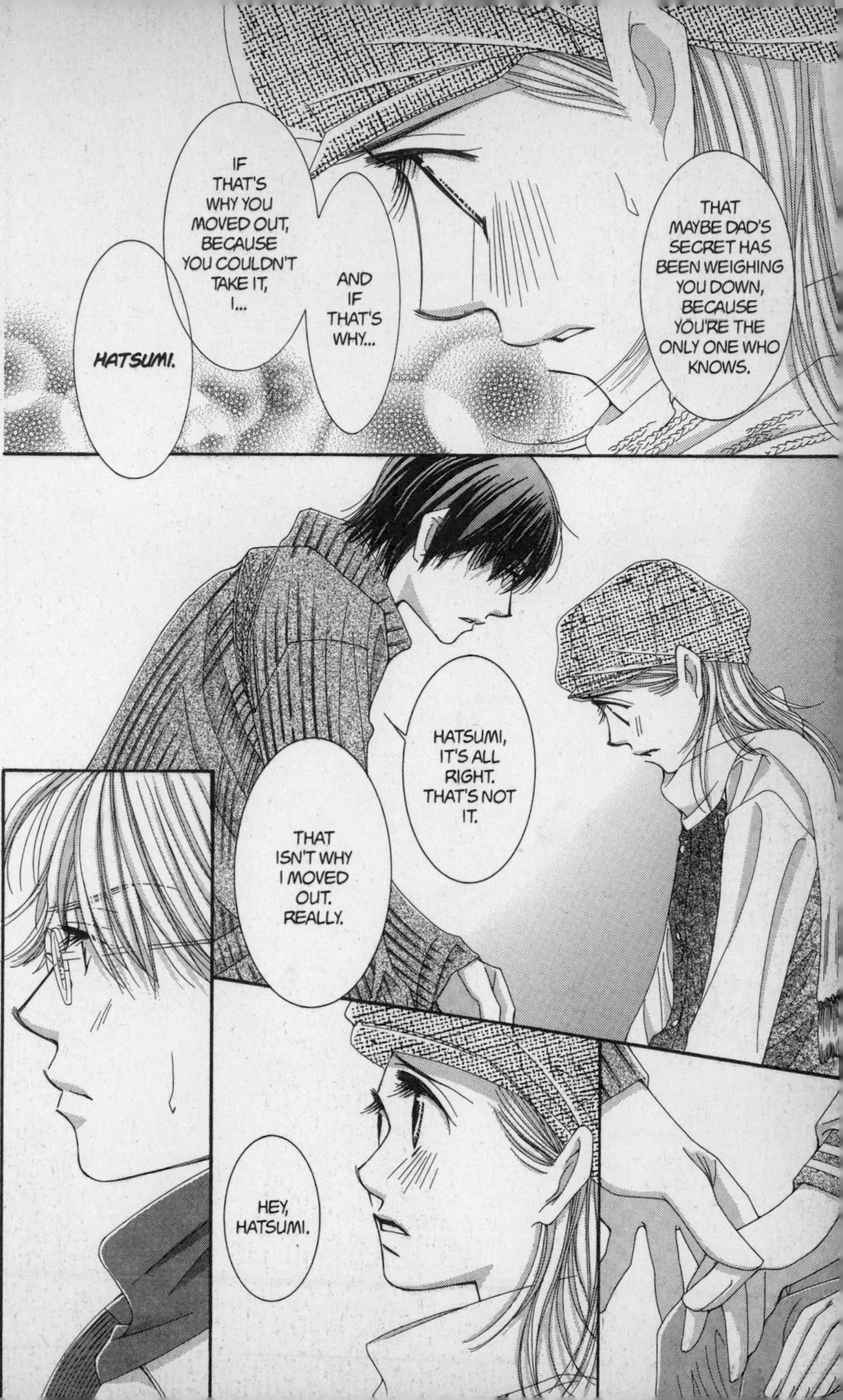
THAT MAYBE DAD'S SECRET HAS BEEN WEIGHING YOU DOWN, BECAUSE YOU'RE THE ONLY ONE WHO KNOWS.
AND IF THAT'S WHY...
IF THAT'S WHY YOU MOVED OUT, BECAUSE YOU COULDN'T TAKE IT, I...
HATSUMI.
HATSUMI, IT'S ALL RIGHT. THAT'S NOT IT.
THAT ISN'T WHY I MOVED OUT. REALLY.
HEY, HATSUMI.

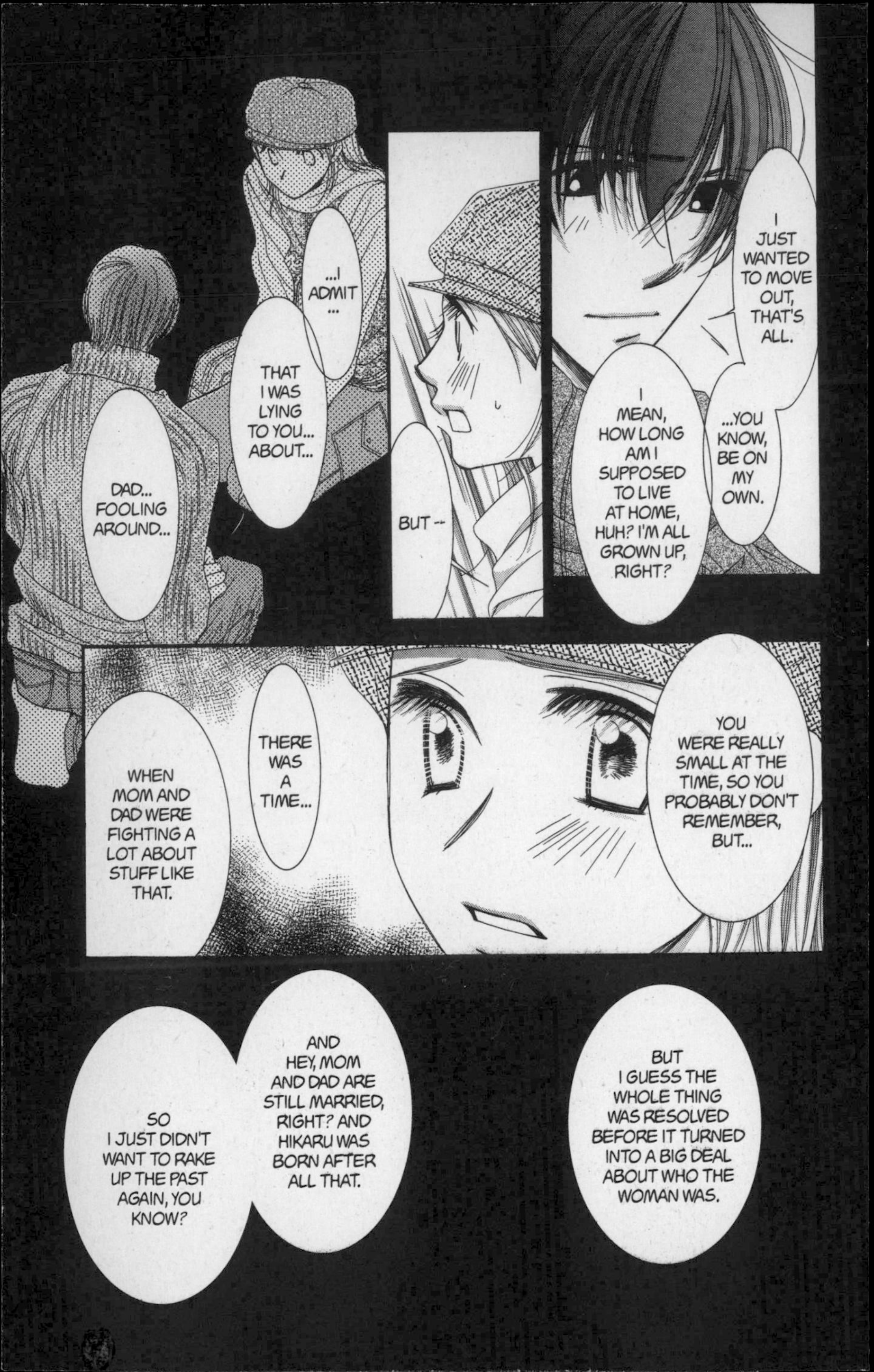
I JUST WANTED TO MOVE OUT, THAT'S ALL.
...YOU KNOW, BE ON MY OWN.
I MEAN, HOW LONG AM I SUPPOSED TO LIVE AT HOME, HUH? I'M ALL GROWN UP, RIGHT?
BUT --
...I ADMIT ...
THAT I WAS LYING TO YOU... ABOUT...
DAD... FOOLING AROUND...
YOU WERE REALLY SMALL AT THE TIME, SO YOU PROBABLY DON'T REMEMBER, BUT...
THERE WAS A TIME...
WHEN MOM AND DAD WERE FIGHTING A LOT ABOUT STUFF LIKE THAT.
BUT I GUESS THE WHOLE THING WAS RESOLVED BEFORE IT TURNED INTO A BIG DEAL ABOUT WHO THE WOMAN WAS.
AND HEY, MOM AND DAD ARE STILL MARRIED, RIGHT? AND HIKARU WAS BORN AFTER ALL THAT.
SO I JUST DIDN'T WANT TO RAKE UP THE PAST AGAIN, YOU KNOW?

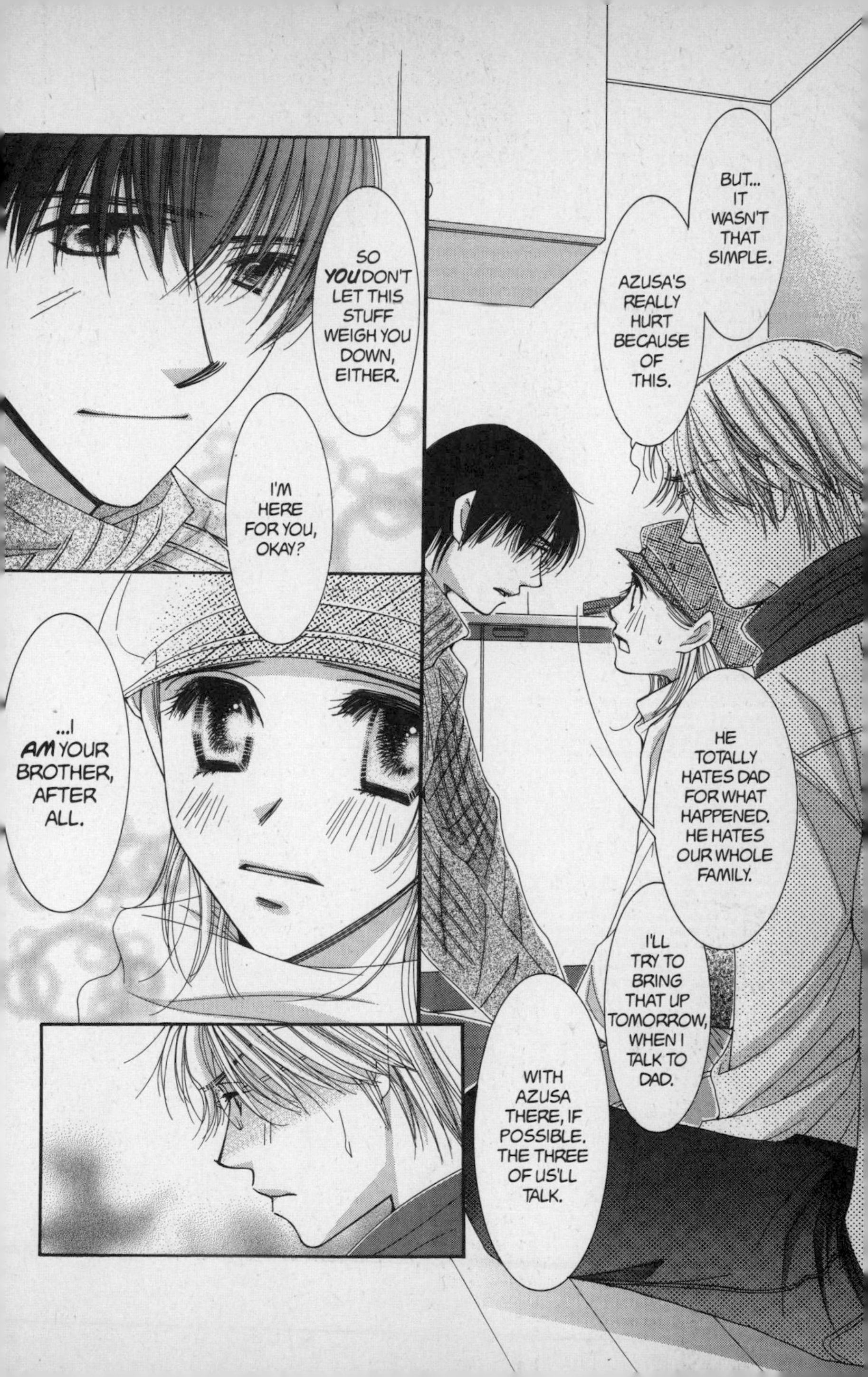
BUT... IT WASN'T THAT SIMPLE.
AZUSA'S REALLY HURT BECAUSE OF THIS.
HE TOTALLY HATES DAD FOR WHAT HAPPENED. HE HATES OUR WHOLE FAMILY.
I'LL TRY TO BRING THAT UP TOMORROW, WHEN I TALK TO DAD.
WITH AZUSA THERE, IF POSSIBLE. THE THREE OF US'LL TALK.
SO **YOU** DON'T LET THIS STUFF WEIGH YOU DOWN, EITHER.
I'M HERE FOR YOU, OKAY?
...I **AM** YOUR BROTHER, AFTER ALL.

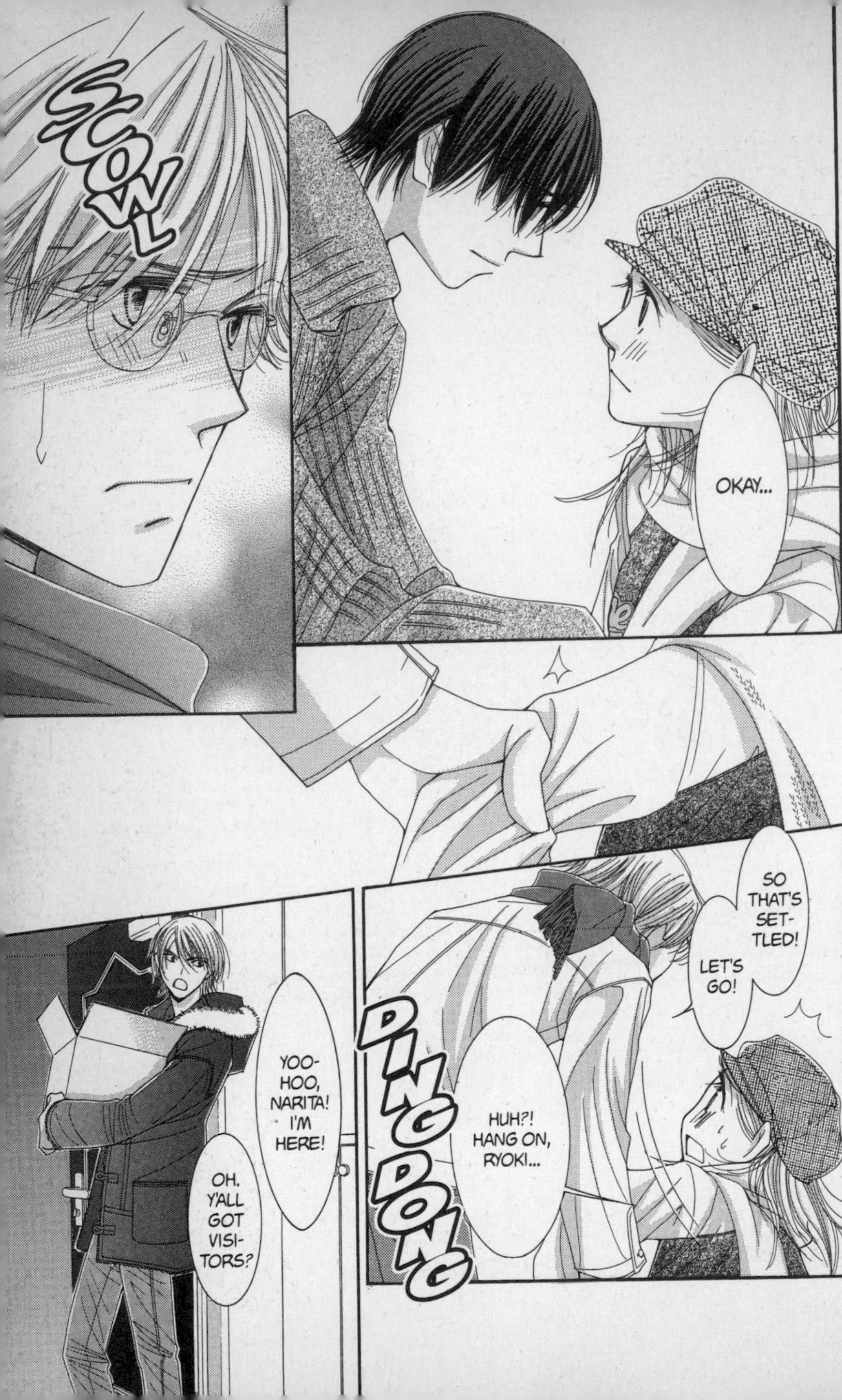
OKAY...
SCOWL
SO THAT'S SET-TLED!
LET'S GO!
HUH?! HANG ON, RYOKI...
DING DONG
YOO-HOO, NARITA! I'M HERE!
OH. Y'ALL GOT VISI-TORS?

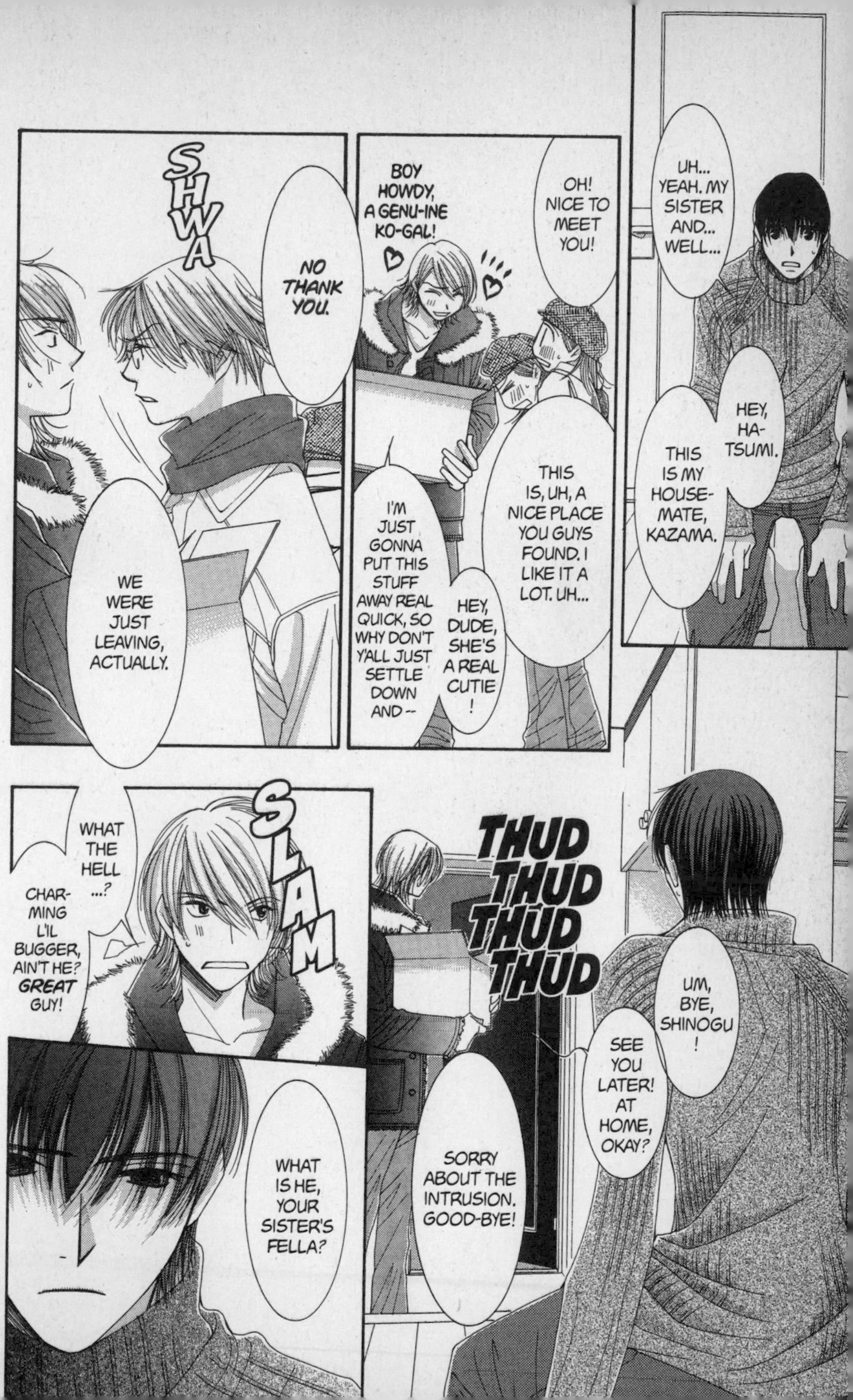
UH... YEAH. MY SISTER AND... WELL...
HEY, HA-TSUMI.
THIS IS MY HOUSE-MATE, KAZAMA.
OH! NICE TO MEET YOU!
BOY HOWDY, A GENU-INE KO-GAL!
THIS IS, UH, A NICE PLACE YOU GUYS FOUND. I LIKE IT A LOT. UH...
HEY, DUDE, SHE'S A REAL CUTIE!
I'M JUST GONNA PUT THIS STUFF AWAY REAL QUICK, SO WHY DON'T Y'ALL JUST SETTLE DOWN AND --
SHWA
NO THANK YOU.
WE WERE JUST LEAVING, ACTUALLY.
UM, BYE, SHINOGU!
SEE YOU LATER! AT HOME, OKAY?
SORRY ABOUT THE INTRUSION. GOOD-BYE!
THUD THUD THUD THUD
SLAM
WHAT THE HELL ...?
CHAR-MING L'IL BUGGER, AIN'T HE? GREAT GUY!
WHAT IS HE, YOUR SISTER'S FELLA?

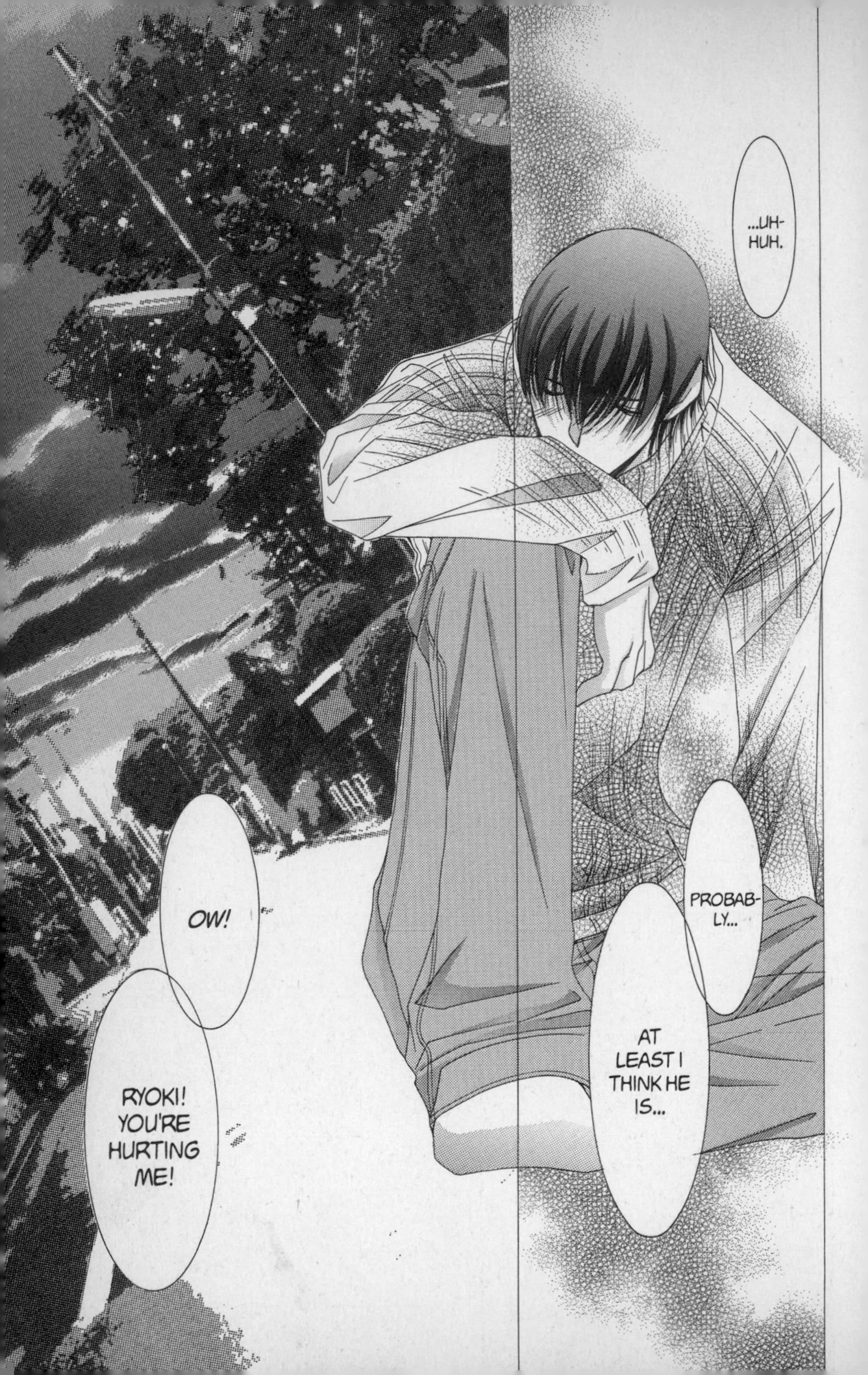
...UH-HUH.
PROBABLY...
AT LEAST I THINK HE IS...
OW!
RYOKI! YOU'RE HURTING ME!

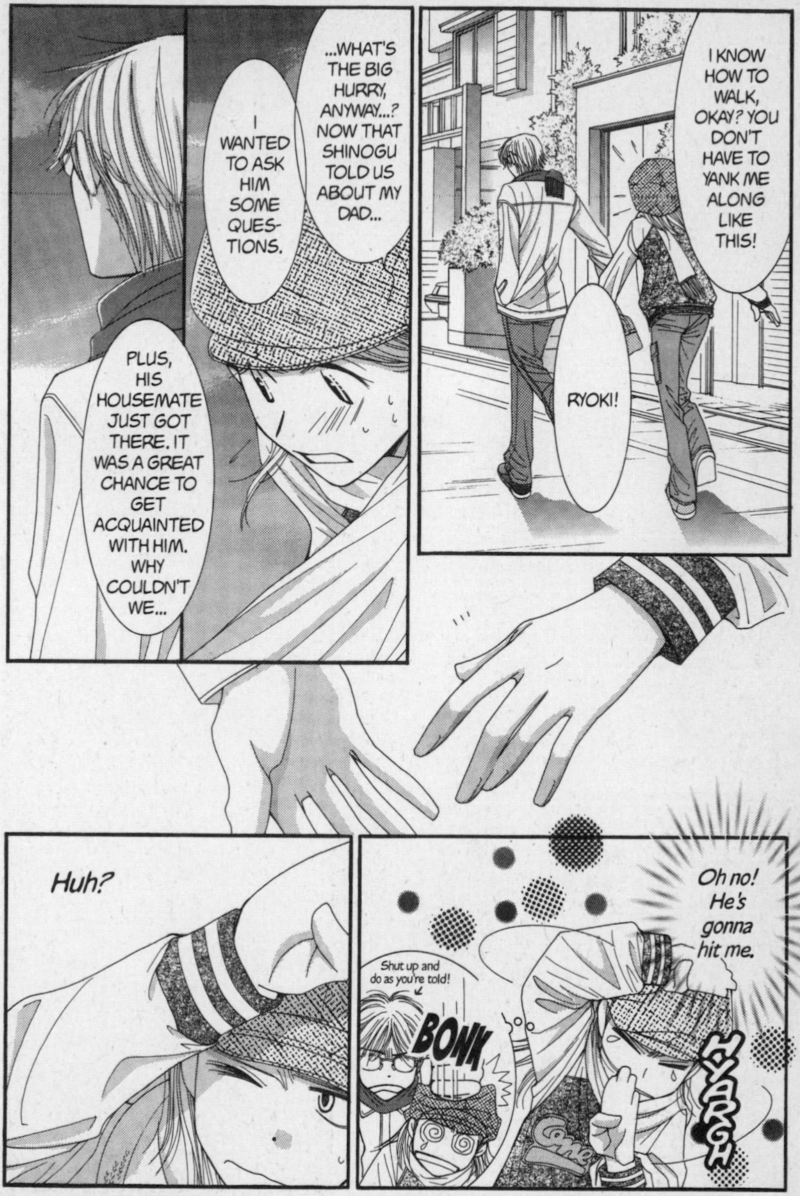
I KNOW HOW TO WALK, OKAY? YOU DON'T HAVE TO YANK ME ALONG LIKE THIS!
RYOKI!
...WHAT'S THE BIG HURRY, ANYWAY...? NOW THAT SHINOGU TOLD US ABOUT MY DAD...
I WANTED TO ASK HIM SOME QUESTIONS.
PLUS, HIS HOUSEMATE JUST GOT THERE. IT WAS A GREAT CHANCE TO GET ACQUAINTED WITH HIM. WHY COULDN'T WE...
Oh no! He's gonna hit me.
HYARGH
Shut up and do as you're told!
BONK
Huh?

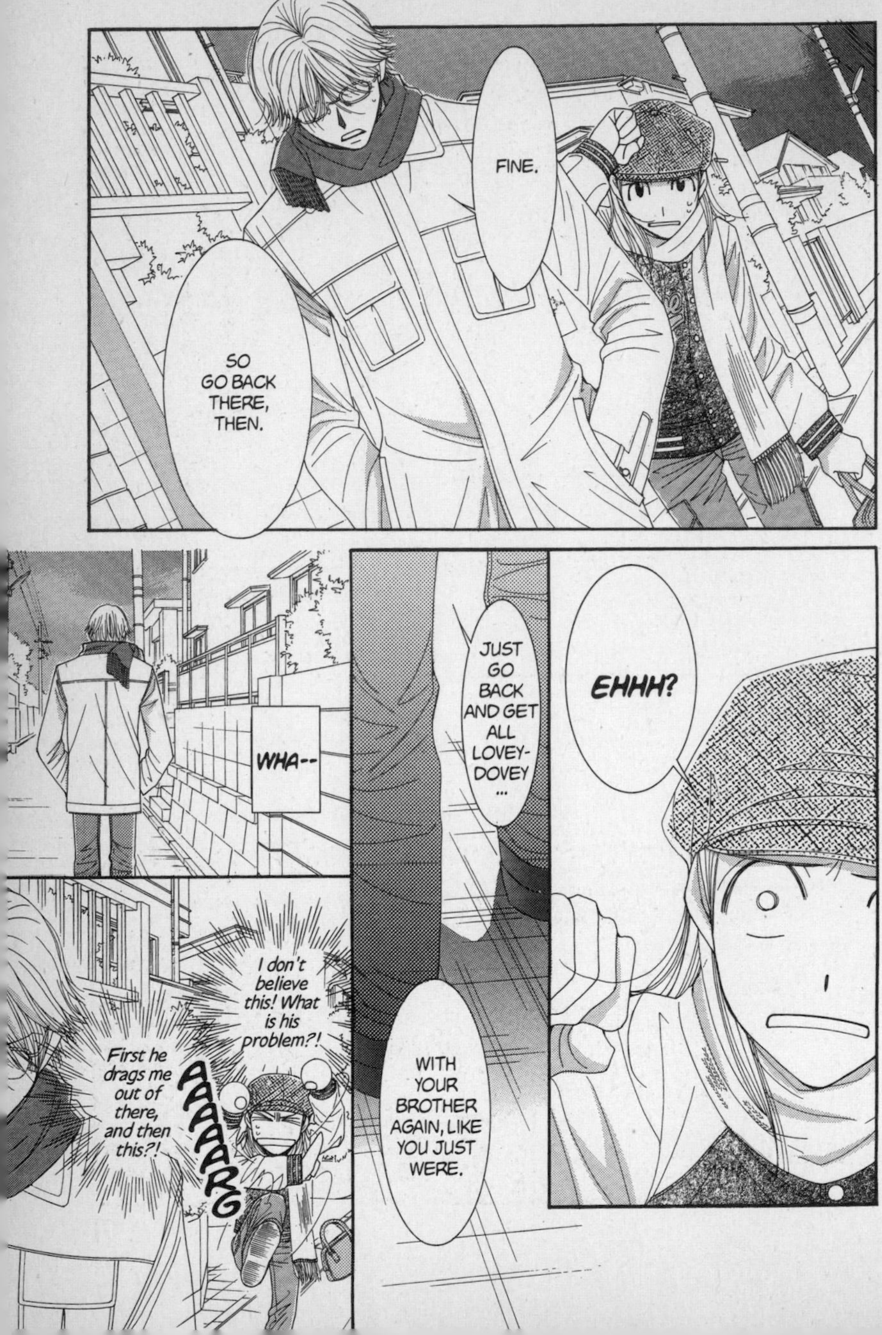
FINE.
SO GO BACK THERE, THEN.
EHHH?
JUST GO BACK AND GET ALL LOVEY-DOVEY...
WITH YOUR BROTHER AGAIN, LIKE YOU JUST WERE.
WHA--
I don't believe this! What is his problem?!
First he drags me out of there, and then this?!
AAAARG

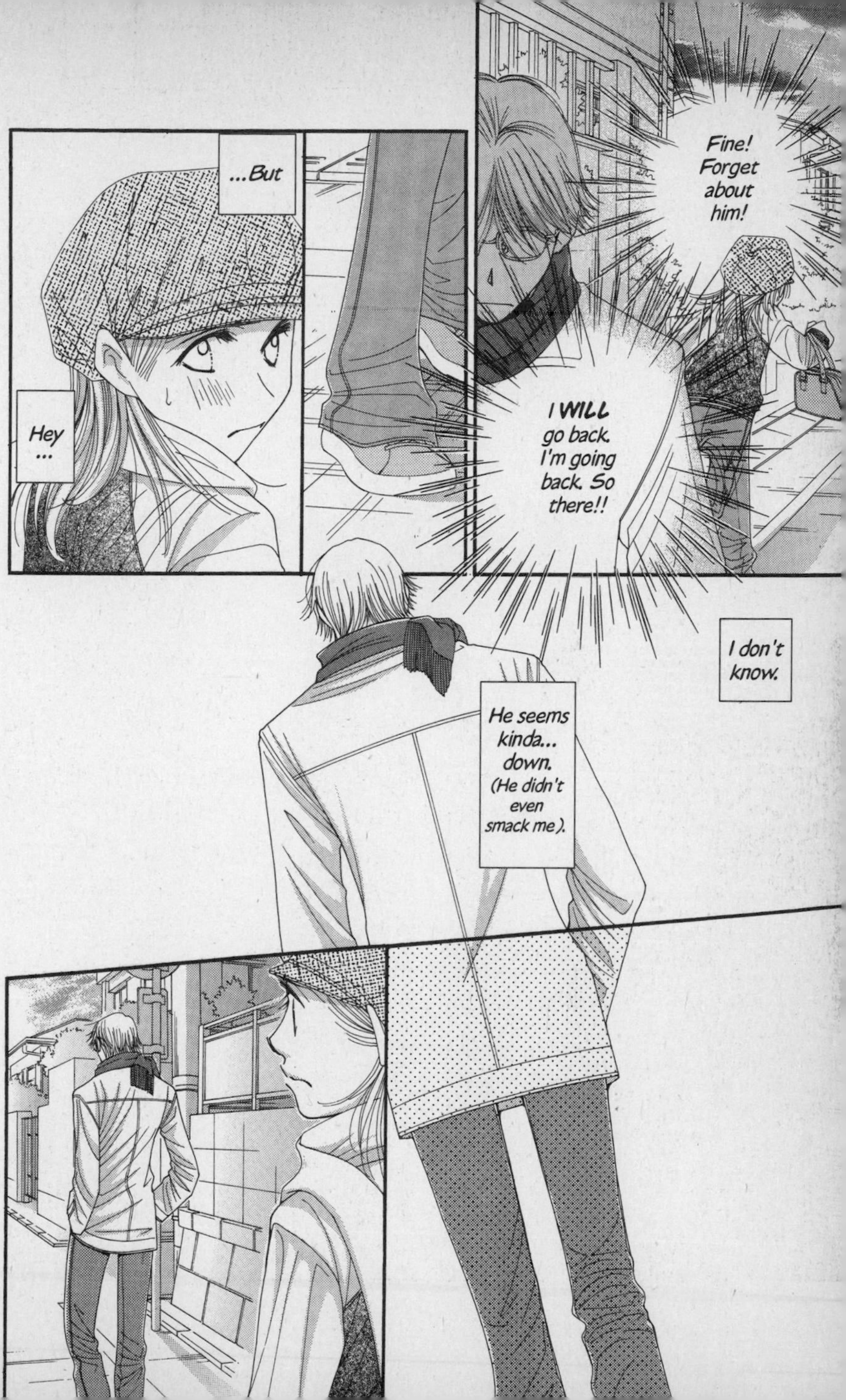
Fine! Forget about him!
I WILL go back. I'm going back. So there!!
...But
Hey...
I don't know.
He seems kinda... down. (He didn't even smack me).

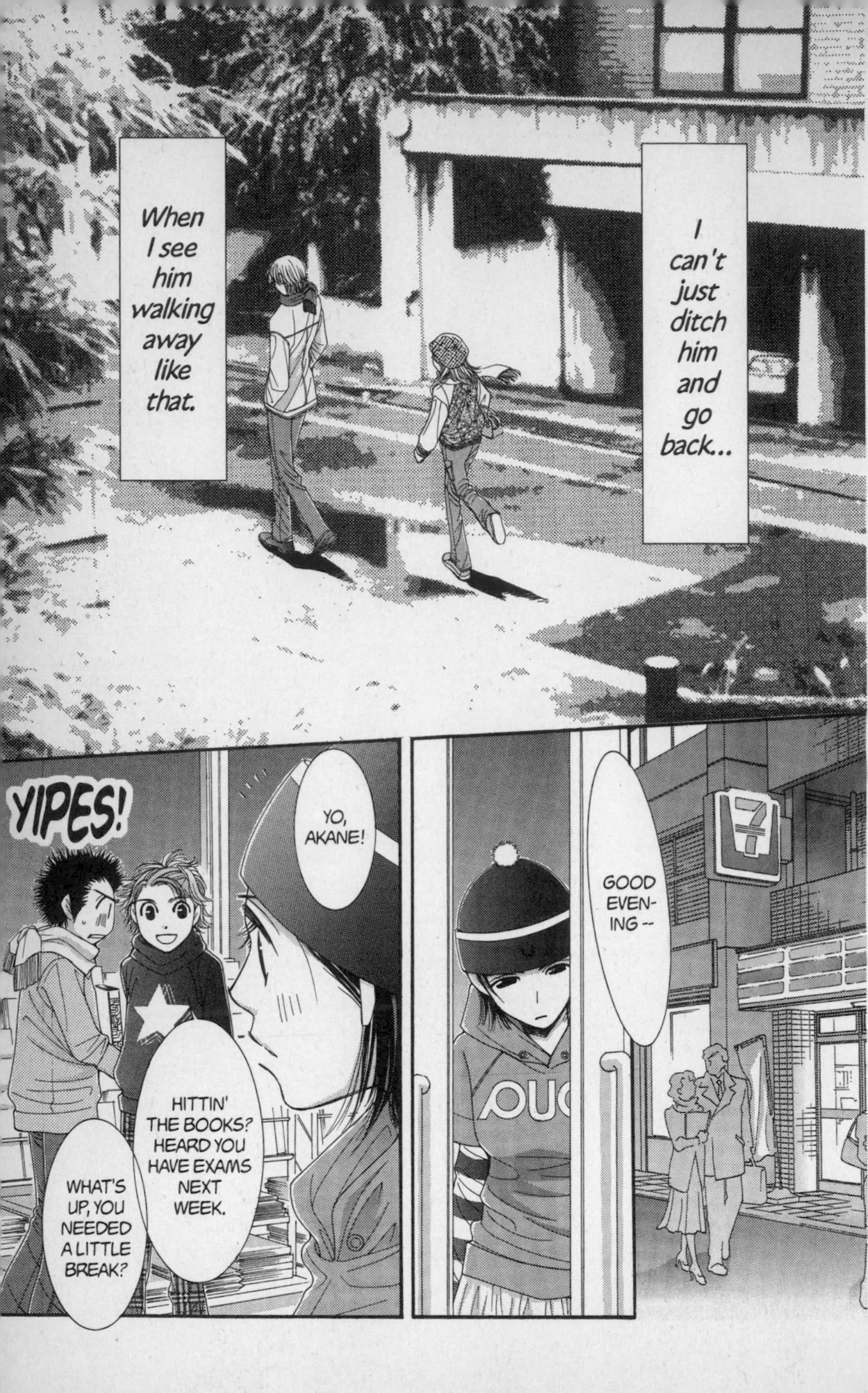
I can't just ditch him and go back...
When I see him walking away like that.
GOOD EVENING --
YO, AKANE!
YIPES!
HITTIN' THE BOOKS? HEARD YOU HAVE EXAMS NEXT WEEK.
WHAT'S UP, YOU NEEDED A LITTLE BREAK?

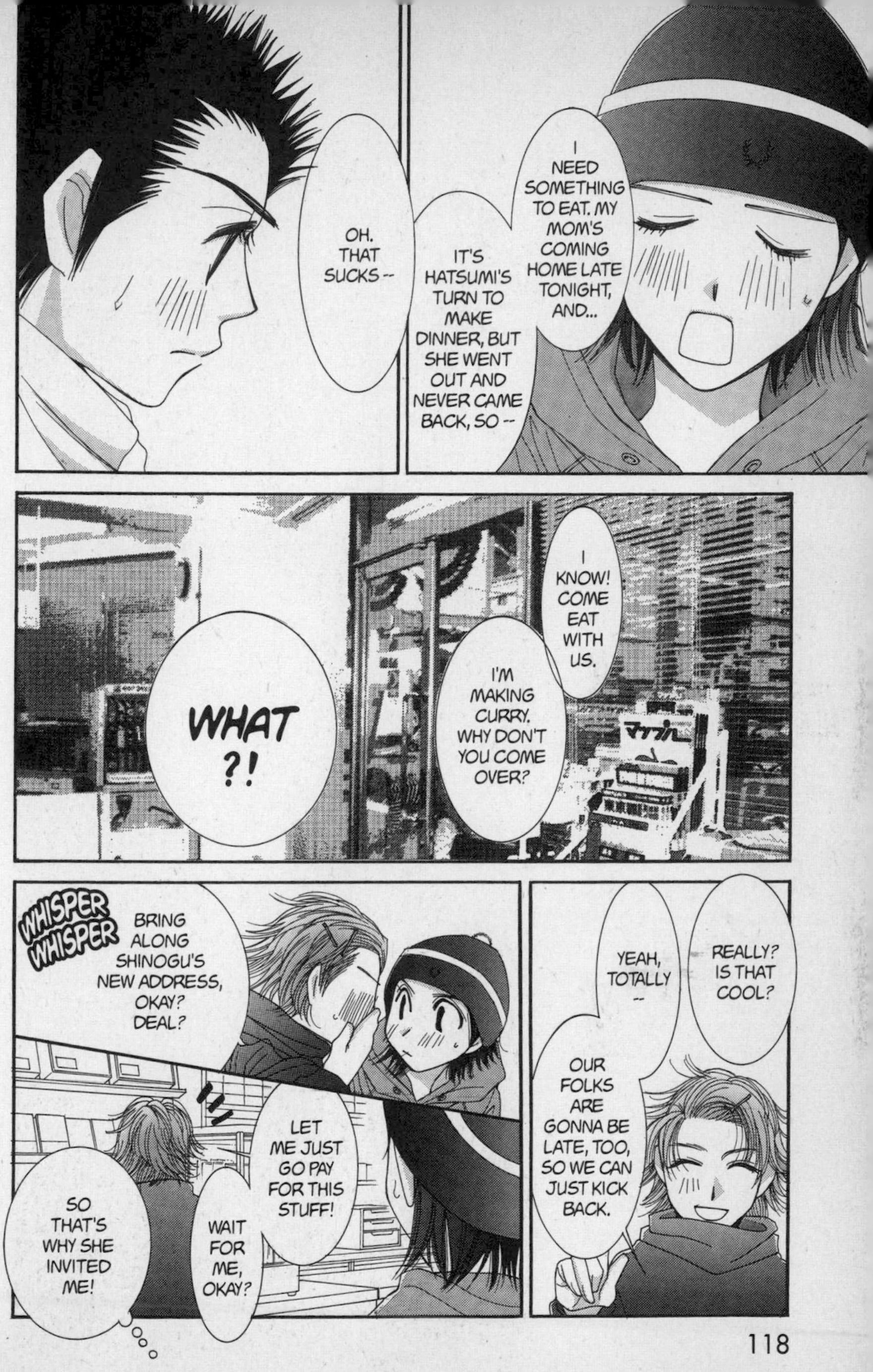
I NEED SOMETHING TO EAT. MY MOM'S COMING HOME LATE TONIGHT, AND...
IT'S HATSUMI'S TURN TO MAKE DINNER, BUT SHE WENT OUT AND NEVER CAME BACK, SO --
OH. THAT SUCKS --
I KNOW! COME EAT WITH US.
I'M MAKING CURRY. WHY DON'T YOU COME OVER?
WHAT?!
REALLY? IS THAT COOL?
YEAH, TOTALLY --
OUR FOLKS ARE GONNA BE LATE, TOO, SO WE CAN JUST KICK BACK.
WHISPER WHISPER
BRING ALONG SHINOGU'S NEW ADDRESS, OKAY? DEAL?
LET ME JUST GO PAY FOR THIS STUFF!
WAIT FOR ME, OKAY?
SO THAT'S WHY SHE INVITED ME!

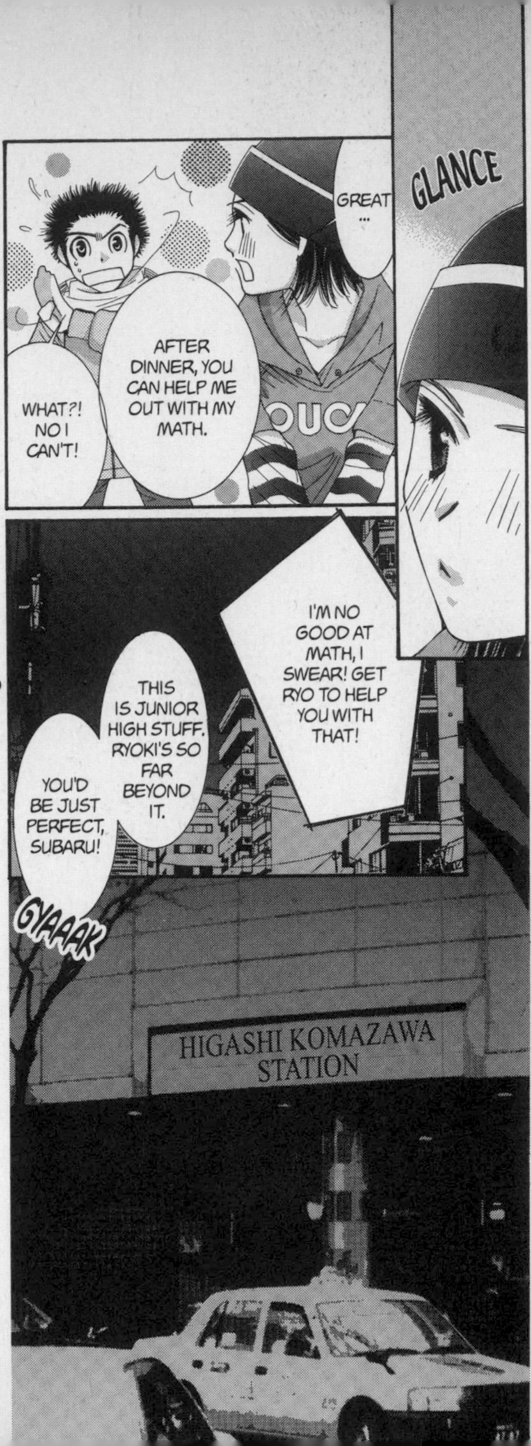
GLANCE
GREAT ...
AFTER DINNER, YOU CAN HELP ME OUT WITH MY MATH.
WHAT?! NO I CAN'T!
I'M NO GOOD AT MATH, I SWEAR! GET RYO TO HELP YOU WITH THAT!
THIS IS JUNIOR HIGH STUFF. RYOKI'S SO FAR BEYOND IT.
YOU'D BE JUST PERFECT, SUBARU!
GYAAAK
HIGASHI KOMAZAWA STATION

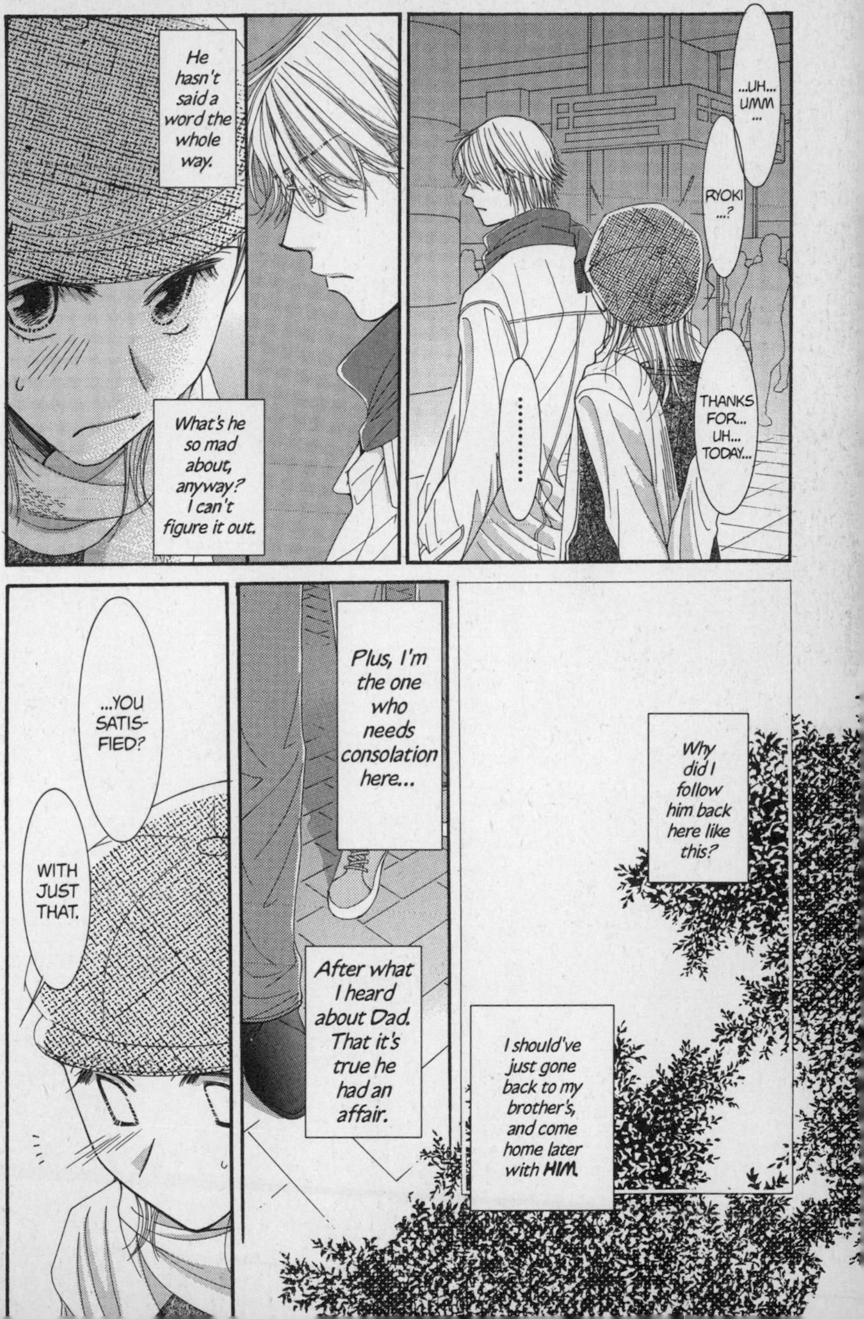
...UH... UMM ...
RYOKI ...?
THANKS FOR... UH... TODAY...
....
He hasn't said a word the whole way.
What's he so mad about, anyway? I can't figure it out.
Why did I follow him back here like this?
I should've just gone back to my brother's, and come home later with HIM.
Plus, I'm the one who needs consolation here...
After what I heard about Dad. That it's true he had an affair.
...YOU SATISFIED?
WITH JUST THAT.

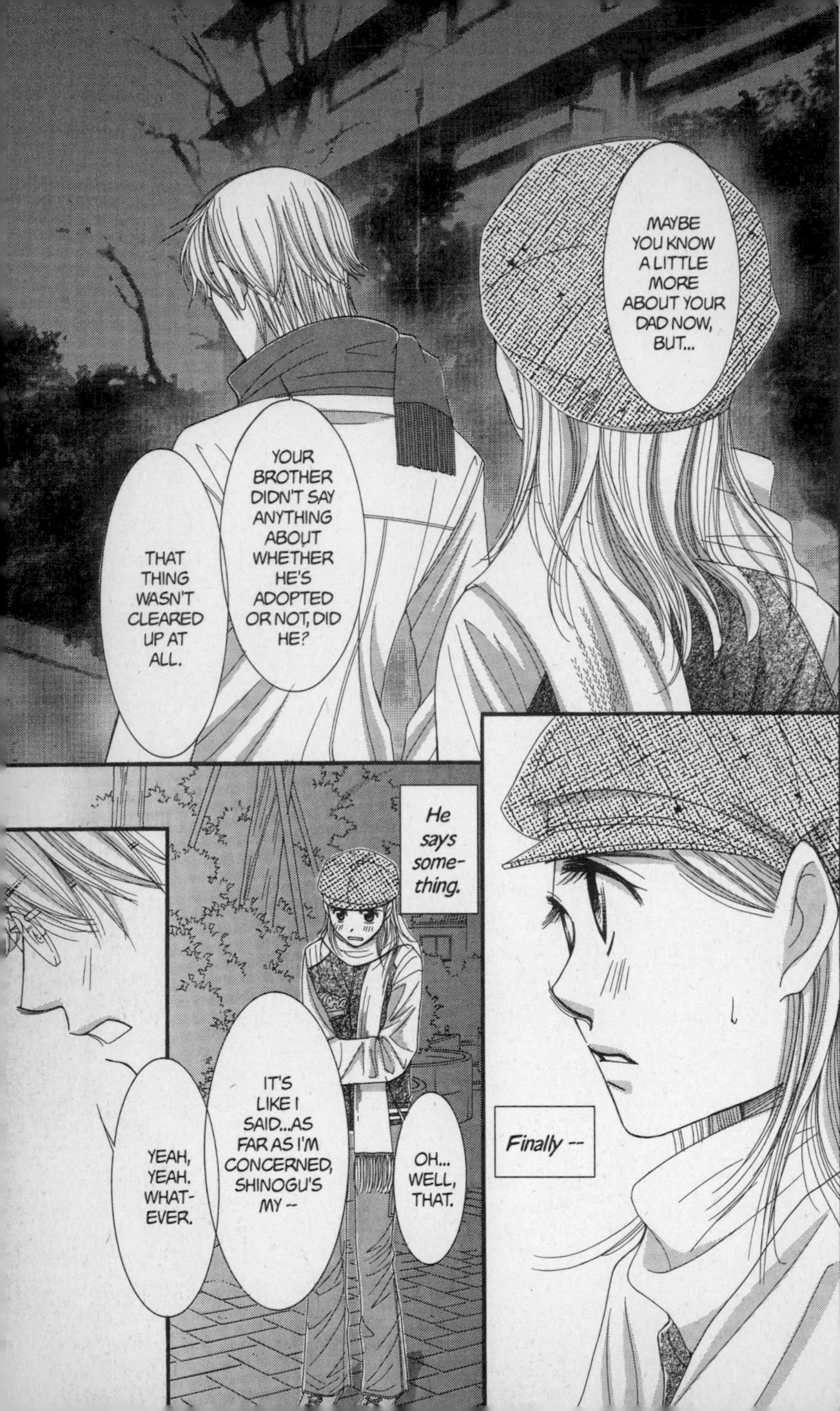
MAYBE YOU KNOW A LITTLE MORE ABOUT YOUR DAD NOW, BUT...
YOUR BROTHER DIDN'T SAY ANYTHING ABOUT WHETHER HE'S ADOPTED OR NOT, DID HE?
THAT THING WASN'T CLEARED UP AT ALL.
Finally --
He says something.
OH... WELL, THAT.
IT'S LIKE I SAID...AS FAR AS I'M CONCERNED, SHINOGU'S MY --
YEAH, YEAH. WHAT-EVER.

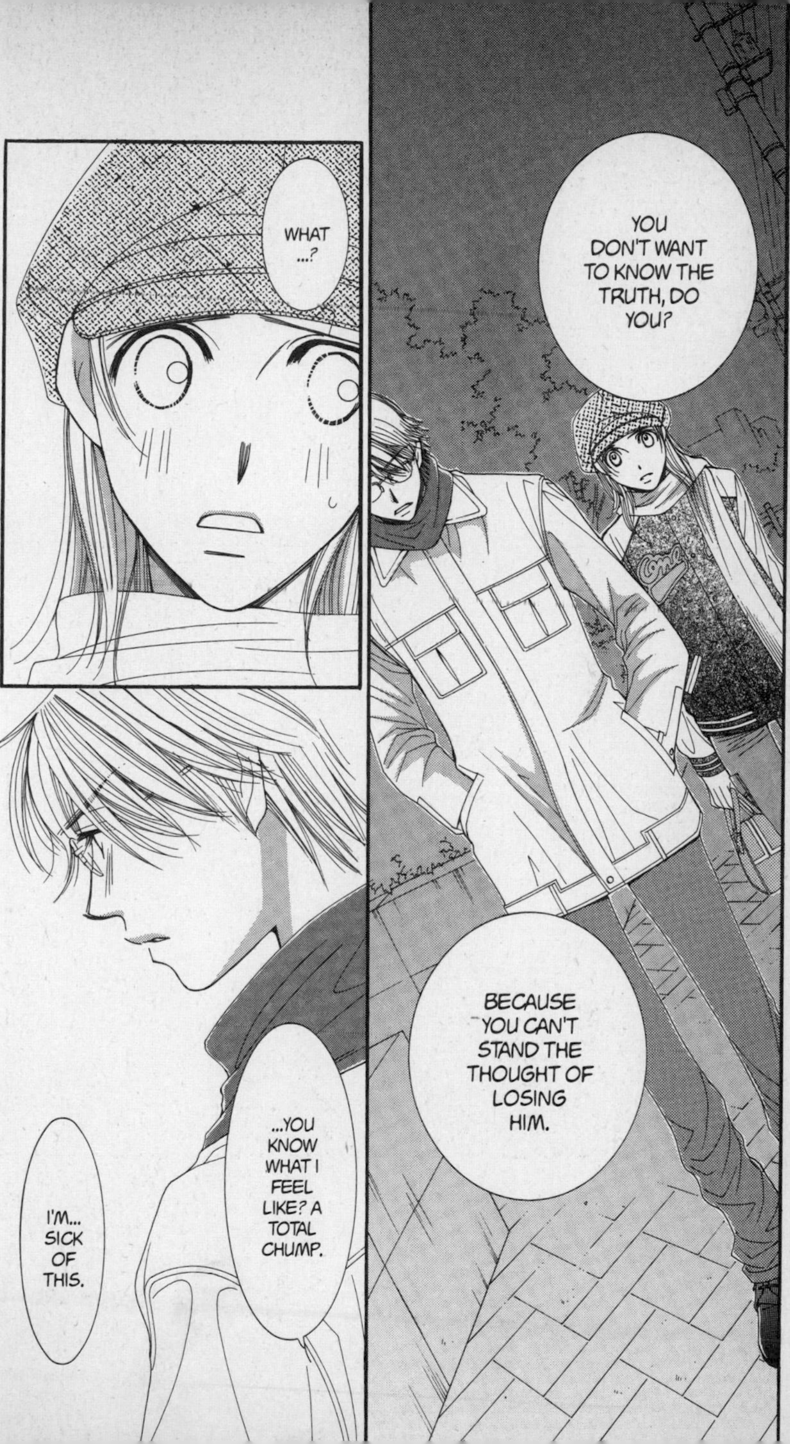
YOU DON'T WANT TO KNOW THE TRUTH, DO YOU?
BECAUSE YOU CAN'T STAND THE THOUGHT OF LOSING HIM.
WHAT ...?
...YOU KNOW WHAT I FEEL LIKE? A TOTAL CHUMP.
I'M... SICK OF THIS.

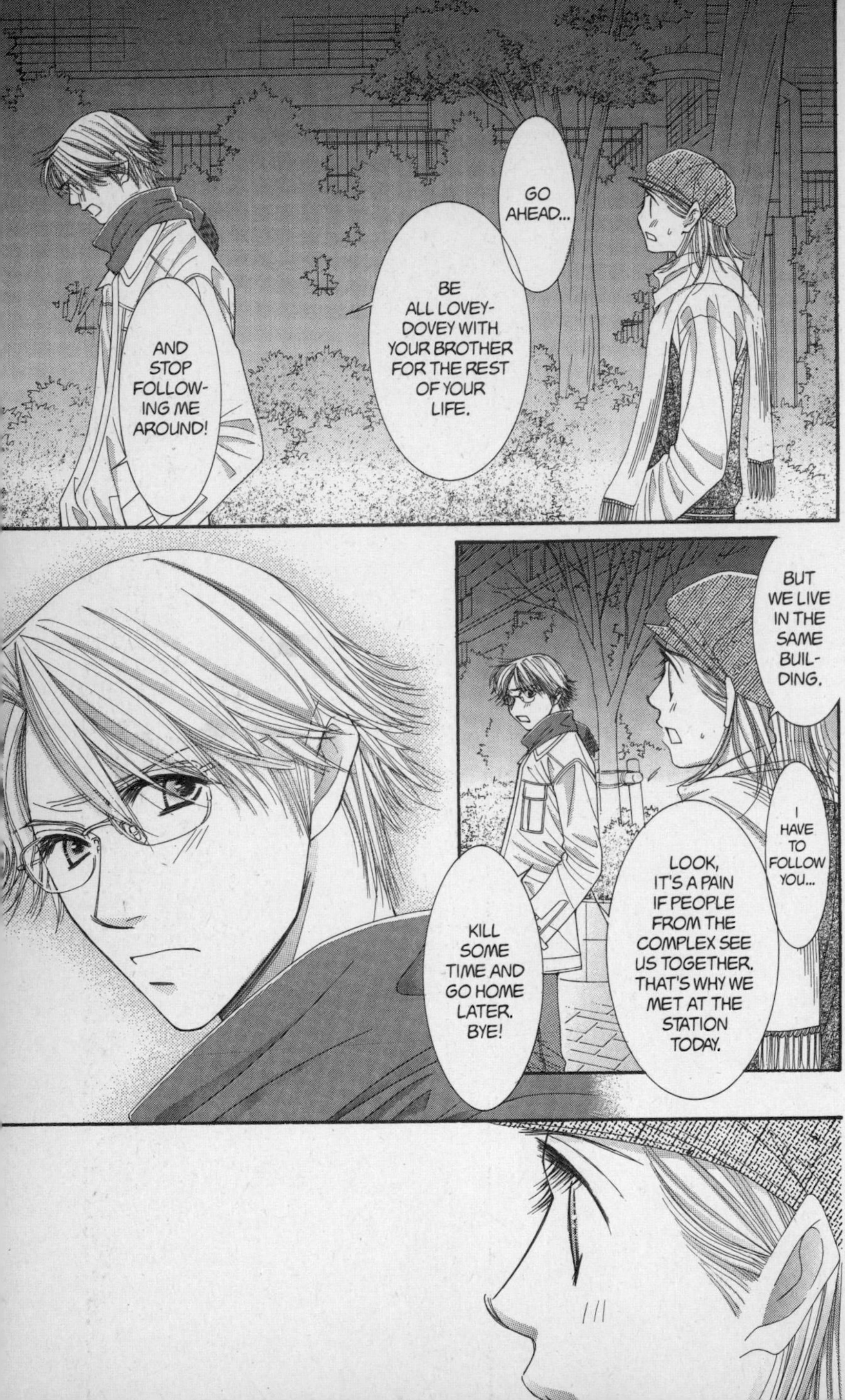
GO AHEAD...
BE ALL LOVEY-DOVEY WITH YOUR BROTHER FOR THE REST OF YOUR LIFE.
AND STOP FOLLOWING ME AROUND!
BUT WE LIVE IN THE SAME BUILDING.
I HAVE TO FOLLOW YOU...
LOOK, IT'S A PAIN IF PEOPLE FROM THE COMPLEX SEE US TOGETHER. THAT'S WHY WE MET AT THE STATION TODAY.
KILL SOME TIME AND GO HOME LATER. BYE!

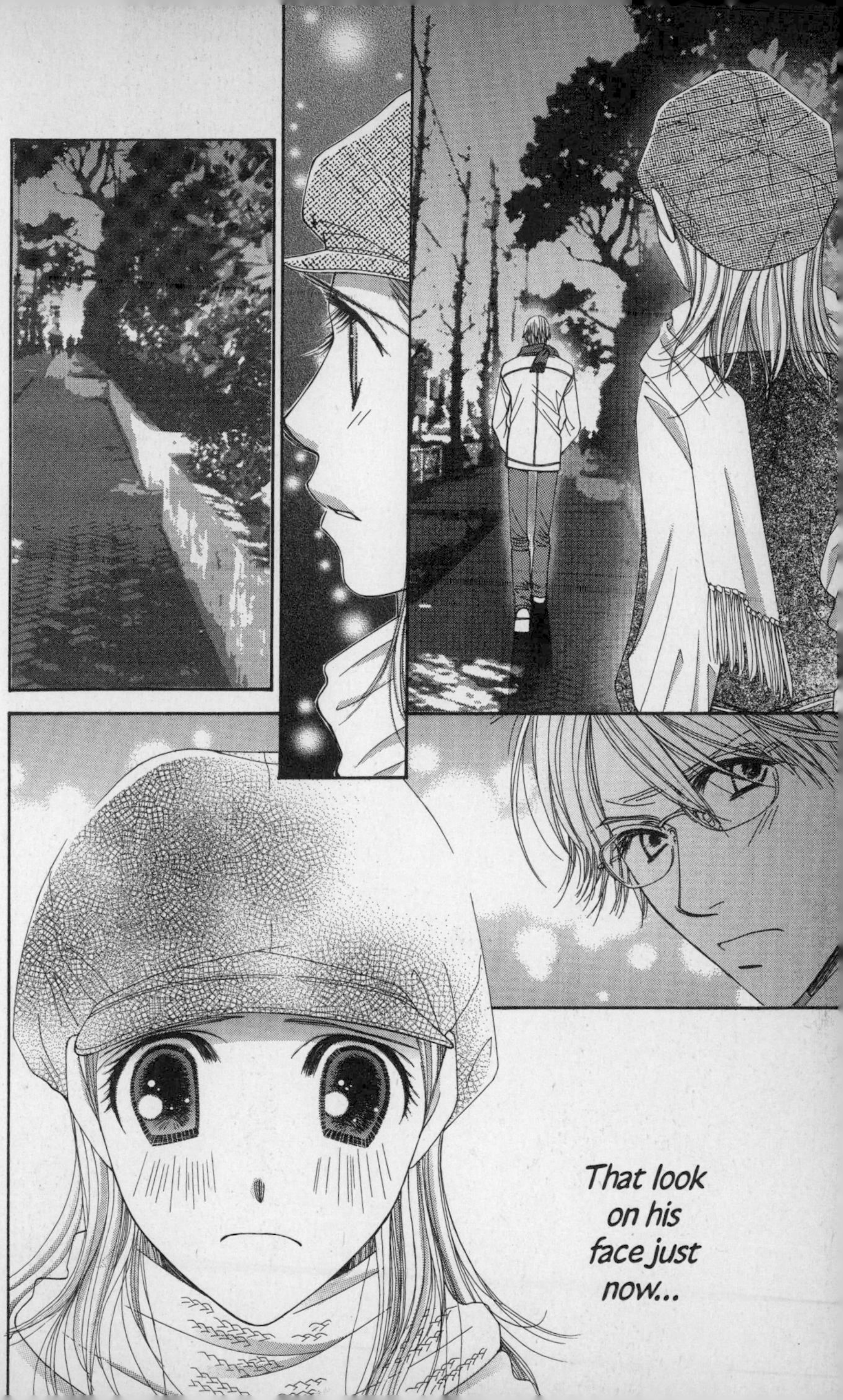
That look on his face just now...

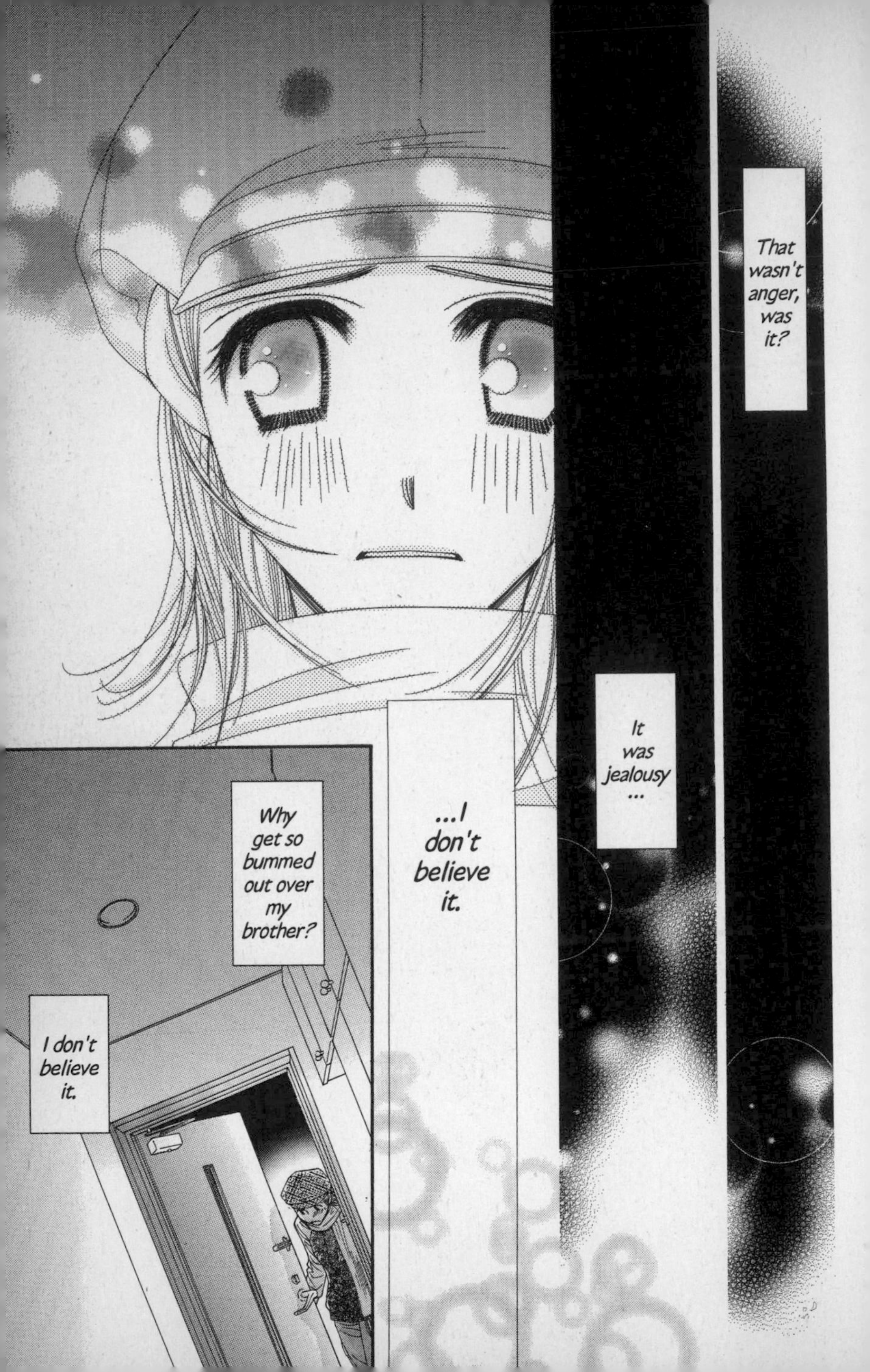
That wasn't anger, was it?
It was jealousy...
...I don't believe it.
Why get so bummed out over my brother?
I don't believe it.

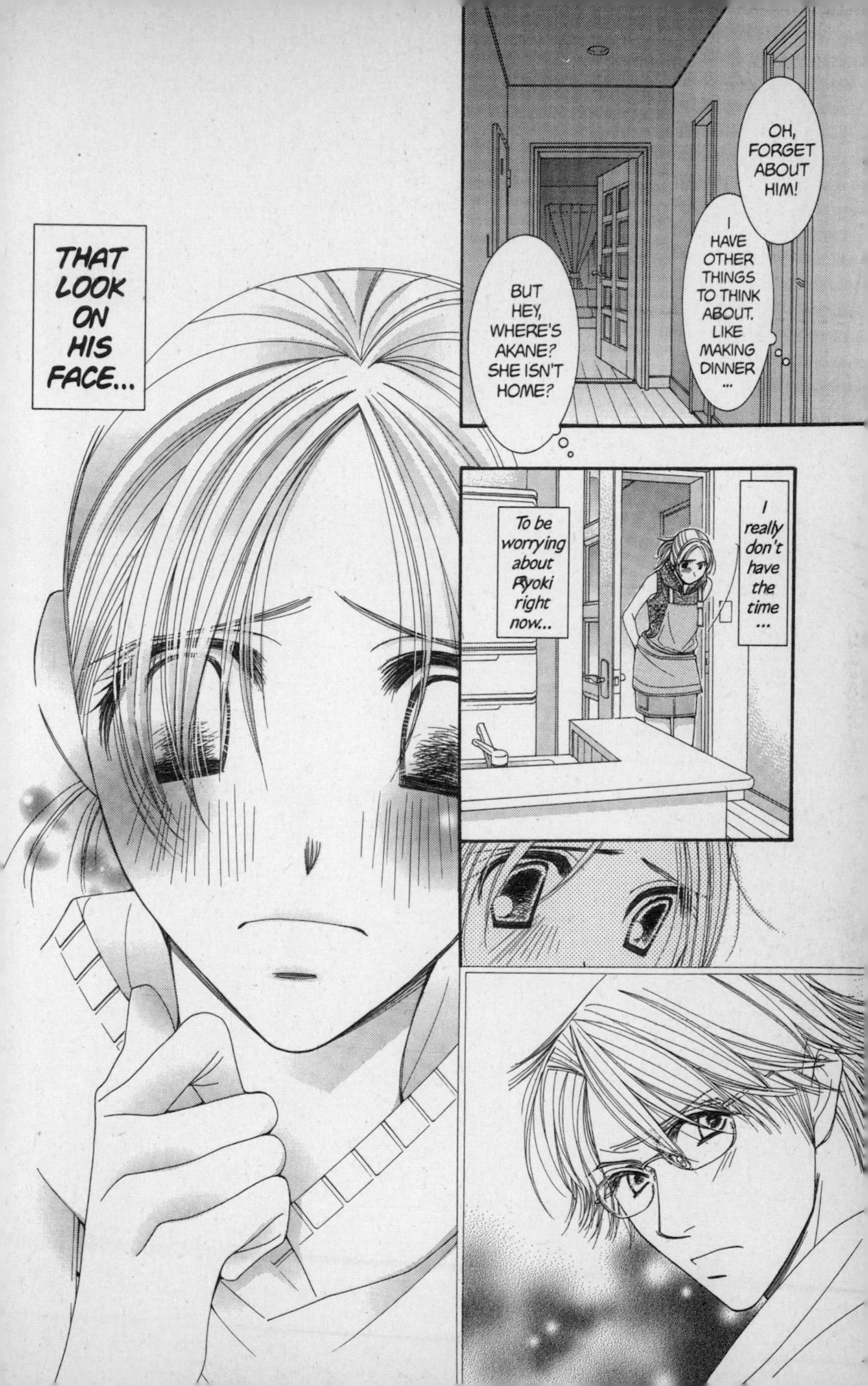
OH, FORGET ABOUT HIM!
I HAVE OTHER THINGS TO THINK ABOUT. LIKE MAKING DINNER...
BUT HEY, WHERE'S AKANE? SHE ISN'T HOME?
I really don't have the time...
To be worrying about Ryoki right now...
THAT LOOK ON HIS FACE...

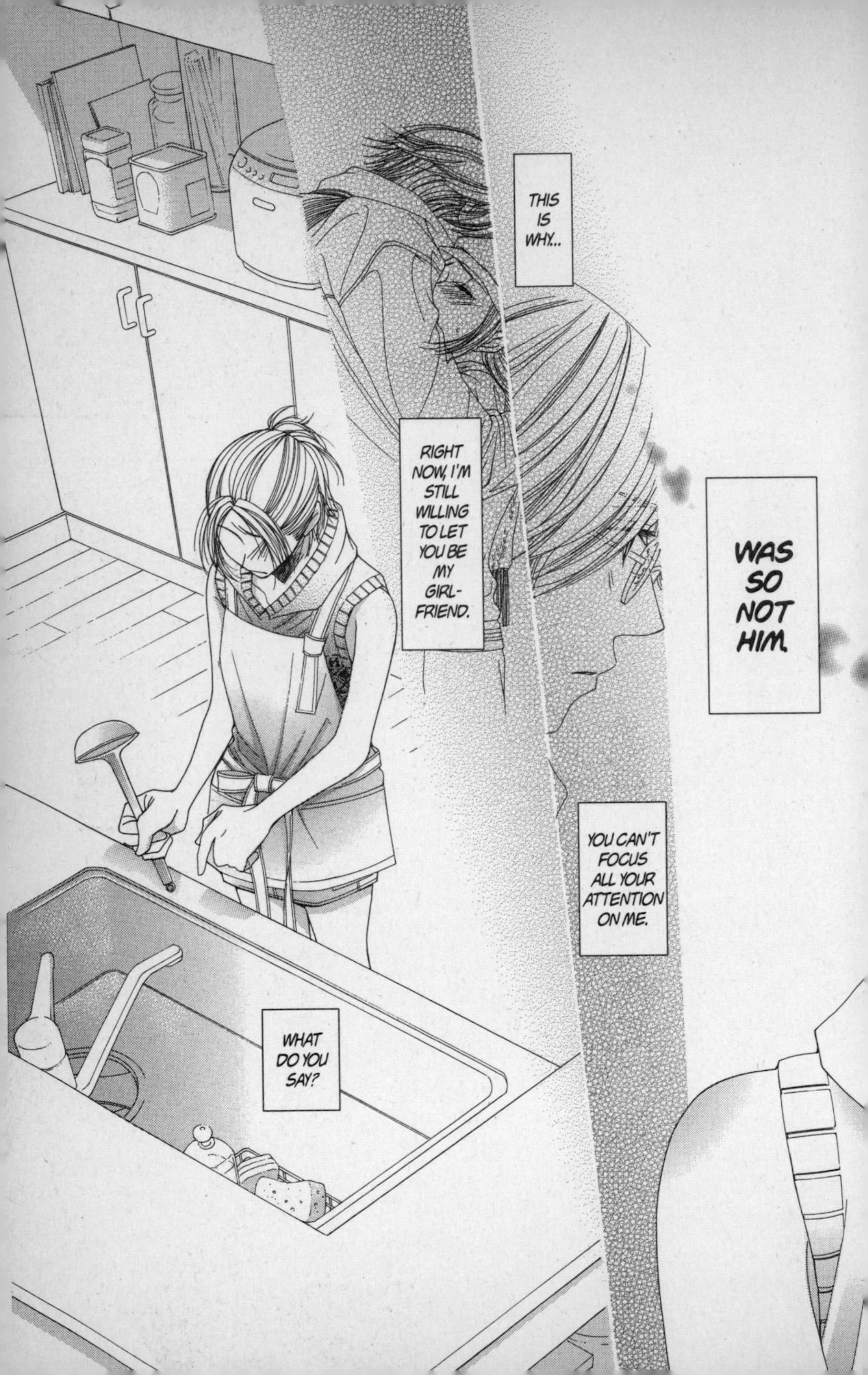
THIS IS WHY...
WAS SO NOT HIM.
YOU CAN'T FOCUS ALL YOUR ATTENTION ON ME.
RIGHT NOW, I'M STILL WILLING TO LET YOU BE MY GIRL-FRIEND.
WHAT DO YOU SAY?

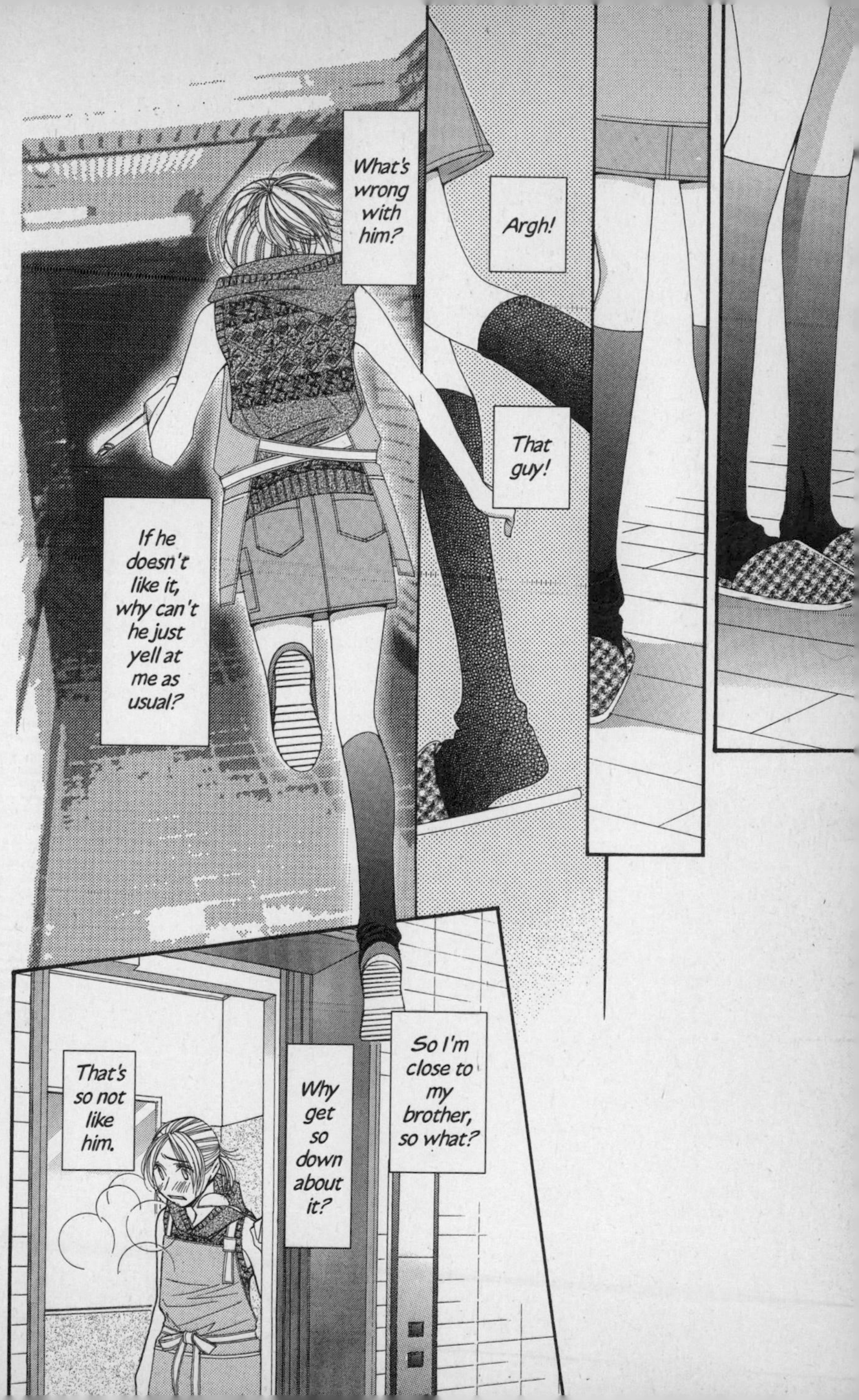
Argh!
That guy!
What's wrong with him?
If he doesn't like it, why can't he just yell at me as usual?
So I'm close to my brother, so what?
Why get so down about it?
That's so not like him.

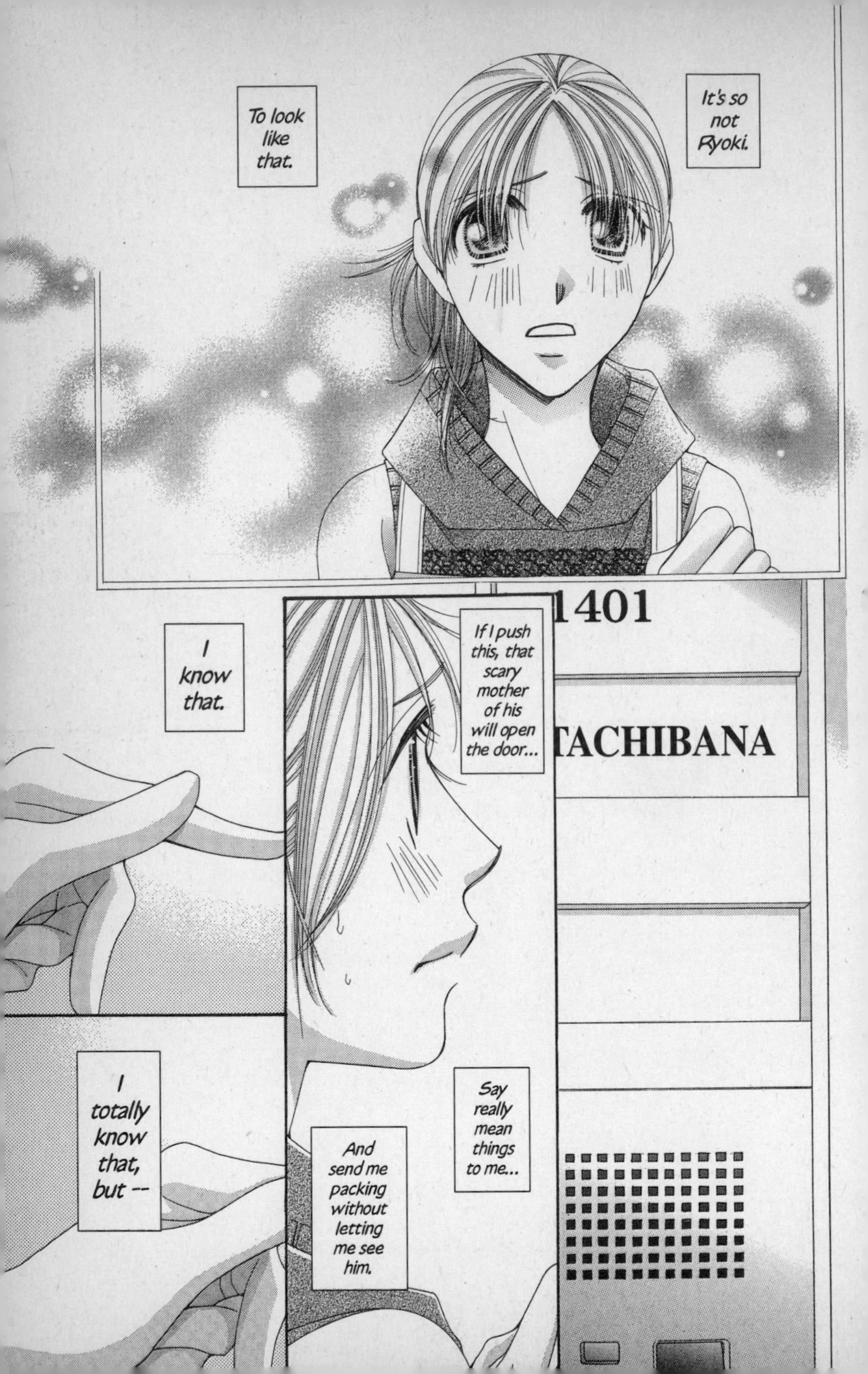
It's so not Ryoki.
To look like that.
1401
TACHIBANA
If I push this, that scary mother of his will open the door...
Say really mean things to me...
And send me packing without letting me see him.
I know that.
I totally know that, but --

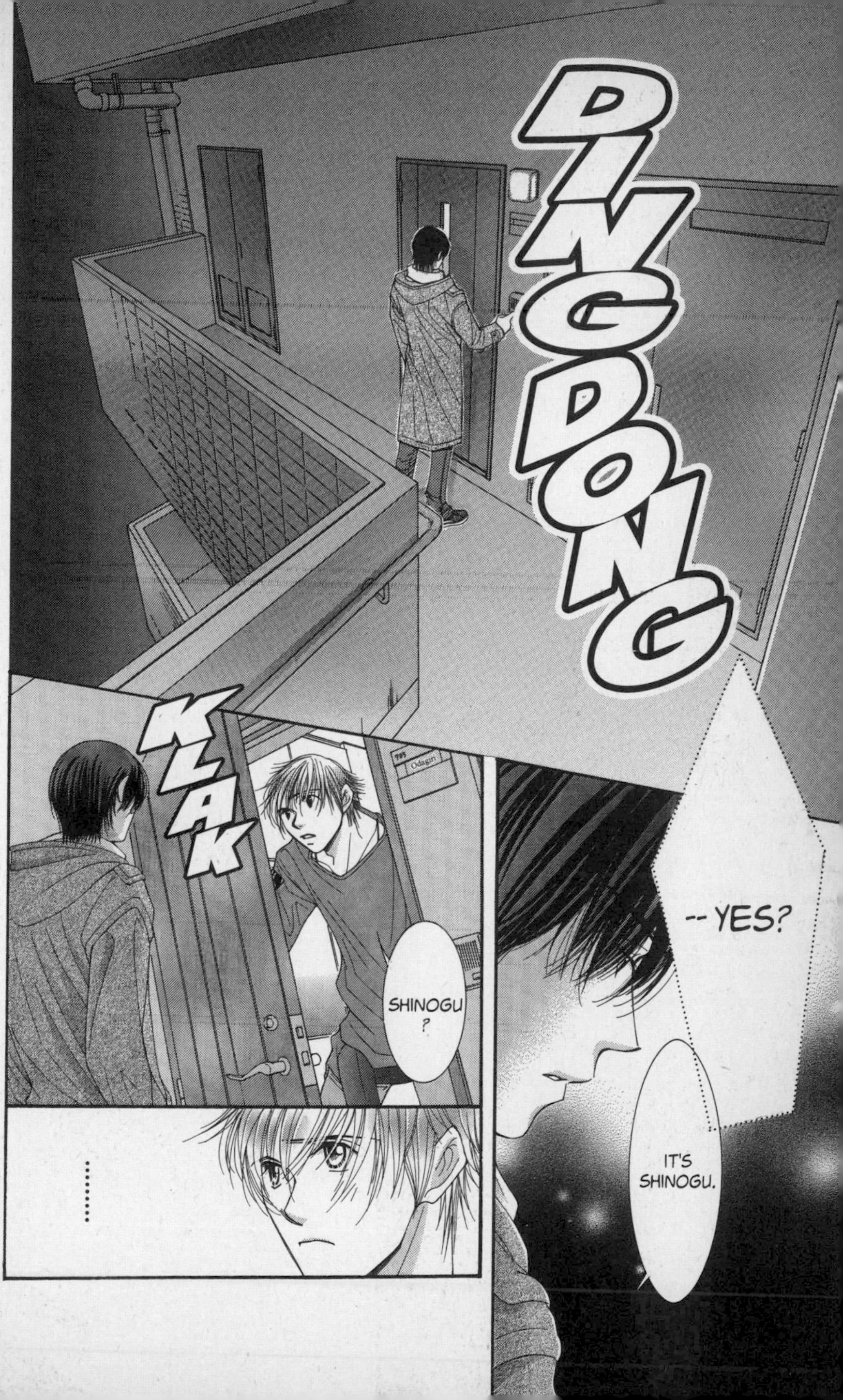
DING DONG
-- YES?
IT'S SHINOGU.
KLAK
SHINOGU ?
……

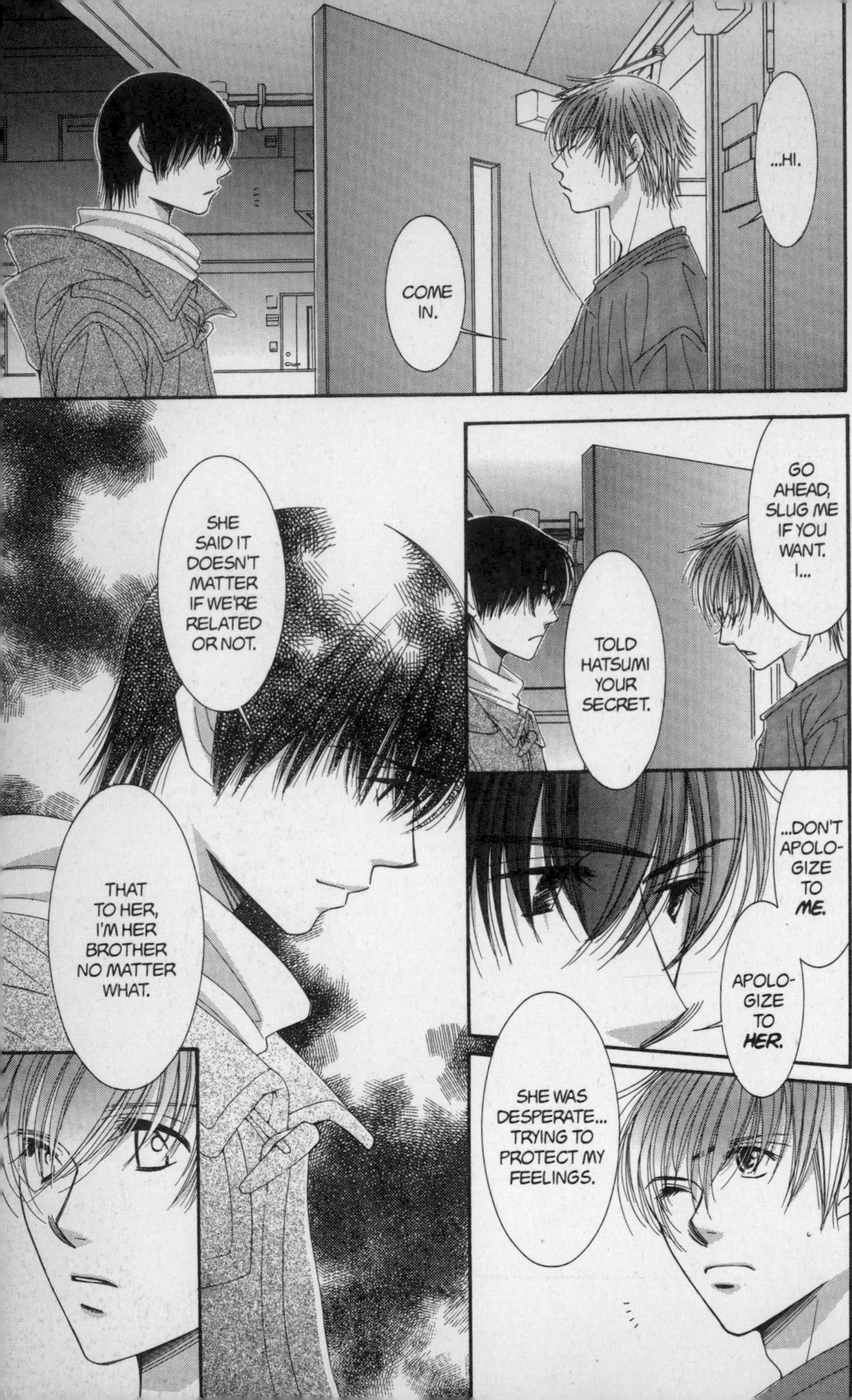
...HI.
COME IN.
GO AHEAD, SLUG ME IF YOU WANT. I...
TOLD HATSUMI YOUR SECRET.
...DON'T APOLOGIZE TO **ME.**
APOLOGIZE TO **HER.**
SHE WAS DESPERATE... TRYING TO PROTECT MY FEELINGS.
SHE SAID IT DOESN'T MATTER IF WE'RE RELATED OR NOT.
THAT TO HER, I'M HER BROTHER NO MATTER WHAT.

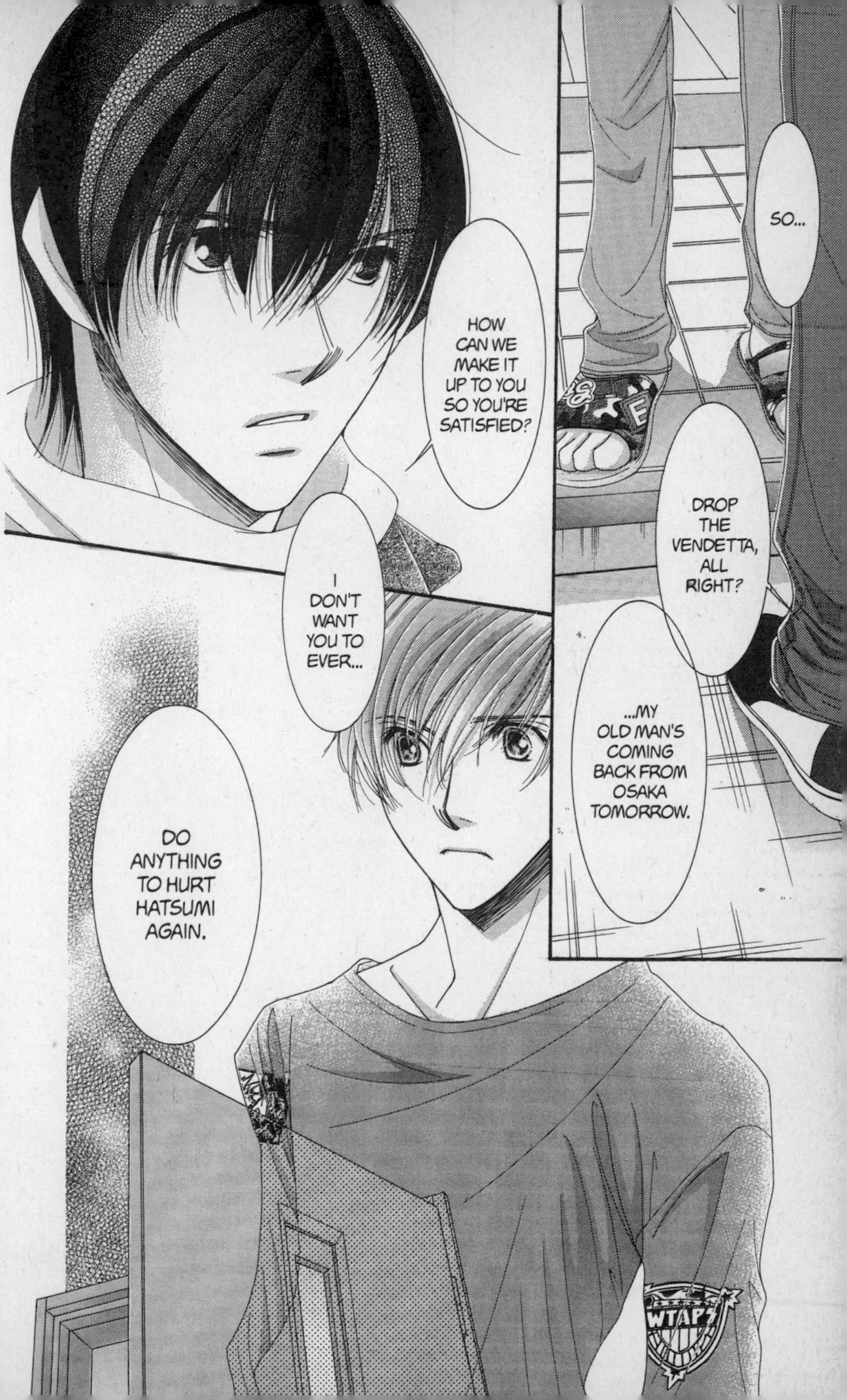
SO...
DROP THE VENDETTA, ALL RIGHT?
...MY OLD MAN'S COMING BACK FROM OSAKA TOMORROW.
HOW CAN WE MAKE IT UP TO YOU SO YOU'RE SATISFIED?
I DON'T WANT YOU TO EVER...
DO ANYTHING TO HURT HATSUMI AGAIN.
WTAPS

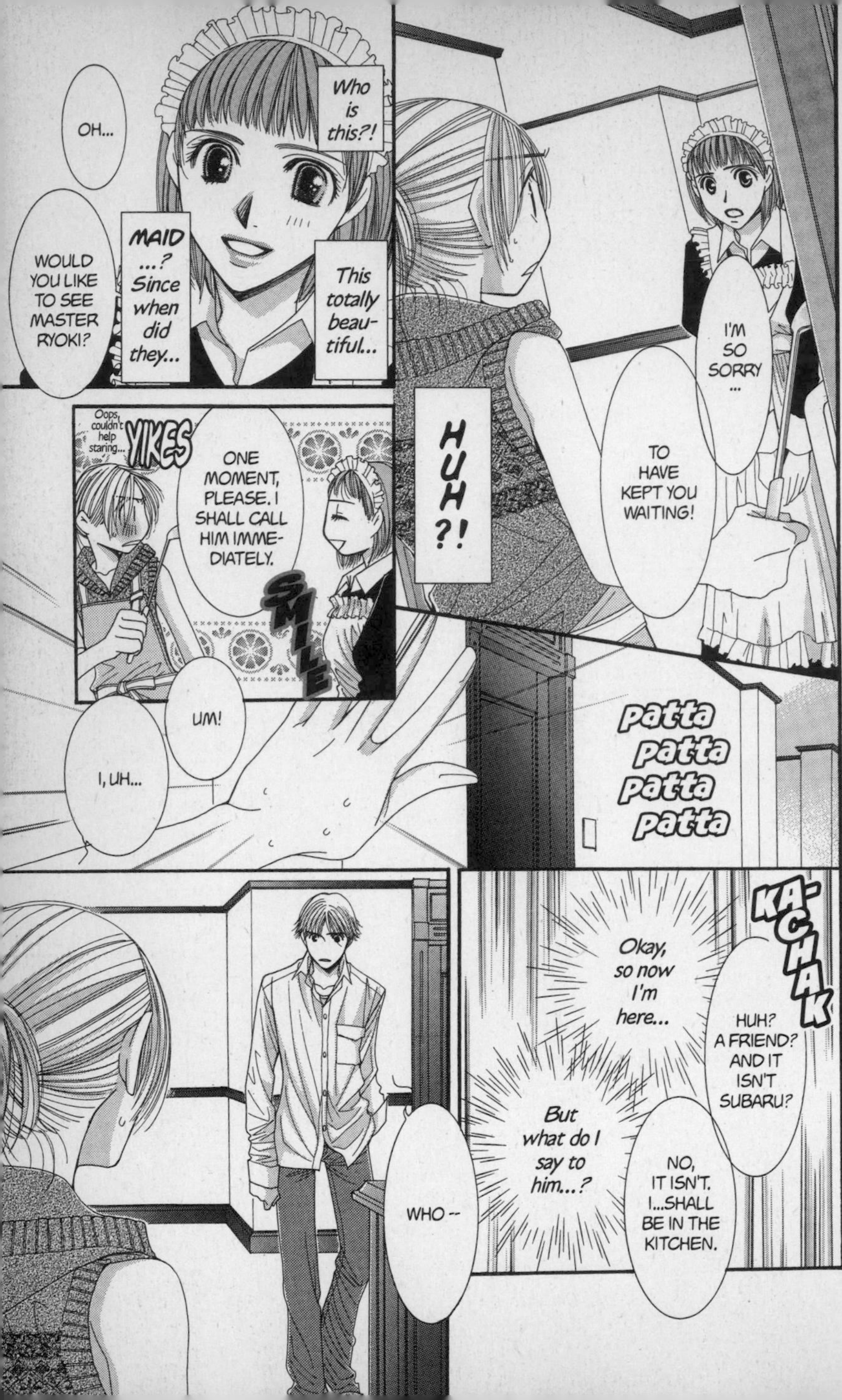
I'M SO SORRY...
TO HAVE KEPT YOU WAITING!
HUH?!
Who is this?!
This totally beautiful...
MAID...? Since when did they...
OH...
WOULD YOU LIKE TO SEE MASTER RYOKI?
Oops, couldn't help staring...
YIKES
ONE MOMENT, PLEASE. I SHALL CALL HIM IMMEDIATELY.
SMILE
UM!
I, UH...
patta patta patta patta
KA-CHAK
HUH? A FRIEND? AND IT ISN'T SUBARU?
NO, IT ISN'T. I...SHALL BE IN THE KITCHEN.
Okay, so now I'm here...
But what do I say to him...?
WHO --

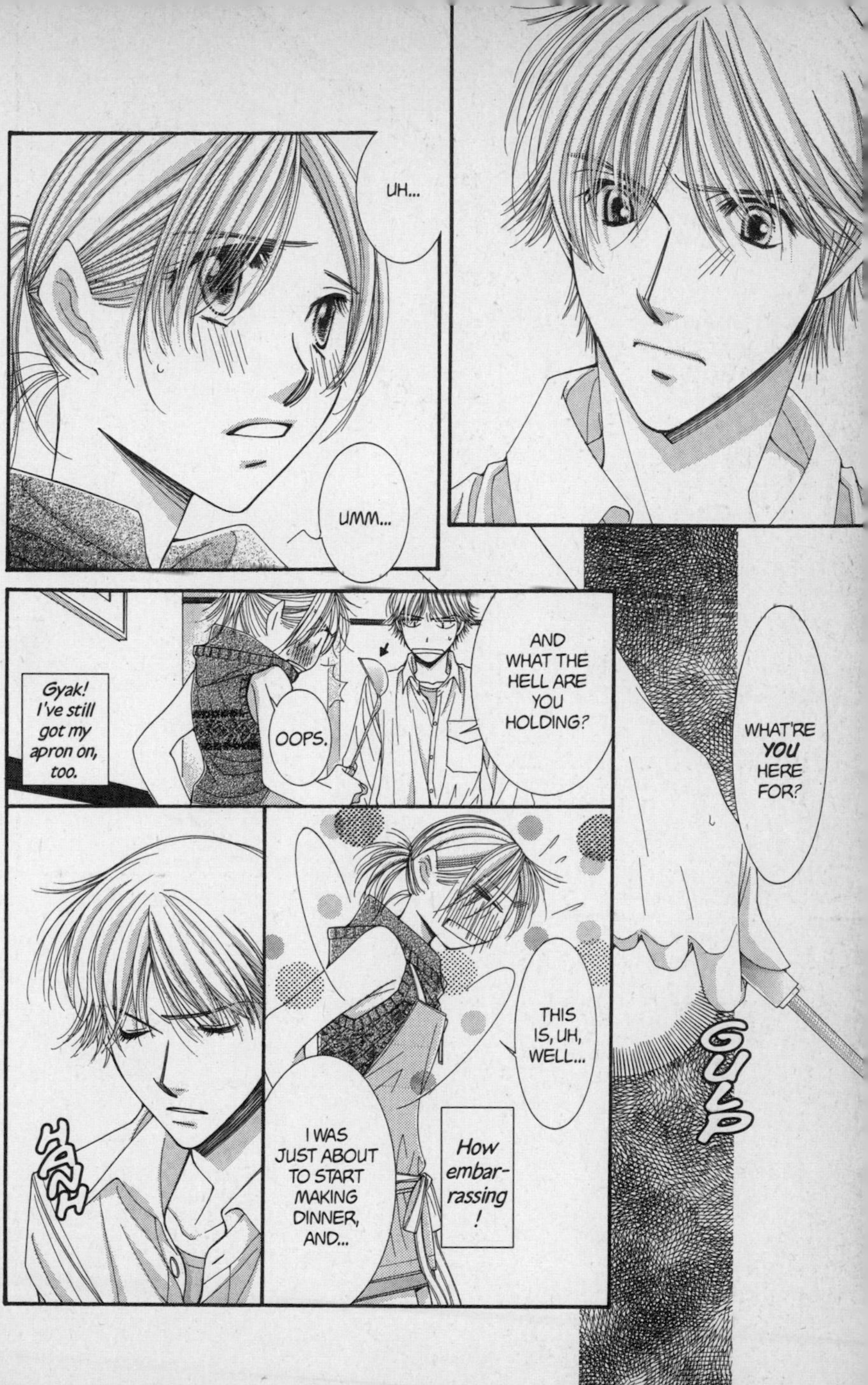
UH...
UMM...
WHAT'RE **YOU** HERE FOR?
GULP
AND WHAT THE HELL ARE YOU HOLDING?
OOPS.
Gyak! I've still got my apron on, too.
THIS IS, UH, WELL...
How embarrassing!
I WAS JUST ABOUT TO START MAKING DINNER, AND...

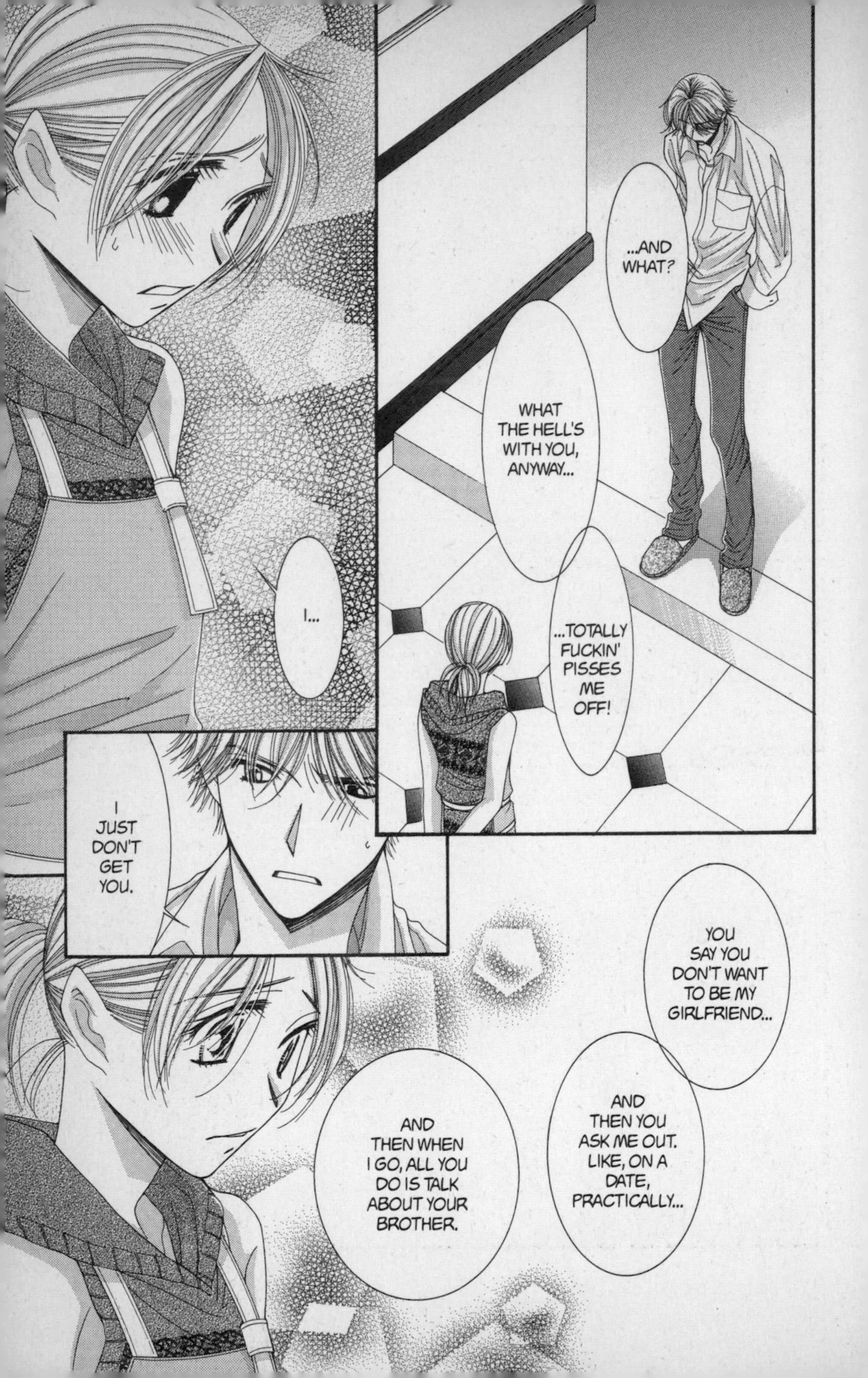
...AND WHAT?
WHAT THE HELL'S WITH YOU, ANYWAY...
...TOTALLY FUCKIN' PISSES ME OFF!
I...
I JUST DON'T GET YOU.
YOU SAY YOU DON'T WANT TO BE MY GIRLFRIEND...
AND THEN YOU ASK ME OUT. LIKE, ON A DATE, PRACTICALLY...
AND THEN WHEN I GO, ALL YOU DO IS TALK ABOUT YOUR BROTHER.

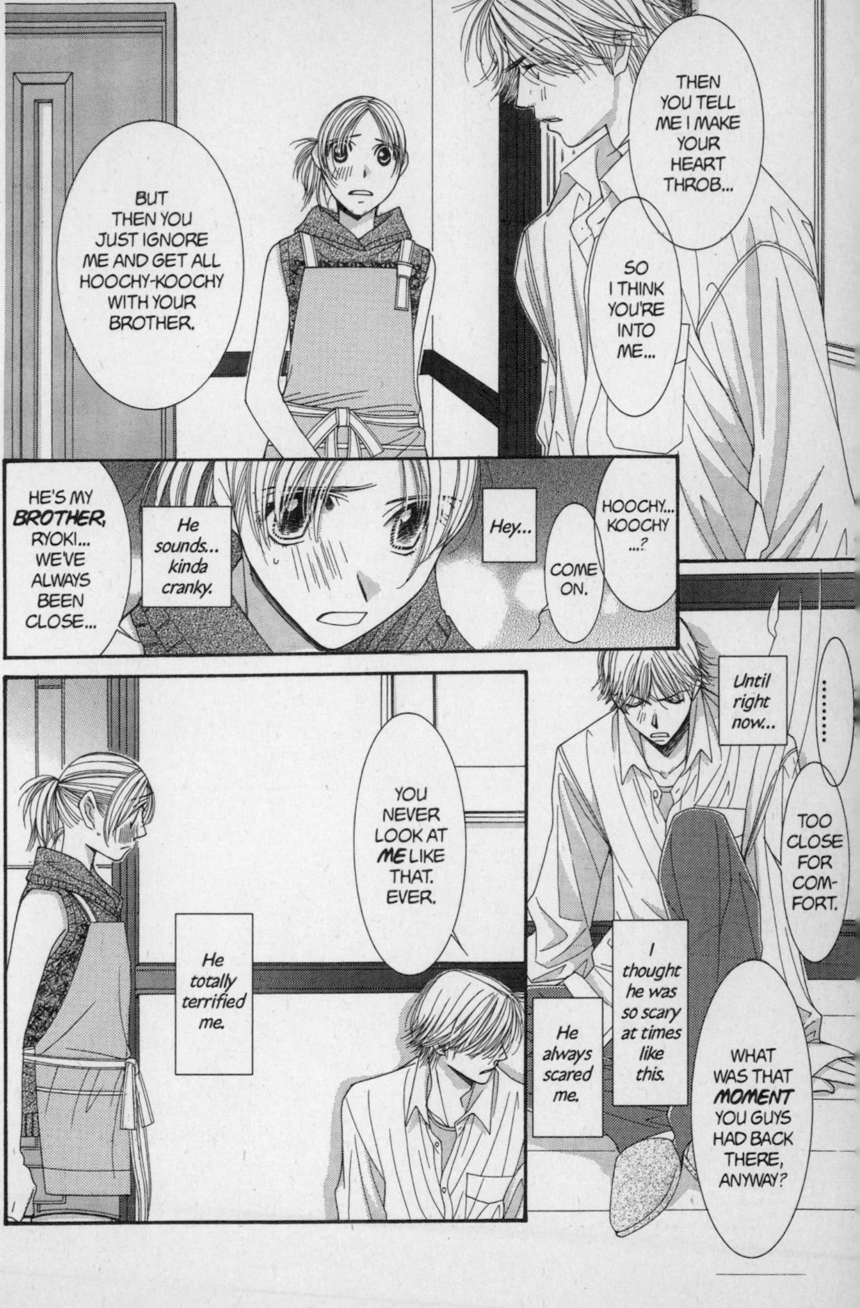
THEN YOU TELL ME I MAKE YOUR HEART THROB...
SO I THINK YOU'RE INTO ME...
BUT THEN YOU JUST IGNORE ME AND GET ALL HOOCHY-KOOCHY WITH YOUR BROTHER.
HOOCHY... KOOCHY ...?
COME ON.
Hey...
He sounds... kinda cranky.
HE'S MY **BROTHER**, RYOKI... WE'VE ALWAYS BEEN CLOSE...
......
Until right now...
TOO CLOSE FOR COMFORT.
WHAT WAS THAT **MOMENT** YOU GUYS HAD BACK THERE, ANYWAY?
I thought he was so scary at times like this.
He always scared me.
YOU NEVER LOOK AT **ME** LIKE THAT. EVER.
He totally terrified me.

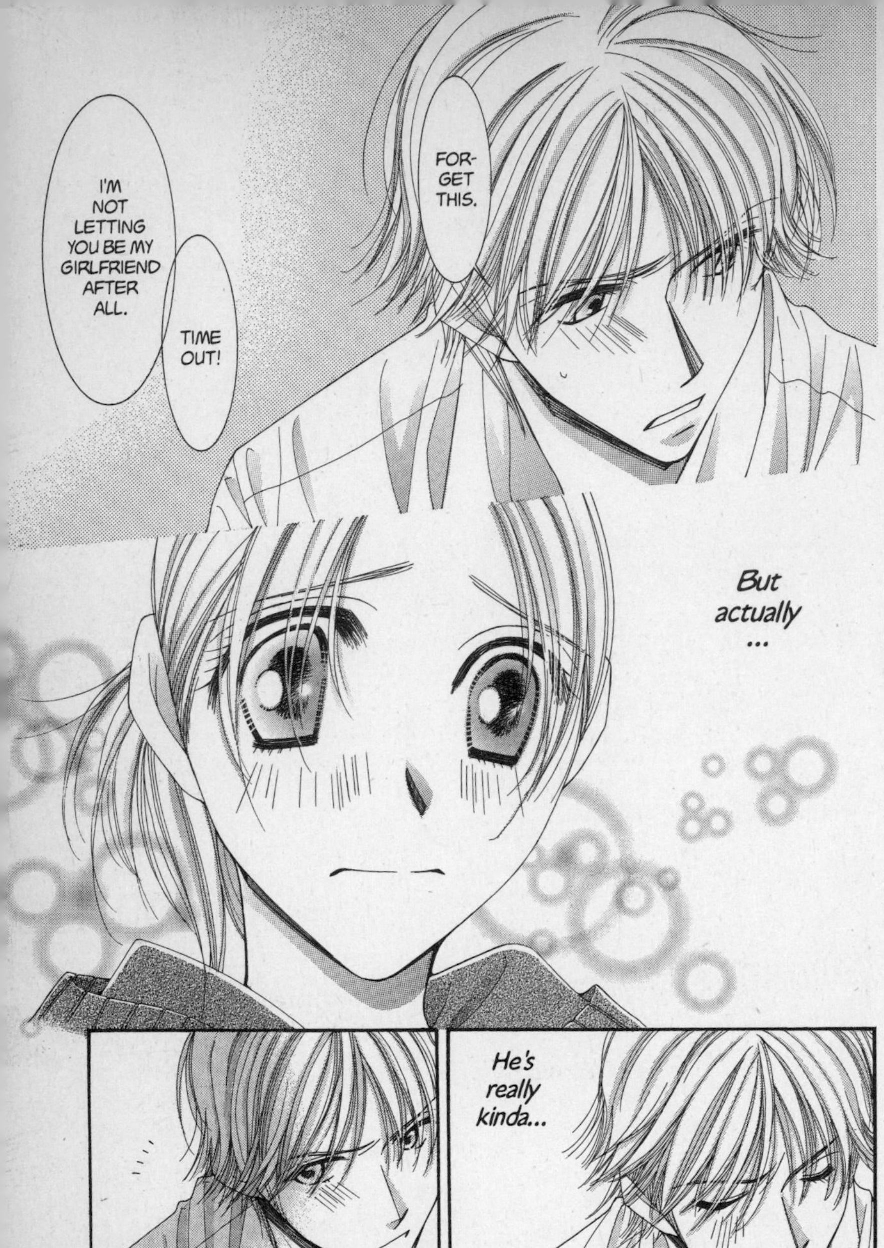
FOR-GET THIS.
TIME OUT!
I'M NOT LETTING YOU BE MY GIRLFRIEND AFTER ALL.
But actually ...
He's really kinda...

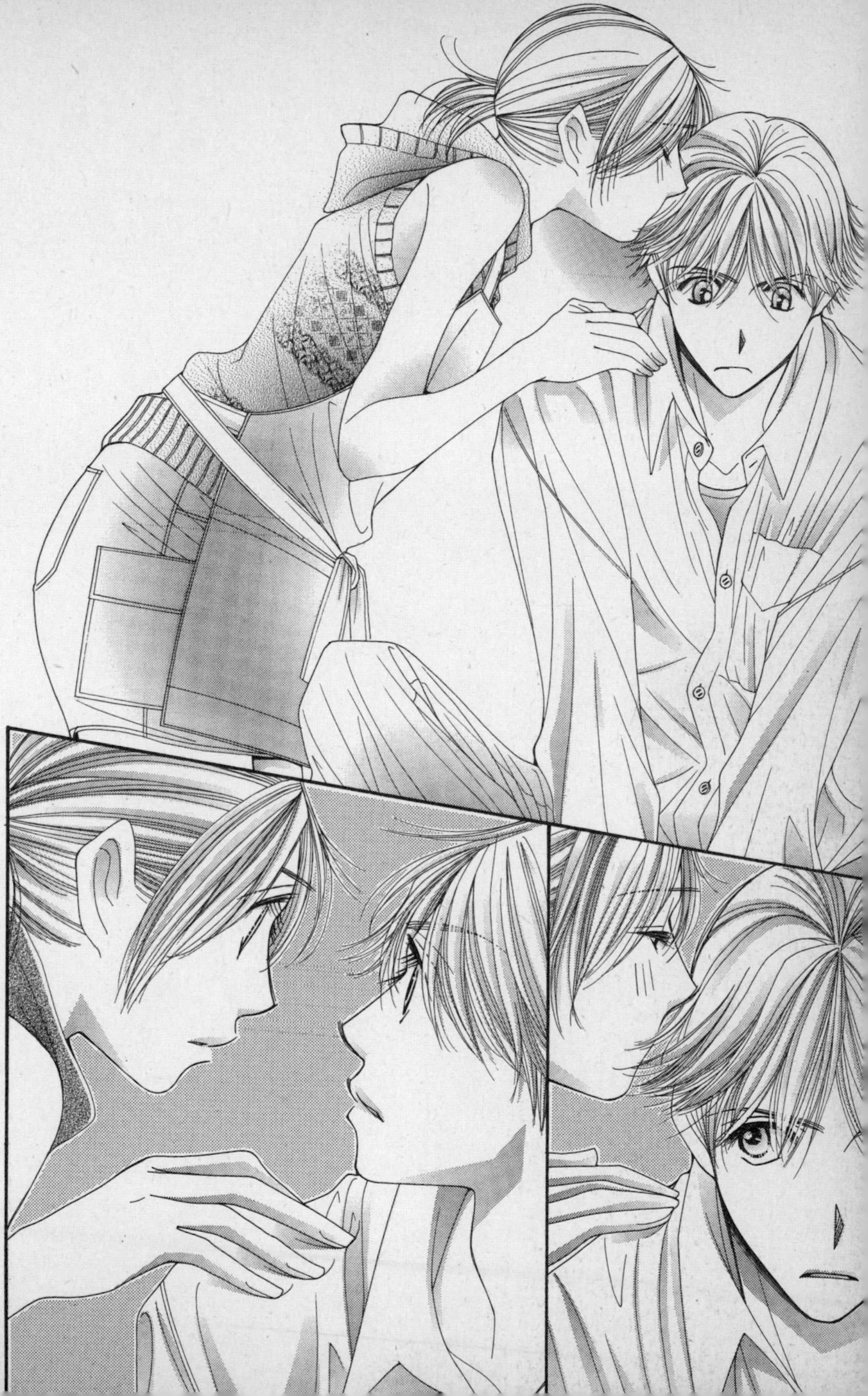

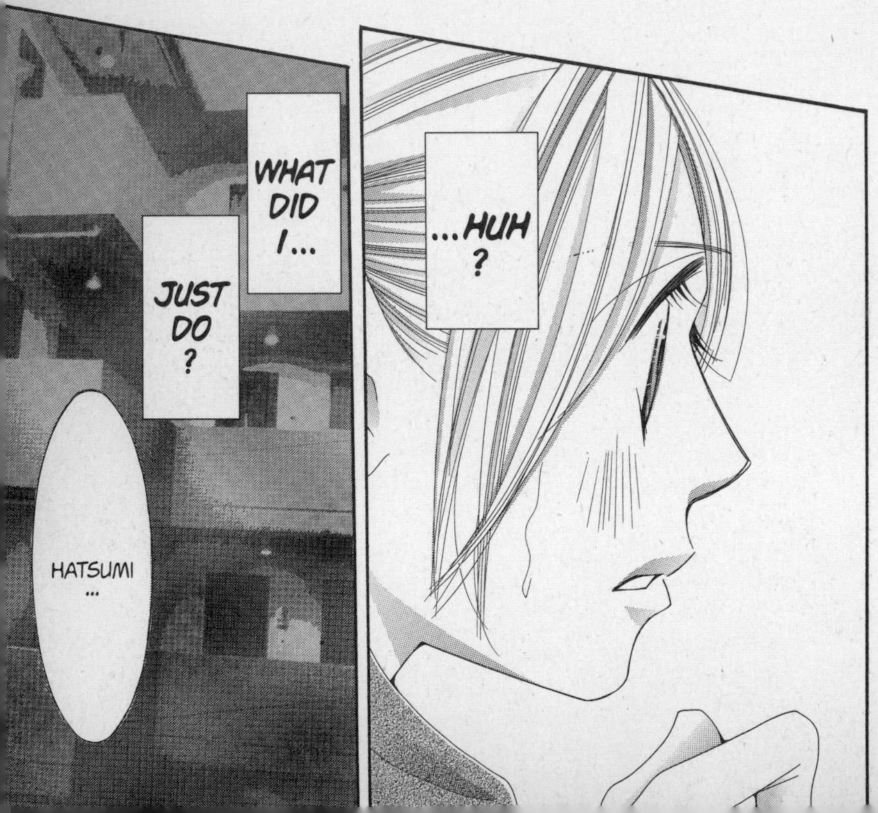
...HUH?
WHAT DID I...
JUST DO?
HATSUMI...

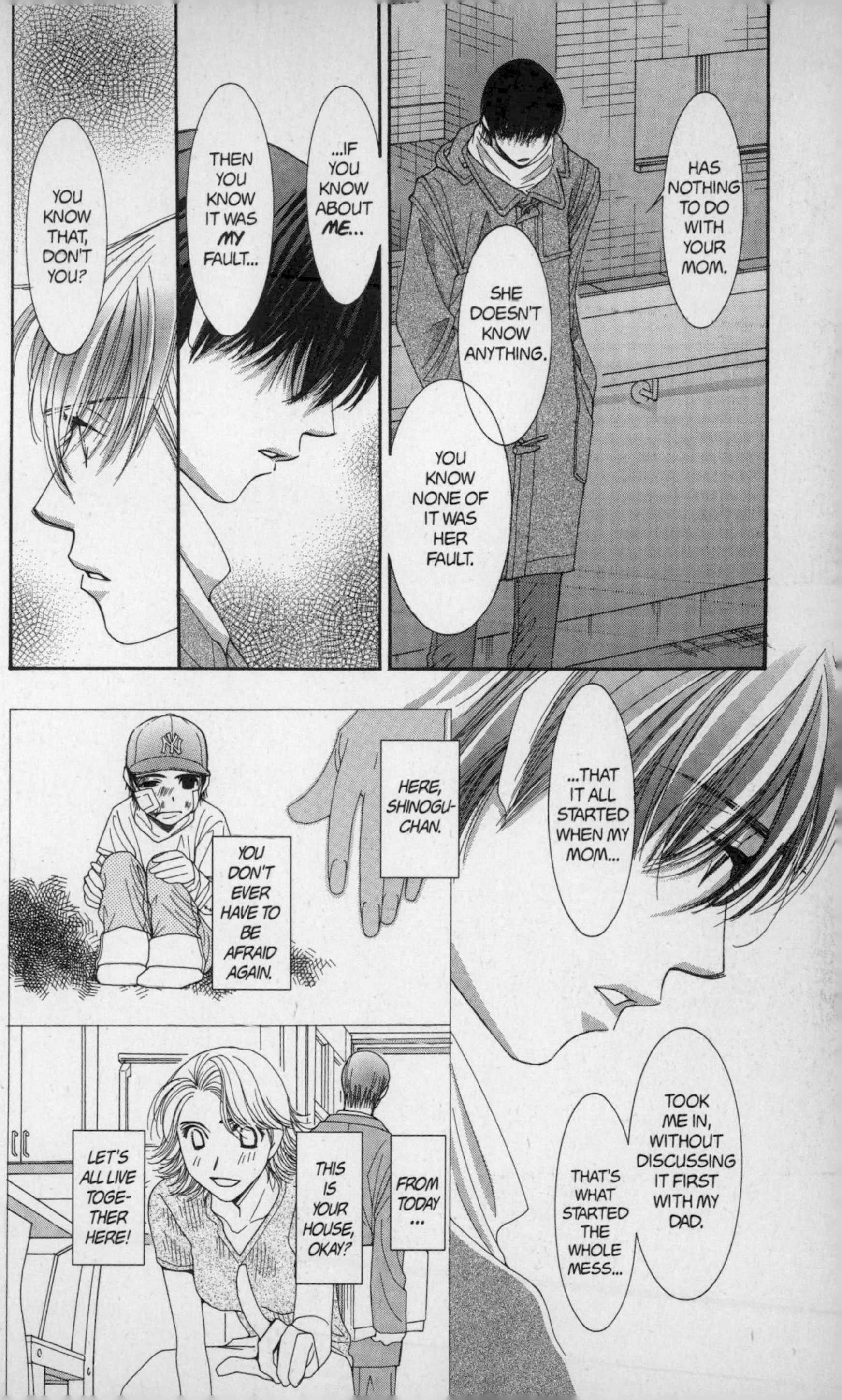
HAS NOTHING TO DO WITH YOUR MOM.
SHE DOESN'T KNOW ANYTHING.
YOU KNOW NONE OF IT WAS HER FAULT.
...IF YOU KNOW ABOUT ME...
THEN YOU KNOW IT WAS MY FAULT...
YOU KNOW THAT, DON'T YOU?
...THAT IT ALL STARTED WHEN MY MOM...
TOOK ME IN, WITHOUT DISCUSSING IT FIRST WITH MY DAD.
THAT'S WHAT STARTED THE WHOLE MESS...
HERE, SHINOGU-CHAN.
YOU DON'T EVER HAVE TO BE AFRAID AGAIN.
FROM TODAY...
THIS IS YOUR HOUSE, OKAY?
LET'S ALL LIVE TOGE-THER HERE!

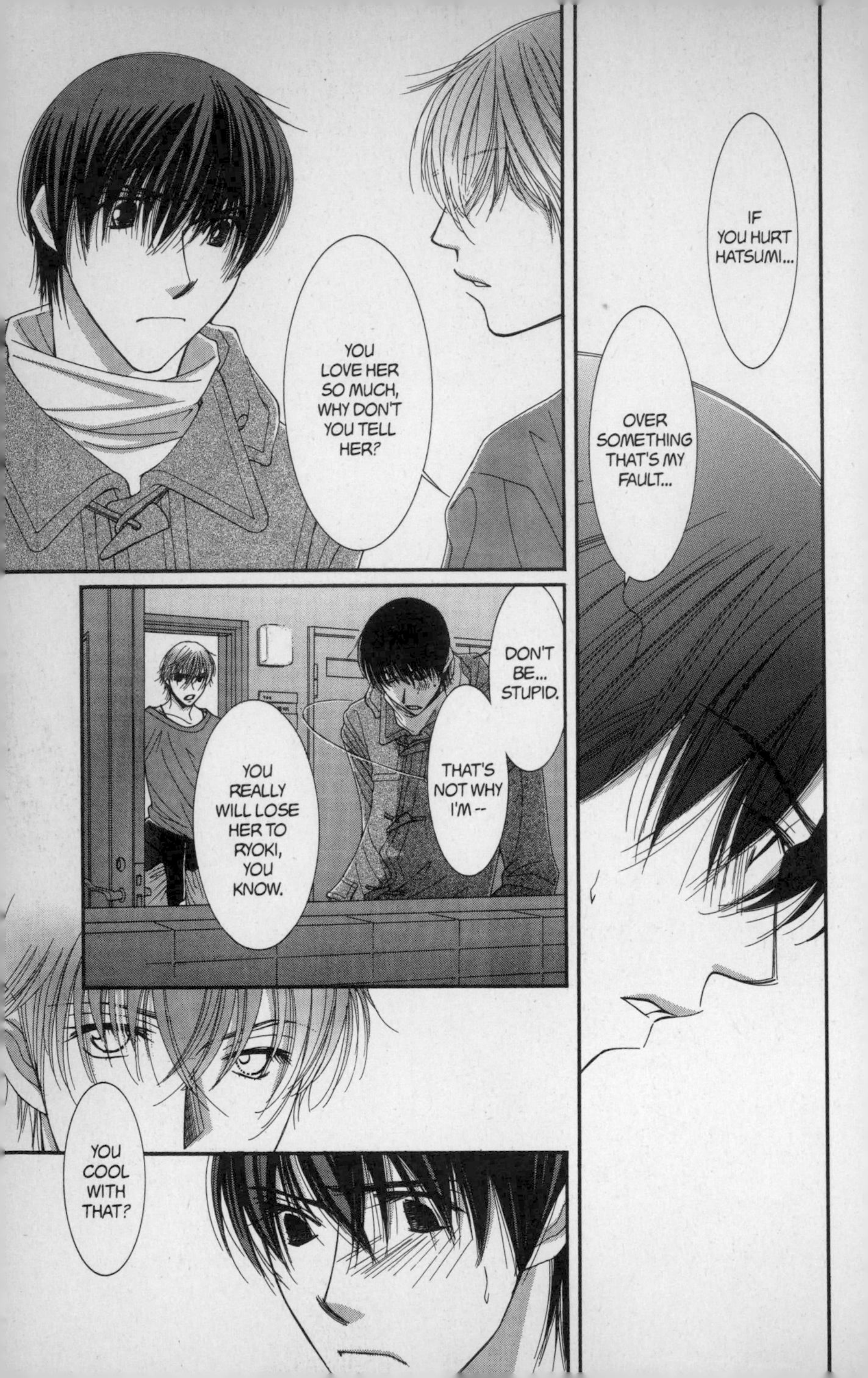
IF YOU HURT HATSUMI...
OVER SOMETHING THAT'S MY FAULT...
YOU LOVE HER SO MUCH, WHY DON'T YOU TELL HER?
DON'T BE... STUPID.
THAT'S NOT WHY I'M --
YOU REALLY WILL LOSE HER TO RYOKI, YOU KNOW.
YOU COOL WITH THAT?

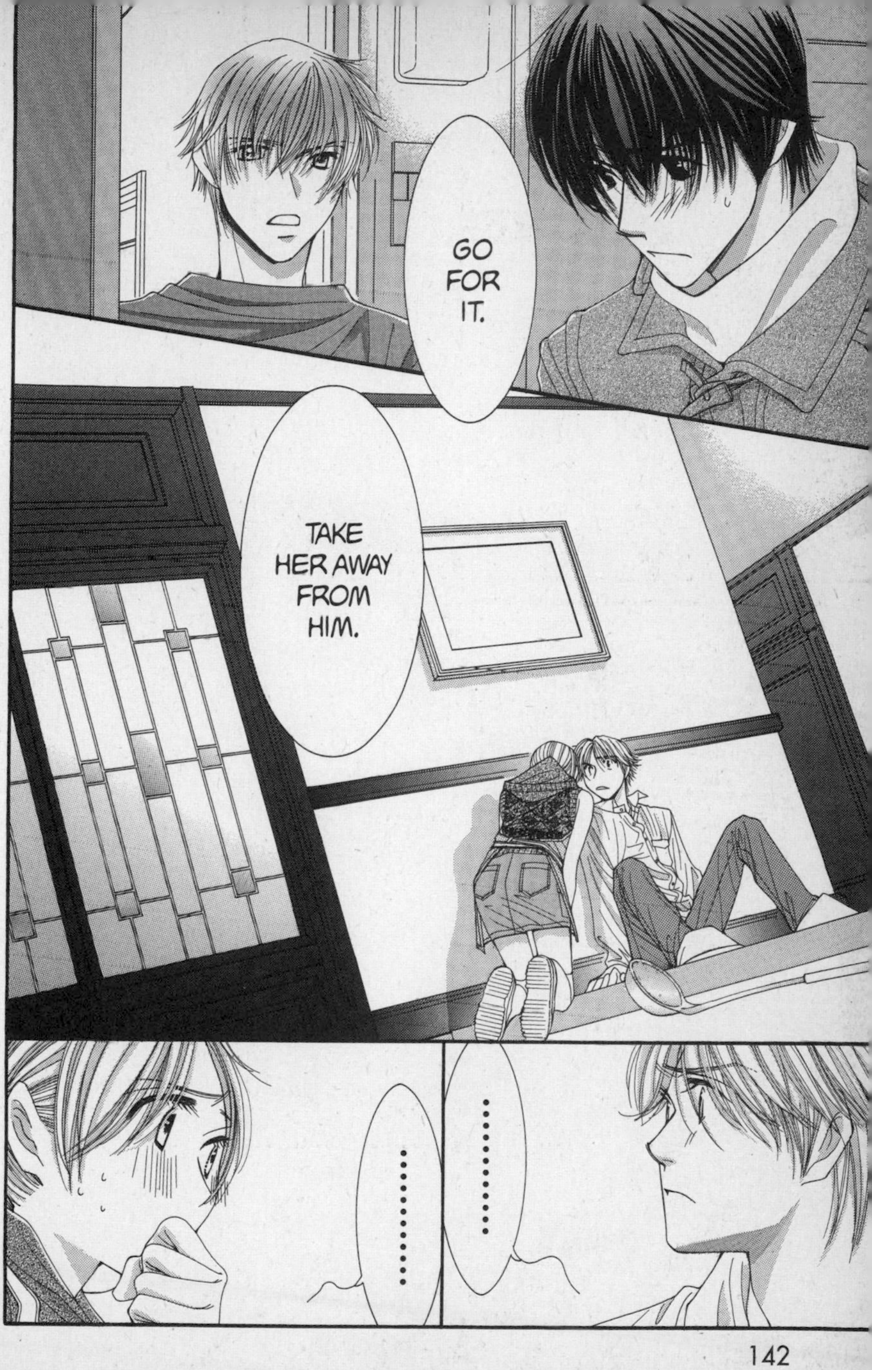
GO FOR IT.
TAKE HER AWAY FROM HIM.
......
......

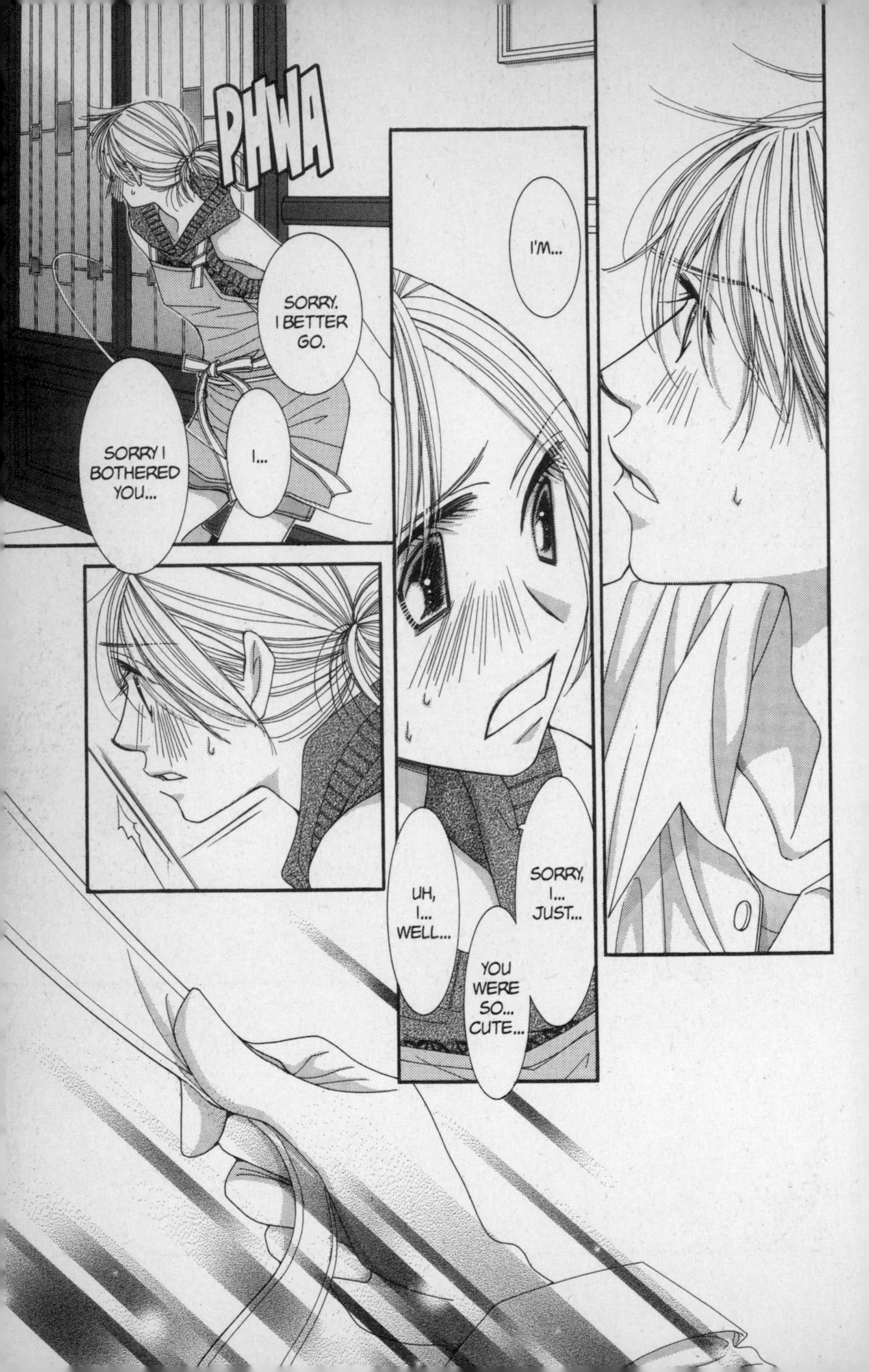
I'M...
SORRY, I... JUST...
YOU WERE SO... CUTE...
UH, I... WELL...
PHWA
SORRY. I BETTER GO.
I...
SORRY I BOTHERED YOU...

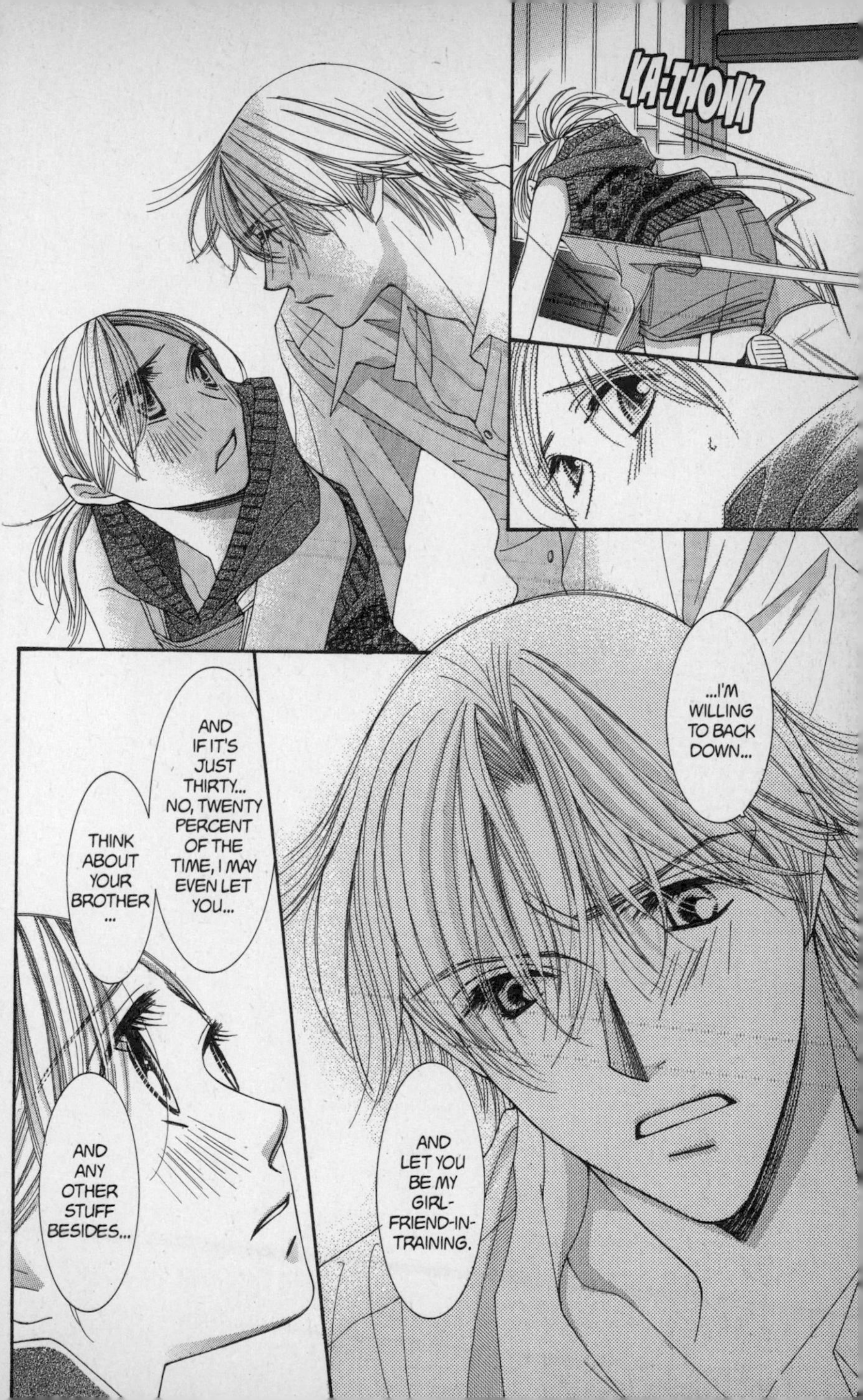
KA-THONK
...I'M WILLING TO BACK DOWN...
AND LET YOU BE MY GIRL-FRIEND-IN-TRAINING.
AND IF IT'S JUST THIRTY... NO, TWENTY PERCENT OF THE TIME, I MAY EVEN LET YOU...
THINK ABOUT YOUR BROTHER...
AND ANY OTHER STUFF BESIDES...

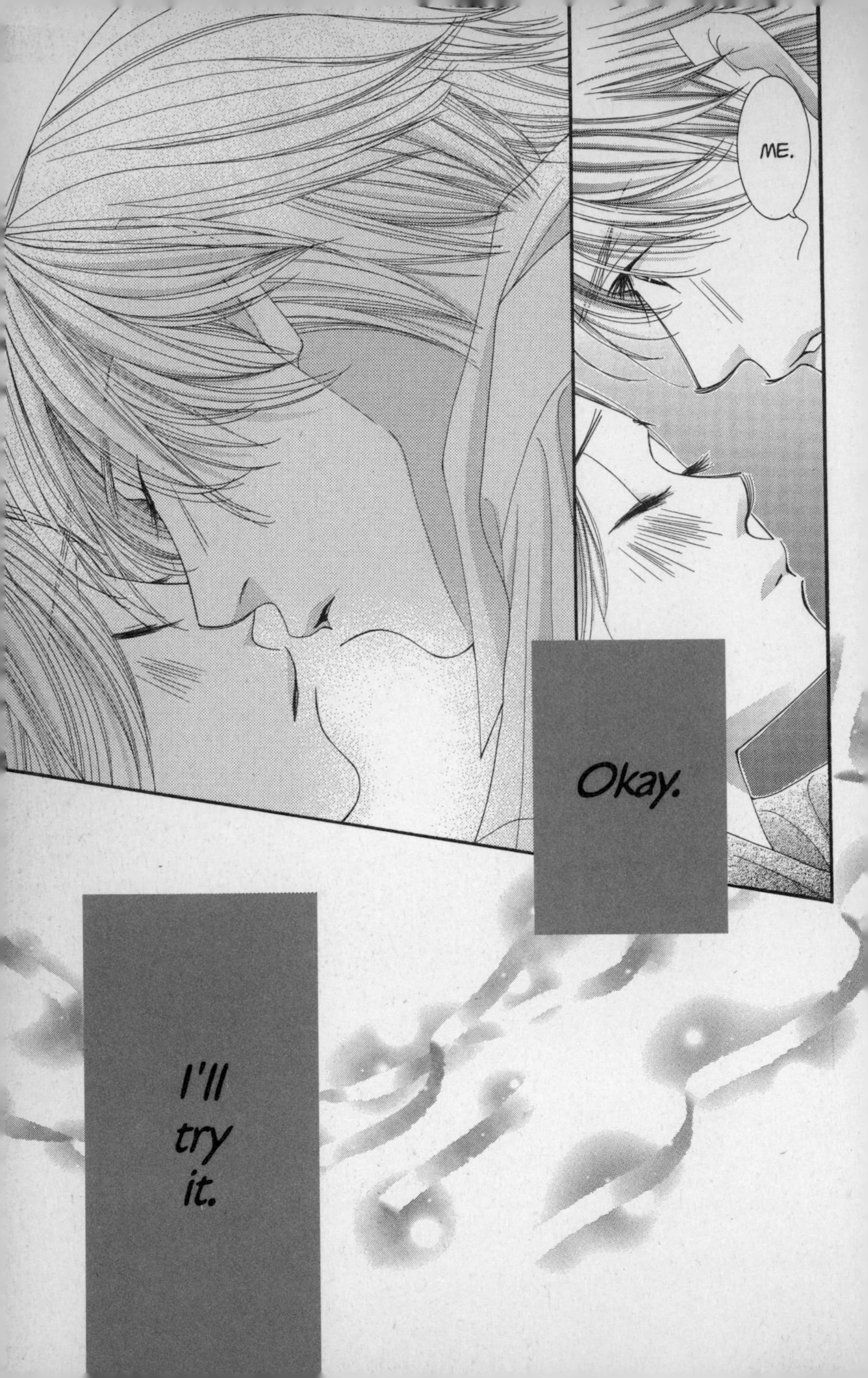
ME.
Okay.
I'll try it.

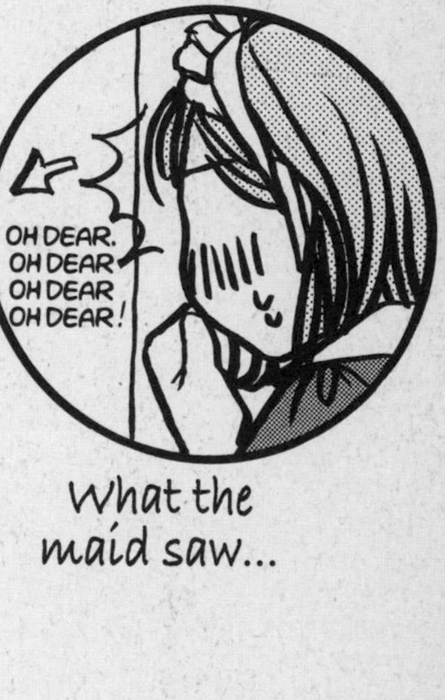
OH DEAR.
OH DEAR
OH DEAR
OH DEAR!

What the maid saw...

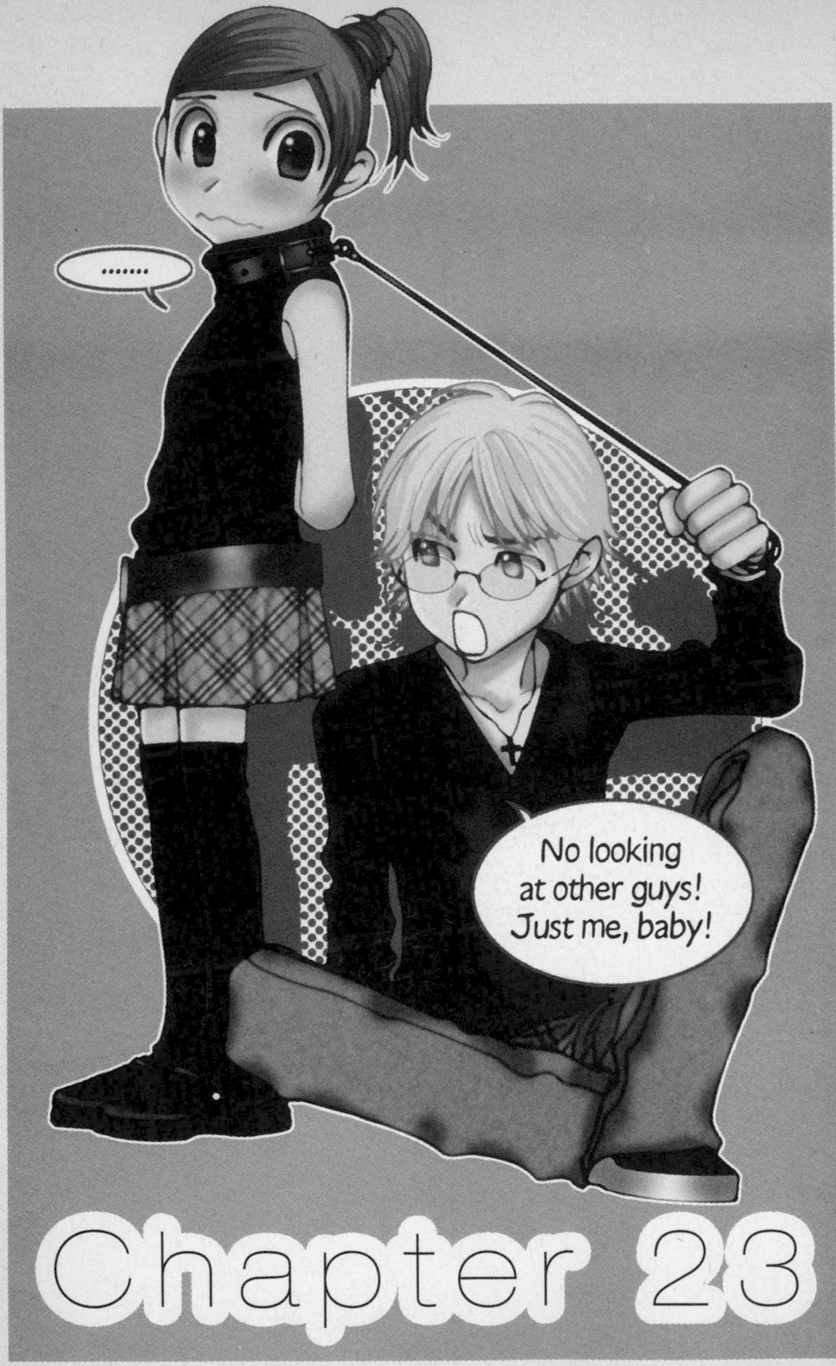
....
No looking at other guys! Just me, baby!
Chapter 23

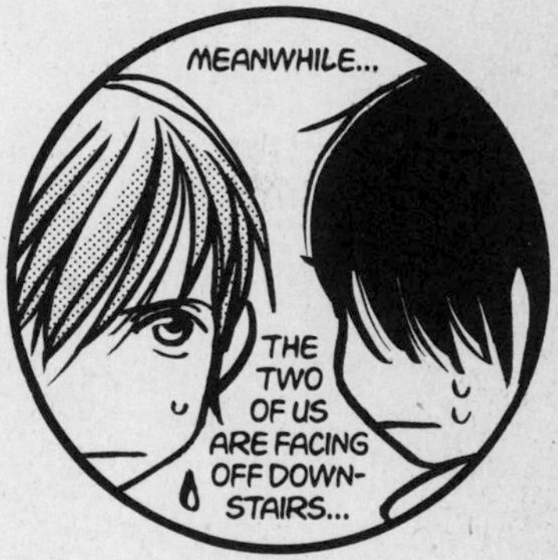
MEANWHILE...
THE TWO OF US ARE FACING OFF DOWN-STAIRS...

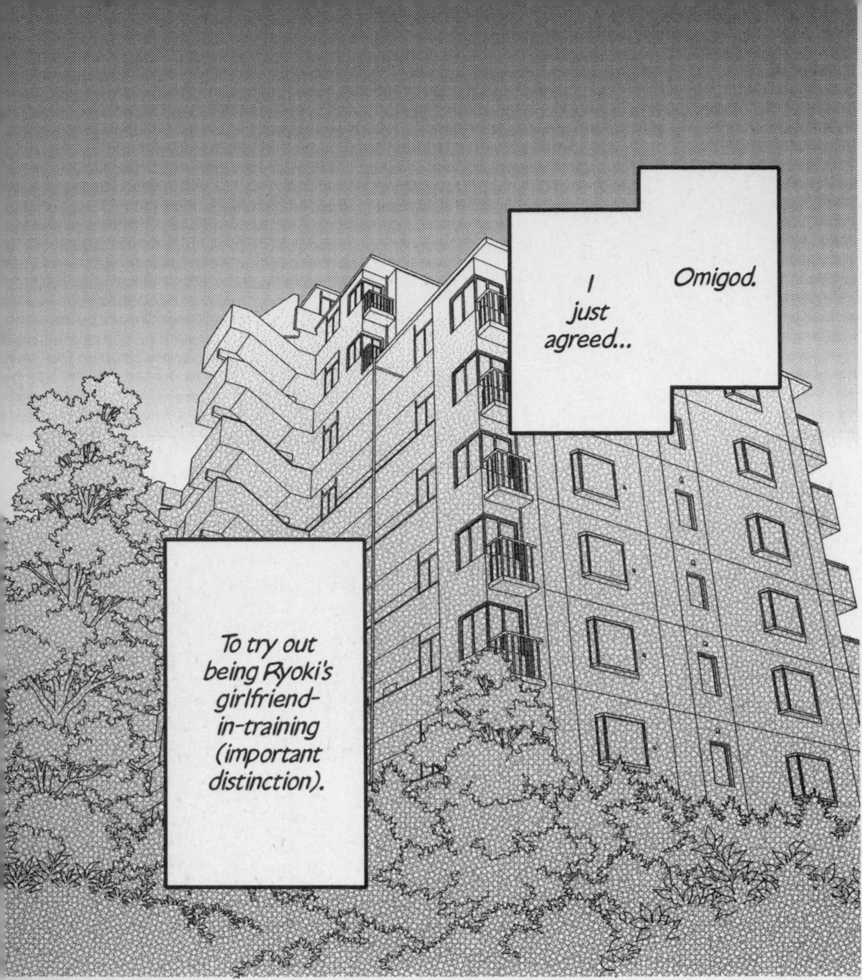
Omigod.
I just agreed...
To try out being Ryoki's girlfriend-in-training (important distinction).

hot gimmick

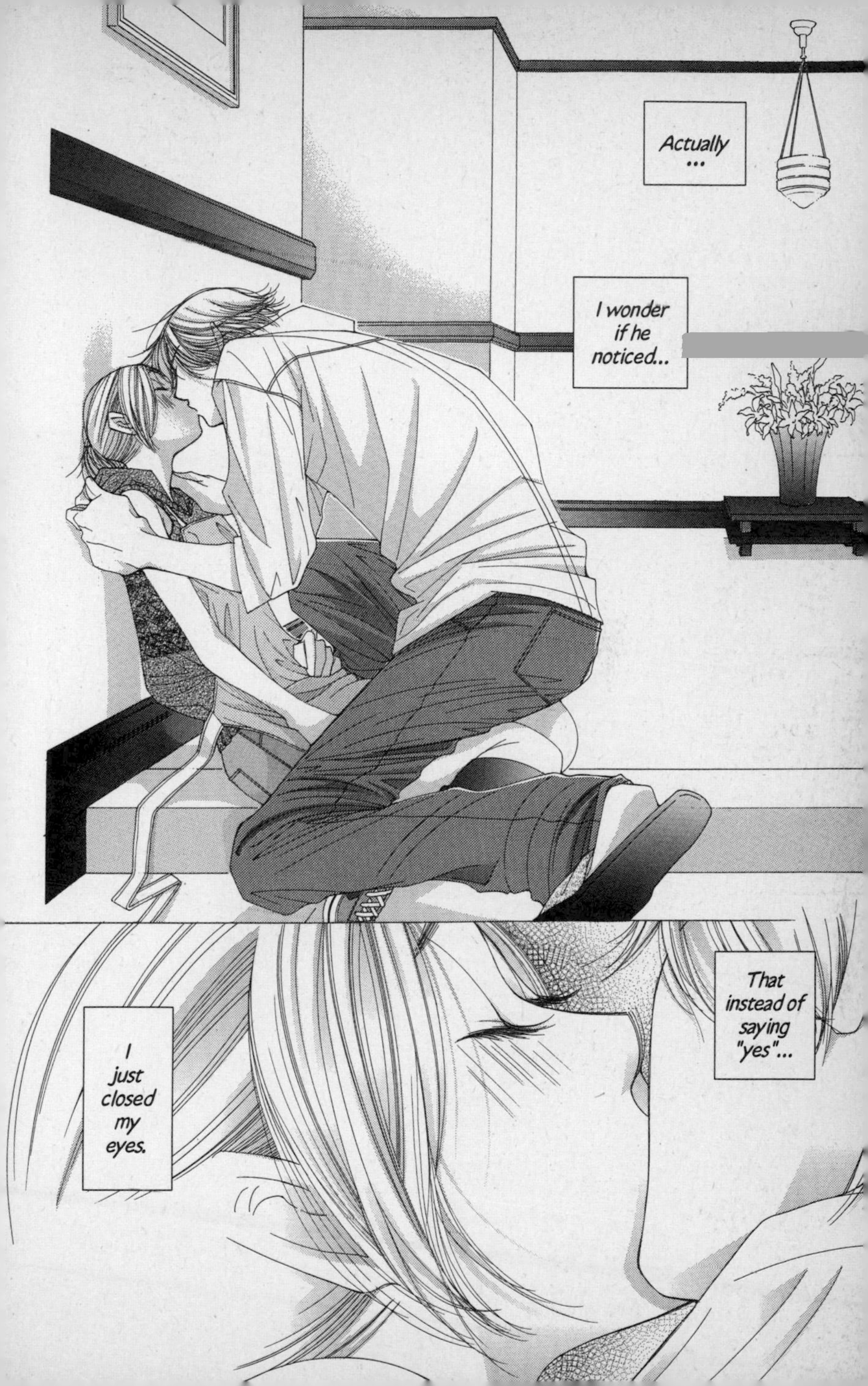

Actually...
I wonder if he noticed...
That instead of saying "yes"...
I just closed my eyes.

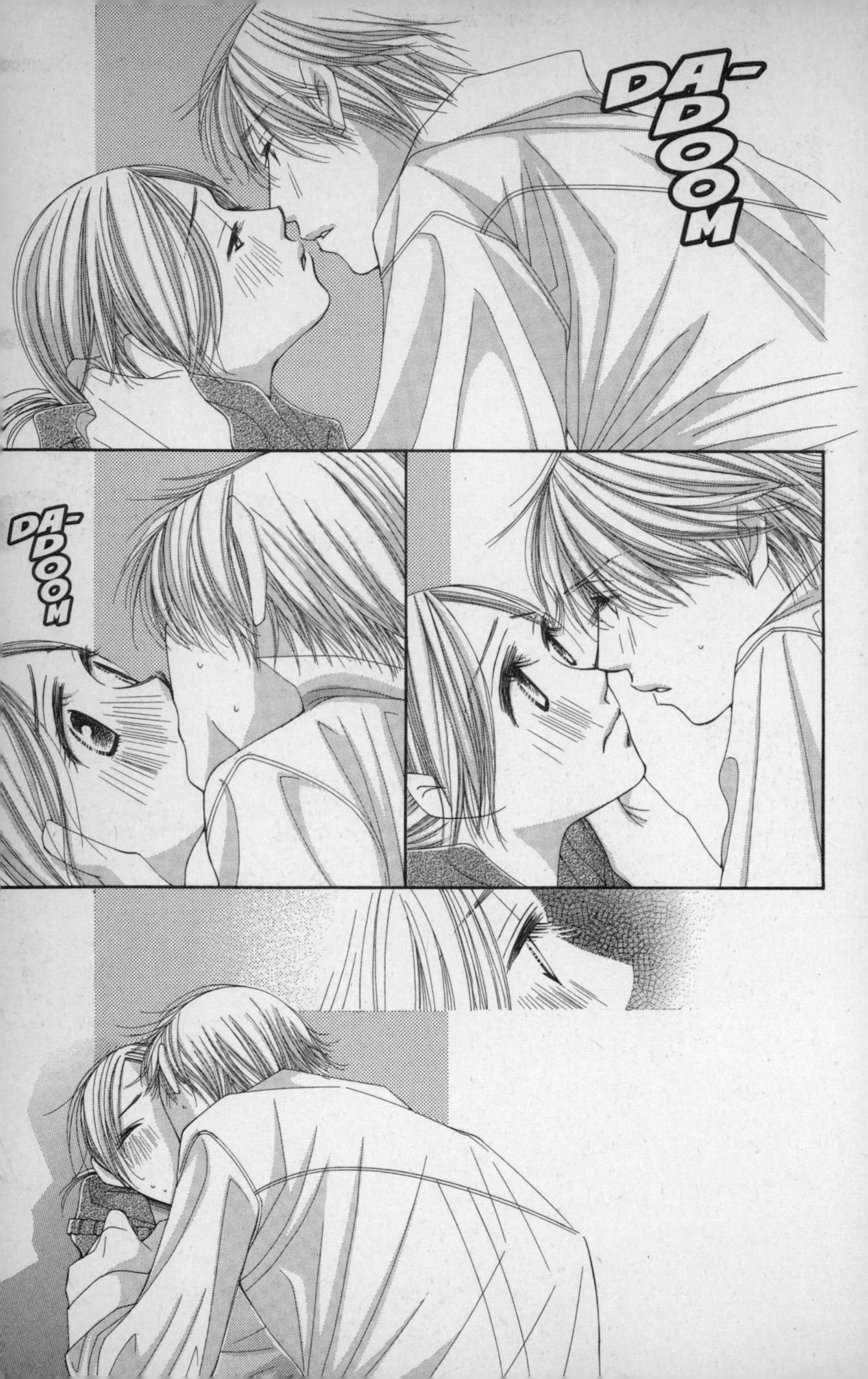
DA-DOOM
DA-DOOM

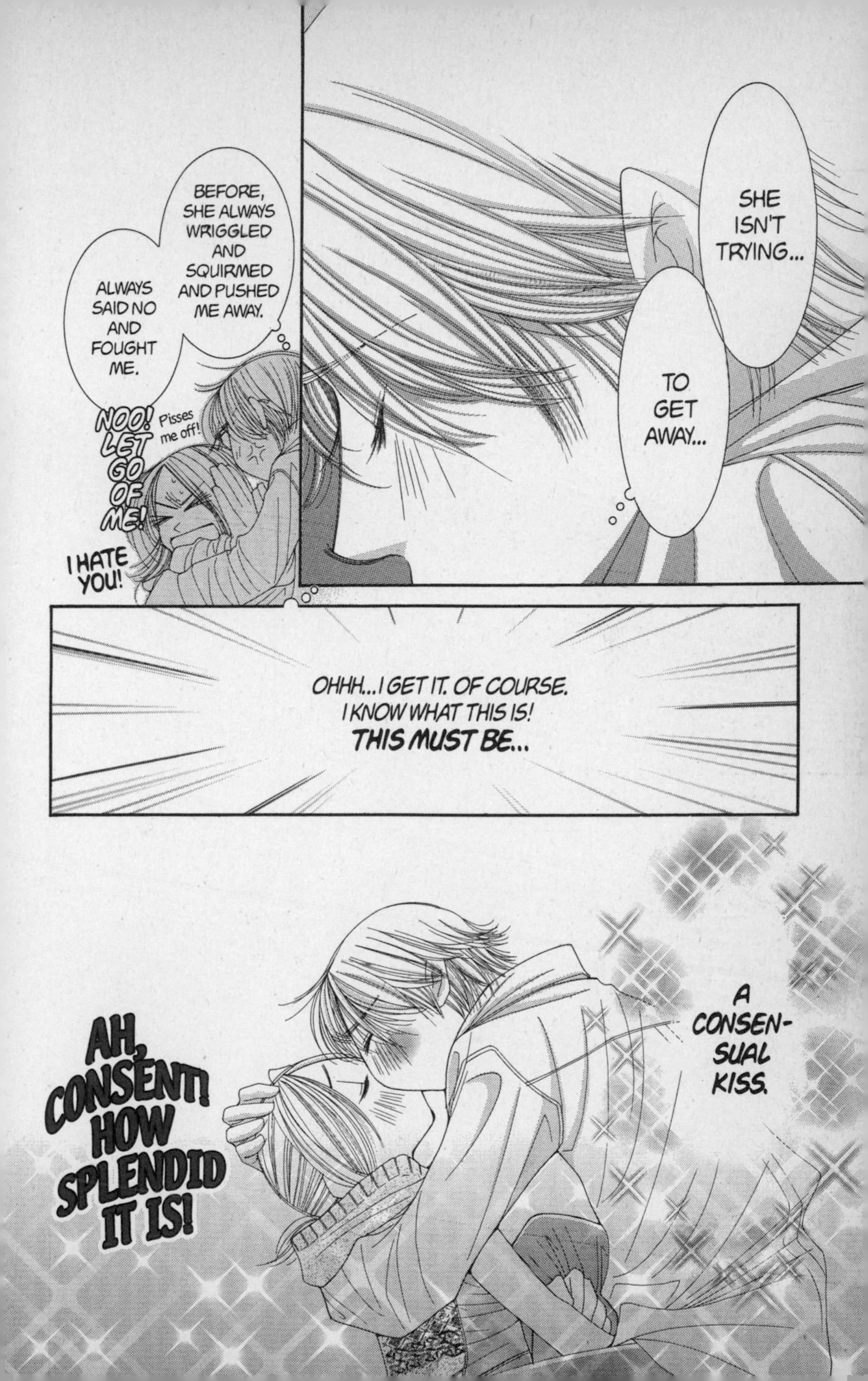
SHE ISN'T TRYING...
TO GET AWAY...
BEFORE, SHE ALWAYS WRIGGLED AND SQUIRMED AND PUSHED ME AWAY.
ALWAYS SAID NO AND FOUGHT ME.
Pisses me off!
NOO! LET GO OF ME!
I HATE YOU!
OHHH...I GET IT. OF COURSE. I KNOW WHAT THIS IS! THIS MUST BE...
A CONSEN-SUAL KISS.
AH, CONSENT! HOW SPLENDID IT IS!

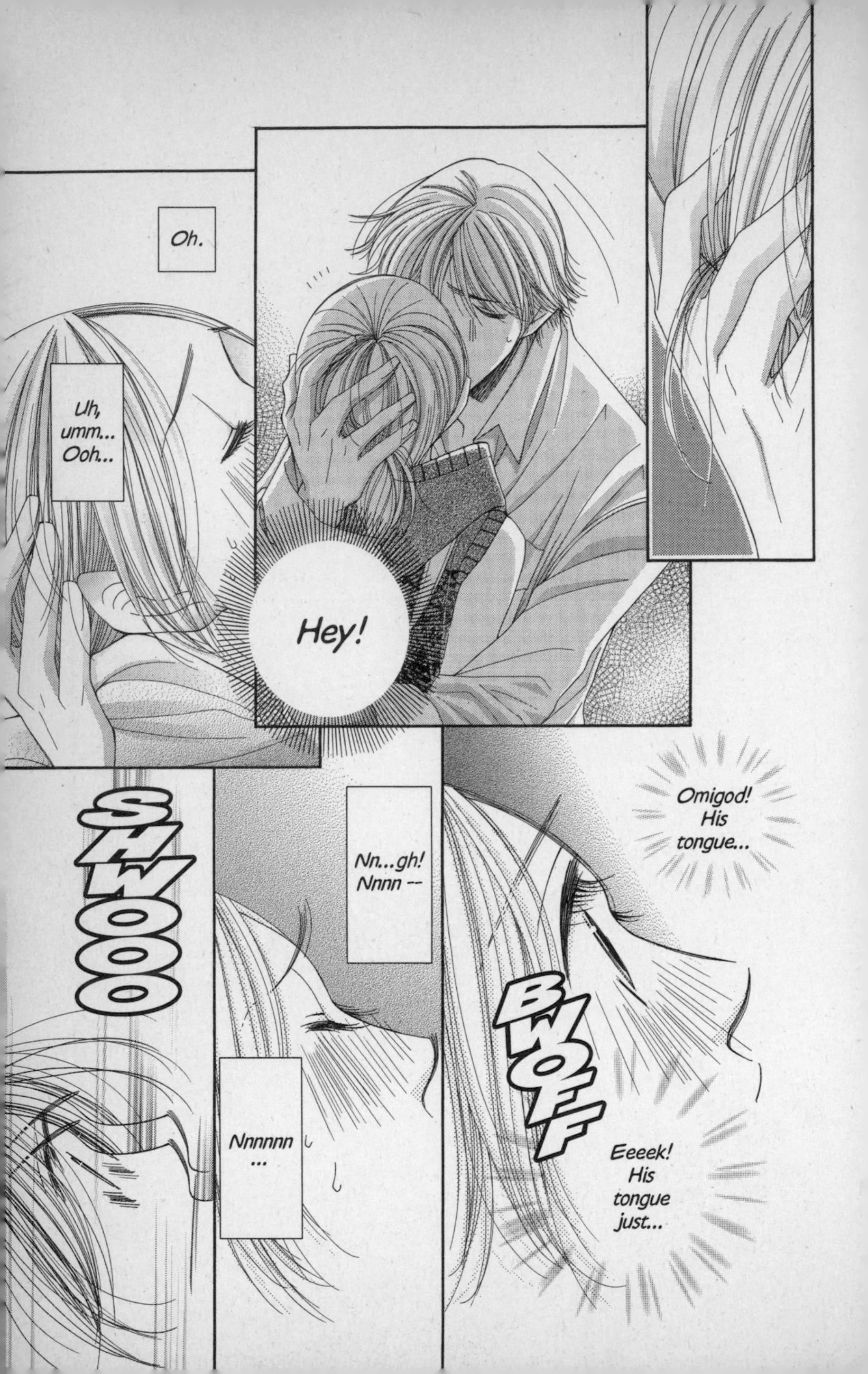
Hey!
Oh.
Uh, umm... Ooh...
Omigod! His tongue...
BWOFF
Eeeek! His tongue just...
Nn...gh! Nnnn --
Nnnnnn ...
SHWOOO

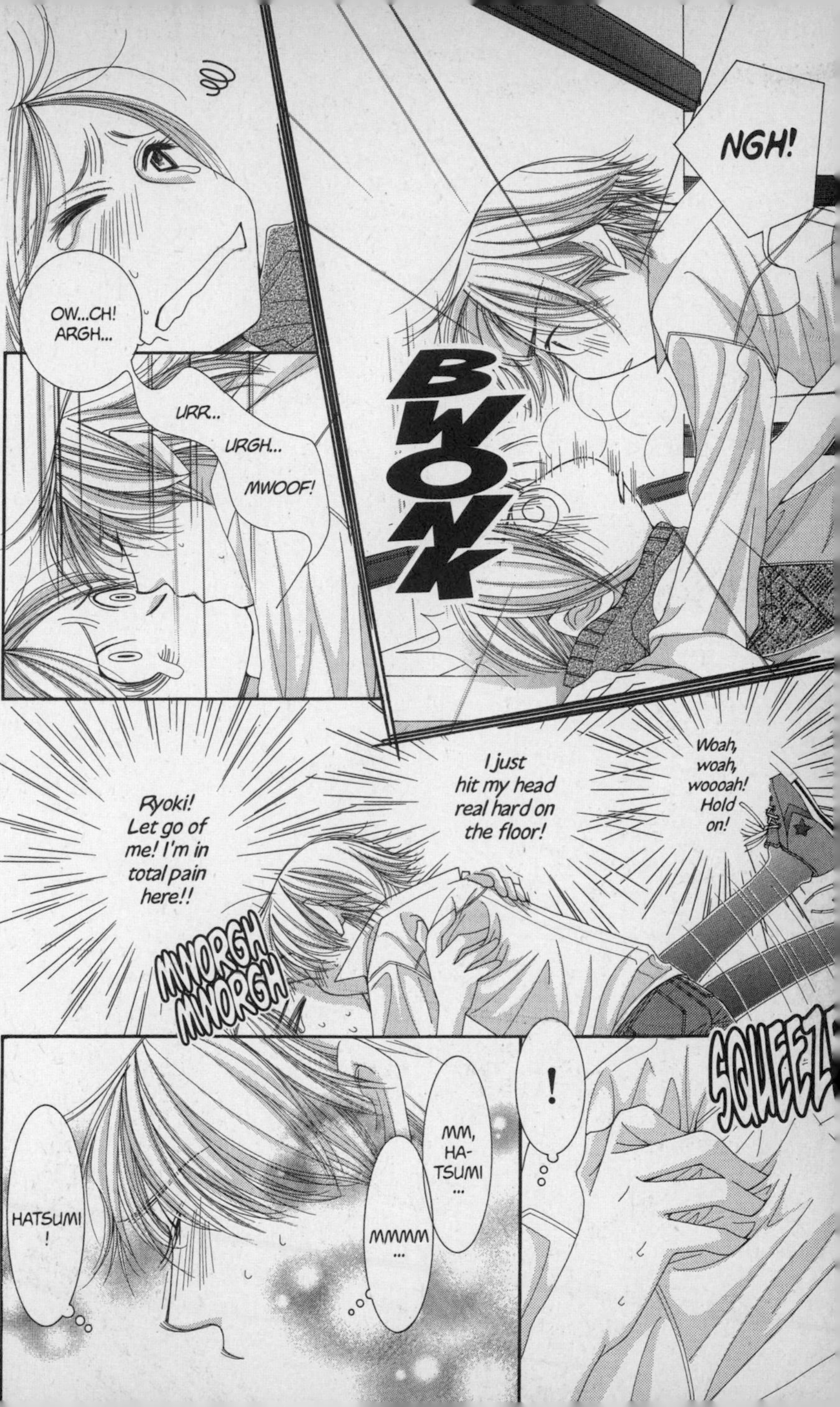
NGH!
BWONK
OW...CH! ARGH...
URR.. URGH... MWOOF!
Woah, woah, woooah! Hold on!
I just hit my head real hard on the floor!
Ryoki! Let go of me! I'm in total pain here!!
MWORGH MWORGH
SQUEEZ
!
MM, HA-TSUMI ...
MMMM ...
HATSUMI !

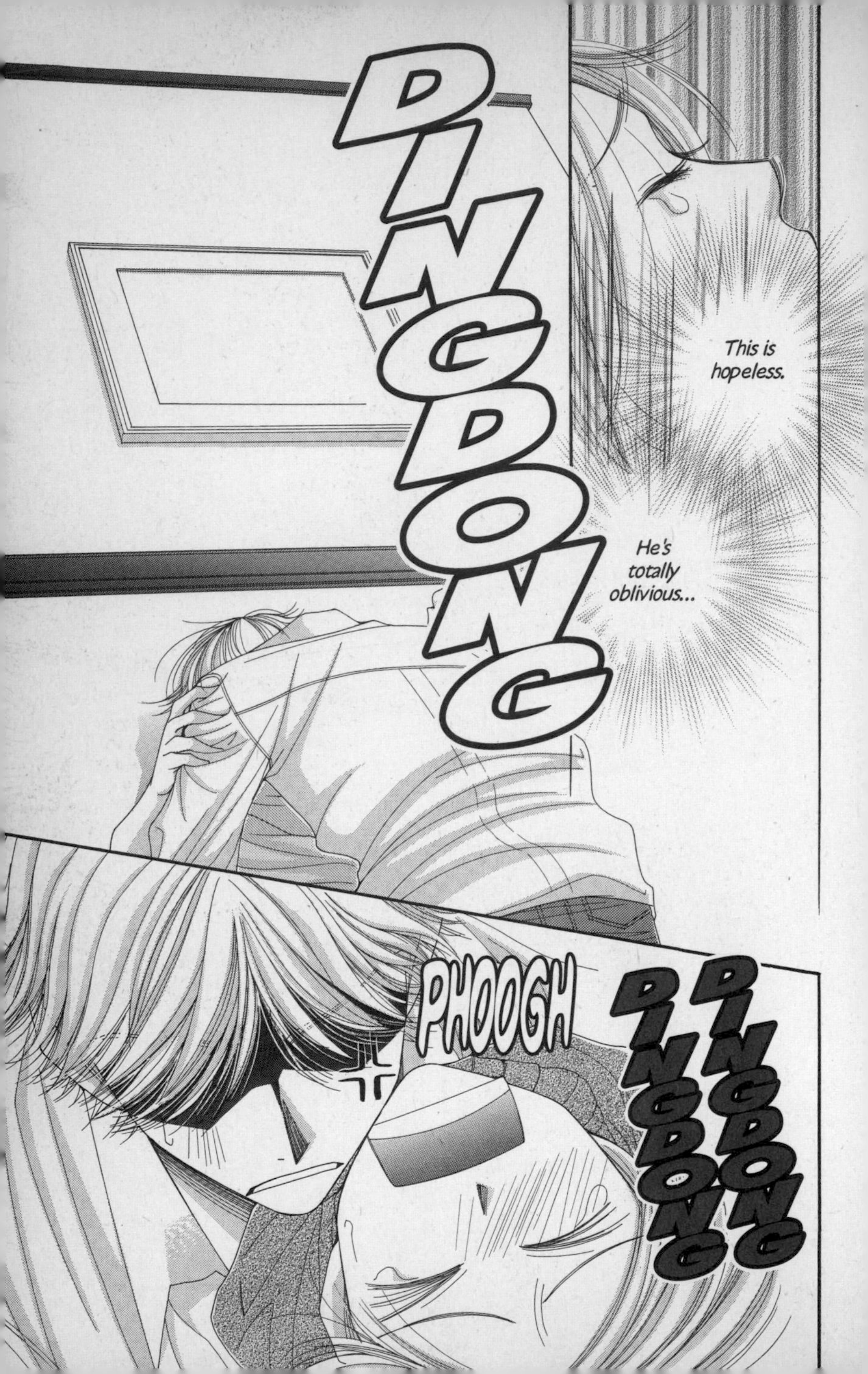
This is hopeless.
He's totally oblivious...
DINGDONG
DINGDONG
DINGDONG
PHOOGH

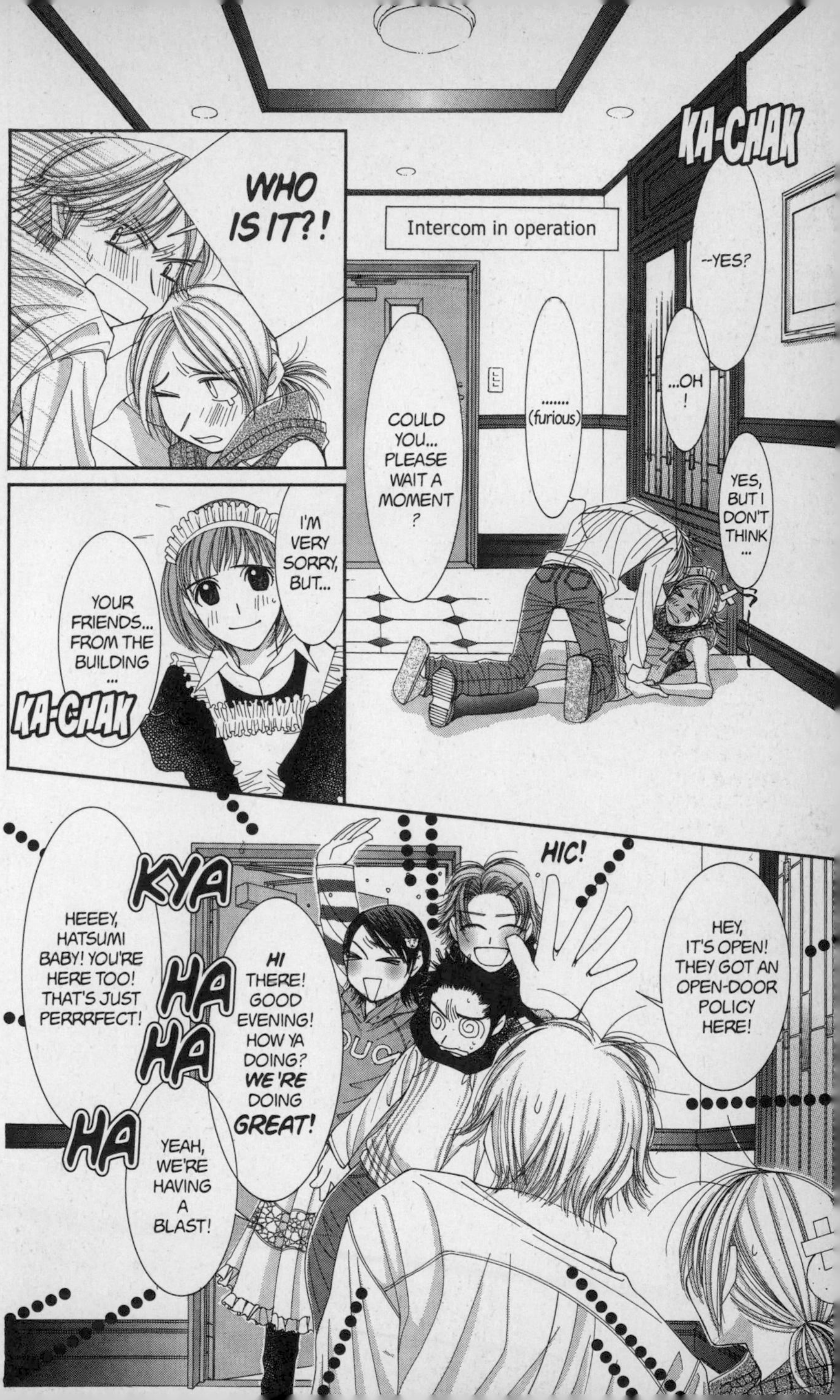
KA-CHAK
Intercom in operation
--YES?
...OH!
YES, BUT I DON'T THINK ...
.... (furious)
COULD YOU... PLEASE WAIT A MOMENT ?
WHO IS IT?!
I'M VERY SORRY, BUT...
YOUR FRIENDS... FROM THE BUILDING ...
KA-CHAK
HIC!
HEY, IT'S OPEN! THEY GOT AN OPEN-DOOR POLICY HERE!
HI THERE! GOOD EVENING! HOW YA DOING? WE'RE DOING GREAT!
KYA HA HA HA
HEEEY, HATSUMI BABY! YOU'RE HERE TOO! THAT'S JUST PERRRFECT!
YEAH, WE'RE HAVING A BLAST!

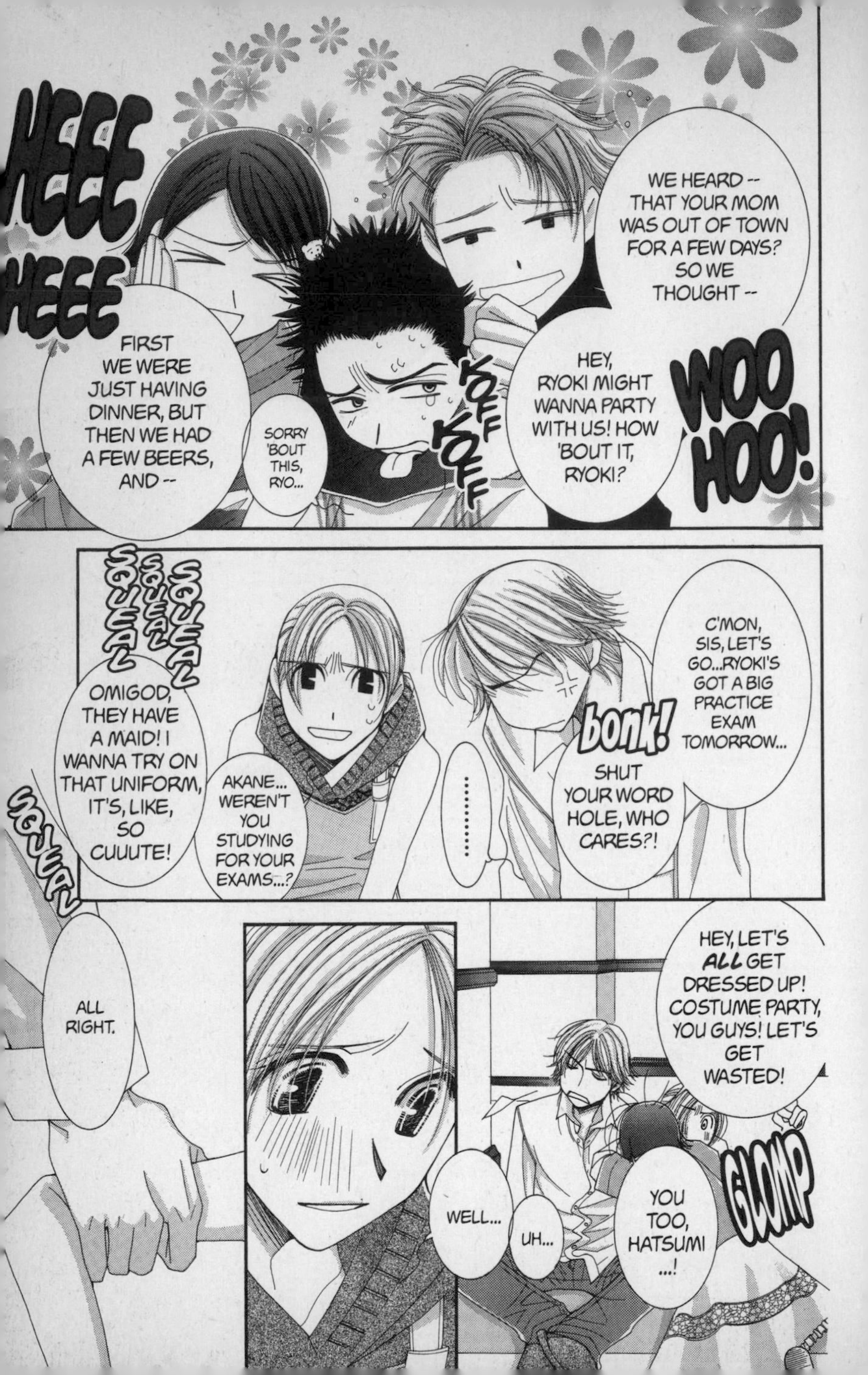
WE HEARD -- THAT YOUR MOM WAS OUT OF TOWN FOR A FEW DAYS? SO WE THOUGHT --
WOO HOO!
HEY, RYOKI MIGHT WANNA PARTY WITH US! HOW 'BOUT IT, RYOKI?
KOFF KOFF
SORRY 'BOUT THIS, RYO...
FIRST WE WERE JUST HAVING DINNER, BUT THEN WE HAD A FEW BEERS, AND --
HEEE HEEE
C'MON, SIS, LET'S GO...RYOKI'S GOT A BIG PRACTICE EXAM TOMORROW...
bonk!
SHUT YOUR WORD HOLE, WHO CARES?!
....
AKANE... WEREN'T YOU STUDYING FOR YOUR EXAMS...?
SQUEAL SQUEAL SQUEAL
OMIGOD, THEY HAVE A MAID! I WANNA TRY ON THAT UNIFORM, IT'S, LIKE, SO CUUUTE!
SQUEAL
HEY, LET'S ALL GET DRESSED UP! COSTUME PARTY, YOU GUYS! LET'S GET WASTED!
GLOMP
YOU TOO, HATSUMI ...!
UH...
WELL...
ALL RIGHT.

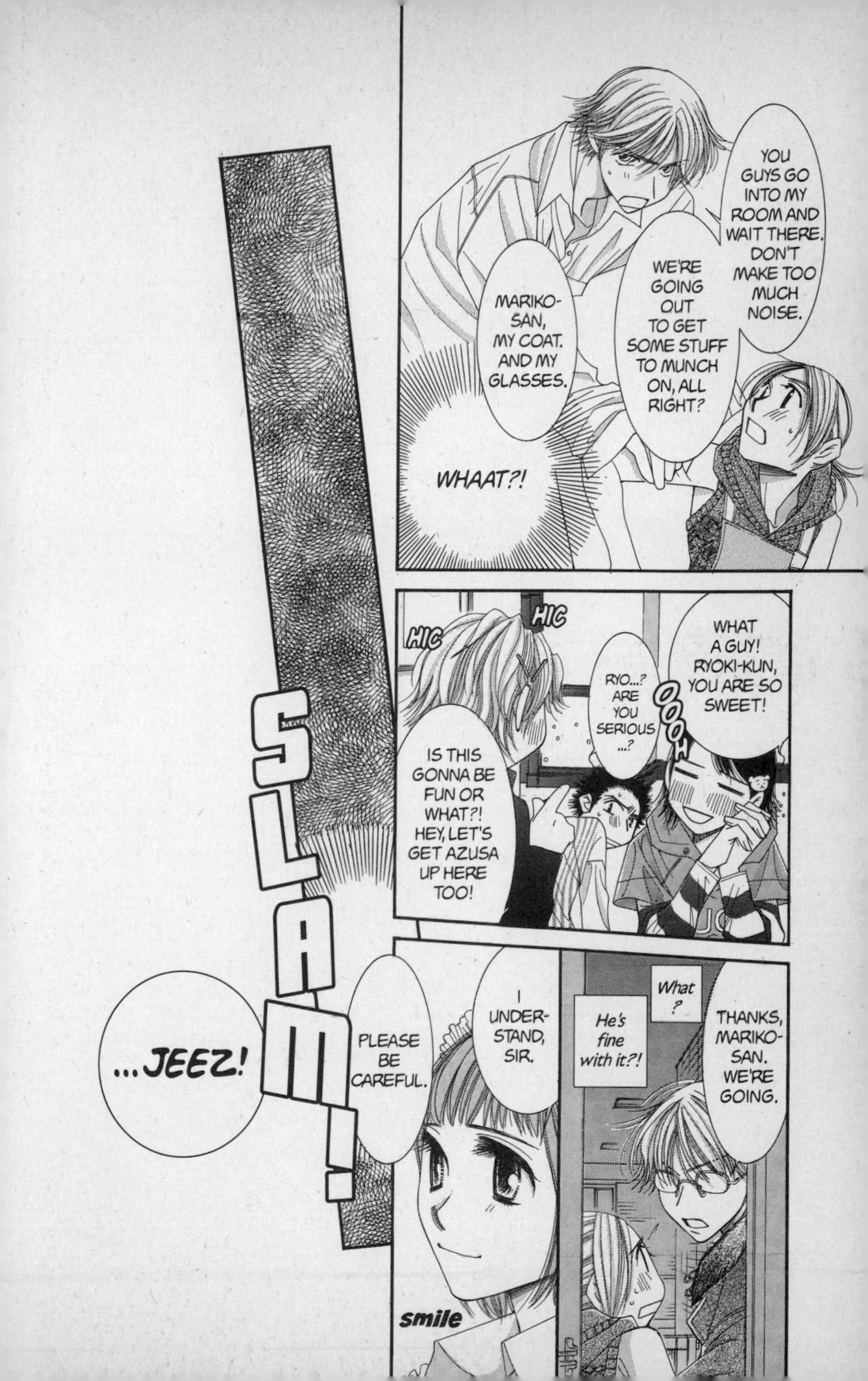

YOU GUYS GO INTO MY ROOM AND WAIT THERE. DON'T MAKE TOO MUCH NOISE.
WE'RE GOING OUT TO GET SOME STUFF TO MUNCH ON, ALL RIGHT?
MARIKO-SAN, MY COAT. AND MY GLASSES.
WHAAT?!
WHAT A GUY! RYOKI-KUN, YOU ARE SO SWEET!
OOOH
RYO...? ARE YOU SERIOUS ...?
HIC
HIC
IS THIS GONNA BE FUN OR WHAT?! HEY, LET'S GET AZUSA UP HERE TOO!
THANKS, MARIKO-SAN. WE'RE GOING.
What?
He's fine with it?!
I UNDER-STAND, SIR.
PLEASE BE CAREFUL.
smile
SLAM!
...JEEZ!

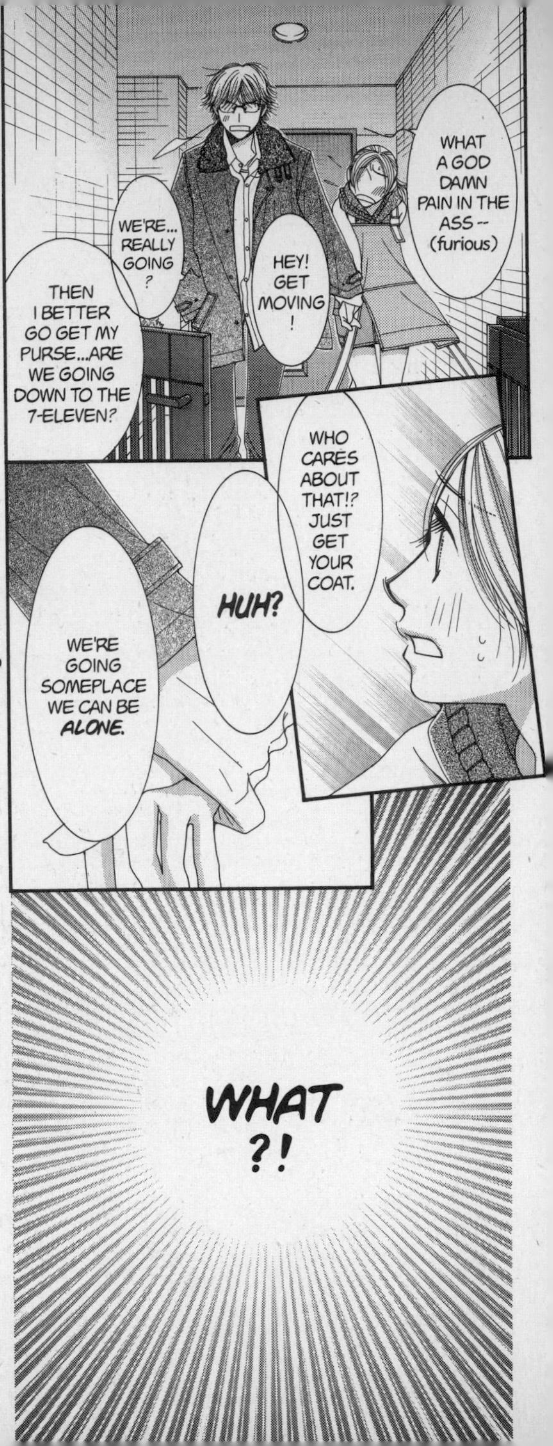
WHAT A GOD DAMN PAIN IN THE ASS -- (furious)
HEY! GET MOVING!
WE'RE... REALLY GOING?
THEN I BETTER GO GET MY PURSE...ARE WE GOING DOWN TO THE 7-ELEVEN?
WHO CARES ABOUT THAT!? JUST GET YOUR COAT.
HUH?
WE'RE GOING SOMEPLACE WE CAN BE ALONE.
WHAT?!

hotgimmick

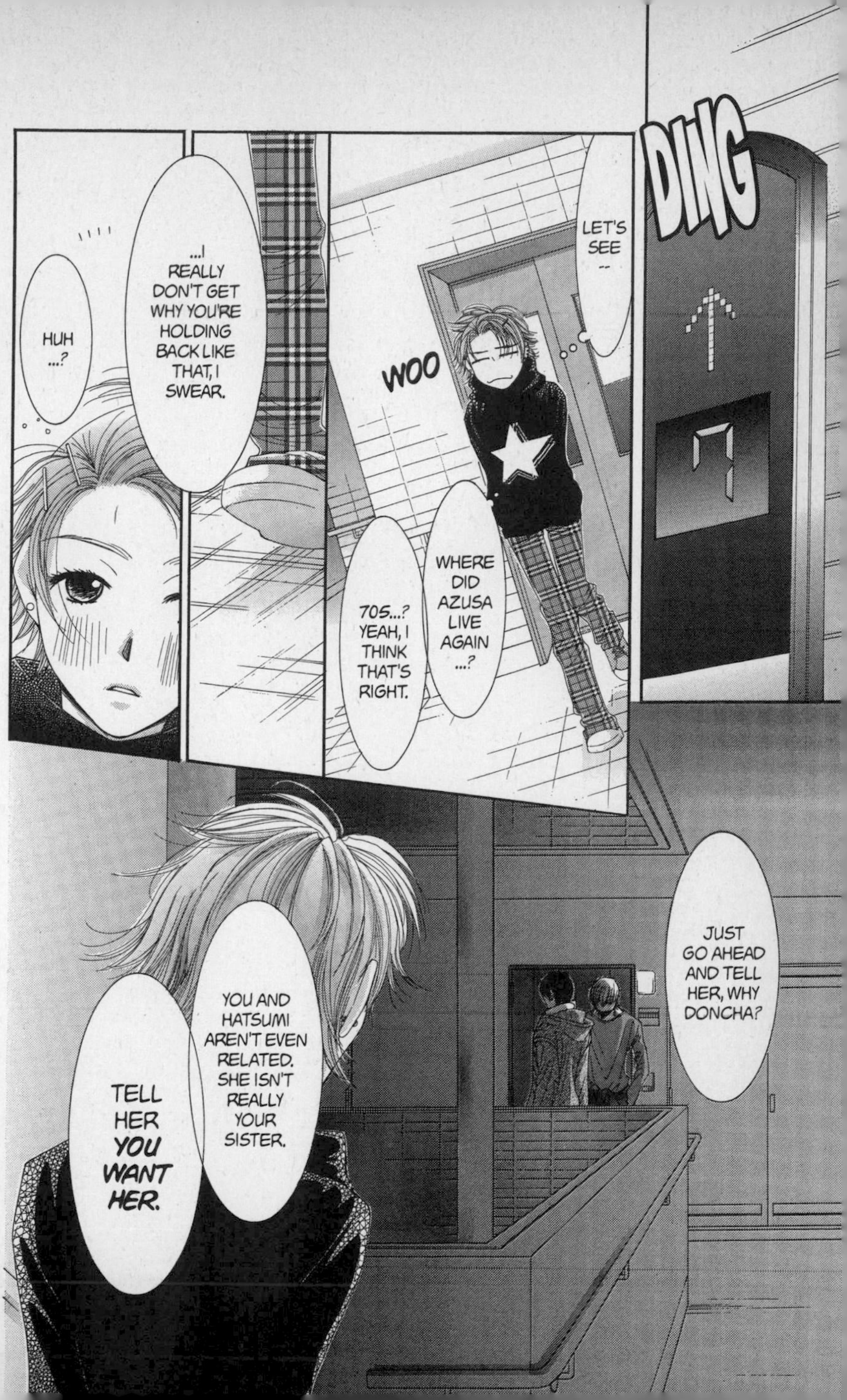
DING
LET'S SEE --
WOO
WHERE DID AZUSA LIVE AGAIN ...?
705...? YEAH, I THINK THAT'S RIGHT.
...I REALLY DON'T GET WHY YOU'RE HOLDING BACK LIKE THAT, I SWEAR.
HUH ...?
JUST GO AHEAD AND TELL HER, WHY DONCHA?
YOU AND HATSUMI AREN'T EVEN RELATED. SHE ISN'T REALLY YOUR SISTER.
TELL HER *YOU WANT* HER.

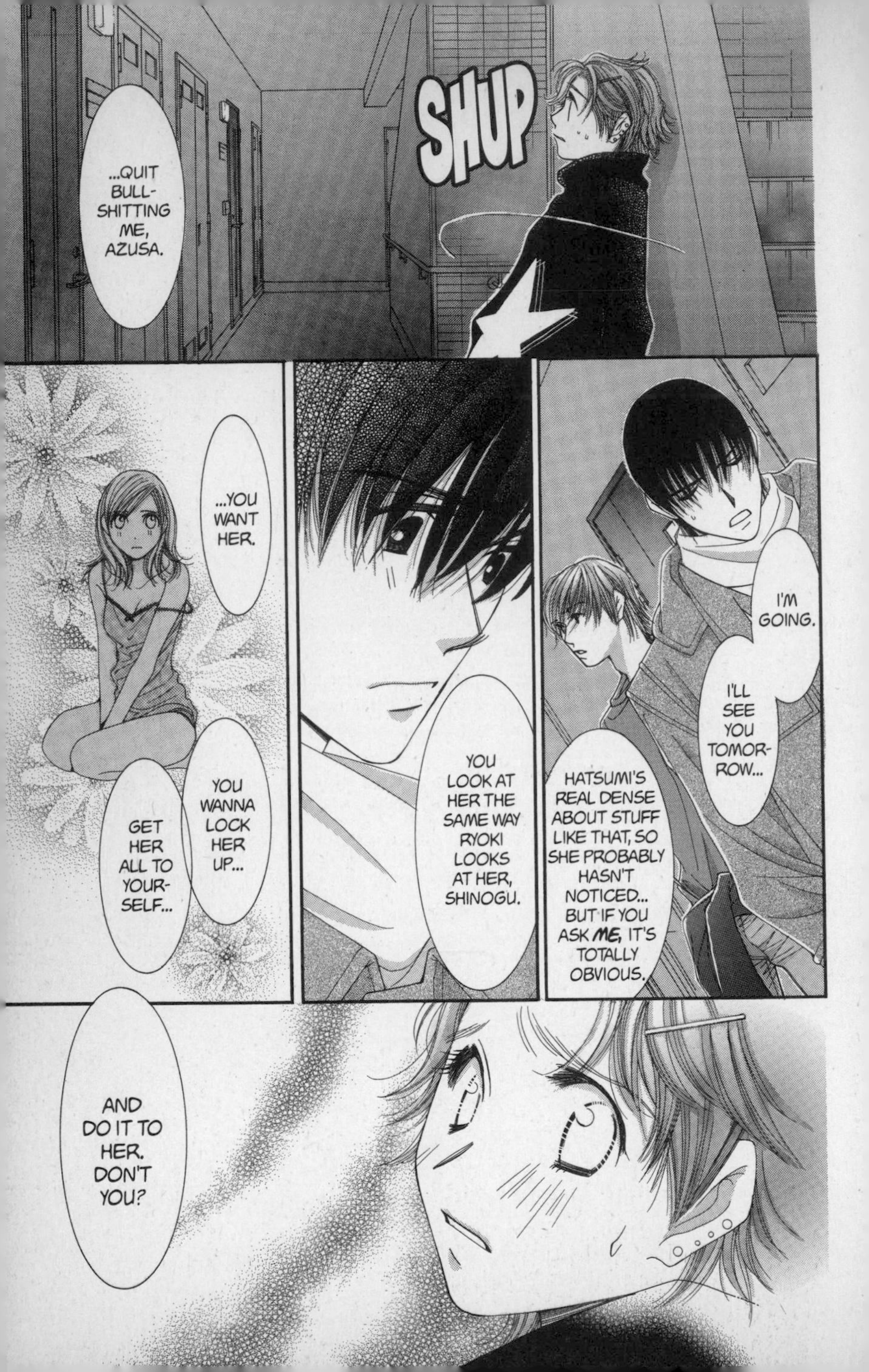
SHUP
...QUIT BULL-SHITTING ME, AZUSA.
I'M GOING.
I'LL SEE YOU TOMOR-ROW...
HATSUMI'S REAL DENSE ABOUT STUFF LIKE THAT, SO SHE PROBABLY HASN'T NOTICED... BUT IF YOU ASK *ME*, IT'S TOTALLY OBVIOUS.
YOU LOOK AT HER THE SAME WAY RYOKI LOOKS AT HER, SHINOGU.
...YOU WANT HER.
YOU WANNA LOCK HER UP...
GET HER ALL TO YOUR-SELF...
AND DO IT TO HER. DON'T YOU?

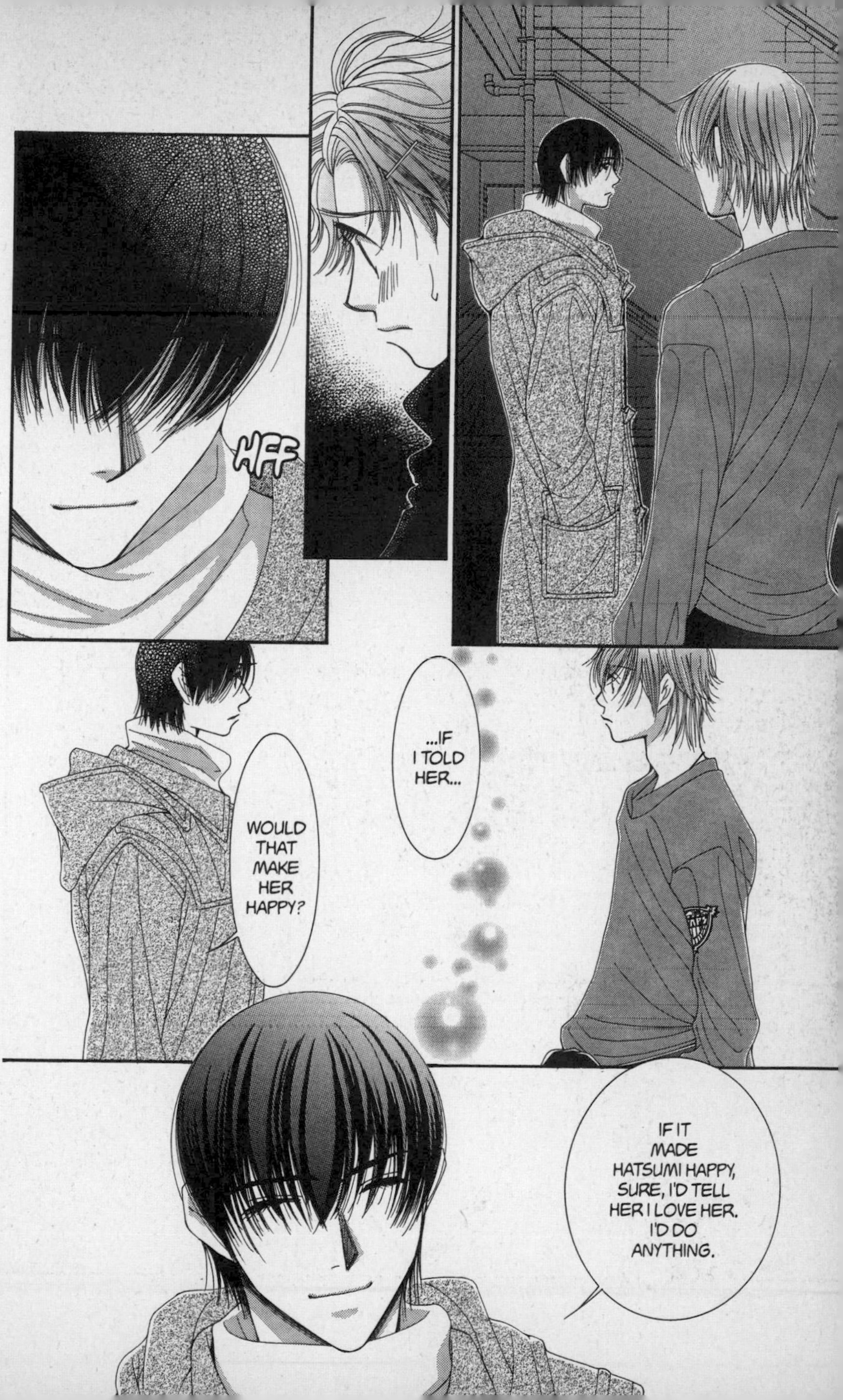
HFF
...IF I TOLD HER...
WOULD THAT MAKE HER HAPPY?
IF IT MADE HATSUMI HAPPY, SURE, I'D TELL HER I LOVE HER. I'D DO ANYTHING.

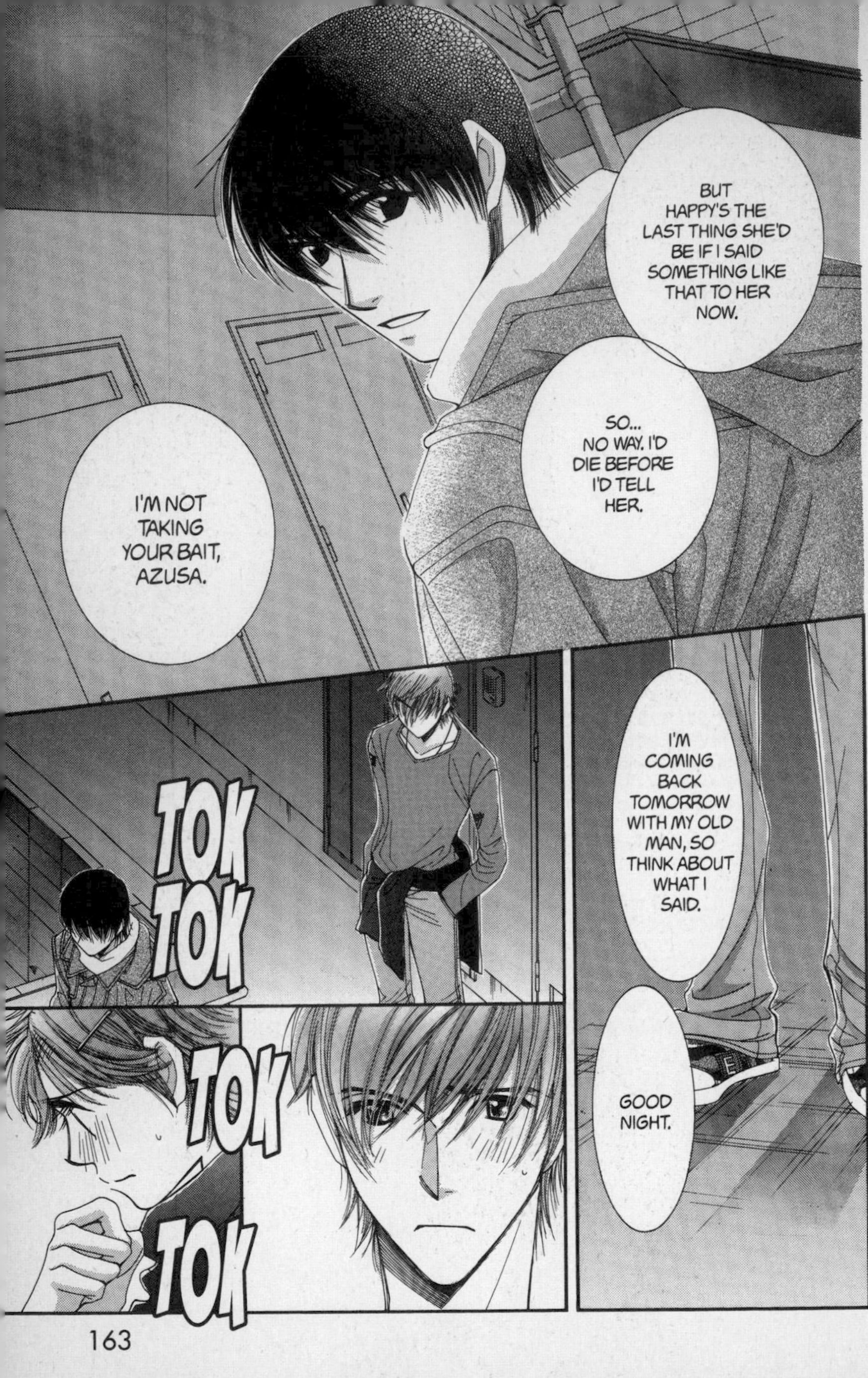
BUT HAPPY'S THE LAST THING SHE'D BE IF I SAID SOMETHING LIKE THAT TO HER NOW.
SO... NO WAY. I'D DIE BEFORE I'D TELL HER.
I'M NOT TAKING YOUR BAIT, AZUSA.
I'M COMING BACK TOMORROW WITH MY OLD MAN, SO THINK ABOUT WHAT I SAID.
GOOD NIGHT.
TOK TOK
TOK
TOK

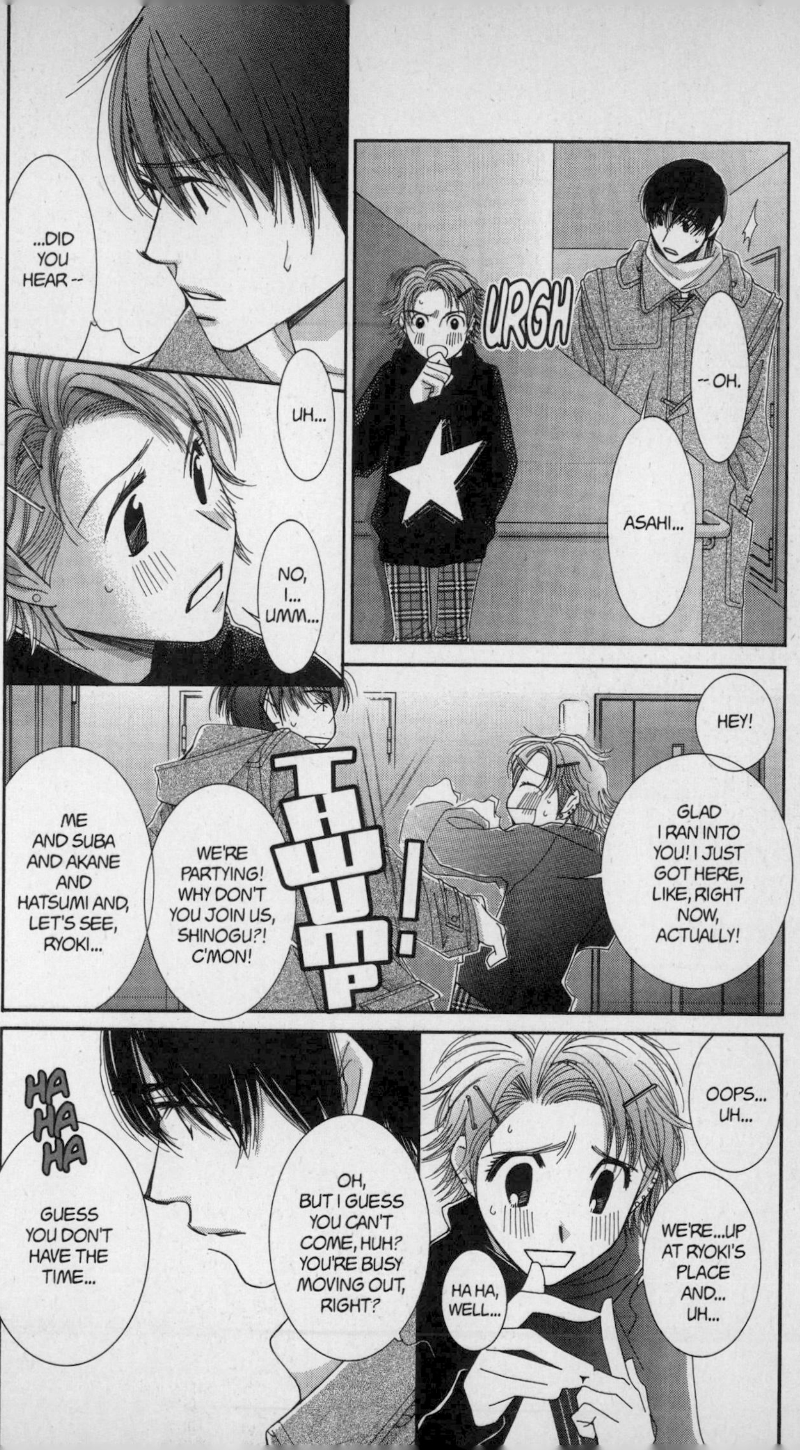

-- OH.
URGH
ASAHI...
...DID YOU HEAR --
UH...
NO, I... UMM...
HEY!
GLAD I RAN INTO YOU! I JUST GOT HERE, LIKE, RIGHT NOW, ACTUALLY!
THUUMP!
WE'RE PARTYING! WHY DON'T YOU JOIN US, SHINOGU?! C'MON!
ME AND SUBA AND AKANE AND HATSUMI AND, LET'S SEE, RYOKI...
OOPS... UH...
WE'RE...UP AT RYOKI'S PLACE AND... UH...
HA HA, WELL...
OH, BUT I GUESS YOU CAN'T COME, HUH? YOU'RE BUSY MOVING OUT, RIGHT?
HA HA HA
GUESS YOU DON'T HAVE THE TIME...

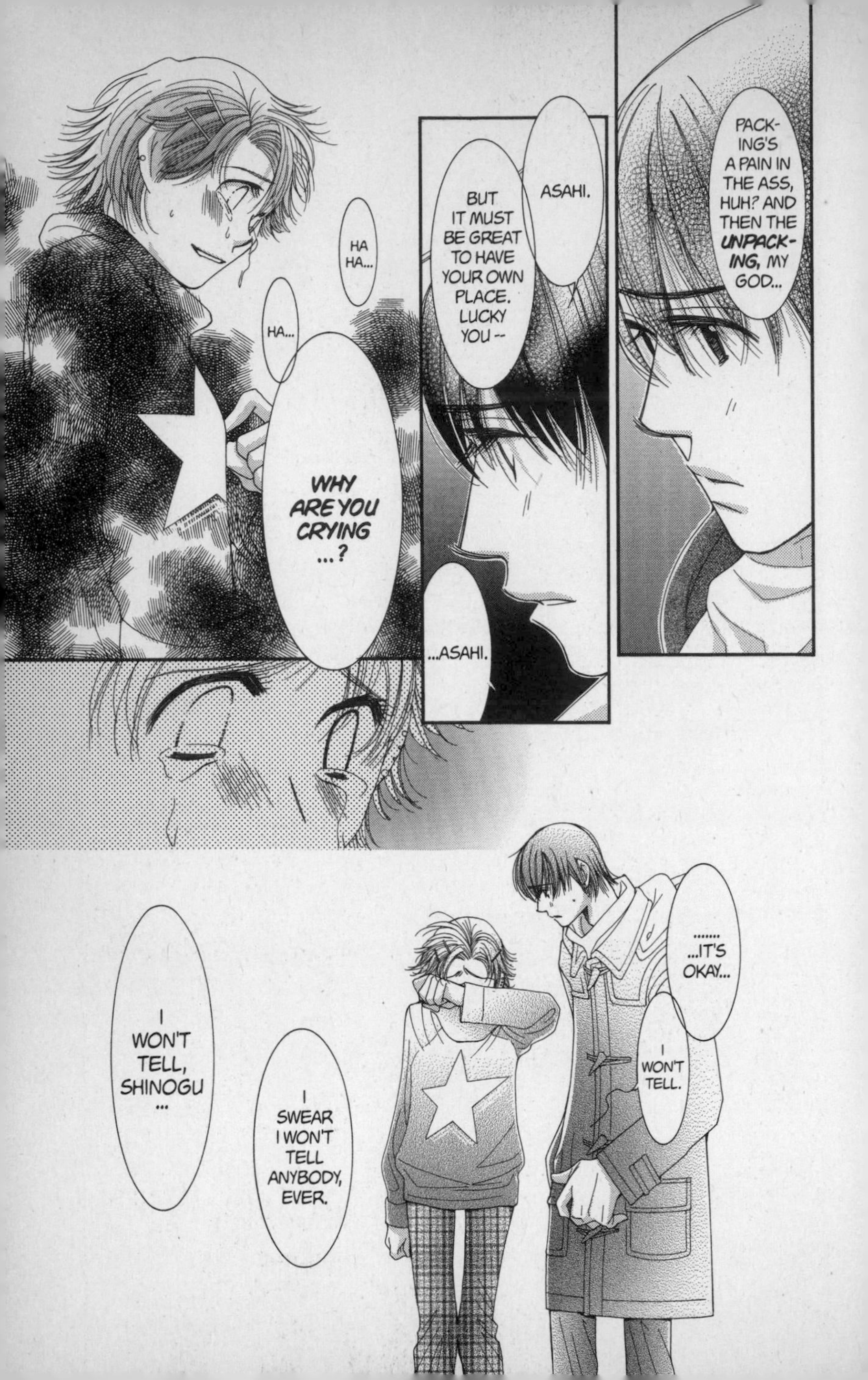
PACK-ING'S A PAIN IN THE ASS, HUH? AND THEN THE **UNPACK-ING,** MY GOD...
ASAHI.
BUT IT MUST BE GREAT TO HAVE YOUR OWN PLACE. LUCKY YOU --
...ASAHI.
HA HA...
HA...
WHY ARE YOU CRYING ...?
....IT'S OKAY...
I WON'T TELL.
I SWEAR I WON'T TELL ANYBODY, EVER.
I WON'T TELL, SHINOGU ...

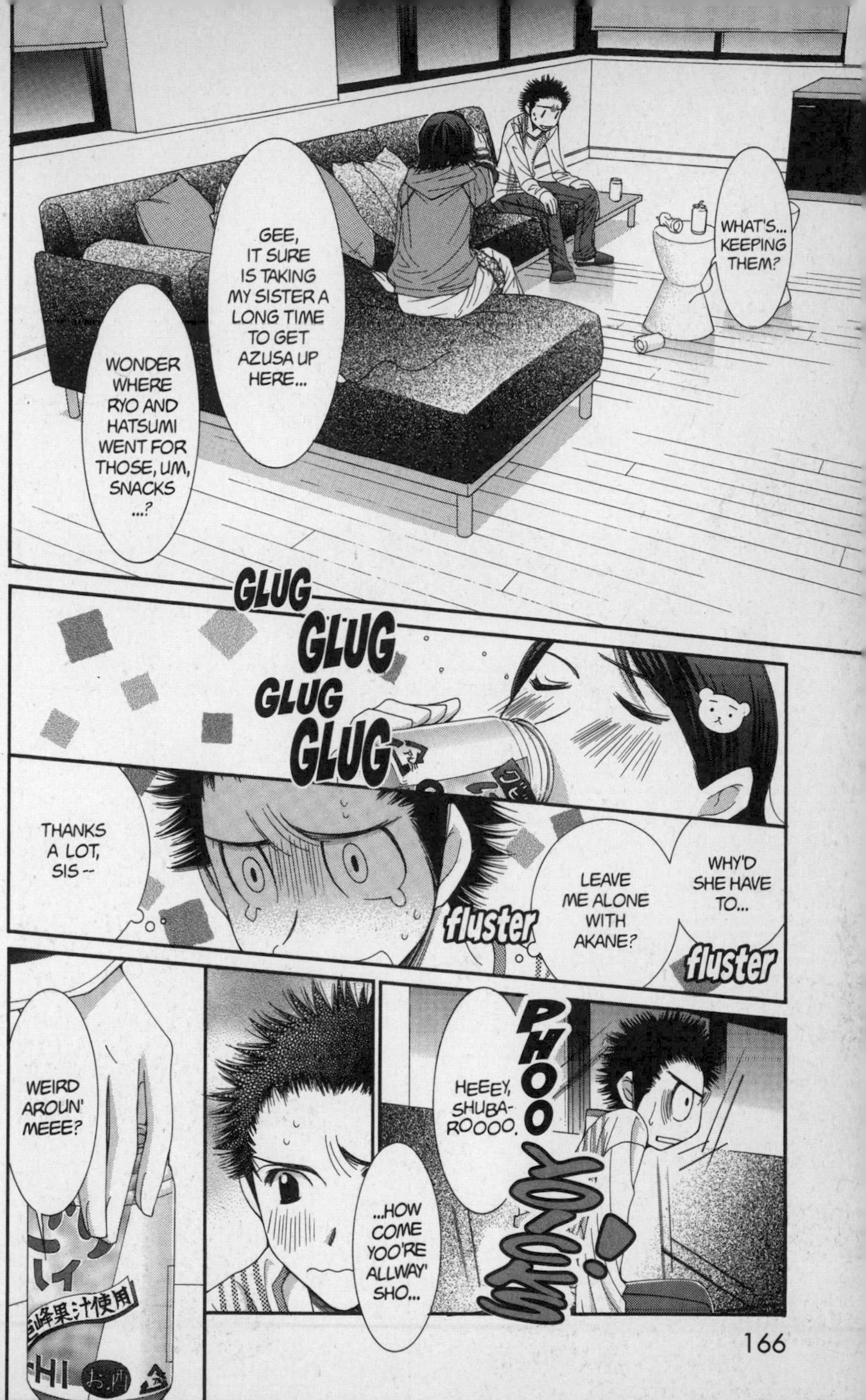
WHAT'S... KEEPING THEM?
GEE, IT SURE IS TAKING MY SISTER A LONG TIME TO GET AZUSA UP HERE...
WONDER WHERE RYO AND HATSUMI WENT FOR THOSE, UM, SNACKS ...?
GLUG GLUG GLUG GLUG
WHY'D SHE HAVE TO...
LEAVE ME ALONE WITH AKANE?
fluster
fluster
THANKS A LOT, SIS --
PHOO
YONG!
HEEEY, SHUBA-ROOOO.
...HOW COME YOO'RE ALLWAY' SHO...
WEIRD AROUN' MEEE?

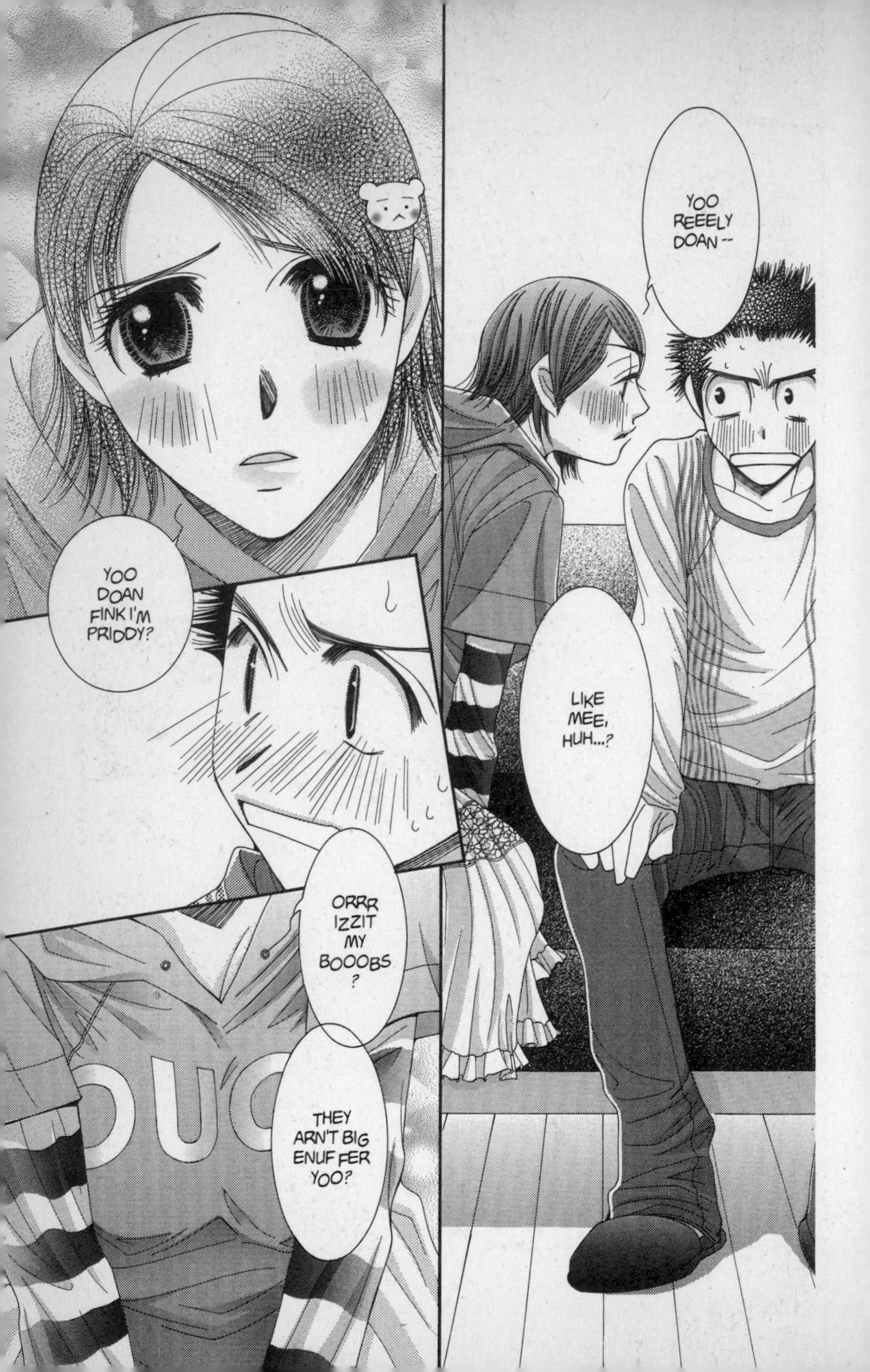
YOO REEELY DOAN --
LIKE MEE, HUH...?
YOO DOAN FINK I'M PRIDDY?
ORRR IZZIT MY BOOOBS?
THEY ARN'T BIG ENUF FER YOO?

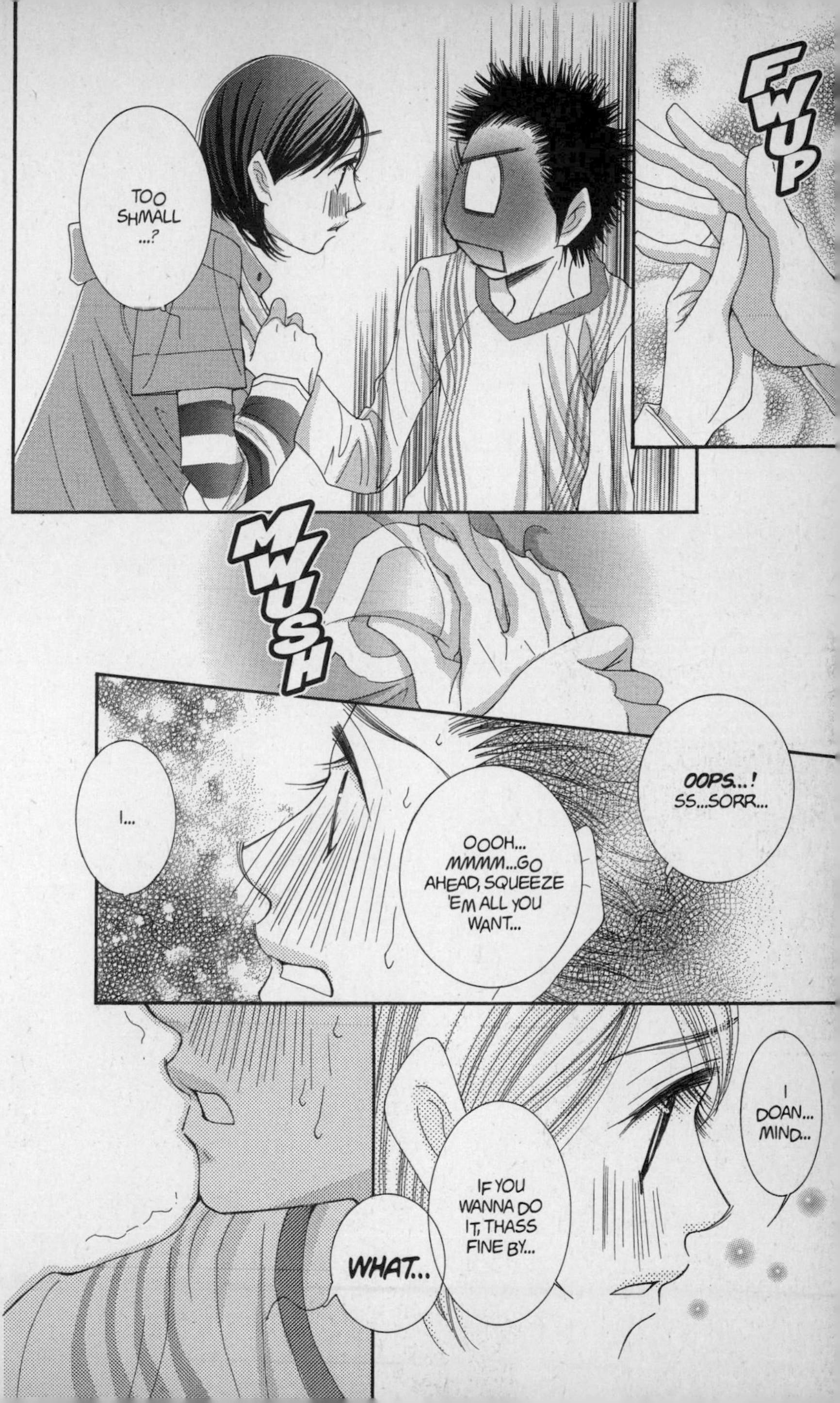
FWUP
TOO SHMALL ...?
MWUSH
OOPS...! SS...SORR...
OOOH... MMMM...GO AHEAD, SQUEEZE 'EM ALL YOU WANT...
I...
I DOAN... MIND...
IF YOU WANNA DO IT, THASS FINE BY...
WHAT...

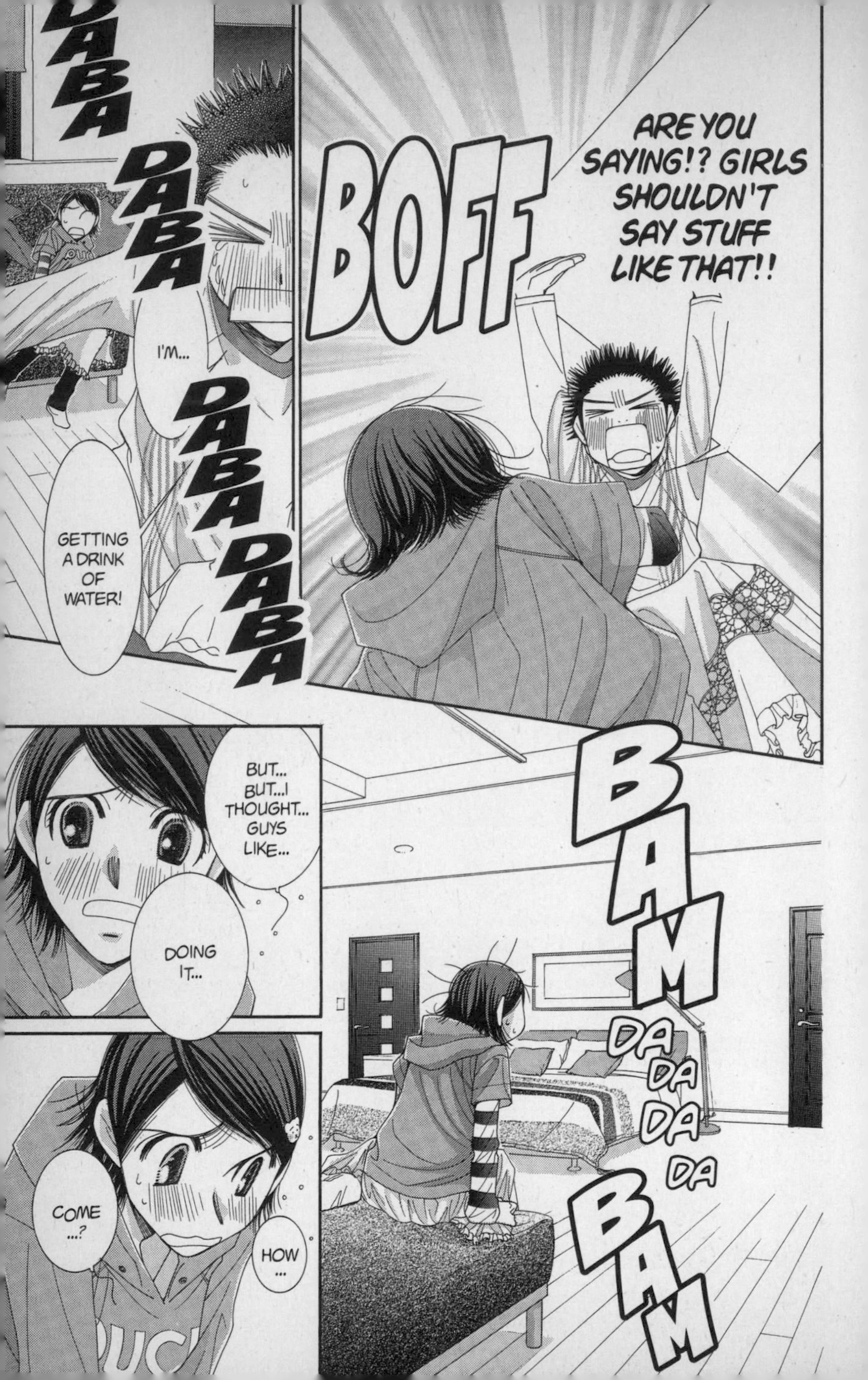
BOFF
ARE YOU SAYING!? GIRLS SHOULDN'T SAY STUFF LIKE THAT!!
DABA DABA BA
I'M...
DABA DABA DABA
GETTING A DRINK OF WATER!
BAM DA DA DA DA BAM
BUT... BUT...I THOUGHT... GUYS LIKE...
DOING IT...
HOW ...
COME ...?

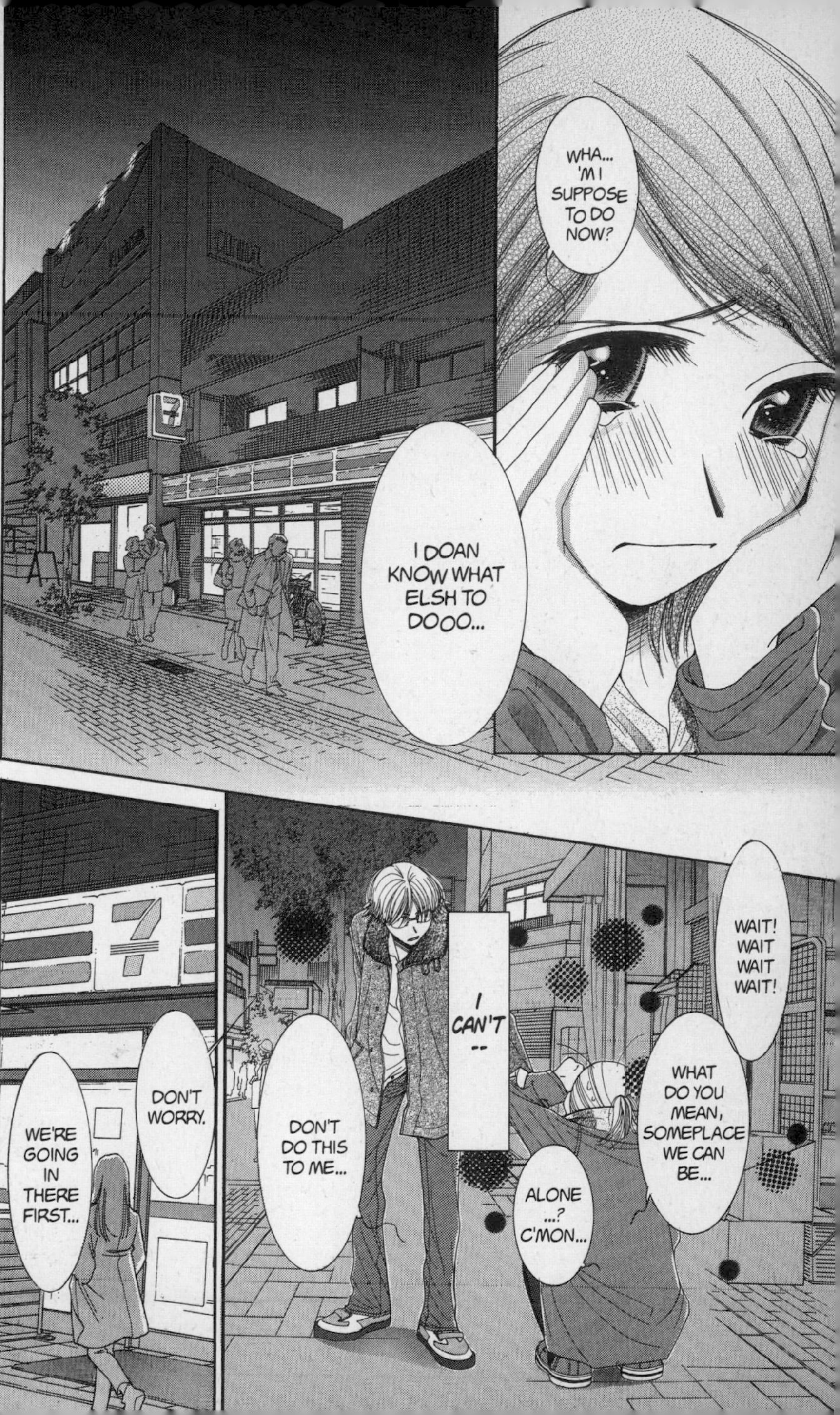
WHA... 'M I SUPPOSE TO DO NOW?
I DOAN KNOW WHAT ELSH TO DOOO...
WAIT! WAIT WAIT WAIT!
WHAT DO YOU MEAN, SOMEPLACE WE CAN BE...
ALONE ...? C'MON...
I CAN'T --
DON'T DO THIS TO ME...
DON'T WORRY.
WE'RE GOING IN THERE FIRST...

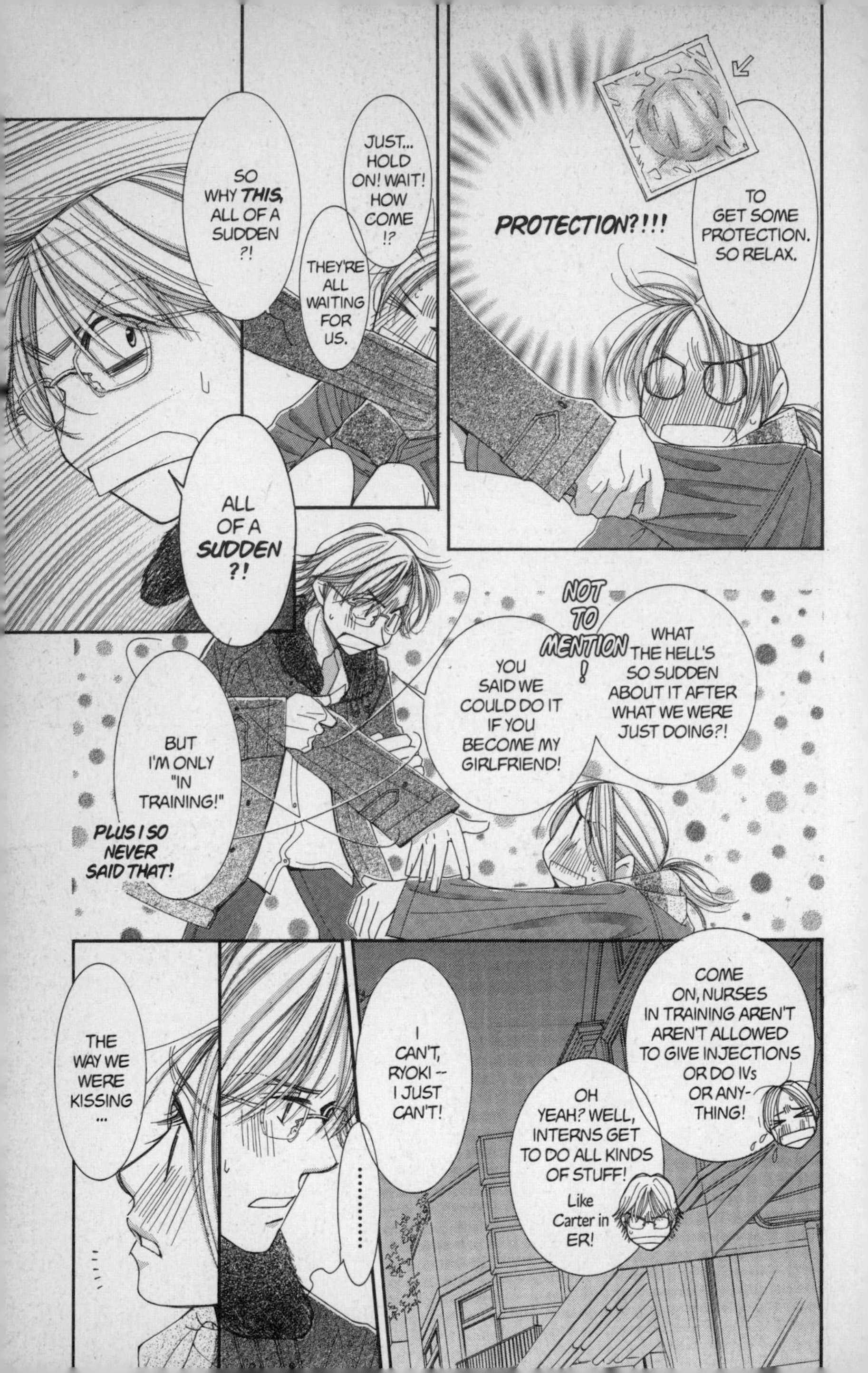
TO GET SOME PROTECTION. SO RELAX.
PROTECTION?!!!
JUST... HOLD ON! WAIT! HOW COME !?
THEY'RE ALL WAITING FOR US.
SO WHY THIS, ALL OF A SUDDEN ?!
ALL OF A SUDDEN ?!
WHAT THE HELL'S SO SUDDEN ABOUT IT AFTER WHAT WE WERE JUST DOING?!
NOT TO MENTION!
YOU SAID WE COULD DO IT IF YOU BECOME MY GIRLFRIEND!
BUT I'M ONLY "IN TRAINING!"
PLUS I SO NEVER SAID THAT!
COME ON, NURSES IN TRAINING AREN'T AREN'T ALLOWED TO GIVE INJECTIONS OR DO IVs OR ANY-THING!
OH YEAH? WELL, INTERNS GET TO DO ALL KINDS OF STUFF!
Like Carter in ER!
I CAN'T, RYOKI -- I JUST CAN'T!
......
THE WAY WE WERE KISSING ...
...

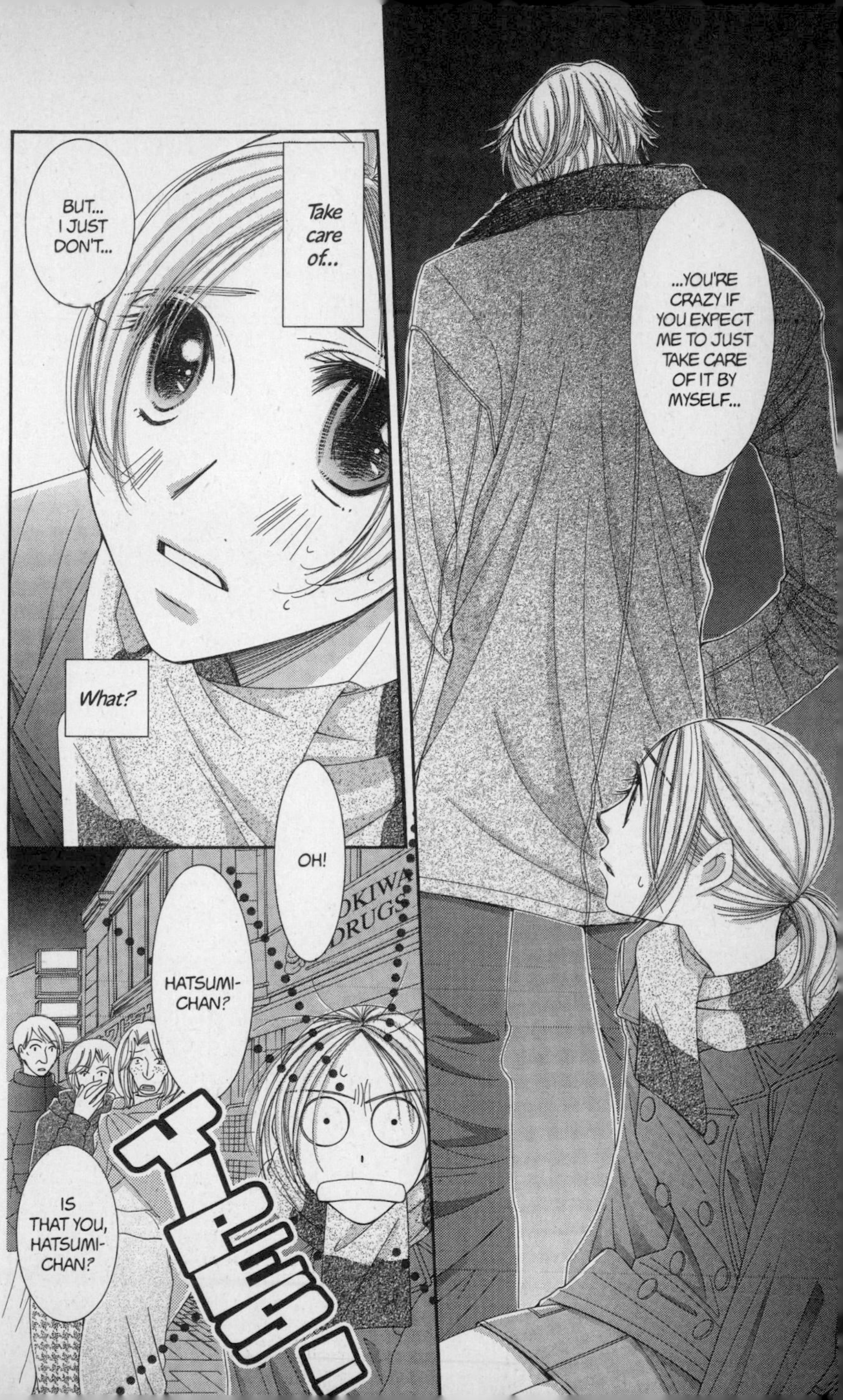
...YOU'RE CRAZY IF YOU EXPECT ME TO JUST TAKE CARE OF IT BY MYSELF...
Take care of...
BUT... I JUST DON'T...
What?
OH!
HATSUMI-CHAN?
DRUGS
IS THAT YOU, HATSUMI-CHAN?

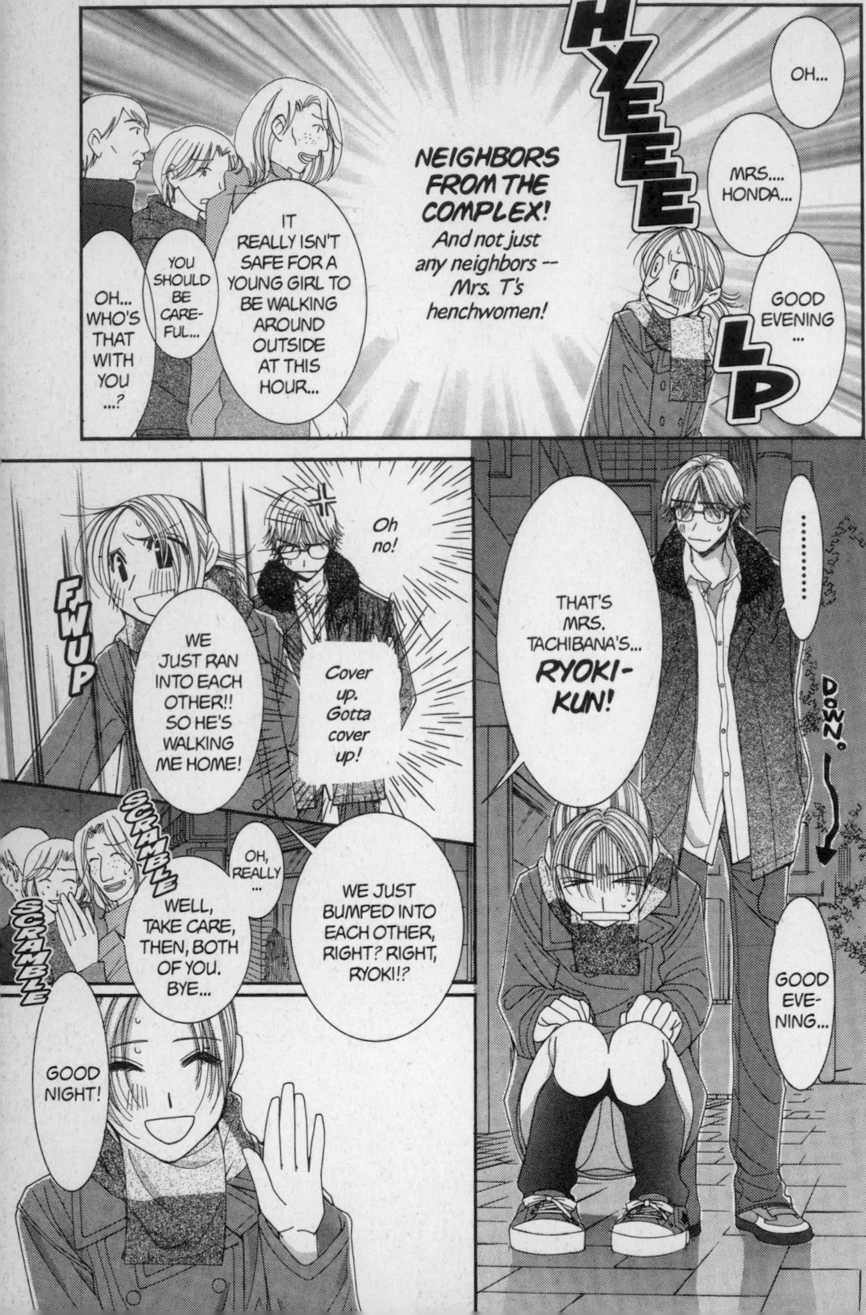
OH...
MRS.... HONDA...
GOOD EVENING ...
HYEEEELP
NEIGHBORS FROM THE COMPLEX! And not just any neighbors -- Mrs. T's henchwomen!
IT REALLY ISN'T SAFE FOR A YOUNG GIRL TO BE WALKING AROUND OUTSIDE AT THIS HOUR...
YOU SHOULD BE CARE-FUL...
OH... WHO'S THAT WITH YOU ...?
....
THAT'S MRS. TACHIBANA'S... RYOKI-KUN!
DOWN
GOOD EVE-NING...
Oh no!
Cover up. Gotta cover up!
WE JUST RAN INTO EACH OTHER!! SO HE'S WALKING ME HOME!
FWUP
WE JUST BUMPED INTO EACH OTHER, RIGHT? RIGHT, RYOKI!?
OH, REALLY ...
WELL, TAKE CARE, THEN, BOTH OF YOU. BYE...
SCRAMBLE
SCRAMBLE
GOOD NIGHT!

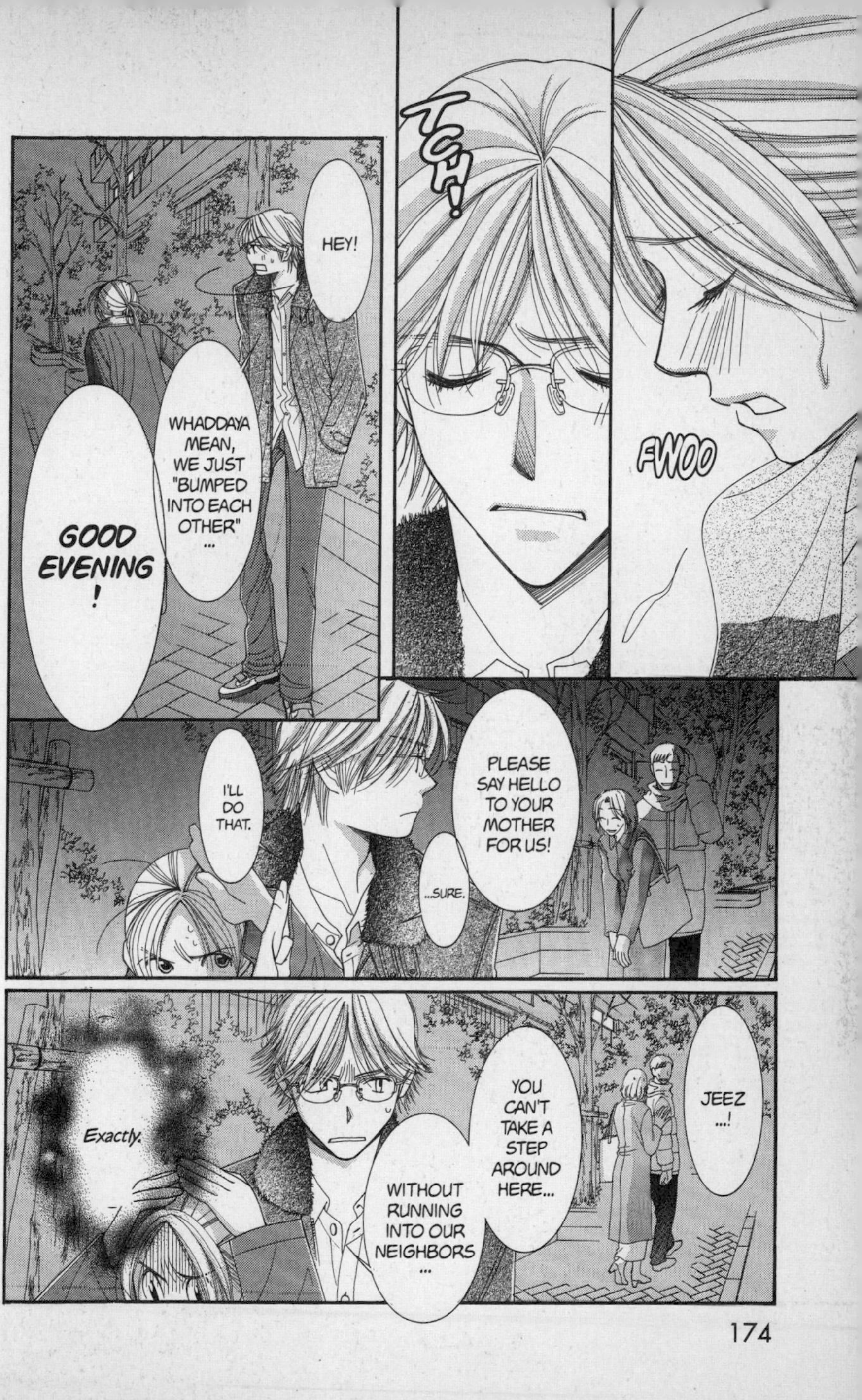
FWOO
TCH!
HEY!
WHADDAYA MEAN, WE JUST "BUMPED INTO EACH OTHER" ...
GOOD EVENING!
PLEASE SAY HELLO TO YOUR MOTHER FOR US!
...SURE.
I'LL DO THAT.
JEEZ ...!
YOU CAN'T TAKE A STEP AROUND HERE...
WITHOUT RUNNING INTO OUR NEIGHBORS ...
Exactly.

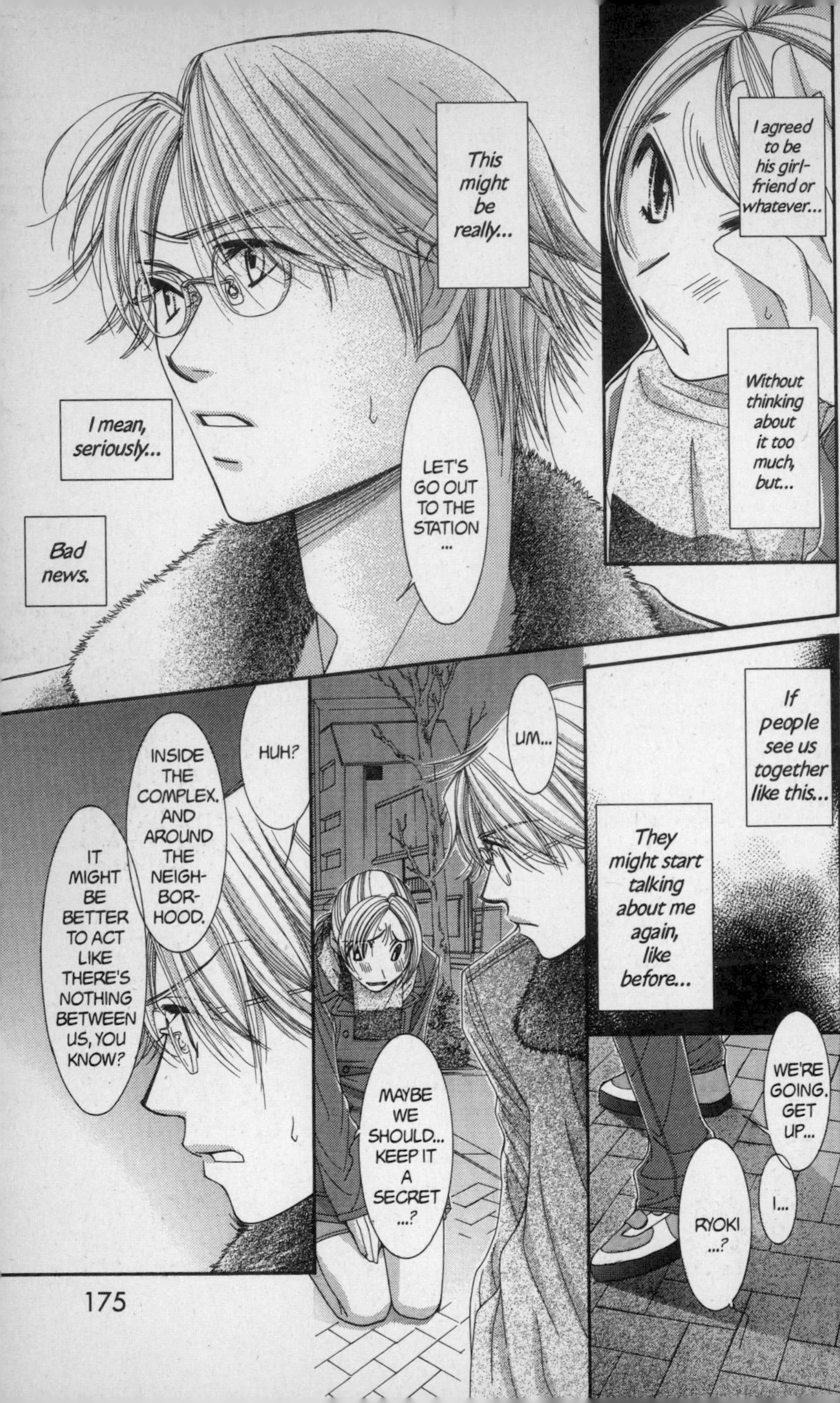
I agreed to be his girl-friend or whatever...
Without thinking about it too much, but...
This might be really...
LET'S GO OUT TO THE STATION...
I mean, seriously...
Bad news.
If people see us together like this...
They might start talking about me again, like before...
WE'RE GOING. GET UP...
I...
RYOKI...?
UM...
MAYBE WE SHOULD... KEEP IT A SECRET...?
HUH?
INSIDE THE COMPLEX. AND AROUND THE NEIGH-BOR-HOOD.
IT MIGHT BE BETTER TO ACT LIKE THERE'S NOTHING BETWEEN US, YOU KNOW?

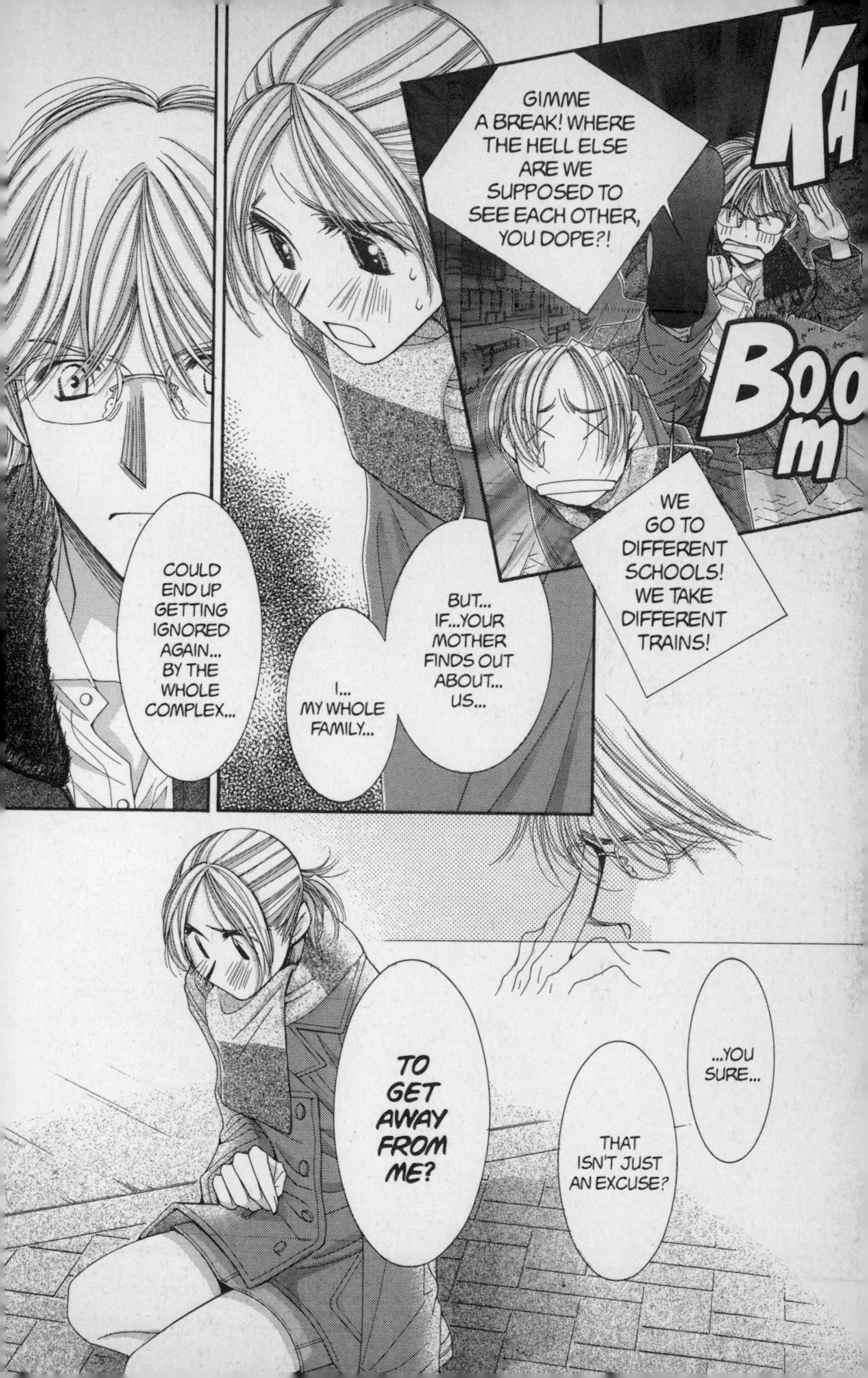
KABOOM
GIMME A BREAK! WHERE THE HELL ELSE ARE WE SUPPOSED TO SEE EACH OTHER, YOU DOPE?!
WE GO TO DIFFERENT SCHOOLS! WE TAKE DIFFERENT TRAINS!
BUT... IF...YOUR MOTHER FINDS OUT ABOUT... US...
I... MY WHOLE FAMILY...
COULD END UP GETTING IGNORED AGAIN... BY THE WHOLE COMPLEX...
...YOU SURE...
THAT ISN'T JUST AN EXCUSE?
TO GET AWAY FROM ME?

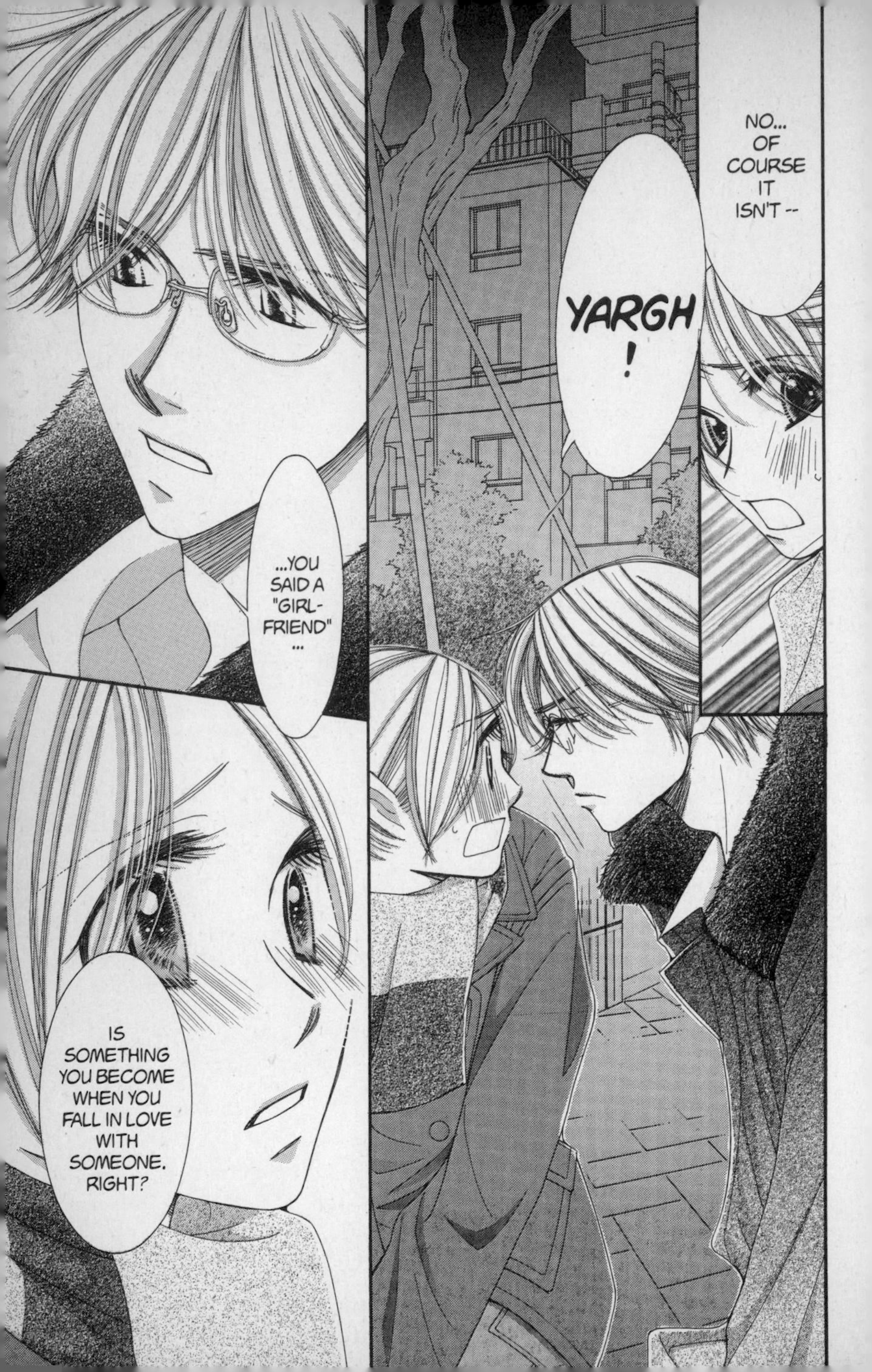
NO... OF COURSE IT ISN'T --
YARGH !
...YOU SAID A "GIRL-FRIEND" ...
IS SOMETHING YOU BECOME WHEN YOU FALL IN LOVE WITH SOMEONE. RIGHT?

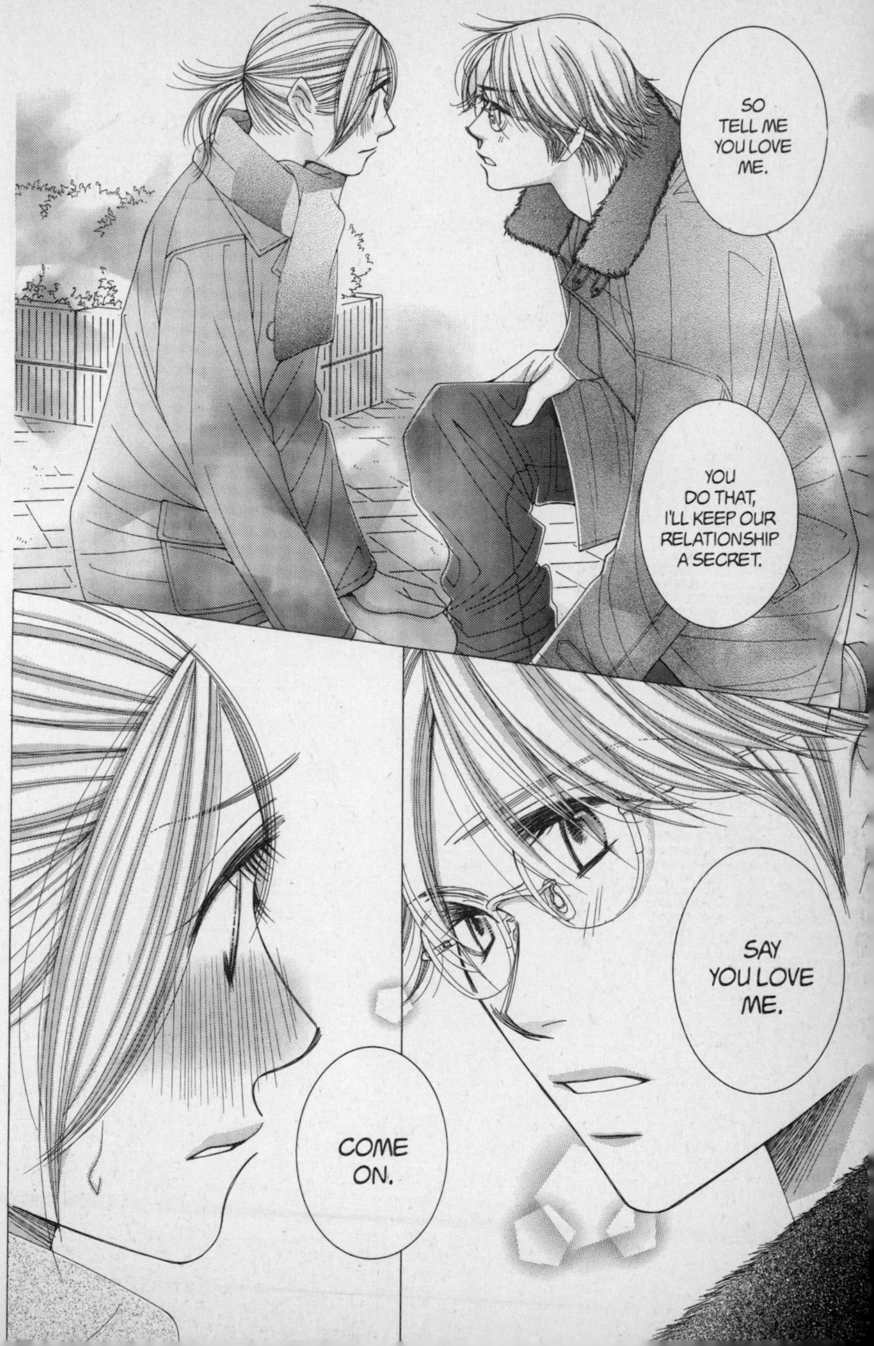
SO TELL ME YOU LOVE ME.
YOU DO THAT, I'LL KEEP OUR RELATIONSHIP A SECRET.
SAY YOU LOVE ME.
COME ON.

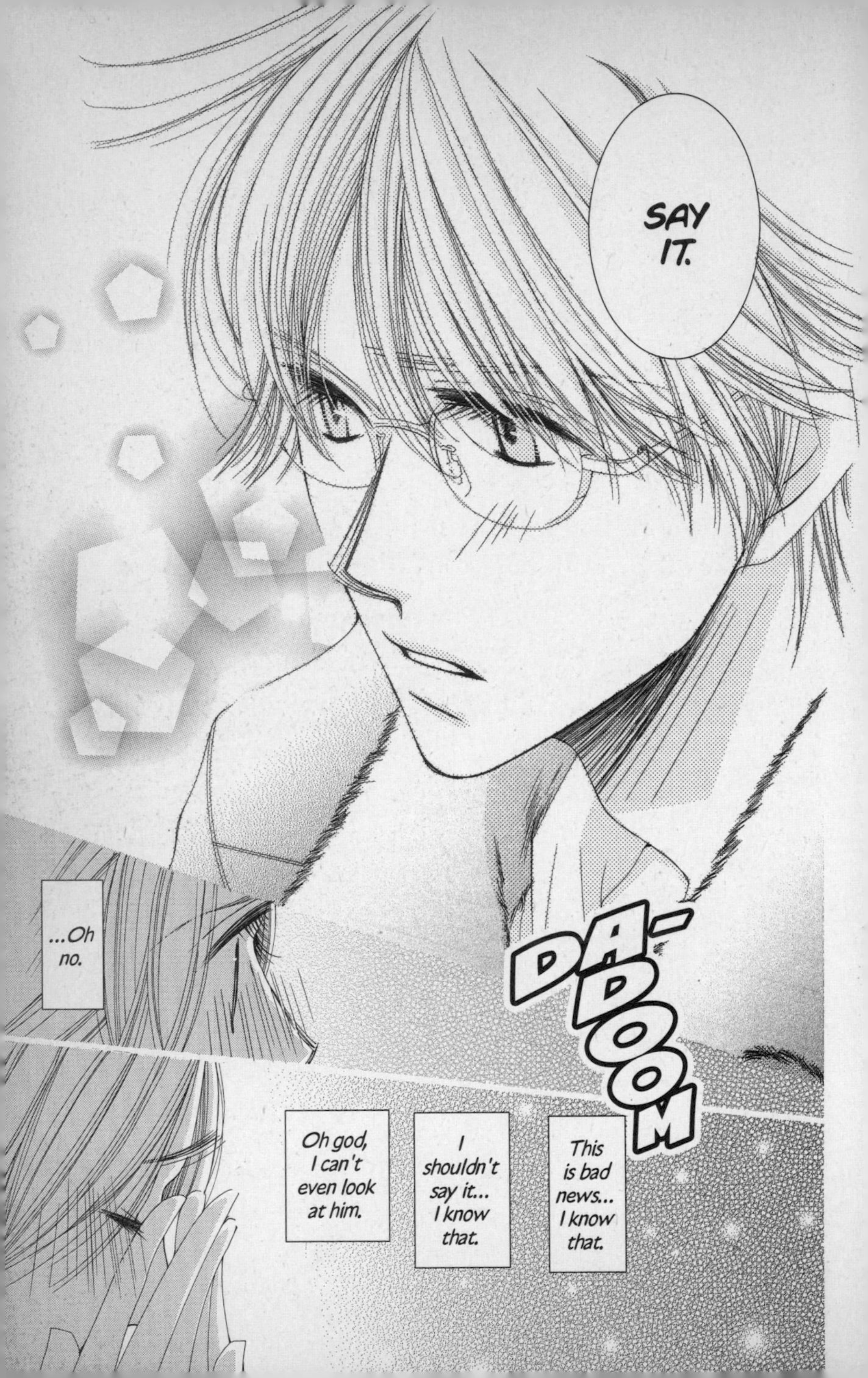
SAY IT.
DA-DOOM
...Oh no.
This is bad news... I know that.
I shouldn't say it... I know that.
Oh god, I can't even look at him.

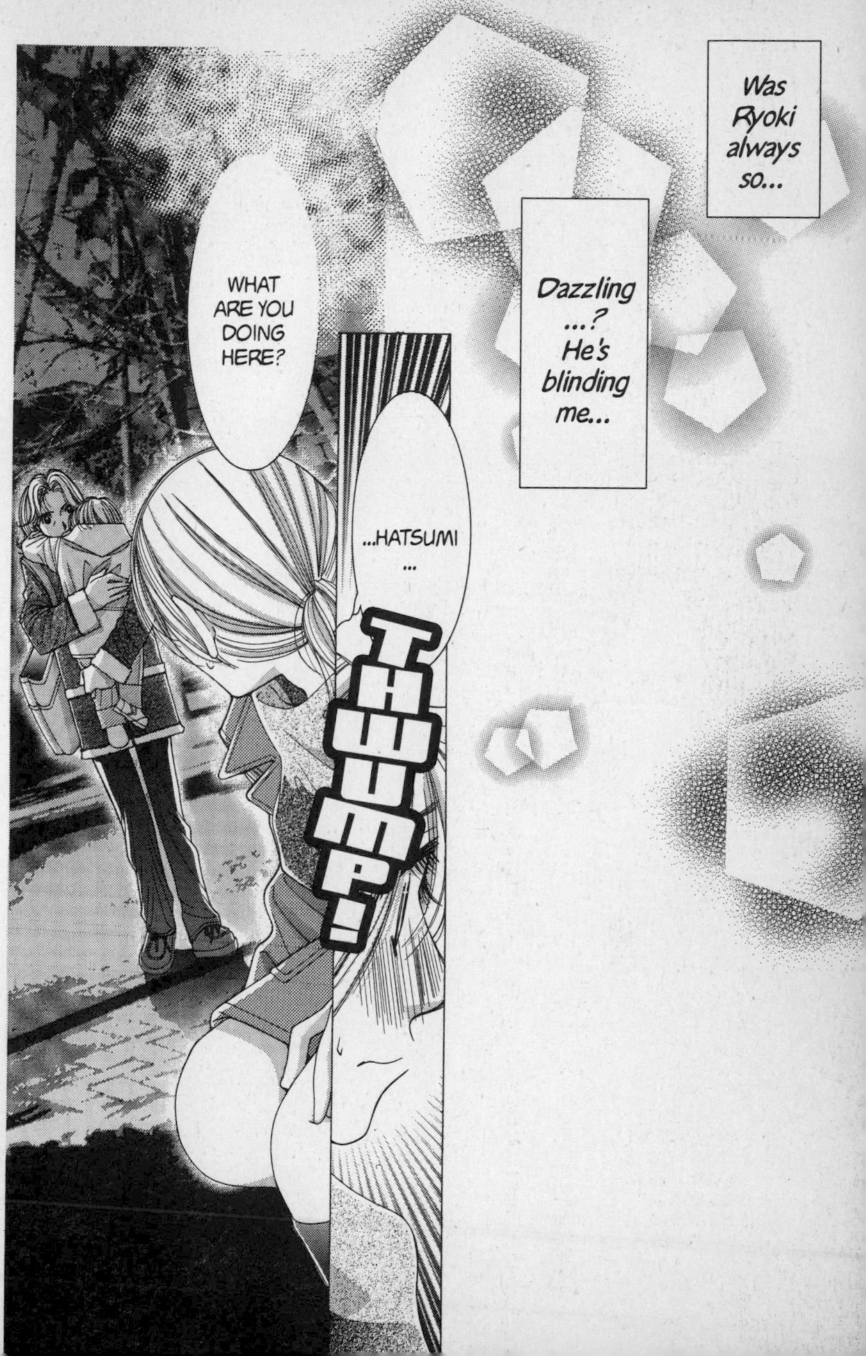
Was Ryoki always so...
Dazzling ...? He's blinding me...
WHAT ARE YOU DOING HERE?
...HATSUMI ...
THUUMP!

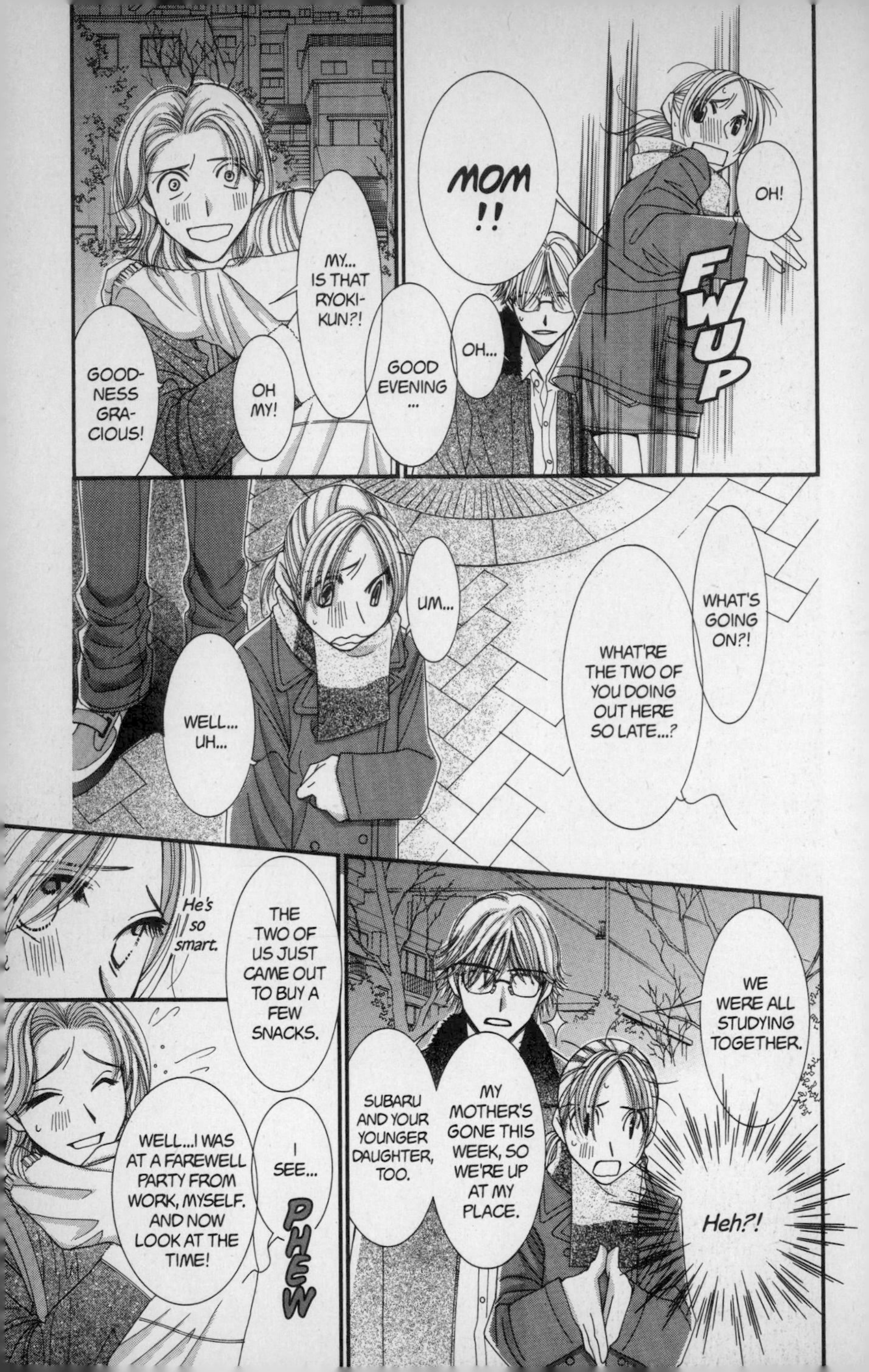
OH!
MOM !!
FWUP
OH...
GOOD EVENING ...
MY... IS THAT RYOKI-KUN?!
OH MY!
GOOD-NESS GRA-CIOUS!
WHAT'S GOING ON?!
WHAT'RE THE TWO OF YOU DOING OUT HERE SO LATE...?
UM...
WELL... UH...
WE WERE ALL STUDYING TOGETHER.
Heh?!
MY MOTHER'S GONE THIS WEEK, SO WE'RE UP AT MY PLACE.
SUBARU AND YOUR YOUNGER DAUGHTER, TOO.
THE TWO OF US JUST CAME OUT TO BUY A FEW SNACKS.
He's so smart.
I SEE...
PHEW
WELL...I WAS AT A FAREWELL PARTY FROM WORK, MYSELF. AND NOW LOOK AT THE TIME!

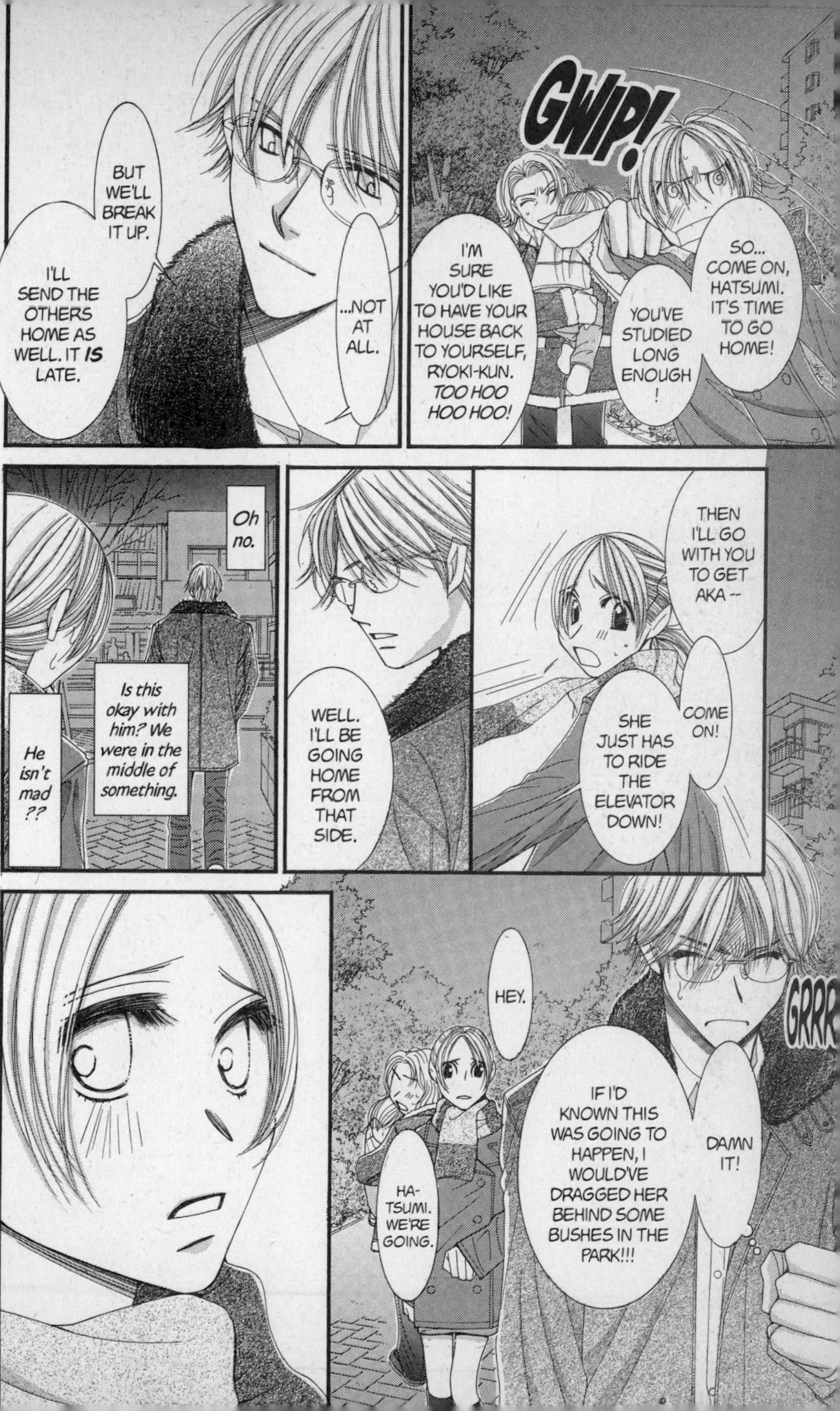
GWIP!
SO... COME ON, HATSUMI. IT'S TIME TO GO HOME!
YOU'VE STUDIED LONG ENOUGH!
I'M SURE YOU'D LIKE TO HAVE YOUR HOUSE BACK TO YOURSELF, RYOKI-KUN. *TOO HOO HOO HOO!*
...NOT AT ALL.
BUT WE'LL BREAK IT UP.
I'LL SEND THE OTHERS HOME AS WELL. IT **IS** LATE.
THEN I'LL GO WITH YOU TO GET AKA --
COME ON!
SHE JUST HAS TO RIDE THE ELEVATOR DOWN!
WELL. I'LL BE GOING HOME FROM THAT SIDE.
Oh no.
Is this okay with him? We were in the middle of something.
He isn't mad??
GRRR
DAMN IT!
IF I'D KNOWN THIS WAS GOING TO HAPPEN, I WOULD'VE DRAGGED HER BEHIND SOME BUSHES IN THE PARK!!!
HEY.
HA-TSUMI. WE'RE GOING.

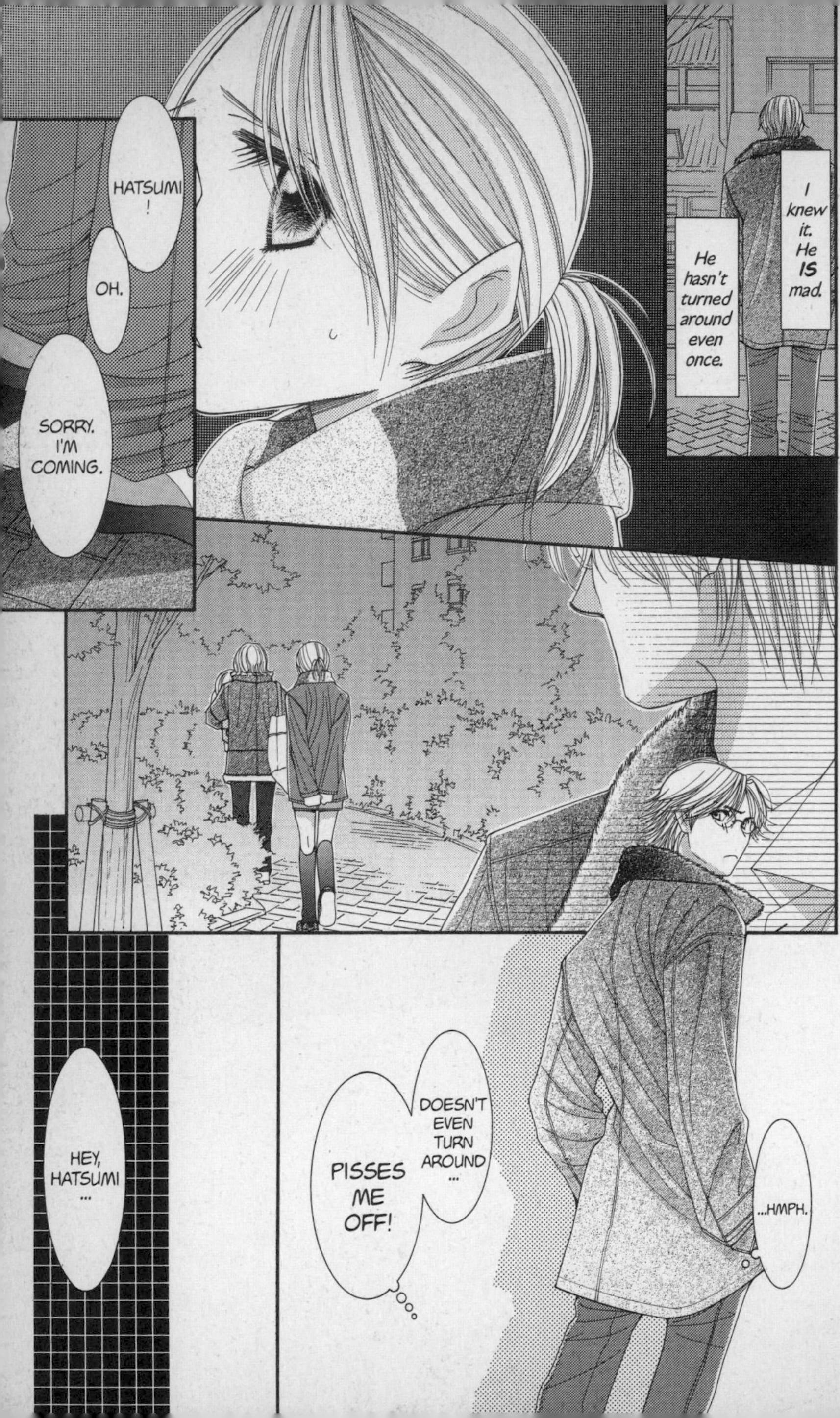
I knew it. He IS mad.
He hasn't turned around even once.
HATSUMI!
OH.
SORRY. I'M COMING.
...HMPH.
DOESN'T EVEN TURN AROUND...
PISSES ME OFF!
HEY, HATSUMI...

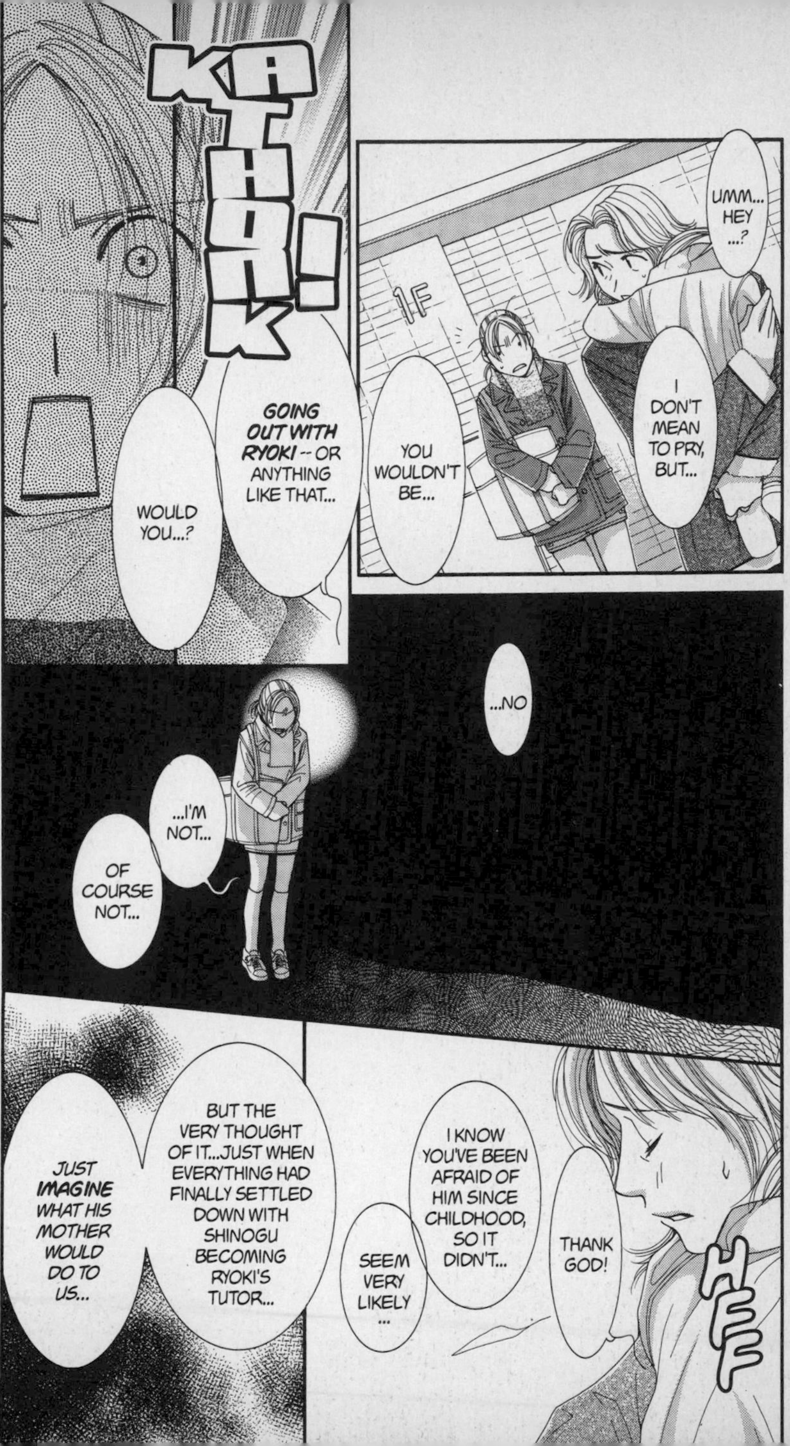
UMM... HEY ...?
I DON'T MEAN TO PRY, BUT...
YOU WOULDN'T BE...
KATHUNK!
GOING OUT WITH RYOKI -- OR ANYTHING LIKE THAT...
WOULD YOU...?
...NO
...I'M NOT...
OF COURSE NOT...
HEF
THANK GOD!
I KNOW YOU'VE BEEN AFRAID OF HIM SINCE CHILDHOOD, SO IT DIDN'T...
SEEM VERY LIKELY ...
BUT THE VERY THOUGHT OF IT...JUST WHEN EVERYTHING HAD FINALLY SETTLED DOWN WITH SHINOGU BECOMING RYOKI'S TUTOR...
JUST IMAGINE WHAT HIS MOTHER WOULD DO TO US...

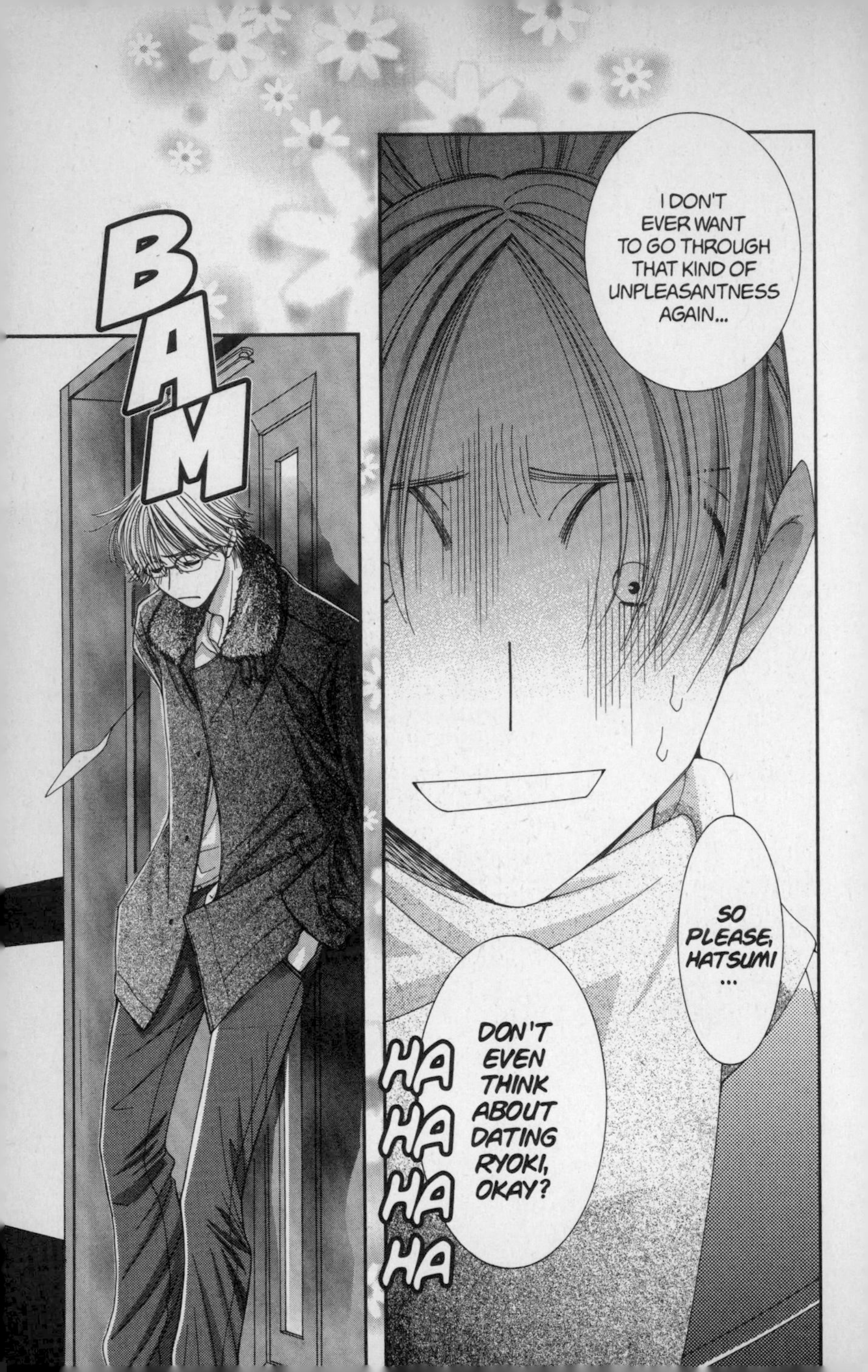
I DON'T EVER WANT TO GO THROUGH THAT KIND OF UNPLEASANTNESS AGAIN...
SO PLEASE, HATSUMI...
DON'T EVEN THINK ABOUT DATING RYOKI, OKAY?
HA HA HA HA
BAM

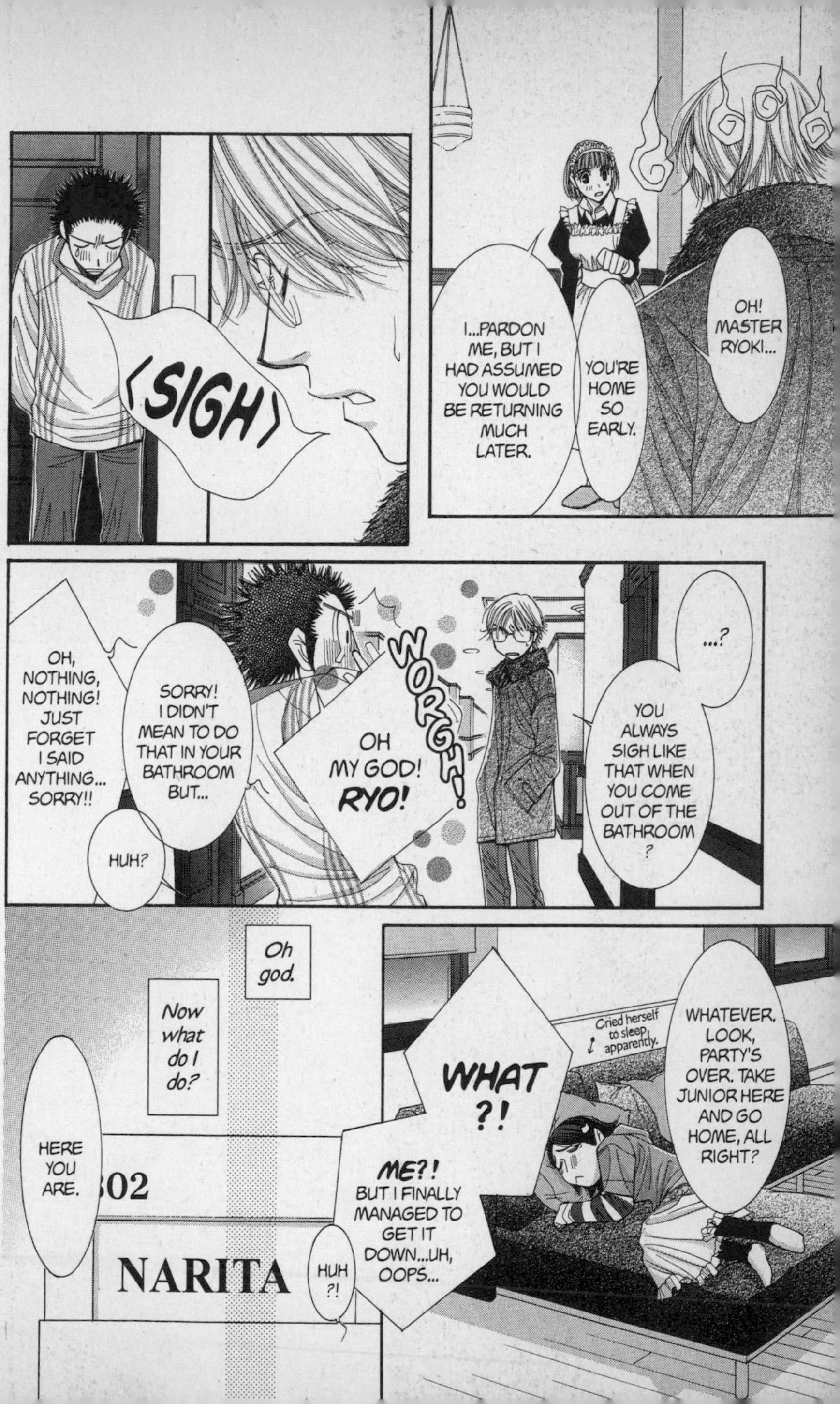
OH! MASTER RYOKI...
YOU'RE HOME SO EARLY.
I...PARDON ME, BUT I HAD ASSUMED YOU WOULD BE RETURNING MUCH LATER.
(SIGH)
...?
YOU ALWAYS SIGH LIKE THAT WHEN YOU COME OUT OF THE BATHROOM?
WORGH!
OH MY GOD! RYO!
SORRY! I DIDN'T MEAN TO DO THAT IN YOUR BATHROOM BUT...
HUH?
OH, NOTHING, NOTHING! JUST FORGET I SAID ANYTHING... SORRY!!
WHATEVER. LOOK, PARTY'S OVER. TAKE JUNIOR HERE AND GO HOME, ALL RIGHT?
Cried herself to sleep apparently.
WHAT?!
ME?! BUT I FINALLY MANAGED TO GET IT DOWN...UH, OOPS...
HUH?!
Oh god.
Now what do I do?
HERE YOU ARE.
302
NARITA

Hot Gimmick

EDITOR'S RECOMMENDATIONS

More manga!
More manga!

Did you like *Hot Gimmick*? Here's what VIZ recommends you try next:

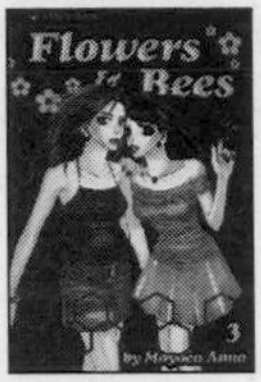

© 2001 Moyoco Anno/ Kodansha Ltd.

FLOWERS & BEES Moyoco Anno's painfully hilarious chronicle of a normal guy attempting to unleash his inner metrosexual is as funny as it is incisive. Hoping to spruce up his image (and at the same time, increase his chances of "gettin' some"), Komatsu becomes a regular at the World of Beautiful Men salon. The salon's proprietresses, a pair of sexy fashionistas, adopt Komatsu as their own private slave and shadow his myriad failed attempts at scoring some points with the opposite sex. Will this equally hapless hero ever get some lovin'? More importantly, will he ever get his act together?

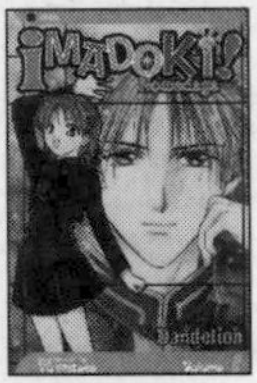

© 2000 Yuu Watase/ Shogakukan, Inc.

IMADOKI! [NOWADAYS] Tanpopo Yamazaki has come a long way from her native Hokkaido to attend prestigious Meiô Academy, and Yû Watase's *IMADOKI! [NOWADAYS]* follows this tenacious horticulturist as she tries to make friends, influence people, and plant flowers. Trouble is, real flowers are strictly verboten at Meiô (the posh student-body suffers from allergies). Tanpopo will have to do a lot more than planting petunias to win over these prudes.

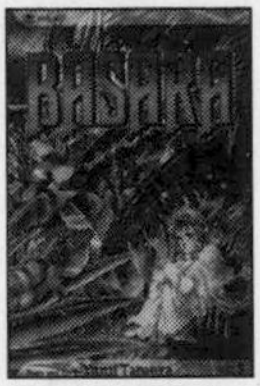

© 1991 Yumi Tamura/ Shogakukan, Inc.

BASARA Yumi Tamura's sprawling epic *BASARA* is one of the most gripping shôjo stories around. A young girl must battle despotic warlords, unearth hidden treasures, and unite a nation, all while impersonating her fallen brother. Is Sarasa truly the child of destiny? Or is her quest doomed to fail? *BASARA* has action, romance, and heart-wrenching drama, all on a grand scale. Not to be missed.

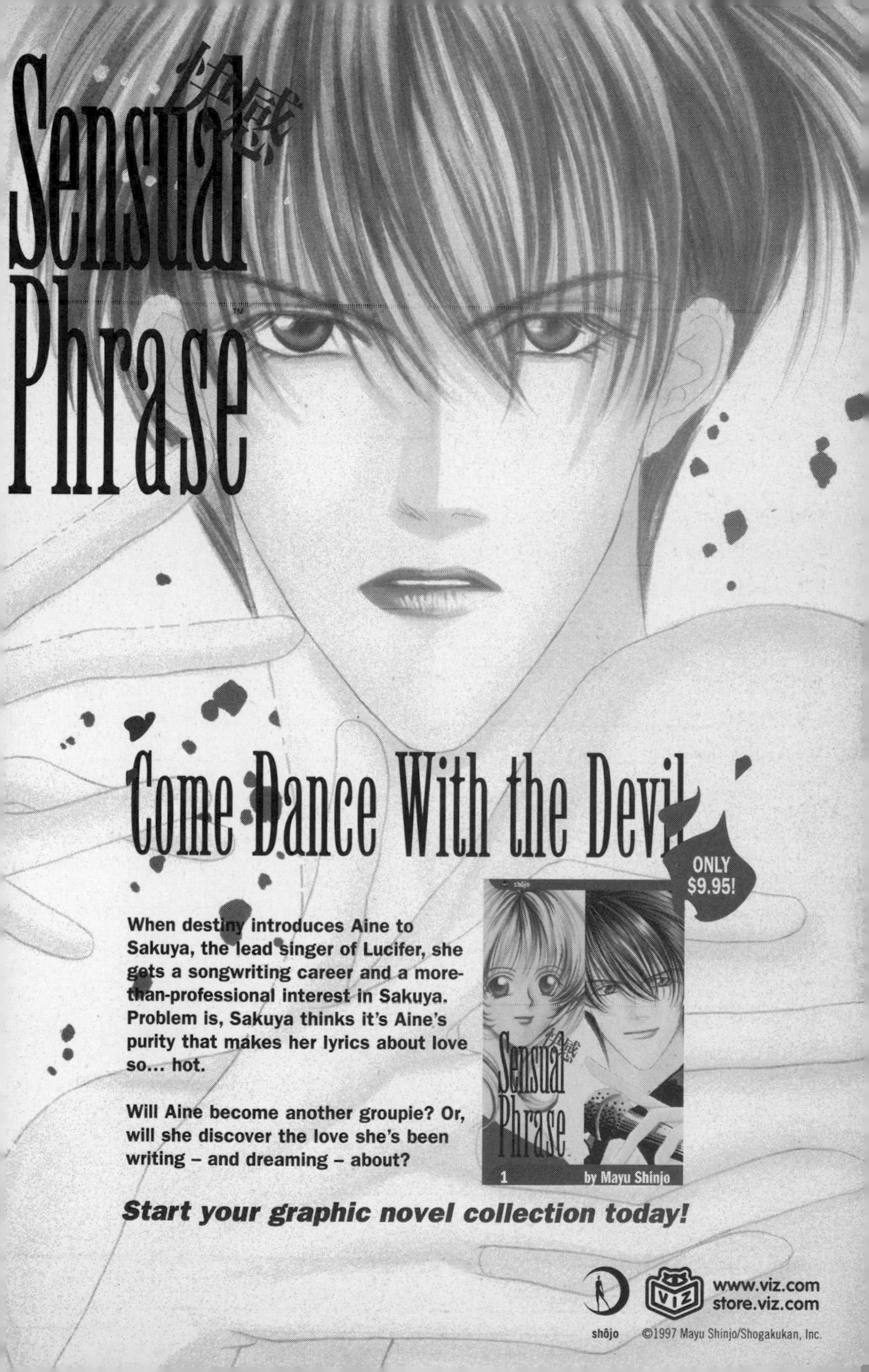
Sensual Phrase™
快感
Come Dance With the Devil
ONLY $9.95!
shôjo
Sensual Phrase
1
by Mayu Shinjo
When destiny introduces Aine to Sakuya, the lead singer of Lucifer, she gets a songwriting career and a more-than-professional interest in Sakuya. Problem is, Sakuya thinks it's Aine's purity that makes her lyrics about love so... hot.
Will Aine become another groupie? Or, will she discover the love she's been writing – and dreaming – about?
Start your graphic novel collection today!
shôjo
VIZ
www.viz.com
store.viz.com
©1997 Mayu Shinjo/Shogakukan, Inc.

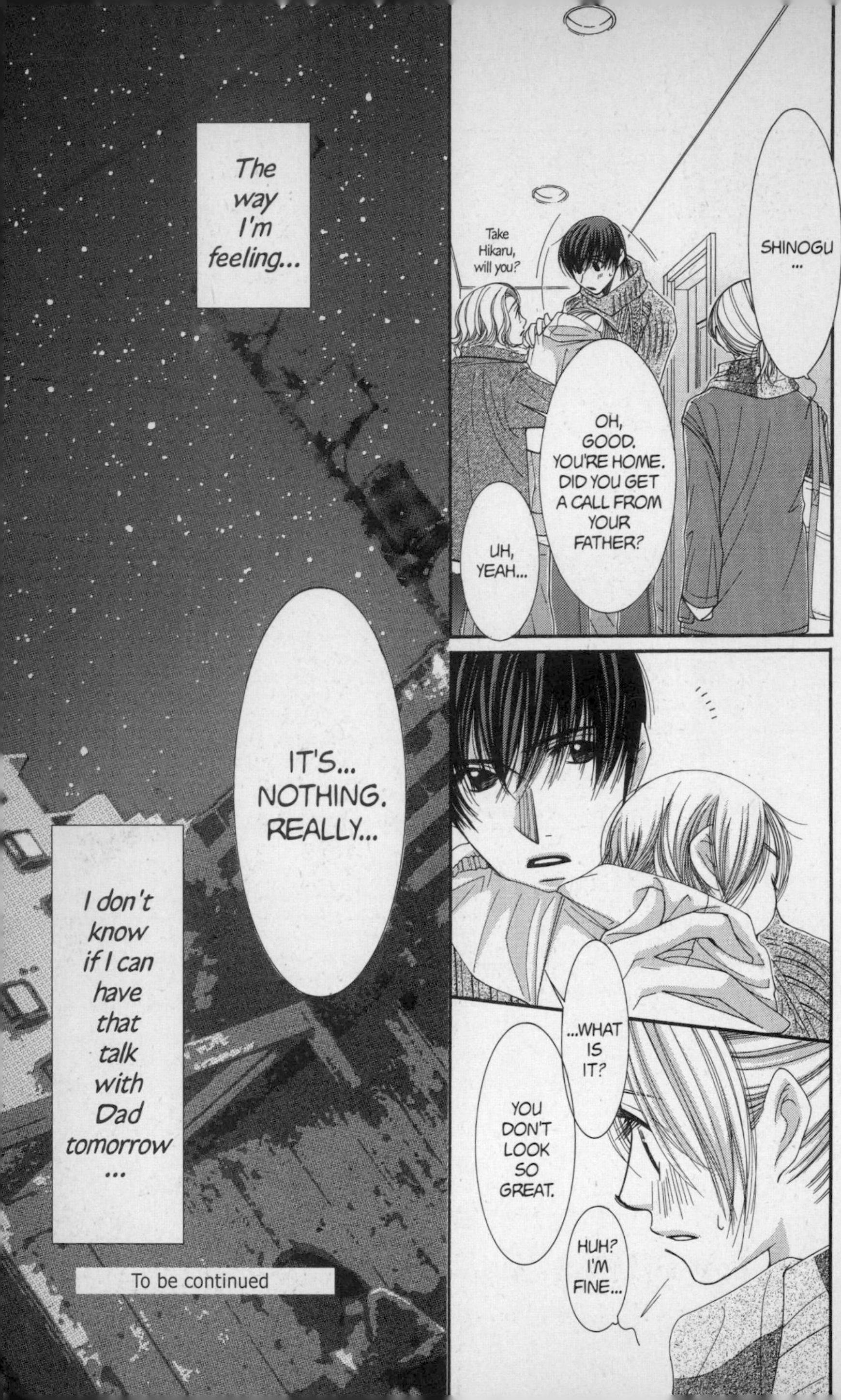
SHINOGU...
Take Hikaru, will you?
OH, GOOD. YOU'RE HOME. DID YOU GET A CALL FROM YOUR FATHER?
UH, YEAH...
...WHAT IS IT?
YOU DON'T LOOK SO GREAT.
HUH? I'M FINE...
The way I'm feeling...
IT'S... NOTHING. REALLY...
I don't know if I can have that talk with Dad tomorrow...
To be continued

HOT GIMMICK
Vol. 5

Shôjo Edition

STORY & ART BY MIKI AIHARA

ENGLISH ADAPTATION BY POOKIE ROLF

Touch-Up Art & Lettering/Rina Mapa
Design/Izumi Evers, Judi Roubideaux
Editor/Kit Fox

Managing Editor/Annette Roman
Editorial Director/Alvin Lu
Director of Production/Noboru Watanabe
Sr. Director of Licensing & Acquisitions/Rika Inouye
V.P. of Sales & Marketing/Liza Coppola
Executive Vice President/Hyoe Narita
Publisher/Seiji Horibuchi

Printed in Canada.

Published by VIZ, LLC, P.O. Box 77010, San Francisco, CA 94107

Shôjo Edition
10 9 8 7 6 5 4 3 2
First printing, June 2004
Second printing, September 2004